terra australis 50

Terra Australis reports the results of archaeological and related research within the south and east of Asia, though mainly Australia, New Guinea and Island Melanesia — lands that remained terra australis incognita to generations of prehistorians. Its subject is the settlement of the diverse environments in this isolated quarter of the globe by peoples who have maintained their discrete and traditional ways of life into the recent recorded or remembered past and at times into the observable present.

List of volumes in Terra Australis

terra australis 50

The Spice Islands in Prehistory

Archaeology in the Northern Moluccas, Indonesia

Edited by Peter Bellwood

Australian
National
University

PRESS

ANU PRESS

Published by ANU Press
The Australian National University
Acton ACT 2601, Australia
Email: anupress@anu.edu.au

Available to download for free at press.anu.edu.au

A catalogue record for this book is available from the National Library of Australia

ISBN (print): 9781760462901
ISBN (online): 9781760462918

WorldCat (print): 1103671384
WorldCat (online): 1103671385

DOI: 10.22459/TA50.2019

Terra Australis Editorial Board: Sue O'Connor, Sally Brockwell, Ursula Frederick, Tristen Jones, Ceri Shipton and Mathieu Leclerc
Series Editor: Sue O'Connor

Cover design and layout by ANU Press. Cover photograph by Peter Bellwood.

Contents

List of figures

List of tables

1

The Indonesian–Australian Archaeological Research Project in the Northern Moluccas

Peter Bellwood

Why the Northern Moluccas?

The Indonesian–Australian Archaeological Research Project in the Northern Moluccas (the Indonesian Province of Maluku Utara), undertaken between 1990 and 1996, illuminated 40,000 years of prehistory in a biogeographical region widely known today as 'Wallacea', named after the pioneer naturalist and explorer Alfred Russel Wallace, author of *The Malay Archipelago* (Wallace 1869). Wallacea, for our purposes, lies between the Sunda and Sahul continental shelves, hence between Borneo/Bali and New Guinea/Australia. For R.E. Dickerson (1928), who first coined the term, Wallacea included the major Philippine and eastern Indonesian archipelagos, the latter comprising Sulawesi, Nusa Tenggara (the Lesser Sundas), Timor, and the Moluccas (Fig. 1.1). Many biogeographers since Dickerson have left out the Philippines (excluding Palawan) and the Moluccas from the definition of Wallacea (e.g. Whitmore 1981:xii), but this monograph is focused upon human rather than natural history. The 'full Wallacea' between the Sunda and Sahul continental shelves (or between Huxley's Line of 1868 and the combined Lydekker (1896) and Weber (1894) Lines, see George 1981: Fig. 2.4) is a far more useful and meaningful concept. No land bridges ever crossed the full expanse of this region of deep seas and steeply plunging coastlines during the Pleistocene Ice Ages, even during glacial maxima, and humans migrating from Taiwan or Sundaland towards New Guinea and Australia always had to cross sea gaps between islands to reach their goals. This monograph is focused on archaeological results from just one small group of islands within this intriguing Wallacean zone of animal and human biogeographical transition, a zone that has always formed both a bridge and a barrier between the Asian and Australian continents.

The original choice of these islands for archaeological research grew from much earlier observations and assumptions about the human prehistory of the Philippine, Indonesian and Oceanic islands, going back at least as far as the voyages of Captain Cook and others during the eighteenth century. By the time volume editor Peter Bellwood emigrated from England to New Zealand in 1967, the simple question *Where did the Polynesians come from?* had been entertaining scholars for a couple of centuries (Howard 1967). By 1967, the consensus had come firmly around to an origin for Polynesians somewhere in the northern islands of Southeast Asia, followed by migrations through Island Melanesia or Micronesia (Green 1967; Howells 1973a). Johann Reinhold Forster, therefore, with his 1770s linguistic and biological observations made during Cook's Second Voyage on similarities between Polynesians, Micronesians, Malays and Filipinos

(Thomas et al. 1996:187), was somewhere close to being right in the opinions of the majority of mid-twentieth-century comparative linguists, physical anthropologists, blood group geneticists, and the small number of archaeologists working in tropical Oceania at that time.

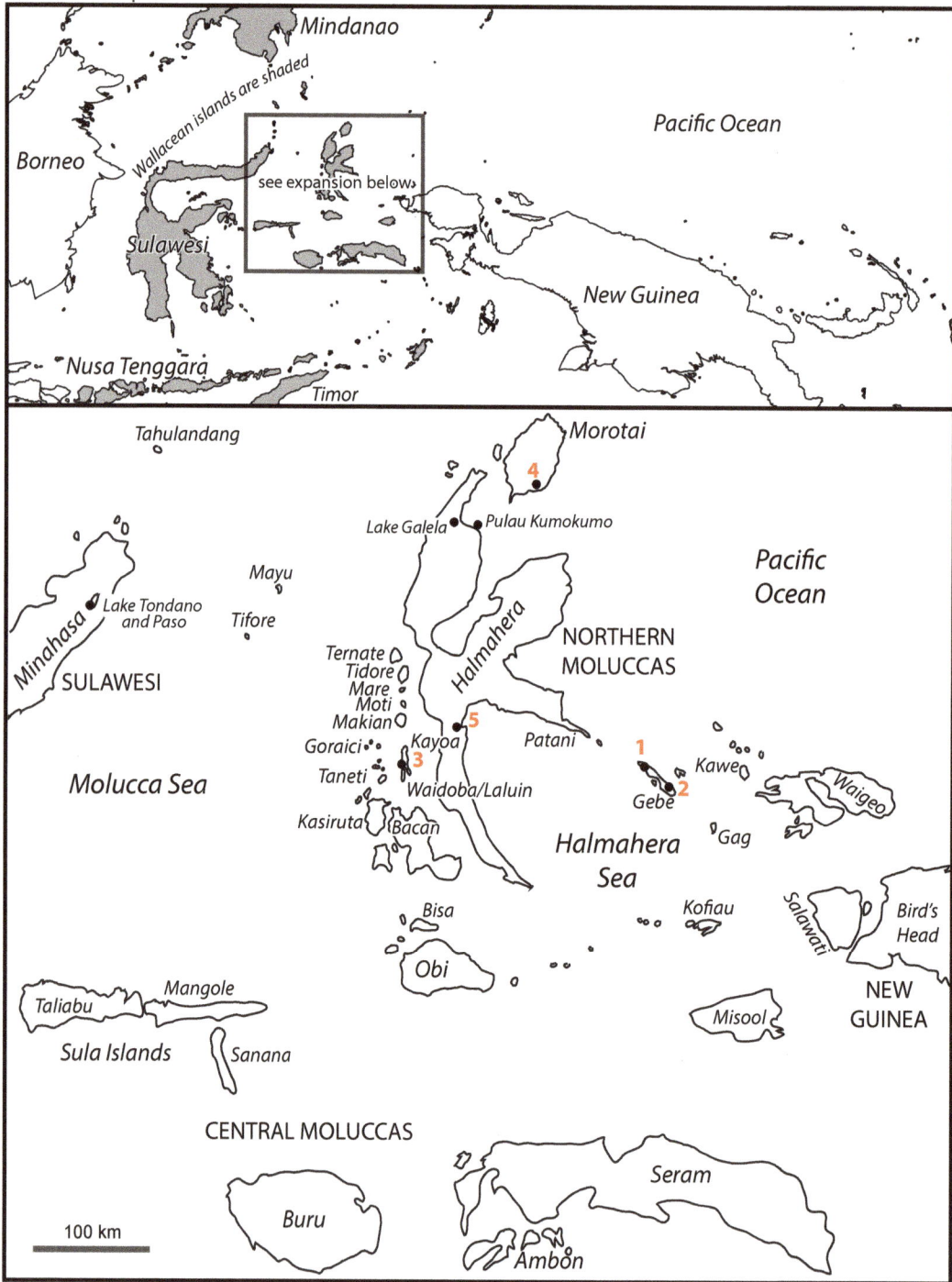

Figure 1.1 The eastern portion of Island Southeast Asia (the Wallacean islands as here defined are shaded) with details of the Northern Moluccas.

Sites and site groups as follows: 1) Golo, Wetef and Buwawansi; 2) Um Kapat Papo and Kaitutsi; 3) Uattamdi and Bukit Keramat; 4) Sabatai Tua, Daeo, Tanjung Pinang, and Sambiki Tua; 5) Gua Siti Nafisah.

Source: Peter Bellwood.

Also by 1967, the Neolithic 'Lapita' decorated pottery style and associated cultural complex of Island Melanesia and western Polynesia (now dated c. 1200 to 800 BCE) had become the main weapon in the archaeological arsenal for those who wished to discuss Polynesian origins, and indeed the origins of all Austronesian-speaking populations in Roger Green's 'Remote Oceania', beyond New Guinea and the Solomons (Green 1991). The Lapita archaeological record at that time suggested very strongly that the first human colonists of the Tongan and Samoan islands in western Polynesia had arrived around 3000 years ago from Island Melanesia, especially Fiji, and went on to become the Polynesians of history as a result of cultural evolution within Tonga and Samoa during the following millennia (Green 1967).

But where were ancestral Polynesian populations located before they reached Fiji? This was not as clear in 1967 as it is now. W.W. Howells (1973a), for instance, was still at that time able to favour a Micronesian route for ancestral Polynesians out of Southeast Asia over the Melanesian one suggested by the Lapita archaeology (Lapita-style pottery has never been found in Micronesia, except for the Marianas; Carson et al. 2013). In a broader perspective, the prehistoric Polynesians were just one group, small in number but remarkably large in geographical distribution, within the vast population of Austronesian-language speakers who are today distributed from Madagascar to Easter Island. More relevant for any consideration of the Northern Moluccas in prehistory was the question *Where did Lapita material culture develop, immediately prior to its arrival c. 3200 years ago in Melanesia?* Given that Lapita sites were located mainly in Island Melanesia, was Lapita purely a home-grown Island Melanesian product with only minor diffusion from Island Southeast Asia, as some archaeologists continued to believe (Allen 1984; Spriggs 1984; Terrell et al. 2001), or did it develop in nascent form somewhere within Island Southeast Asia itself, as had often been suggested during the 1970s (Bellwood 1978; Golson 1972; Howells 1973a)?

In 1975, I published some early conclusions of my own on this issue in the pages of *Current Anthropology* (Bellwood 1975:13):

> Lapita pottery seems likely to be attributable to a mobile group of Austronesian seafarers and traders who were expanding in central and eastern Melanesia after 1300 B.C. The degree of emphasis on dentate stamping appears to be a localized Melanesian development, but the general Lapita combinations of dentate stamping, circle stamping, red-slipping and lime infill, carinated body forms, and absence of painting, cord-marking, and tripod feet quite clearly link it with similar and contemporary ceramics in the Marianas (Spoehr 1957), in the Batungan sites on Masbate in the central Philippines (Solheim 1968: Fig. 5), and in the Yüan-shan culture in northern Taiwan (Chang 1969). There are no grounds at all for deriving the Lapita ceramic style from anywhere on the Southeast Asian mainland; there are clearly no close similarities with the Lungshanoid cultures of mainland China or Taiwan (Chang 1969), and the well-known Sa-huynh site in South Vietnam (Parmentier 1924, Solheim 1959) may perhaps be regarded as a record of Chamic settlement in South Vietnam from the Island Southeast Asian jar-burial province of the 1st millennium B.C. The Austronesian languages themselves have no traceable mainland origin, and, to keep closely to the point, there are no grounds for seeking possible extra-Melanesian connections for Lapita pottery beyond Taiwan, the Philippines, and northeastern Indonesia. It is possible to trace Yüan-shan origins back to the earlier cord-marked and incised pottery of Taiwan, and this of course in turn may have a mainland origin (Chang 1969: chap. 10), but the relevance of this connection for Lapita origins remains to be demonstrated.

When I wrote this piece as a first draft in 1973, my main interest was to trace Lapita origins back into an archaeologically and linguistically documented trail of settlement extending eastward into Island Melanesia from eastern Indonesia and the Philippines, ultimately perhaps from a Neolithic and Proto-Austronesian homeland in Taiwan. My 1974 excavations with I Made Sutayasa in Minahasa and the Talaud Islands (Bellwood 1976) were my first fieldwork foray into this question. The research in the Northern Moluccas was basically a continuation of this, two decades later, with similar goals in mind.

My basic views on the *overall* significance of Austronesian population and language dispersal have changed little since those years, despite variations in detail, and now receive support from the major growth in the quantity of available archaeological information from recent Neolithic excavations in Taiwan (e.g. Tsang and Li 2015), the Batanes Islands and the Cagayan Valley in the northern Philippines (Bellwood and Dizon 2013; Hung et al. 2011), the Mariana Islands (Carson 2014; Carson and Hung 2017; Carson et al. 2013), and Sulawesi (Anggraeni et al. 2014; see also Bellwood 2011, 2017; Bellwood et al. 2011). The recent discovery of the most widespread Polynesian mitochondrial DNA haplotype, and a northern Island Southeast Asian autosomal ancestry signature, in the DNA of three 3000-year-old Lapita crania from the site of Teouma in Vanuatu (Bedford et al. 2018; Lipson et al. 2018; Posth et al. 2018; Skoglund et al. 2016) strongly supports a biological genesis of Polynesians somewhere northwest of New Guinea. Modern archaeological data also indicate that the closest parallels for Lapita pottery occur in the Philippine and Mariana Islands (Carson et al. 2013), with a possible extension into northern Sulawesi (Ono, Aziz et al. 2017:118; Ono, Oktaviana et al. 2017; Ono, Sofian et al. in press).

However, neither the Northern Moluccas nor the Talaud Islands have so far produced any archaeological materials that are closely related to Lapita or early Marianas pottery decoration. Therefore, while in 1990 I might have considered the Northern Moluccas and the northern coastline of New Guinea to have offered a major passageway into Oceania for the migrations of the Austronesian-speaking peoples, and especially the ancestral Polynesians, I have to state that I am no longer so enthusiastic about this likelihood today (Bellwood 2017:Chapter 8). Moluccan archaeology in 2018 needs to find its own relevance from other sources, and hopefully this monograph will show how it can. One aspect of particular relevance is that these islands were a meeting place for speakers of Papuan and Austronesian languages between 3500 and 2000 years ago, and the archaeological record related to the first appearance of pottery seems to reflect this meeting fairly clearly (Ono, Aziz et al. 2017; Ono, Oktaviana et al. 2017).

There is, of course, a lot more to Northern Moluccan archaeology than Neolithic pottery and possible links with Lapita and New Guinea. Fifty years ago, rather little was known also about the Late Palaeolithic in Island Southeast Asia, beyond the schematically published findings from the Tabon and Niah Caves, in Palawan and Sarawak respectively (see contemporary summaries in Bellwood 1978). So, it is gratifying to note that the North Moluccan project described in this monograph has contributed not just to Neolithic issues, but also much information on the putatively modern human (*Homo sapiens*) colonisation of Wallacea as much as 40,000 years ago (Szabó et al. 2007). Golo and Wetef Caves on Gebe Island, in particular, have yielded important Palaeolithic data.

As well as site reports, this monograph also contains specialist reports on the human remains, animal bones and shell artefacts that were recovered from many sites, and we are now considering the implications of ancient human DNA data from the sites of Uattamdi and Tanjung Pinang, courtesy of the Max Planck Institutes for Evolutionary Anthropology in Leipzig and the Science of Human History in Jena, Germany. Although the excavations described in this monograph took place more than 20 years ago, there are sufficient new data to encourage a thorough presentation of all the results, new and old, in a single venue. This monograph is that venue.

The Indonesian–Australian Archaeological Research Project in the Northern Moluccas, 1990 to 1996

In 1977, three years after my first Indonesian research project with I Made Sutayasa in Minahasa and the Talaud Islands, I approached the late Professor R.P. Soejono, former head of the National Archaeological Research Centre in Jakarta (then called Lembaga Purbakala dan Peninggalan Nasional), with a proposal to commence research in the Northern Moluccas. Soejono indicated that permits would be hard to obtain for various reasons beyond his control, connected with the general political atmosphere between Indonesia and Australia at that time. I decided to move my interests for the next decade to Sabah (Bellwood 1988). By 1990, the situation in Indonesia had brightened, and while I was a member of the Comparative Austronesian Project at The Australian National University (ANU), led by James Fox (Bellwood et al. 2006), I was able to apply successfully for a research permit from Lembaga Ilmu dan Pengetahuan Nasional (LIPI) and the Archaeological Research Centre in Jakarta (by this time renamed Pusat Penelitian Arkeologi Nasional). Geoffrey Irwin and I landed in Ternate to begin our research in December 1990, in company with Gunadi Nitihaminoto, Agus Waluyo, Gunadi Kusnowihardjo and the late Haji Syamsuddin Tukuboya. Four field seasons followed, in 1990–91, 1994 (twice), and 1995–96.

During the 1990s, and up until 2007, a number of excavation and other specialist reports were published on the results of the North Moluccan archaeological project (see the list below), but the results have never been brought together as a whole into one single definitive publication. This scattering of data has been a little unfortunate, especially since a 40,000-year record of prehistoric human activity from one close-set group of relatively small Wallacean islands has not exactly been an everyday occurrence in the archaeology of Island Southeast Asia. This retrospective account of the North Moluccan archaeological project, prepared during 2013–18, or roughly 25 years after the project's commencement, will attempt to make the data (much previously unpublished) accessible and useful for future generations of archaeologists, especially Indonesian archaeologists who might wish one day to continue research in the region. It is intended to provide a kind of road map for those who wish to access the existing published reports, as well as offering some conclusions of an interpretative and chronological nature. Many new perspectives are apparent 25 years after the actual field research, and now is the time to bring them forth.

The monograph opens with a full account of the many excavations undertaken by the project, presenting basic field data and chronologies. Successive chapters are focused on pottery, lithic artefacts, shell artefacts, zooarchaeology, and human skeletal analysis and health. The volume finishes with a review chapter by Bellwood on the whole prehistoric record of the Northern Moluccas in its Island Southeast Asian and Oceanic setting. Detailed information that has been published previously is not necessarily always repeated, but a conscious attempt is made to bring all pertinent data together in a single presentation format, using references to other published material as necessary.

No attempt is made in this monograph to give an overall introduction to Moluccan natural history, but a few preliminary generalisations are warranted. The Northern Moluccas are entirely equatorial, located within 3 degrees north and south of the Equator, with no marked dry season. Monsoon winds vary seasonally, blowing generally from the north or northeast in the northern hemisphere winter (January) and from the south or southeast in the southern hemisphere winter (July). Vegetation is wet rainforest, except on very poor soils.

A major volcanic arc runs down the western side of Halmahera Island, and the Jailolo region of Halmahera, plus the islands of Ternate, Tidore and Makian, still have active volcanoes. Halmahera itself has rugged uplifted interior terrain incorporating sedimentary and metamorphic rocks of late Mesozoic age and onwards (Hall et al. 1988). Along the eastern coastlines of

Morotai, Halmahera and Gebe, raised coral reefs are common. The Halmahera island complex can therefore be conceptualised as a westerly arc of active volcanoes, against which a separate uplifted easterly arc, without current volcanic activity, has been forced by subduction and plate movement. The result is the unusual spider shape of the island of Halmahera, rather similar to that of the much larger Sulawesi that lies to the west.

Native mammals prior to human arrival were possibly restricted to placental rodents and bats of ultimate Eurasian (Sunda) origin, and marsupial sugar gliders and cuscuses of ultimate Australasian (Sahul) origin (Flannery 1995a). Question marks hover around marsupial wallabies and bandicoots, as discussed in Chapter 10. Did the marsupials, including perhaps even the cuscuses, arrive by natural means or by human translocation?

By 1500 CE, the Spice Islands were entering the consciousness of Western civilisations as a source of spices, especially cloves and nutmegs. Hence the arrivals of Portuguese, Dutch, and eventually Indonesian systems of political interference and control (Andaya 1993; Cortesão 1944; Wallace 1869). The post-1500 historical era is not particularly relevant for the contents of this monograph, and none of the excavated sites have significant material culture from this time. However, questions are raised about the role of the Moluccas in spice trading (especially cloves, of Northern Moluccan origin) much earlier, especially with the inception of contacts between Indonesia and India around 2000 years ago.

It remains to list the personnel and funding agencies that made the project a success. The research project formally entitled 'Archaeological Survey and Excavation in the Halmahera Islands, Moluccas, Indonesia', with fieldwork carried out between 1990 and 1996, was funded by the National Geographic Society and the Australian Research Council. It involved cooperation between five institutions: the Department of Archaeology and Anthropology at ANU, the Indonesian National Research Centre of Archaeology (then termed Pusat Penelitian Arkeologi Nasional), the Department of Anthropology at Auckland University, the (then) Indonesian Directorate of Protection and Development of Historical and Archaeological Heritage, and the Sultan Palace Museum in Ternate. The fieldwork was undertaken in four phases: December 1990 to February 1991, January to February 1994, May to June 1994, and December 1995 to January 1996. Major team members were as follows, with their places of residence at the time of the research: Peter Bellwood (Canberra), Geoffrey Irwin (Auckland), Agus Waluyo (Jakarta), Gunadi Nitihaminoto, Gunadi Kusnowihardjo, Daud Tanudirjo (all Yogyakarta), the late Haji Syamsuddin Tukuboya (Ternate), and Joko Siswanto (Manado). Analytical expertise was also provided during the 1990s by Tim Flannery (identification of marsupials and rodents), Peter White (analysis of animal bones), Doreen Bowdery (analysis of phytoliths), and David Bulbeck (analysis of human remains). The ANU, ANSTO (Australian Nuclear Science and Technology Organisation), New Zealand and Waikato Radiocarbon Dating laboratories analysed the radiocarbon dates, as listed in Table 1.1 below. We thank Stewart Fallon and Rachel Wood of the ANU Dating Laboratory for recent discussions about matters of C14 date interpretation.

Many of the figures were originally drawn on tracing paper by hand during the 1990s, with some of the lettering replaced for clarity using Adobe Illustrator. Some figures are completely new, and most (except where otherwise credited) were prepared using Illustrator or digital scans of original 35 mm slides by Peter Bellwood. Some of the illustrations therefore have an 'archival' feel, but to maintain accuracy no unnecessary redrawing has been attempted.

This *Terra Australis* monograph has been published with the aid of a subsidy from the ANU Publication Subsidy Committee.

Articles previously published from this project on the archaeology of the Northern Moluccas

At this point in the introductory chapter, it will be useful to present a list of all the previous publications related to this project. Most date from the 1990s and represent opinions published quite soon after the completion of the relevant fieldwork. Not all reflect completely the current perspectives that are presented in this monograph, and it can often be informative to observe just how interpretations can change as new information appears. The articles are in chronological order, from 1992 onwards.

Bellwood, P. 1992. New discoveries in Southeast Asia relevant for Melanesian (especially Lapita) prehistory. In J.C. Galipaud ed., *Poterie Lapita et Peuplement*, pp. 49–66. Nouméa: ORSTOM. (This article was the first to be published on the Maluku Project, following the first period of fieldwork in 1990–91, when excavations took place in the important sites of Uattamdi, Tanjung Pinang, and Gua Siti Nafisah.)

Bellwood, P., A. Waluyo, Gunadi, G. Nitihaminoto and G. Irwin 1993. Archaeological research in the Northern Moluccas; interim results, 1991 field season. *Bulletin of the Indo-Pacific Prehistory Association* 13:20–33.

Bellwood, P. 1995. Archaeological research in the Northern Moluccas 1991–1994: a preliminary report. *Southeast Asian Archaeology International Newsletter* 7:3–12.

Flannery, T., P. Bellwood, P. White, A. Moore, Boeadi and G. Nitihaminoto 1995. Fossil marsupials (Macropodidae, Peroryctidae) and other mammals of Holocene age from Halmahera, North Moluccas, Indonesia. *Alcheringa* 19:17–25.

Mahirta 1996. The development of the Mare pottery tradition. *Bulletin of the Indo-Pacific Prehistory Association* 20: 124–132.

Bellwood, P. 1998. From Bird's Head to bird's eye view: long term structures and trends in Indo-Pacific Prehistory. In J. Miedema, C. Odé and R. Dam (eds), *Perspectives on the Bird's Head of Irian Jaya, Indonesia*, pp. 951–975. Amsterdam: Rodopi.

Flannery, T., P. Bellwood, J.P. White, T. Ennis, G. Irwin, K. Schubert and S. Balasubramanian 1998. Mammals from Holocene archaeological deposits on Gebe and Morotai Islands, Northern Moluccas, Indonesia. *Australian Mammalogy* 20/3:391–400.

Bellwood, P., G. Nitihaminoto, G. Irwin, Gunadi, A. Waluyo and D. Tanudirjo 1998. 35,000 years of prehistory in the Northern Moluccas. In G.-J. Bartstra (ed.), *Bird's Head Approaches*, pp. 233–275. *Modern Quaternary Research in Southeast Asia* 15. Rotterdam: Balkema.

Bellwood, P. 1998. Between Southeast Asia and Oceania: preceramic occupation in the Northern Moluccas and associated mysteries. In *Jejak-Jejak Budaya II: Persembahan untuk Prof. Dr. R.P. Soejono*, pp. 323–369. Yogyakarta: Asosiasi Prehistorisi Indonesia Rayon II.

Bellwood, P. 1998. The archaeology of Papuan and Austronesian prehistory in the Northern Moluccas, Indonesia. In R. Blench and M. Spriggs (eds), *Archaeology and Language, Volume 2: Correlating Archaeological and Linguistic Hypotheses*, pp. 128–140. London: One World Archaeology Series, Routledge.

Irwin, G., P. Bellwood, G. Nitihaminoto, D. Tanudirjo and J. Siswanto 1999. Prehistoric relations between Island Southeast Asia and Oceania: recent archaeological investigations in the Northern Moluccas. In J.-C. Galipaud and I. Lilley eds, *The Pacific from 5000 to 2000 BP*, pp. 363–374. Paris: Institut de Recherche pour le Développement.

8   The Spice Islands in Prehistory

Bellwood, P., G. Nitihaminoto, Gunadi, A. Waluyo and G. Irwin 2000. The Northern Moluccas as a crossroads between Indonesia and the Pacific. In Sudaryanto and A.H. Rambadeta (eds), *Antar Hubungan Bahasa dan Budaya di Kawasan Non-Austronesia*, pp. 195–254. Yogyakarta: Pusat Studi Asia Pasifik.

Pasveer, J. and P. Bellwood 2004. Prehistoric bone artefacts from the Northern Moluccas, Indonesia. *Modern Quaternary Research in Southeast Asia* 18:301–359.

Bellwood, P. and P. White 2005. Domesticated pigs in eastern Indonesia. *Science* 309:381.

Szabó, K., A. Brumm and P. Bellwood 2007. Shell artefact production at 32,000 BP in Island Southeast Asia: thinking across media? *Current Anthropology* 48:701–724.

Szabó, K. and B. Koppel 2015. Limpet shells as unmodified tools in Pleistocene Southeast Asia: an experimental approach to assessing fracture and modification. *Journal of Archaeological Science* 54:64–76.

There are in addition three Master's theses:

Mahirta. 2000. The Development of Mare Pottery in the Northern Moluccas Context. Unpublished MA thesis, The Australian National University.

Hull, Jennifer R. 2014. The Vertebrate Remains Recovered During the 1990–1996 Excavations of the Northern Moluccan Islands. Unpublished Master of Archaeological Science subthesis, The Australian National University.

Wyatt, Bronwyn 2017. Health and Disease in Prehistoric Indonesia: Placing the Northern Moluccas Islands into Context Within Broader Southeast Asian Prehistory. Unpublished Master of Biological Anthropology subthesis, The Australian National University.

Checklist of radiocarbon dates from the Northern Moluccas (Peter Bellwood and Rachel Wood)

A total of 77 radiocarbon dates were assembled during the course of this project, and these are referred to frequently throughout the text and in the tables for each excavated site. For convenience, the total series is listed here, by site, in Table 1.1. Many are listed again in the tables in the following excavation chapters.

Within tables that list radiocarbon dates, the convention cal. BP (for calibrated years before present) is used for calibrated dates. In the general text, the abbreviations BCE and CE (Before Common Era and Common Era) are used to replace BC and AD.

The information in this table has been updated where relevant by Rachel Wood (Radiocarbon Dating Laboratory, Research School of Earth Sciences, The Australian National University) and Fiona Petchey (Radiocarbon Dating Laboratory, Waikato University, New Zealand).

Table 1.1 C14 dates from the Northern Moluccas, listed in stratigraphical order where possible for each site.

*Lab. Number	Site and Layer or Depth (cm)	C14 age BP (uncal.)	OxCal 4.2 (IntCal 13) at 95.4%, ΔR =0 (cal. BP)	δ13C (if measured)	Pretreatment and quality assurance details for ANU dates, if available	Material	Cultural context (more details are given in Chapters 2–5)
Golo Cave, Gebe							
ANU 11818	Golo skeleton	1900±190	2314–1415			Human bone	Burial placed from base of Layer 1
OZD 773	Golo M6 30–35	9580±70	10,621–10,246	2.36		Cassis adze	Adze, using old shell for manufacture
ANU 9448	Golo M5 45–55	3230±180	3900–2975	−26.4±0.2	1	Charcoal	Terminal preceramic
ANU 9449	Golo M4 50–55	7400±110	8100–7641		2	Turbo sp., 9 shells	Preceramic
ANU 11006	Golo M5 60–65	18,440±140	22,269–21,474		2	Turbo sp.	Disturbance? (seems too old)
S-ANU 36407#	Golo 75–80	6745±45	7675–7516	−21.8±2.0	3	Wallaby tooth enamel	Wallaby presence on Gebe
S-ANU 36409#	Golo 80–90	7050±60	7982–7738	−37.1±2.0	3	Wallaby tooth enamel	Wallaby presence on Gebe
ANU 9769	Golo M5 135–40	10,540±70	12,044–11,376	−1.9±0.2	4	Nerita sp., multiple shells	Preceramic
OZD 775	Golo M5 135–40	32,800±950	38,984–34,638	5.03		Tridacna adze	Adze, using old shell for manufacture
ANU 9512	Golo M5 145–50	11,480±70	13,131–12,756	−3.0±0.2	4	Nerita sp., multiple shells	Preceramic
OZD 774	Golo M5 145–50	6430±80	7176–6771	2.95		Hippopus adze	Adze, presumably buried in a pit
ANU 11053	Golo M5 185–90	19,080±140	22,919–22,285		7	Marine shell	Preceramic
ANU 11005	Golo LM6 190–195	7750±80	8369–8029			Turbo sp., number not recorded	Disturbance? (seems too young)
ANU 9768	Golo M5 195–200	9250±80	10,243–9794		4	Turbo sp., 2 shells	Disturbance? (seems too young)
Wk 17763	Golo M4 200–205	28,740±474	33,485–31,324	0.8±0.2	XRD 98.60± 0.3% aragonite	Drupa clathrata, two fragments◆	Preceramic
Wk 17762	Golo LM6 205–210	16,236±101	19,401–18,864	3.1±0.2		Turbo marmoratus, multiple pieces	Preceramic◆
ANU 11007	Golo LM6 205–210	21,780±160	25,982–25,351			Turbo sp. operculum	Preceramic
Wk 17761	Golo LM6 210–215	28,251±305	32,593–31,142	3.4±0.2	XRD 97.50± 0.25% aragonite	Turbo marmoratus, single shell	Preceramic operculum artefact◆
Wk 4629	Golo M4 210–215	32,210±320	36,350–35,001			Marine shell	Preceramic

*Lab. Number	Site and Layer or Depth (cm)	C14 age BP (uncal.)	OxCal 4.2 (IntCal 13) at 95.4%, ΔR =0 (cal. BP)	δ^{13}C (if measured)	Pretreatment and quality assurance details for ANU dates, if available	Material	Cultural context (more details are given in Chapters 2–5)
ANU 9447	Golo M5 230–235A	31,030±400	35,390–33,910		2	*Turbo* sp. 3 shells	Preceramic
ANU 9447	Golo M5 230–235B	32,490±1070	39,003–34,173		2	*Turbo* sp. 3 shells	Preceramic
Wetef rockshelter, Gebe							
NZA 8369	Wetef K4 Layer A	791±67	906–570	−20.8		Wallaby bone	Youngest date for wallabies on Gebe
Wk 4618	Wetef K3 45–50	4920±60	5425–5025	2.2±0.2		Marine shell	Preceramic
Wk 4619	Wetef K3 75–80	5250±60	5742–5467	2.3±0.2		Marine shell	Preceramic
NZA 8387	Wetef K4 Layer B	5521±77	6487–6182	−24.9		Wallaby bone	Wallaby presence on Gebe
Wk 4620	Wetef K4 100–105	7260±70	7874–7580	3.1±0.2		Marine shell	Preceramic
Wk 4621	Wetef K3 110–115	6560±70	7239–6901	2.7±0.3		Marine shell	Preceramic
Wk 4622	Wetef K4 140–145	7710±70	8327–8011	2.2±0.2		Marine shell	Preceramic
Wk 4623	Wetef K3 145–150	7710±70	8327–8011	2.2±0.3		Marine shell	Preceramic
Wk 4624	Wetef K3 170–175	8510±70	9340–8974	1.7±0.2		Marine shell	Preceramic
Wk 4625	Wetef K4 200–205	11,310±80	12,962–12,626	0.0±0.2		Marine shell	Preceramic
Wk 4626	Wetef K4 240–245	21,290±170	25,610–24,614	2.8±0.2		Marine shell	Preceramic
Wk 4627	Wetef K4 250–255	25,540±420	30,299–28,381	3.0±0.2		Marine shell	Preceramic
Um Kapat Papo, Gebe							
ANU 9316	UKP 2: 15–20 cm	2030±60	1765–1437		2	*Turbo* sp., number not recorded	Incised pottery
ANU 9317	UKP layer 3: 5–15	4830±70	5300–4900		2	*Turbo* sp. operculum	Preceramic
ANU 9318	UKP layer 3: 55–65	6670±60	7330–7028		2	*Turbo* sp., 4 shells, 1 very weathered, 3 slightly weathered	Preceramic
Buwawansi site complex, Gebe							
ANU 9319	Buwawansi 2: 10–15	1930±70	1655–1319		2	*Turbo* sp., 1 shell	Red-slipped and incised pottery
Wk 4630	Buwawansi 5A: 35	1940±60	1646–1341			Marine shell	Red-slipped and incised pottery

*Lab. Number	Site and Layer or Depth (cm)	C14 age BP (uncal.)	OxCal 4.2 (IntCal 13) at 95.4‰, ΔR =0 (cal. BP)	δ13C (if measured)	Pretreatment and quality assurance details for ANU dates, if available	Material	Cultural context (more details are given in Chapters 2–5)
ANU 9454	Buwawansi 6: 15-20	2230±70	2008–1640		2	Hippopus sp., 3 shells	Red-slipped and incised pottery
ANU 9770	Buwawansi 5: 25-30	3160±60	3128–2789	2.5±0.2	2	Hippopus sp., very weathered whole shells and fragments	Red-slipped and incised pottery
ANU 9453	Buwawansi 3B: 130-135	4010±80	4271–3811		2	Cardium sp., 1 shell	Preceramic
Wk 4628	Buwawansi 1B, 35-45	8550±70	9379–9007			Marine shell	Preceramic (with Tridacna adze?)
Tanjung Pinang rockshelter, Morotai							
ANU 8439#	Tanjung Pinang A2	2090±180	2684–1618		5	Human bone, apatite fraction	Secondary burials, incised pottery
ANU 7778	T. Pinang A2	3390±70	3426–3061		4	Turbo sp. opercula	Preceramic
ANU 7779	T. Pinang A6	4090±70	4356–3930		4	Turbo sp. opercula	Preceramic
ANU 7780	T. Pinang A7	4720±70	5210–4815		4	Turbo sp. opercula	Preceramic
ANU 7781	T. Pinang A11	5390±70	5901–5604		4	Turbo sp. opercula	Preceramic
ANU 7782	T. Pinang A14	8860±110	9860–9284		4	Turbo sp.	Preceramic
ANU 7783	T. Pinang A19-20	37,510+650/-600	42,595–40,450		2	Mixed marine shell, with excessive carbonate build up.	Pre-human
ANU 9455	T. Pinang A42-46	37,510±1860	46,172–38,325		2	Mixed marine shell, 13 shells	Pre-human (1.3 m below ANU 7783)
Sambiki Tua, Morotai							
ANU 7784	Sambiki Tua 20 cm	720±180	1054–325		1	Charcoal	Pottery manufacture
Daeo Cave 2, Morotai							
ANU 9452	Daeo 2 20-25	5530±70	6463–6194	-27.5±0.2	1	Charcoal	Preceramic
OZD768	Daeo 2 E4/5 50-55	10,820±90	12,920–12,571	-24.81		Canarium charcoal	Preceramic
ANU 9450	Daeo 2 60-65	13,930±140	16,767–15,889		2	8 Turbo sp. opercula	Preceramic
ANU 9451	Daeo 2 55-60	1420±150	1691–986	-25.8±0.2	1	Charcoal	Disturbance? (seems too young)

*Lab. Number	Site and Layer or Depth (cm)	C14 age BP (uncal.)	OxCal 4.2 (IntCal 13) at 95.4%, ΔR =0 (cal. BP)	δ13C (if measured)	Pretreatment and quality assurance details for ANU dates, if available	Material	Cultural context (more details are given in Chapters 2-5)
Gua Siti Nafisah, Halmahera							
S-ANU 42627	Siti Nafisah F7 DI	1330±20	1299-1187	-20.4±1.0	6. 1‰, 4.8 mg, collagen yield, 43.4%C, C:N 3.1, δ13C 20.4‰, δ15N 5.0‰	Sus scrofa ulna, cut-marked	Disturbed context
ANU 7790	Siti Nafisah J10 ceramic midden	1870±80	1598-1268	0.7±0.1	2	Anadara sp.	Incised and red-slipped pottery
S-ANU 43339	Siti Nafisah J10 C2	1825±25	1825-1699	-20.8±1.0	6. 2. 0.3‰, 1.3mg, collagen yield, 43.7%C, C:N 3.3, δ13C 20.8‰, δ15N 4.6‰. Low yield but other QA indicators are typical of collagen.	Sus scrofa humerus	Incised and red-slipped pottery
ANU 7785	Siti Nafisah A2	2540±70	2351-2007		2	Anadara sp.	Incised and red-slipped pottery
ANU 7786	Siti Nafisah B1	3410±70	3443-3080		2	Anadara sp., several 5 cm fragments in a range of diagenetic states	Preceramic midden, extinct marsupials
ANU 7787	Siti Nafisah C3	4690±120	5280-4623		4	Anadara sp., several fragments	Preceramic midden, extinct marsupials
ANU 7788	Siti Nafisah D2	4890±70	5409-4979		2	Anadara sp., 4 shells	Preceramic midden, extinct marsupials
ANU 7789	Siti Nafisah D4	5120±100	5692-5268		2	Anadara sp.	Preceramic midden, extinct marsupials
Uattamdi, Kayoa							
OxA 35201	Uattamdi cranium	1915±27	1932-1813	-16.28		Human bone	Early Metal phase jar burial
ANU 7772	Uattamdi A5	900±100	1094-666		1	Charcoal fragments	Chinese coins
ANU 7773	Uattamdi B1	1190±70	1269-969		1	Charcoal fragments	glass beads
ANU 9322	Uattamdi B2	2330±70	2136-1782		2	Turbo sp., 1 shell 15-20 cm	Jar burial, glass beads
ANU 7774	Uattamdi B4	390±190	(overlaps modern)		1	Charcoal fragments	Disturbance? (too young)
ANU 7775	Uattamdi C3	2610±170	3160-2324		1	Ash, which may have included charcoal	Ash from hearth. Red-slipped pottery, shell beads
ANU 9323	Uattamdi D1	3260±70	3293-2882		2	Cardium sp., 1 shell	Red-slipped pottery, shell beads
S-ANU 60005	Uattamdi C6	2928±29	3144-2964	-12.6	3a	Sus scrofa tooth enamel	Red-slipped pottery, shell beads

*Lab. Number	Site and Layer or Depth (cm)	C14 age BP (uncal.)	OxCal 4.2 (IntCal 13) at 95.4%, ΔR =0 (cal. BP)	δ13C (if measured)	Pretreatment and quality assurance details for ANU dates, if available	Material	Cultural context (more details are given in Chapters 2–5)
S-ANU 60006	Uattamdi C6	2884±35		-12.7	3b	As above, same sample	Red-slipped pottery, shell beads
ANU 10959	Uattamdi D2	3410±140	4080–3362		1	Charcoal, from old wood?	Charcoal from hearth. Red-slipped pottery, shell beads
ANU 10957	Uattamdi D3	2850±120	3330–2753		1	Charcoal	Red-slipped pottery, shell beads
ANU 9320	Uattamdi D3	650±180	937–306		1	Charcoal	Cooking hearths. Disturbance?
ANU 7776	Uattamdi D4	3440±110	3579–3014		2	Marine shell	From hearth. Red-slipped pottery, shell beads
ANU 9321	Uattamdi E	3530±70	3590–3239		2	Marine shell	Pre-human beach deposit

* In the left-hand column, ANU = The Australian National University (all ANU dates listed here were measured conventionally), S-ANU = Single Stage Accelerator of The Australian National University, Wk = Waikato, OZO = ANSTO AMS Laboratory, Lucas Heights. Marine shell samples are calculated with ΔR as zero (Marine13 in OxCal 4.2 set at 100%).

◆ See Szabó et al. 2007.

Radiocarbon dates on apatite, whether from enamel or bone, were only undertaken if no collagen was present. These dates very likely underestimate the true age of the sample as contamination cannot be fully removed from these sample types (Wood et al. 2016; Zazzo 2014).

Pretreatment descriptions where available for ANU and S-ANU samples:

1. Charcoal: Physically cleaned, and washed in hot 10% HCl, rinsed.

2. Shell: Surface cleaned with dental drill, washed in ultrasonic bath and rinsed in demineralised water.

3a. Enamel apatite: Surface and dentine removed with dental drill. Hand ground, 1M acetic acid for 20 hours under a weak vacuum (Wood et al. 2016).

3b. Enamel apatite: Surface and dentine removed with dental drill. Micronised in a McCrone microniser for 30 minutes, 1M acetic acid for 20 hours under a weak vacuum (Wood et al. 2016).

4. Shell: Surface cleaned with dental drill, washed in ultrasonic bath and rinsed. Acid etched.

5. Bone apatite: Surfaces cleaned with dental drill. Crushed. Treated with acetic acid, rinsed and dried.

6. Bone, ultrafiltered collagen: Surfaces cleaned with dental drill, acid, base, acid, gelatinisation, ultrafiltration (Wood et al. 2014).

7. Shell: Surface cleaned with dental drill and washed in demineralised water.

Comments on quality assurance for tooth enamel samples S-ANU 60005 and 60006. Both samples were screened for calcite and brushite by FTIR before and after treatment. Neither was visible. Tooth enamel IRSF of 5.0: S-ANU 60005 0.8‰ C, δ13C - 12.6, δ15N - 6.1, S-ANU 60006 0.6‰ C, δ13C -12.7, δ15N - 6.1.

Sources: Peter Bellwood, Geoffrey Irwin, Rachel Wood and Fiona Petchey, plus the radiocarbon laboratories as listed.

2

Investigations on Gebe Island

Peter Bellwood, Geoffrey Irwin, Daud Tanudirjo,
Gunadi Nitihaminoto, Joko Siswanto, and Doreen Bowdery

The island of Gebe is 43 km long by a maximum of 7.5 km wide (Fig. 2.1). It occupies an important geographical position as a 'stepping stone' between the eastern tip of Halmahera at Patani and the islands that fringe the western side of Waigeo Island and the Bird's Head region of New Guinea. The islands of Kawe and Gag (West Papua) are visible from it on clear days (both are shown in Fig. 1.1). Unfortunately, the island was left off most of the topographic and geological maps of the Northern Moluccas that were available to us in the 1990s, and all our detailed geographical information was derived from maps kindly provided to us by the Aneka Tambang mining company, which at that time was operating a nickel mine on Gebe (mining operations ceased in 2005). These maps included a 1:25,000 relief map with contours at 25 m intervals, and a partial geological map at a scale of 1:50,000.

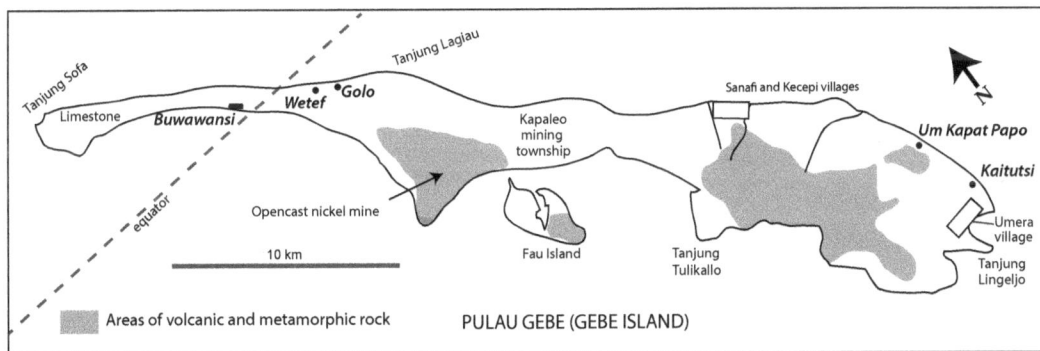

Figure 2.1 Map of Gebe Island showing geological formations (as known in 1994) and site locations.
Raised coral limestone (with caves and rockshelters) occurs along much of the northern coast, but no map of the outcrops exists.
Source: Peter Bellwood.

Geologically, Gebe has a narrow northern peninsula of raised coral that straddles the equator and contains the most important of our excavated sites. The central and southern parts of the island contain extensive deposits of lateritic nickel ore, overlying volcanic and metamorphic rocks, which include gabbro and serpentinite. These outcrops have been partially mapped, and approximate boundaries as known in 1994 are shown in Figure 2.1. The highest points, which occur in the southeastern part of the island, are all less than 400 m above sea level. The island has rather an infertile appearance from an ecological viewpoint, and much of the native vegetation is stunted. Agricultural land, mostly under tree crops or shifting cultivation, is of very restricted extent. The indigenous population is small and in 1994 inhabited only two villages; Sanafi with Kecepi (two villages in one complex), and Umera. Many of the indigenous people at that time had moved for employment into the large mining settlement of Kapaleo, which occupied the centre of the island near the nickel mine and airstrip. Mining ceased in 2007, and none of the authors have revisited the island since 1996.

The island has two markedly different sides with respect to sea conditions. The northeast-facing shore receives swells from the open Pacific and thus has rough sea conditions for much of the year, especially between November and March when monsoon winds blow from the northeast. The more protected southwest-facing shore (Fig. 2.2) has gentler seas and much more accessible fishing grounds, except during the southeast monsoon period between May and August. The northeast-facing shore is difficult for fishing by canoe owing to the presence of a rather severe barrier reef with few safe passages or anchorages (almost none at all during rough seas). Boats only travel this shoreline during the period of quietest sea, around May to August, when this side of the island is in the lee. Available fish and shellfish resources are much more prolific along the southwest-facing shore, which has much less raised coral than the north coast and which contains the important archaeological open site and rockshelter complex of Buwawansi.

Observations of the island from the air and on the ground suggest that Gebe has been tilted to some degree along its longitudinal axis, with the southwest-facing coast being partly submerged and fringed by extensive mangrove swamps. The uplifted northeast-facing coast is backed for much of its length by an eroded and frequently scree-encased cliff of raised coral. This attains heights (albeit rarely) of up to 20 m.

Figure 2.2 The Buwawansi narrow coastal flat from the south.
Source: Peter Bellwood.

The rather impoverished non-domesticated 'native' mammal fauna of the island contains a species of sugar-glider (*Petaurus breviceps*—its bones have never been found archaeologically in the Northern Moluccas), a species of rat (*Rattus praetor*) and several species of bat (Flannery 1995a:414). The single species of cuscus that occurs on the island has been classified taxonomically as *Phalanger alexandrae* by Flannery and Boeadi (1995), who regarded it as a native species most closely related to *P. ornatus* of Halmahera. A species of *Dorcopsis* wallaby found in the Gebe Holocene archaeological deposits, and now absent on the island, was initially regarded as a translocation from Misool Island off the Bird's Head of New Guinea (Flannery et al. 1995, 1998), although this is still not an absolute certainty owing to the absence of any truly Pleistocene bone assemblages from Gebe. The issue of translocation is discussed further in Chapter 10.

Gebe was first visited by our team in January 1994, when preliminary surveys were carried out, resulting in discovery of the open air and rockshelter sites at Buwawansi and the cave of Um Kapat Papo. In May–June 1994 we discovered the caves of Wetef and Golo, and continued research at Buwawansi. Further research on these last three sites was undertaken in December 1995–January 1996. Gebe is thus the only region of the Northern Moluccas to have received three periods of fieldwork, but the results have certainly repaid the investment of time.

Golo Cave

Golo Cave turned out to be one of the most important sites excavated in the Northern Moluccas. It was shown to us, together with the rockshelters at nearby Wetef, by Ramalan Marsaoly on 5 June 1994. Excavations were then carried out in Golo by Peter Bellwood and Goenadi Nitihaminoto from 10–14 June 1994, and later from 23 December 1995 to 3 January 1996. The large rockshelter at Wetef was excavated by Geoffrey Irwin and Daud Tanudirjo in 1995–96, and a report on this site follows in the next section.

Golo lies about 60 m inland from the head of the beach, in a low coral cliff. Its present-day earth floor lies between 8 and 9 m above high tide level. Like Um Kapat Papo (below), Golo Cave is essentially a creation of underwater solution processes that must have occurred when the reef was still below sea level. It has a high and uneven ceiling approximately 3–4 m high. In extent, it measures about 12 m from drip-line to back wall, and occupies a similar width (Figs 2.3 and 2.4). In the rear of the cave there is a dark passage that runs about 50 m into the rock. Adjacent to this is a kind of limestone gallery, formed by a long horizontal alcove fronted by a series of free-standing stalactite columns.

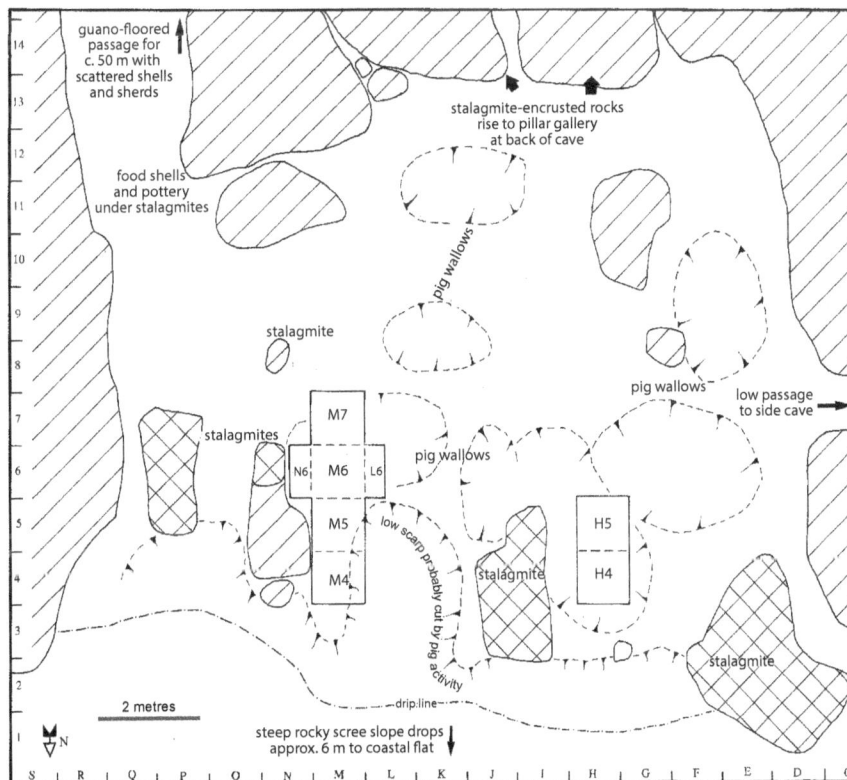

Figure 2.3 Plan of Golo Cave, showing excavation units and their component squares (each 1x1 m).
Limestone bedrock features are hatched in one direction only, stalactite floor to ceiling pillars are cross-hatched.
Source: Peter Bellwood.

When first entered, the floor of the cave was seen to consist of a dark brown deposit disturbed in places by shallow pits made by feral pigs. Very few artefacts were seen on the surface. In cross-section, the earthen floor of the cave rises slightly through about 50 vertical cm inwards from the drip-line towards the centre, and then drops down again into the back of the cave. In the semi-dark inner part of the cave, near the back wall, the floor is generally quite low and significant human occupation here seems never to have occurred. Excavation was restricted to the front half of the cave, to those areas where the deposits seemed to be deep and relatively undisturbed.

Figure 2.4 Golo Cave, from outside (above) and inside before excavation (below).
The stalagmite pillar that divides the mouth into two parts can be seen in both photographs.
Source: Peter Bellwood.

A grid of 1 m squares was imposed over the site in 1994, prior to excavation. In that year, Square M5 (visible in Fig. 2.3) was dug to bedrock at 240 cm, whereas M4 was stopped at only 70 cm below the surface due to shortage of time. The other squares delineated in Figure 2.3 were laid out and dug in 1995–96, at which time M4, L6 and M6 were also taken to bedrock. Excavation in M7 was halted by a large boulder. L6 and N6 were opened as small extensions to recover an extended skeleton, which lay at a depth of 65–80 cm in M6 (Fig. 2.6). N6 was not dug below the level of the skeleton for safety reasons connected with the nearby presence of a very large limestone boulder on the modern surface. Squares H4 and H5 were also excavated in 1995–96, but found to contain a stratigraphy only 90–140 cm deep owing the presence of high sloping bedrock.

Layer boundaries were not clearly visible during the excavation process, so the deposits were removed continuously in 5 cm spits and dry-sieved through 2.5 mm meshes. In 1994 some limited wet-sieving was carried out in the sea (the nearest fresh water lies a 1 km walk away down the beach towards Tanjung Lagiau), but this did not add very much to the data recoverable by careful hand sorting, except possibly for the recovery of small fragments of bone, and the procedure was not continued because of the logistical difficulties. In terms of stratigraphy, a very careful inspection of sections after excavation, and of photographs taken under different light conditions, leads to a conclusion that only two sedimentary layers (1 and 2) can be clearly identified, together with a single burial pit. These features are shown in section in Figure 2.5.

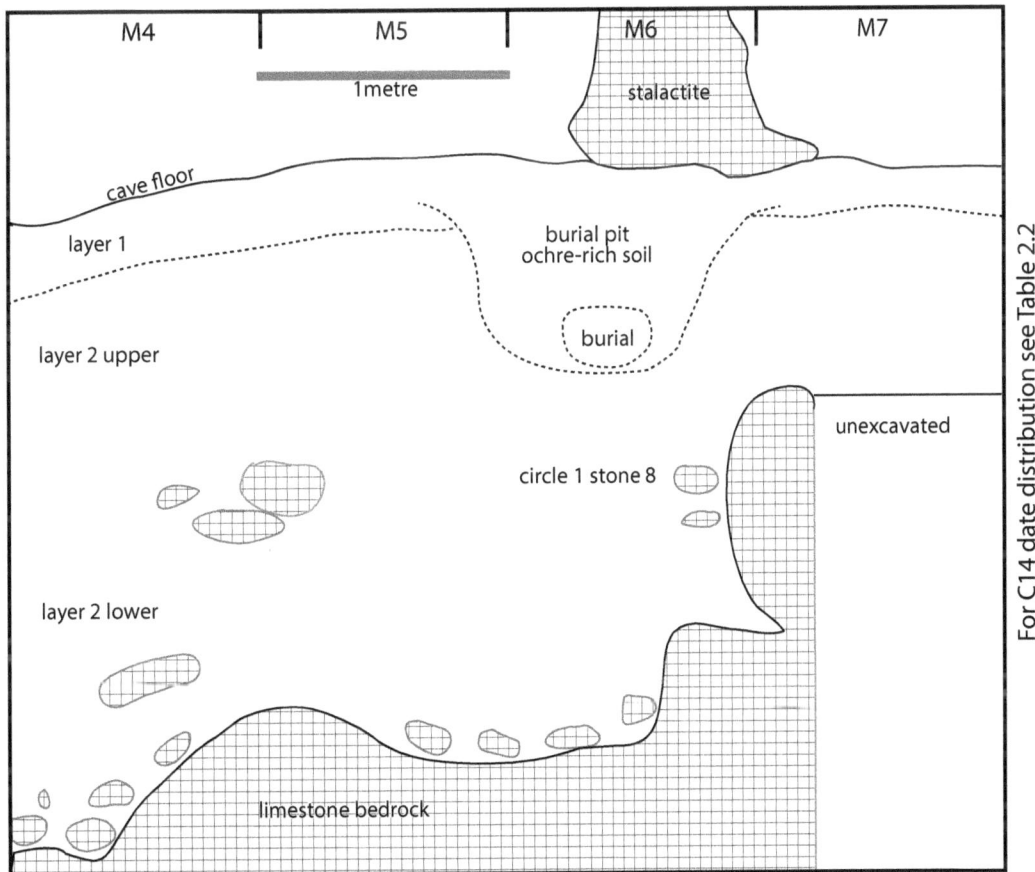

Figure 2.5 Section of the east walls of Squares M4 to M7, Golo Cave.
The hanging stalactite is projected on to the top of the section from the east wall of N6.
Source: Peter Bellwood.

The question arises of whether Golo Cave contains essentially one continuously deposited profile, or whether sharply different depositional phases can be identified. One way to examine this question is through recording grain size distributions by depth, calculated (see Table 2.1) following advice from John Magee, then of the Division of Archaeology and Natural History at ANU. A quantity of soil from each 10 cm depth was paddle-agitated for about 5 minutes in 300 mL of water mixed with 10 mL of NaOH and 10 mL of NaPO$_3$. For Golo, this was sufficient time to disaggregate material concreted with CaCo$_3$, so these figures are thus an accurate record of actual grain size.

Table 2.1 Grain size distributions and colours of Golo sediments by depth, excavation unit L6–M6.

Depth below surface (cm)	Per cent coarse > 0.063 mm	Per cent fine < 0.063 mm	Munsell colour*
10 (Layer 1)	51	49	10YR5/2
40	49	51	10YR6/2
60	56	44	10YR5/3
70	45	55	10YR5/3
80	49	51	10YR6/2
90	43	57	10YR6/2
100	43	57	10YR6/2
120	38	62	10YR6/2
140	44	56	10YR6/2
150	39	61	10YR6/2
160	41	59	10YR6/2
170	61	39	10YR6/2
180	52	48	10YR6/2
190	48	52	10YR6/2
200	52	48	10YR6/2
210	55	45	10YR6/1
220	63	37	10YR6/1
230	67	33	10YR7/2

* Fine fractions after oven drying.
Source: Peter Bellwood.

No major trend occurred in grain size distribution with depth at Golo, except for a slight accumulation of coarser particles in the two lowest spits (220 and 230 cm). Much of the fine fraction was probably derived from bat guano, which still falls in the cave today. The coarse fractions of these deposits, upon hand examination, can be seen to consist of limestone nodules, shell grit, dark (presumably mineral) grains, and grains of coral sand of a similar size range as those in the modern beach. These beach sand grains are most visible in the lowest two spits, as might be expected since the cave was possibly uplifted with a quantity of coral beach sand trapped within it. These lowest spits, however, show no signs of any separate and sterile basal beach sand layer, unlike those visible in the bases of the nearby Wetef rockshelter and Uattamdi rockshelter on Kayoa. Cultural deposits continued right to bedrock in Golo, suggesting that any former beach sand deposit had been mostly washed out of the cave before human occupation began.

The fine fractions generally become lighter in colour with depth, from greyish-brown at the top to light grey at the base. The transition zone between Layers 1 and 2 is rather diffuse (certainly more diffuse than can be indicated in Fig. 2.5), and subdivision of the 2 m depth of Layer 2 into more than one stratigraphic layer seems unwarranted. Its contents are discussed therefore purely in terms of depth below the surface inside the single long excavation unit, which includes squares LMN4–7 (Table 2.2).

Golo excavation units LMN4–7, Layer 1 and the burial pit

This upper layer in Golo Cave is 30 cm thick, dark brown in colour and relatively rich in limestone pieces and concretions. It is rather deficient in cultural materials above its bottom 5 cm, but it contains almost all the potsherds and seven of the 14 *Cassis* shell adzes (Table 2.2). Immediately to the east of N6, the cave floor (i.e. the top of Layer 1) is sealed by a massive stalactite pillar, which drops down to the present floor level of the cave and then stops. Excavation under its edge revealed no trace of an underlying stalagmite. This pillar would presumably have existed in almost its present form during the formation of Layer 1, and it appears to have served as a focal point for the caching of the *Cassis* shell adzes. No less than 12 of these were found concentrated close to the stalactite in excavation unit LMN6–7, in situations that suggest they were cached deliberately in shallow holes dug in Layer 1 and into the top of Layer 2. Only one was found in Square M5, and none at all in M4. Layer 1 postdates a charcoal C14 determination of 3900–2975 cal. BP (ANU 9448), so the *Cassis* adzes are clearly of quite recent date, presumably Neolithic or Early Metal Phase, and perhaps buried by the same inhabitants as those who buried the supine human skeleton with the red ochre, to be described next. The *Cassis* adzes are described in Chapters 8 and 9.

In 1994, during the excavation of M5, it was observed that a soil zone with a marked reddish tinge occurred in the south wall of the square, within upper Layer 2. This feature disappeared towards the north. At that time, its significance was not understood. In 1995–96, during the excavation of Square M6, it became apparent that this reddish soil lay around and above a complete extended adult burial, placed supine at a depth of 65–80 cm below the surface, with head turned towards the south (Fig. 2.6). Part-squares L6 and N6 were opened to reveal the full length of this burial, which had an elongated coral pebble, placed below its feet, presumably laid deliberately as a grave offering. No other grave goods occurred.

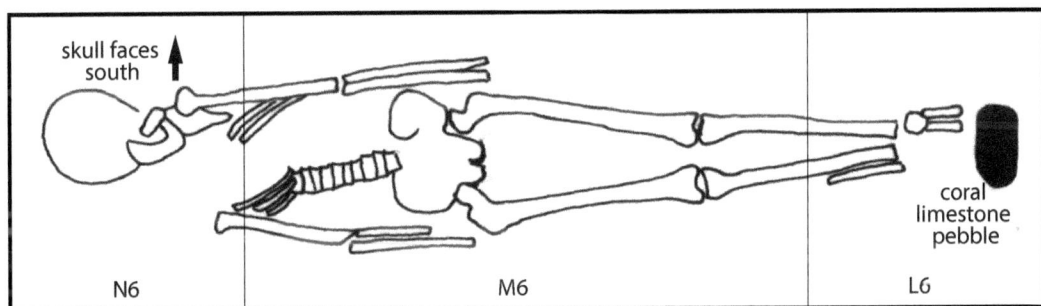

Figure 2.6 Field sketch plan of the Golo L6–M6 skeleton (not all bones recovered are shown).
M6 is 1 m long.
Source: Peter Bellwood.

Although no burial pit was noticed, partly because M6 was excavated prior to discovery of the skeleton itself, careful consideration of the whole situation on site and in photographs (unfortunately, none of sufficient clarity for publication) made it clear that the reddish soil and the burial were connected with each other. Unfortunately, no section was left across the burial by which to check the relationship. But matters became clearer when the distribution of red ochre pieces within the site was considered. Ochre, which occurs in small quantities throughout all layers, is present in red and yellow varieties, the latter being quite rare. The red ochre often occurs in amorphous lump form, but many pieces were very definitely faceted and shaped (Fig. 8.5). When distributions were examined, it turned out that the faceted pieces of red ochre were concentrated markedly in the vicinity of the skeleton, adjacent to and above it, especially between 35–70 cm below the ground surface (Table 2.3). In addition, the reddish layer was of restricted extent and did not continue into M7. This concentration so close to the burial seemed beyond the range of coincidence.

It is thus likely that the reddish soil formed the filling of a burial pit dug from quite close to the base of Layer 1. Interestingly, there were no signs of any decrease in densities of occupation materials such as shellfish, oven stones or stone flakes in the ochre-rich deposit. This indicates that occupation-rich Layer 2 material was dug out initially, and then redeposited around the corpse while being mixed with the scraped and powdered ochre. The burial, which had an artificially deformed cranium, is described by David Bulbeck in Chapter 11.

Golo excavation units LMN4–7, Layer 2

Layer 2 is brown, with the same texture as Layer 1, up to 2 m thick, but lighter in colour and with a slightly lesser concentration of small limestone pieces. However, it contains many large limestone pieces in its lower part, close to the bedrock. The upper part of Layer 2, especially between 30–70 cm below the cave surface, contains the densest remains in the Golo sequence in terms of animal bones, cooking stones, flaked lithics and shells (Table 2.2). In contrast, the middle and lower parts of Layer 2, from about 100 cm down to 240 cm, have only fairly sparse evidence of human occupation, but a fairly marked increase occurs below 200 cm in densities of flaked stones and shell (including worked shell). It is not absolutely clear if all of the cultural materials at the base of the site reflect a true stratigraphic presence or simply downwards movement through gravity—some of the lowest volcanic pebble cooking stones are large and heavy, as can be seen in Table 2.2.

Table 2.2 Distribution of the cultural contents of Golo Cave by depth, for all excavated units, except where stated otherwise.

Golo Cave, depth in cm	Animal bone gm	Shell gm, M5 only	Shell adzes	Bone points#	Facetted ochre tablets◆	Volcanic cook stones (no./gm), unit LM6	Sherds	Flaked stone, (no./gm), unit LMN4-7	C14 date (cal. BP) ms = marine shell
0-10	15	600	2 Cassis	1			6	0	
10-20	90	890	2 Cassis	3		4/700	6	1/175	2314-1415 human bone
20-30	128	2150	3 Cassis	4		1/50	12	3/17	
30-40	1967	3050	3 Cassis	39	6	7/350	3	3/30	10,621-10,246 Cassis adze
40-50	1631	3800		34	7	33/1010		13/114	3900-2975 charcoal
50-60	904	2085	2 Cassis	33	14	24/1000		18/317	8100-7641 ms
60-70	379	1875	2 Cassis	5	10	28/1125	1	29/443	22,269-21,474 ms
70-80	139	1275		2	5	17/1350		16/215	7675-7516 wallaby bone
80-90	63	1050			3	29/1650		13/448	7982-7738 wallaby bone
90-100	34	1350	1 indet.			18/1000		3/68	
100-110	15	775	1 Hippopus		2	29/2250		4/200	
110-120	7	800			1	10/575		6/37	
120-130	40*	575	1 Tridacna			3/100		6/129	
130-140		550	1 Tridacna			5/210		4/157	12,044-11,376 ms 38,984-34,638 Tridacna adze
140-150	7*	825	1 Hippopus			1/400		7/197	13,131-12,756 ms 7176-6771 Hippopus adze
150-160		775				3/1000			
160-170		600			1	5/95		1/3	
170-180		950				1/165			
180-190		550						1/55	22,919-22,285 ms
190-200		350						2/56	8369-8029 ms 10,243-9794 ms
200-210		325						10/160	19,401-18,674 ms 25,982-25,351 ms 33,485-31,324 ms
210-220		690				2/220		4/125	32,593-31,142 ms 36,350-35,001 ms
220-230		1050				1/10		7/255	35,390-33,910 ms 39,003-34,173 ms
230-240		375				1/410		3/31	

*Human bones, described by David Bulbeck in Chapter 11.
See Pasveer and Bellwood 2004. ◆ Most are from the burial pit surrounding the skeleton directly dated to 2314-1415 cal. BP (ANU 11818).

The chronology for the site is considered to be best expressed through the shaded radiocarbon dates (see Table 1.1 for full details) in the right-hand column.
Source: Peter Bellwood.

Table 2.3 Distribution of ochre pieces, Golo Cave.

Depth in cm	H4–5	M4	M5	LMN6	M7
30–40	R	RR		R	RR
40–50	R		RR	RRRry	Rr
50–60	Rrr		RRRRRR	RRRRRR	
60–70	R		RRRRRRRRR	**BURIAL**	RR
70–80	RRR	Rr	R	**BURIAL**	r
80–90	r		r	R	RRy
90–100		r		rrr	
100–110			RR		r
110–120			Rry	rrrr	
130	rr			y	
140				rrrr	
150			r		
160					
170	r		R		
180					
190					
200					
210				ry	

Notation is for individual pieces. R = facetted/grooved red; r = amorphous red; y = amorphous yellow.

Source: Peter Bellwood.

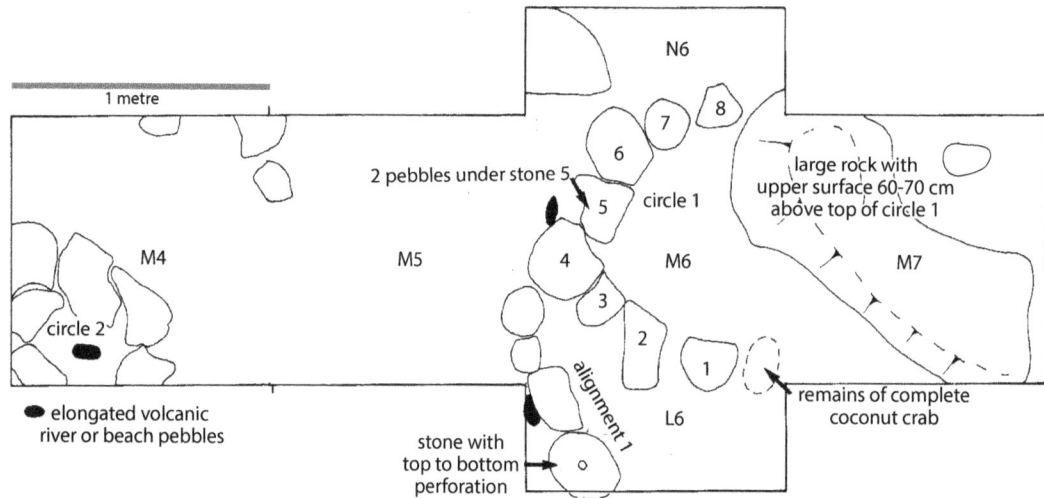

Figure 2.7 Circular stone arrangements (circles 1 and 2) in Layer 2 at 115–135 cm, Golo Cave.

Source: Peter Bellwood.

The middle portion of Layer 2 is of particular importance owing to the presence of circular structures of coral limestone blocks placed on the cave floor. The two clearest of these were the two uppermost, which both lay at the same depth below surface. The largest, termed circle 1 for recording purposes, lay in M6 with the bases of its stones at 135 cm depth, the stones themselves being up to 20 cm high (Figs 2.7 and 2.8). There are eight coral stones in all, one of which (stone 3) had been displaced sideways in antiquity but which fitted perfectly back into the adjacent hole. The vertical location of stone 8 is shown in the trench section, Figure 2.5. In shape, this structure is actually a semicircle with an internal diameter of 80 cm, but it appears to be built outwards from the side of a large limestone boulder that occupies most of Square M7. This boulder rose to about 70 cm above the top of the circle 1 stones and thus would have formed a prominent feature of the cave floor at the time (it has since been buried, such that its top is today about 60–70 cm below ground level).

A striking feature of circle 1 was the finding of three elongated volcanic beach pebbles in direct association with it, presumably brought to Golo from the southern half of Gebe Island. Two were buried together under stone 5 (weights 400 and 500 gm), the third (weight 1250 gm) lay just outside the circle next to stone 4. None of these pebbles showed signs of deliberate working.

At the same level in M4, about 1.4 m north of the M6 circle, lay another much smaller feature termed circle 2. This was a complete circle of coral blocks of the same general size as those in circle 1. However, in this case the inner diameter was only about 30 cm. The feature did not contain any sign of a post hole, but precisely in its middle and about halfway down the soil fill lay another elongated volcanic beach pebble, this time weighing 340 gm and having one apparently smoothed side, possibly artificial.

Close to circle 1 in M6, but lying on a surface about 10 cm below it, lay part of another apparent stone alignment—in this case called alignment 1 in Figure 2.7 since no particularly circular shape was evident. This alignment could possibly have been part of a straight line—it has four stones in M6 with a fifth visible inside the section, and so is of unknown total length. One stone was perforated right through by a small hole about 5 cm in diameter. Since the stone is crumbly reef coral, it is difficult to know whether the hole was intentional or natural—there are no signs of human workmanship surviving. Again, alignment 1 produced a beach pebble, in this case a similar elongated one weighing 800 gm and placed next to one of the stones.

Figure 2.8 Golo stone circles 1 and 2 (photos not to same scale, and see Figure 2.7 for actual scale).
These photos are archival and are slightly blurred.
Source: Peter Bellwood.

So far, the three structures described can be seen as part of one constructional phase, with alignment 1 perhaps being superseded after a short interval by circle 1. The recurrent association of elongated beach pebbles of volcanic rock is interesting. Such pebbles are not common in the site as a whole and the association cannot be coincidental. Most of the other volcanic stones in the upper part of the site are shattered oven stones, and the vast majority lie at higher levels.

About 25 cm below these structures in M6 and lying at 160 cm below the surface, parts of two other possible structures were located (Fig. 2.9). These are not so clear as the ones above, possibly because some of their stones had been removed. One possible alignment consists of four stones in a line, two on either side of a 50 cm gap. The other is a part-circle of five stones, like circle 1, which also lies close to the large rock in M7. However, because it is so much closer to the rock than was circle 1, the possibility arises that this is just rubble that has accumulated around its base. Yet, once again, we have an elongated beach pebble in association, this time lying alone between the two structures. Given the fact that the blocks that make up these alignments are all on one level, and few blocks occurred scattered elsewhere at this level, the assumption that both were deliberate human constructions seems to be quite reasonable. Because the upper structures were so obviously deliberately constructed, the chances that these lower ones were also would appear to be quite high.

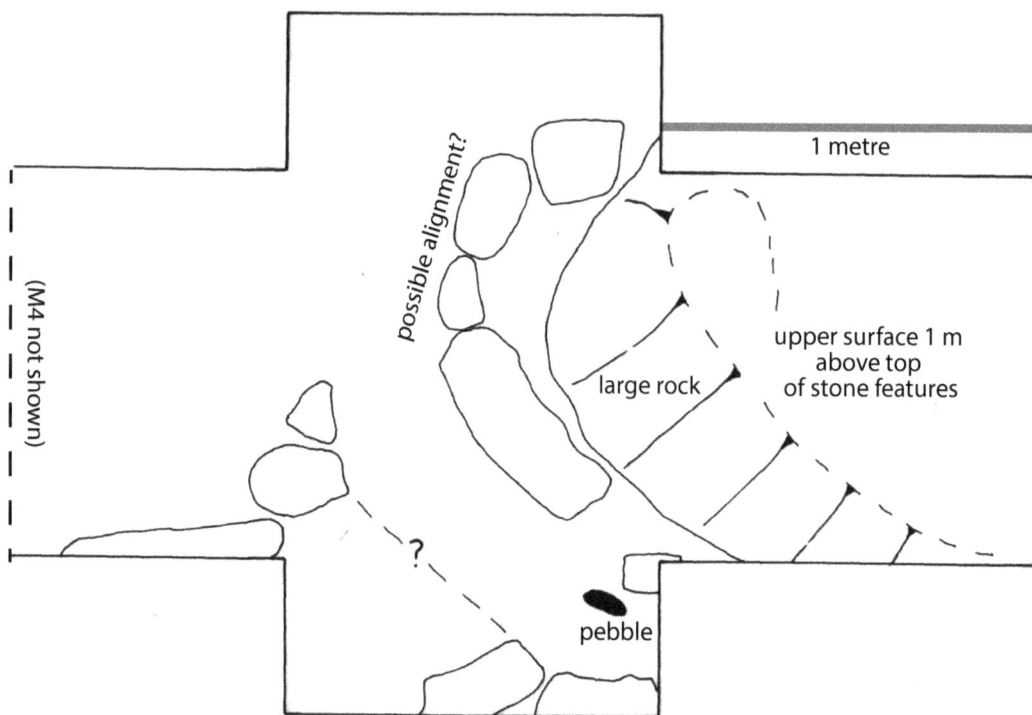

Figure 2.9 Possible stone arrangements in Layer 2 at c. 140–160 cm, Golo Cave.
Source: Peter Bellwood.

In terms of chronology, the stone construction activity in Golo Cave is clearly dated by samples ANU 9769 and 9512, which form a close-set pair. Both are on marine shell, with results of 12,044–11,376 and 13,131–12,756 cal. BP. They suggest a time span for the constructions centred on 12,500 years ago, at the end of the Pleistocene, and perhaps a little older for the lower alignments. In this case, because of the size and weight of these blocks and the unlikelihood of post-depositional movement, the adjacent marine shell C14 dates most probably do relate directly to them.

Between about 90–170 cm below the surface, and during the overall period of construction of these stone circles, Layer 2 had only a limited occurrence of cultural materials, with only approximately one-third to one-half of the shell densities present in the upper part of Layer 2, no bone, and relatively few flaked lithics and cooking stones (Table 2.2). Ochre quantities were also very limited. On the other hand, between 100–150 cm below the cave surface there occurred the remarkable series of four (perhaps five) adzes made on *Tridacna* or *Hippopus* shells, all probably cached in pits dug from higher levels and almost certainly younger in date than the stone circles. One *Hippopus* adze from a level immediately below the circles is only 7000 years old in terms of its actual shell C14 date (OZD 774). The typology and dating for these items will be discussed in Chapters 8 and 9, but *Tridacna* and *Hippopus* (giant clam) adzes are a very important tool type that many consider to belong to preceramic and pre-Neolithic contexts in Island Southeast Asia and Melanesia. One *Tridacna* example also occurs in the Buwawansi 1 rockshelter, to be described below.

The lowest 40–50 cm of Layer 2, at about 190–240 cm below the cave surface, produced some further surprises in the form of a small rise in the density of cultural materials, particularly worked and/or burnt marine shell, flaked stone, and volcanic cooking stones. Because the flaked shell and stone materials have been discussed in full elsewhere (Szabó et al. 2007), they are not described again here, except to note the significance of finding both worked stone and worked shell at a date extending back to beyond 35,000 cal. BP, this being highly relevant for discussions of the handiwork of early *Homo sapiens* in Island Southeast Asia. Two concentrations of possible burnt coral cooking stones were observed in M6 at about 190 cm below the surface, each being approximately 40 cm in diameter. A large elongated volcanic pebble and a single example of a *Canarium* anvil also occurred at this level, the latter pitted on either side exactly like the examples from elsewhere in the Northern Moluccas (Figs 8.1(l) and 8.2). However, caution should perhaps address any claim that this anvil is truly 35,000 years old. Downwards movement through disturbance is possible.

The actual date of uplift of Golo Cave above sea level is unknown, so it is not clear if the basal occupation in the cave is likely to represent the first human occupation of the island. However, it should be emphasised again that the basal part of Layer 2 shows no evidence for a layer of clean beach sand. The deposit at the bottom on bedrock is the same in colour and texture as the higher portions, and it contains cultural material. This suggests that the cave was not actually at beach level when it was first occupied, and probably contained very little natural soil/sand matrix before human occupation began.

Phases of occupation at Golo Cave

To recap on all the above, the occupation in Golo Cave can be divided into the following four major phases:

- Phase 1, c. 36,000 to perhaps 25,000 BP, represented by the lower occupation at approximately 200–240 cm below ground level in basal Layer 2, with worked *Turbo* opercula (Szabó et al. 2007), use of *Scutellastra flexuosa* limpet shells as scrapers (Szabó and Koppel 2015), flaked stone, and use of volcanic and possibly coral cooking stones.

- Phase 2, c. 25,000 to 11,000 BP, represented by intermittent occupation with construction of the stone circles and alignments with volcanic beach pebble 'offerings' towards the end of the phase, but otherwise with a diminished density of occupation in terms of shell and flaked stone.

- Phase 3, Early and Middle Holocene, mostly between 8000 and 3000 BP, represented by upper Layer 2 with bones of cuscus and wallaby (Chapter 10), the densest period of shell midden deposition, numerous flaked lithics and cooking stones, and possibly the burial of the *Tridacna* and *Hippopus* adzes in pits dug in the cave floor.

- Phase 4, post 3000 BP, represented by Layer 1, with an extended and cranially deformed burial dated to about 2000 years ago associated with prolific use of red ochre, caching of *Cassis* adzes, and sparse pottery. By this time, wallabies had disappeared from Golo Cave, but their bones continued to be deposited in nearby Wetef rockshelter. Phase 4 can be classified as Neolithic.

The question arises of variation in the intensity of occupation within Golo Cave through time. It will already be evident from the above discussion, combined with the contents of Table 2.2, that fluctuations occurred in the densities of various cultural materials with depth. In particular, occupation was generally rather thin between 140 and 200 cm. But was the island of Gebe actually abandoned during that time?

In 2000, an analysis of 22 phytolith samples from Golo, taken at 10 cm depth intervals, was undertaken by Doreen Bowdery in the School of Archaeology and Anthropology at ANU. Although precise identification of economically important plants was not undertaken, Bowdery was able to present data on numbers of classified phytolith groups and on microfossil counts by 10 cm spit. Her results are presented in Figures 2.10 and 2.11, in which it can be seen that the distributions of phytoliths, starch and charcoal particles (both in the soil samples and trapped inside phytoliths) match to some degree the distributions of cultural materials in Golo shown in Table 2.2. There are fluctuations, especially through the middle layers of the cave, although if phytoliths, starch and charcoal really do relate to a presence of humans in the site, then there was clearly no long hiatus in occupation at any time, but rather a continuous fluctuation that might just reflect sampling factors. This suggests that humans were always in the vicinity of Golo Cave, even if not in actual occupation of the site. The phytolith evidence from Golo does not indicate that Gebe Island was abandoned for any long periods of time during the past 35,000 years.

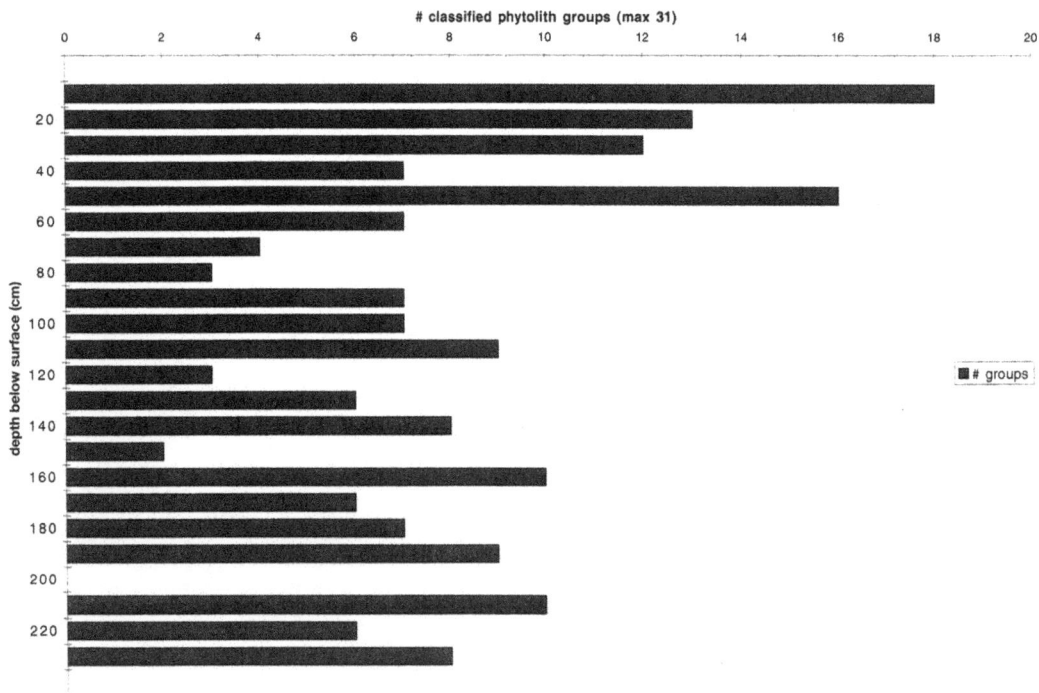

Figure 2.10 Classified phytolith morphological groups, expressed as percentages of an identified total of 31, by 10 cm spit in Golo Cave.

Actual species are not identified. Depths are below surface.

Source: Doreen Bowdery.

Microfossil summary

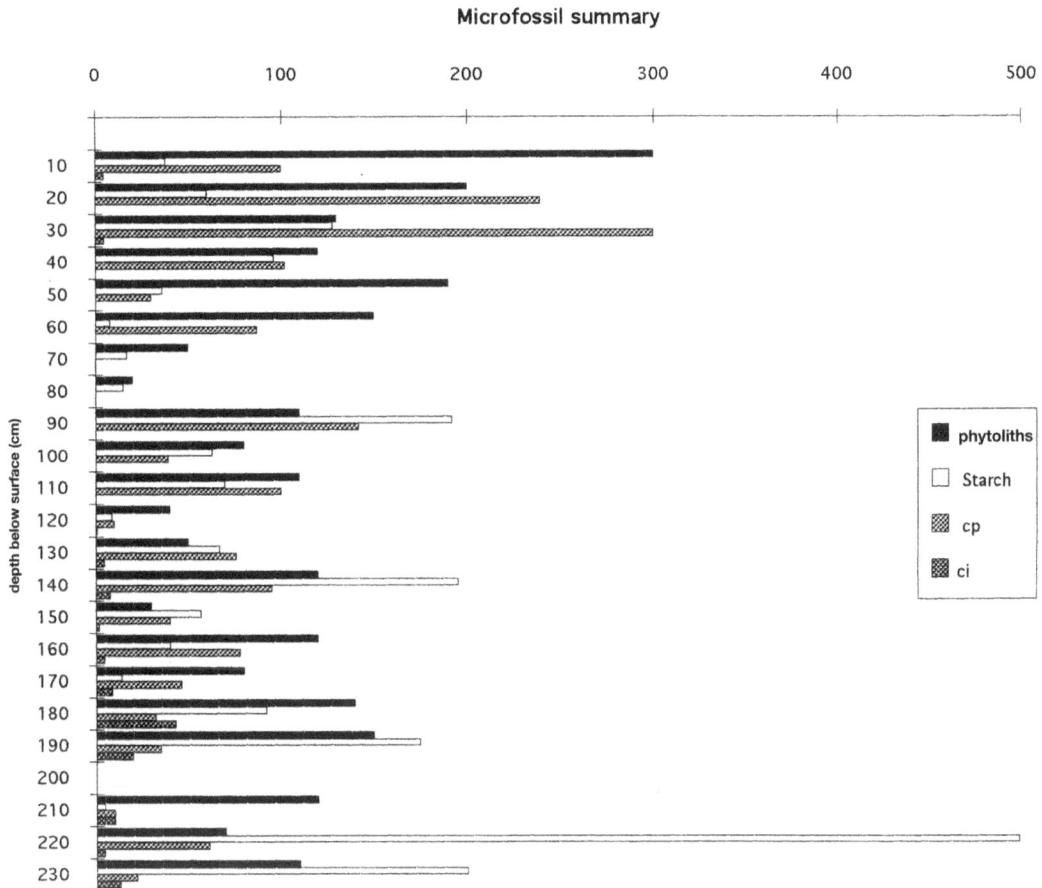

Figure 2.11 Counts for phytoliths, starch grains, carbon particles recovered from soil samples during phytolith extraction, and cytoplasmic carbon inclusions in phytoliths, by 10 cm spit in Golo Cave.

Depths are below surface. cp = carbon particle count; ci = carbon inclusion count.

Source: Doreen Bowdery.

Wetef rockshelter

Wetef is a large rockshelter on the north coast of Gebe Island, a kilometre west of Golo Cave and just south of the Equator. Like Golo it was formed by undersea and underground solution processes rather than wave action, and it now lies 60 m inland from the current beach in a low coral cliff, with its floor at 8 m above sea level. The shelter is 18 m wide and 7 m deep inside the drip-line (Fig. 2.12).

An excavation trench, 2x1 m, was located towards the front of the shelter, inside the drip-line (Fig. 2.13). Wetef was well exposed to daylight and the stratigraphy was discernible. Excavation was by stratigraphic unit and collection by 5 cm spits, separately for Squares K3 and K4. All material was passed through 4 mm screens. Depths below the surface shown in the figures and tables (below) were measured at the junction of K3 and K4.

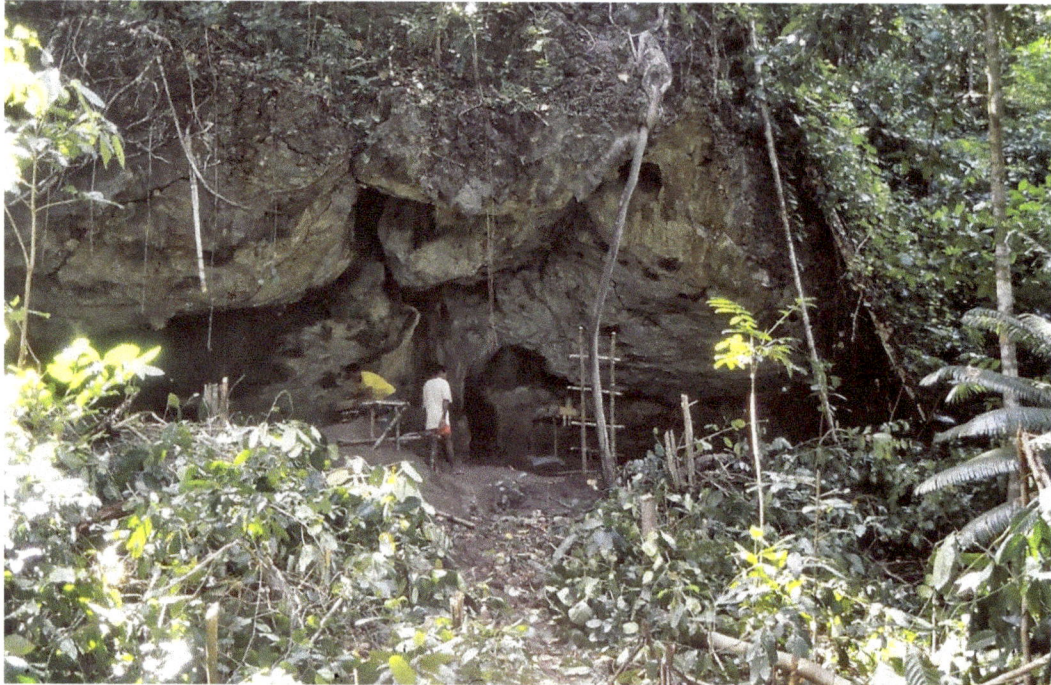

Figure 2.12 Wetef rockshelter during excavation in 1996–97.
Source: Geoffrey Irwin.

Wetef stratigraphy and C14 dating

Figure 2.14 is a photograph of the excavation after completion, and Figure 2.15 is a drawing of the excavated section. The deposit was similar to that described for Golo Cave (above). It was mildly alkaline and composed largely of roof limestone, guano, decayed plant material and cultural remains.

The upper Layer A was a soft brown soil, subject to disturbance from the surface, with dry leaf litter and land snails trapped in the deposit. There were intact lenses of compacted white wood ash from fires in the vicinity. Table 2.4 and Figure 2.16 show the distribution of cultural materials by depth, and it is clear that all seven undecorated potsherds discovered in the site belonged to this upper and recent part of the deposit. Marine shell was associated with this layer also, but the very small number of animal bones and cooking stones could have been carried up from the top of Layer B, below. The evidence points to only intermittent and slight use of the shelter at this time.

The interface between Layers A and B was virtually sterile and marked by a scatter of limestone pieces, 5 cm in diameter or less, in the same brown soil matrix. Effectively sealed below this was a rich midden in Layer B. There was an abundance of animal bone, marine shell, and cooking stones of diverse volcanic and metamorphic rocks, available from further east on the island. Three complete *Cassis* shell adzes and many broken pieces were found in Layer B1 and there were a small number of stone flakes.

A further lens of roof-fall limestone pebbles at around 70 cm below the surface separated Layers B1 and B2, and could have represented some slight interruption in occupation. The midden continued in Layer B2 in a matrix of scattered ash and charcoal, and some of the shell was burnt.

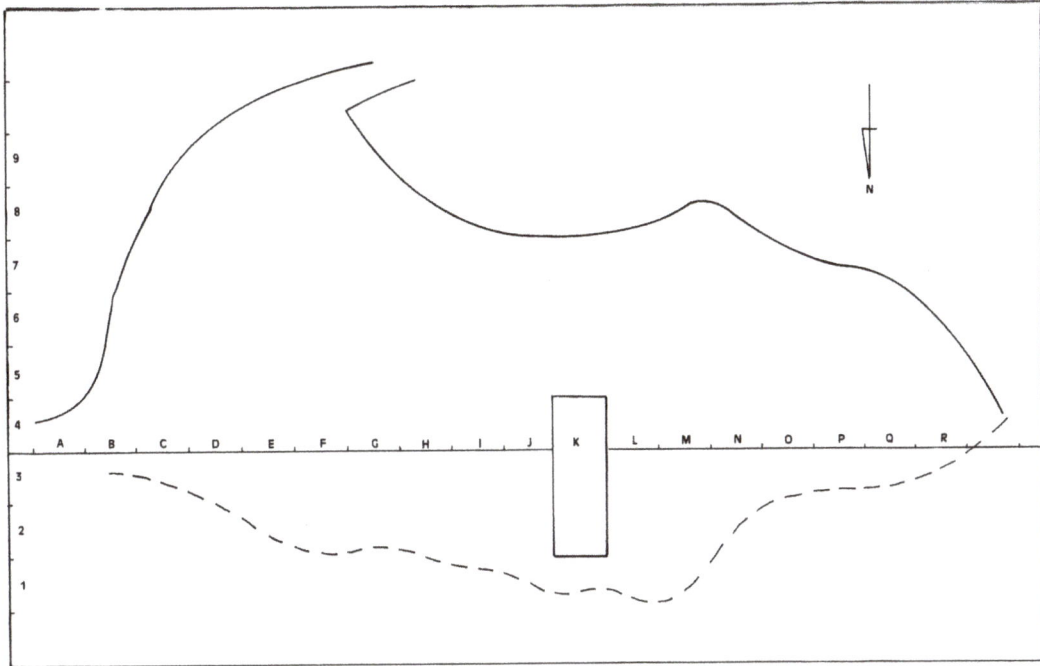

Figure 2.13 Plan of the Wetef rockshelter (grid is 1x1 m).
Source: Geoffrey Irwin.

Figure 2.14 The Wetef excavation on completion in 1996 (the excavation is 2.4 m deep).

Clean beach sand is visible in the base of the excavation at the rear, as are the ash layers in Layer C2.

Source: Peter Bellwood.

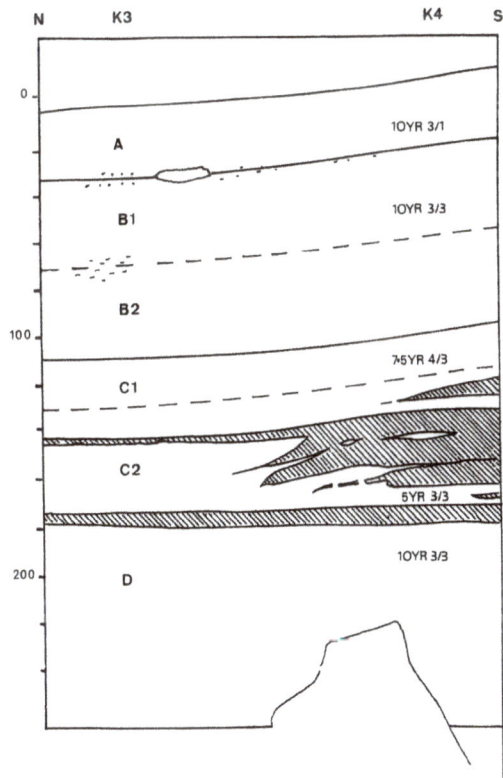

Figure 2.15 The Wetef section, east wall, 2 m across.

Shaded layers are ash.

Source: Geoffrey Irwin.

Table 2.4 The distribution of cultural remains by depth in Wetef Squares K3 and K4 (shell only for K4).

cm	Bone gm	Shell (K4) gm	Cooking stones no.	gm	Sherds no.	Shell adzes no.	Flaked stone no.	gm	Bone points no.	C14 date cal. BP (Tables 1.1 and 2.7)
0–10		145			2					780–670
10–20	14	260	1	10	3				1	
20–30	8	200			1		1	9	2	
30–40	166	265	3	50	1					
40–50	1151	580	10	80		2	1	6		5425–5025
50–60	801	610	3	240			1	10	3	
60–70	475	1100	6	310		2			7	
70–80	508	1300	1	40		3			2	5742–5467
80–90	408	640				3			4	
90–100	265	470	3	140					1	
100–110	36	380								7874–7580
110–120	18	320	9	570						7239–6901
120–130	45	510	21	850						
130–140	38	430	1	20					1	
140–150	43	460	5	460			4	79		8327–8011
150–160	71	260	13	1010					2	8327–8011
160–170	87	440	33	1160			3	63	1	
170–180	83	320	18	660					1	9340–8974
180–190	4	210	14	310						
190–200	15	490	7	290			5	62	1	
200–210	5	370	11	370			3	43		12,962–12,626
210–220	1	410	3	140			2	15		
220–230		290	3	70			1	16		
230–240		220	13	200			1	16		
240–250		40	19	400						25,610–24,614
250–260			6	60						30,299–28,381
260–270			2	20						

Source: Geoffrey Irwin.

Four radiocarbon dates on marine shell (Table 2.5) bracket this period of intensive use of Wetef between 5425–5025 cal. BP (Wk 4618), near the top of Layer B, and 7874–7580 cal. BP (Wk 4620) near the bottom.

The next layer moving downwards in the profile, Layer C, is also divided into upper and lower zones; C1 was a lighter brown soil with a finer texture and C2 had a reddish hue. Between them, at around 125–130 cm depth, there was an encrusted lens of small stones and shells, many apparently sterile, which marked a minor stratigraphic event. Two radiocarbon dates from Layer C1, each on a separate shell from Squares K3 and K4, gave the same age of 8327–8011 cal. BP (Wk 4622 and Wk 4623).

Layer C2 featured lenses of compacted grey ash, some restricted to K4, but two intact layers of ash extended across both K3 and K4 (Fig. 2.15, shaded). The upper ash layer at about 140 cm below the surface had a fine lens of charcoal immediately beneath and represented a particular burning event. Another radiocarbon date, sealed between this and a lower intact ash at about 175–180 cm, gave an age of 9340–8974 cal. BP (Wk 4624).

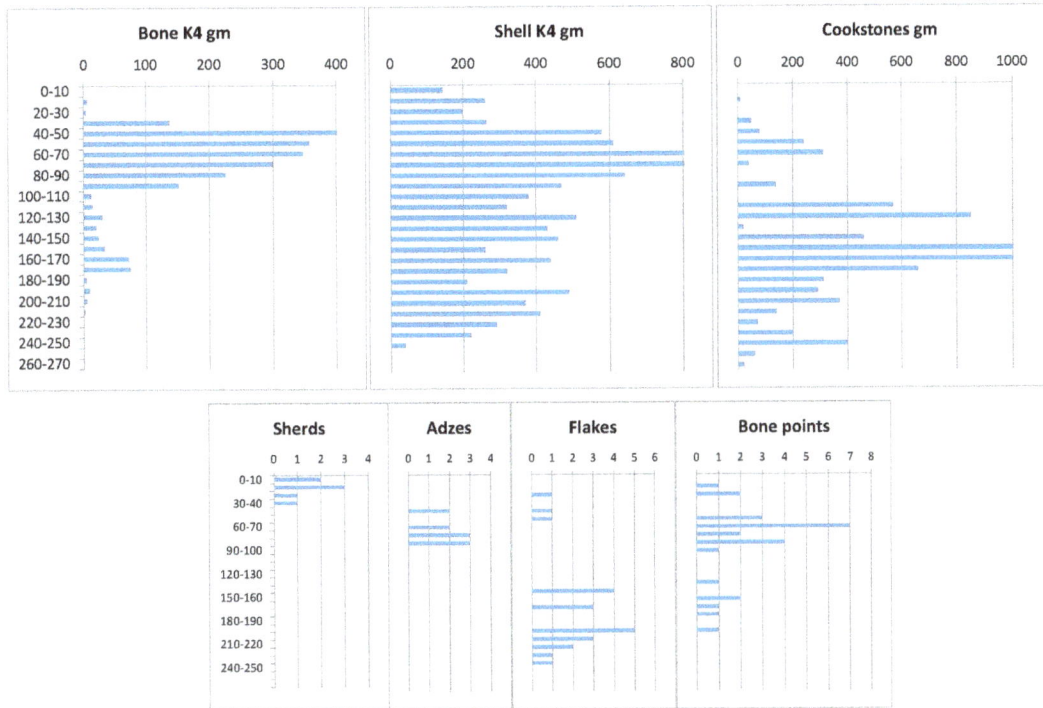

Figure 2.16 Histograms to illustrate the distribution of cultural remains in Wetef Squares K3 and K4.

Source: Geoffrey Irwin.

Table 2.5 Radiocarbon dates from excavations in Wetef rockshelter.

Lab No.	Loc.	Depth cm	Material	δC13	C14 age BP (uncal.)	OxCal 4.2 (IntCal 13) at 95.4% (cal. BP)
Wk 4618	K3	45–50	shell	2.2±0.2	4920±60	5425–5025
Wk 4619	K3	75–80	shell	2.3±0.2	5250±60	5742–5467
Wk 4620	K4	100–105	shell	3.1±0.2	7260±70	7874–7580
Wk 4621	K3	110–115	shell	2.7±0.3	6560±70	7239–6901
Wk 4622	K4	140–145	shell	2.2±0.2	7710±70	8327–8011
Wk 4623	K3	145–150	shell	2.2±0.3	7710±70	8327–8011
Wk 4624	K3	170–175	shell	1.7±0.2	8510±70	9340–8974
Wk 4625	K4	200–205	shell	0.0±0.2	11,310±80	12,962–12,626
Wk 4626	K4	240–245	shell	2.8±0.2	21,290±170	25,610–24,614
Wk 4627	K4	250–255	shell	3.0±0.2	25,540±420	30,299–28,381
NZA 8369	K4	Layer A	wallaby bone	–20.8	791±67	906–570
NZA 8387	K4	Layer B	wallaby bone	–24.9	5521±77	6487–6182

Wk = Waikato University Radiocarbon Laboratory; NZA = Rafter Radiocarbon Laboratory.

Marine13 curve for shell (ΔR=0); IntCal13 curve for bone.

Source: Geoffrey Irwin.

Marine shell and cooking stones remained abundant through Layer C. However, there was a sharp decline in animal bone in Layer C1, following an earlier increase in Layer C2. It can be seen in Figure 2.16 that the distribution of animal bone in Wetef was bimodal, with the earlier mode in Layer C being much smaller than the later one in Layer B.

Close to the base of the section, below the deposition of the lower ash at the base of Layer C, there was no disturbance of the lower part of the site in Layer D. A radiocarbon date of 12,962–12,626 cal. BP (Wk 4625) below the ash indicated that this depth was close in date to the Pleistocene/Holocene boundary. Below this date the soil was very moist. Only very small quantities of animal bone were found in the top 20 cm of Layer D and, if bone formerly existed deeper in the site, it has not survived, perhaps due to water passing through the deposit.

Much of the small assemblage of stone flakes came from Layer D, down to a depth of 235 cm. Marine shell and crab continued to 245 cm and cooking stones to the bottom of the deposit at 260–270 cm. Two radiocarbon dates of 25,610–24,614 cal. BP (Wk 4626) and 30,299–28,381 cal. BP (Wk 4627) came from the lower part of Layer D, but the lowest part of the layer still remains undated. Layer D thus represented intermittent occupation in the terminal Pleistocene.

Below 250 cm, Layer D contained mixed beach sand and the cultural deposit bottomed out at 270 cm (Fig. 2.15). At the base of Golo was coral rock, but at Wetef there was sterile yellow coralline marine sand underlying the deposit (Layer E), which presumably dated from a time when the site was closer to sea level. The beach sand was tested to a depth of 60 cm in a narrowing space between large rocks, but we did not reach bedrock.

Phases of occupation at Wetef

The evidence from Wetef complements, and adds to, the evidence from Golo. While a handful of sherds was found in the top of Wetef, the site was essentially preceramic. The evidence for the age of the *Cassis* shell adzes is equivocal, although it is likely that those from Golo date to within the past 3000 years, as discussed in Chapter 8. Through the occupation sequence much of the economic evidence from the site relates to strandline exploitation, inshore fishing and hunting, the latter of *Dorcopsis* wallabies and phalangers.

The Wetef sequence can be summarised in terms of the phases of settlement established for Golo (above), commencing from the base upwards. Golo Phase 1 was either not present at Wetef, or it was not found. The bottom of the cultural deposit was not dated and the area sampled was small, but it was laid down on clean beach sand, which indicates that the site was closer to sea level then than now.

Phase 2 was characterised by intermittent occupation during the terminal Pleistocene. Shellfish and cooking stones were abundant and much of the small collection of stone flakes from Wetef occurred in these levels. Bone of all animals represented in the site, including macropod and phalanger, survived only in small quantities from the end of the period, but it is considered likely that groundwater passing through the deposit could have removed former evidence of a bone presence.

Golo Phases 3 and 4 are hardly separable at Wetef and together cover the Holocene. The evidence for Golo Phase 3 at Wetef is finer grained than that at Golo itself. Layer C covered the earlier part of the period to around 6000 BC, and Layer C2 had extensive evidence for fires and cooking in association with animal bone and marine shell. Bone, ash lenses, and cooking stones were fewer in Layer C1. Layer B dates to the mid to late Holocene, and presumably overlaps with Golo Phase 4. It is marked by a major peak in animal bone and marine shell, although no traces of domesticated animals were found. All of the *Cassis* adzes, both complete and broken, were found in Layer B1. A stratigraphic interface at the top of Layer B indicates a sharp reduction in the use of the site from this time onwards.

Layer A contained just a few potsherds but no stone flakes, shell adzes or animal bones. Evidence for fires was slight and there were no cooking stones. However, marine shell was still brought to the site. Elsewhere on Gebe during this period there was ceramic occupation, presumably dogs were present, and the *Dorcopsis* wallaby survived until at least the date (direct on wallaby bone) of 906–570 BP (NZA 8369). Wallabies no longer exist on Gebe, or elsewhere in the Northern Moluccas.

Um Kapat Papo

Um Kapat Papo, with the nearby but less significant cave of Kaitutsi, was the first site to be discovered on Gebe. It lies in a coral cliff behind the beach about 4–5 km along the southeast-facing coast of the island from the village of Umera. The approximate position of the site could only be ascertained by taking a compass bearing on the nearby island of Yu, to the north of Gebe. The present cave floor lies about 13 m above high tide level, up a fairly steep scree slope of coral blocks and soil, and then up a 3 m sheer cliff, which has to be scaled by ladder (Fig. 2.17). The name of the cave was given to us as 'Um Kapat Papo' by informants from Umera, but on further questioning it turned out that this simply meant 'cave' in the Gebe language, i.e. 'house beneath the rock', the parallel phrase being *rumah di bawah batu* in Bahasa Indonesia. Other informants during a later fieldwork period told us that the land name for the land on which the cave is located is 'Sanjin', so the cave should perhaps be called 'Um Sanjin' in the Gebe language. However, because of some uncertainty over this, and because we had already started labelling the finds from the cave with the initials UKP (for Um Kapat Papo), this name will be kept.

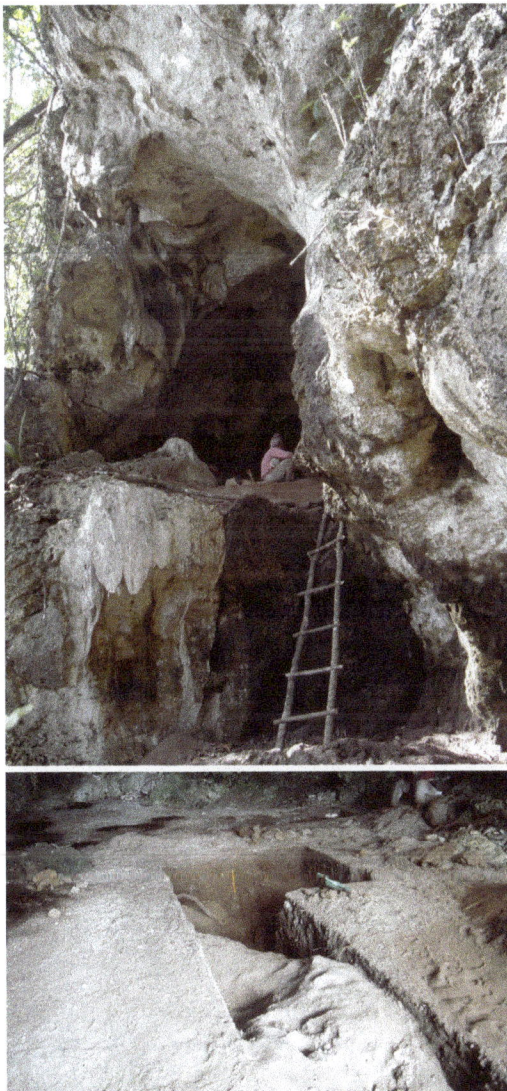

Figure 2.17 Um Kapat Papo, exterior and interior views.

Source: Peter Bellwood.

Upon first entering the cave, an archaeologist's dream seemed to have come true. The floor is entirely of earth, quite flat, 17 m long by a maximum of 8 m wide. It had been covered by a thin layer of white coral gravel by people hiding in the cave during the period of hostility between Indonesia and the Netherlands in 1962–63, when Irian Jaya (now Papua and West Papua provinces) was relinquished into Indonesian control by the Dutch. In one part of the cave there were flat constructions of bamboo, which were believed by our informants to be rafts used for fleeing from Dutch control in Gag Island, a nearby island within West Papua (although in reality these constructions seemed much too small for such a purpose). They were left alone. Here and there in the rear of the cave are small piles of black bat guano, indicating the presence of bat colonies and suggesting how the soil deposit within the cave came to exist. There are no external sources visible for the sediments within the cave, so presumably all is derived from decomposed bat guano, plus the products of coral reef limestone dissolution and materials brought in by humans.

The cave itself is partly of underwater (presumably undersea) solution origin, hence phreatic, as witnessed by high roof chimneys in its rear. A horizontal notch all around the wall inside was probably formed during a pre-human phase of sea level stability, when the cave was located at sea level and the sea entered it. As will be seen below, the deposits in the cave only date back to the early Holocene. This raises the questions of why UKP has no Pleistocene deposits, unlike the caves of Golo and Wetef described above. The answer may lie in the location of the cave, up a sheer cliff. If this cliff was higher in the past (i.e. prior to formation of the scree slope against its base), the cave could have lain a vertical 10 m or much more above the ground below, inaccessible to all except skilled rock-climbers and thus unsuitable for normal habitation.

Within the cave, two excavation units were laid out, denoted H6–8, and KL8/9 plus M–P9, according to the grid (Fig. 2.18). Eleven square metres were thus excavated in total. The deposits turned out to be disappointingly shallow, especially in Squares M9 to P9 where bedrock actually reached the surface. The KL8/9 unit was deeper, to a maximum of 70 cm, and the most interesting material was recovered here. Layer 3 is everywhere alkaline (pH between 7 and 8.5), but Layer 2 in the rear of the cave, where there are active falls of bat guano, is quite acid (pH 4.5 to 5). This is quite significant because most of the animal bone was recovered from the forward trenches, and was presumably dissolved soon after deposition in unit H6–8 in the back of the cave.

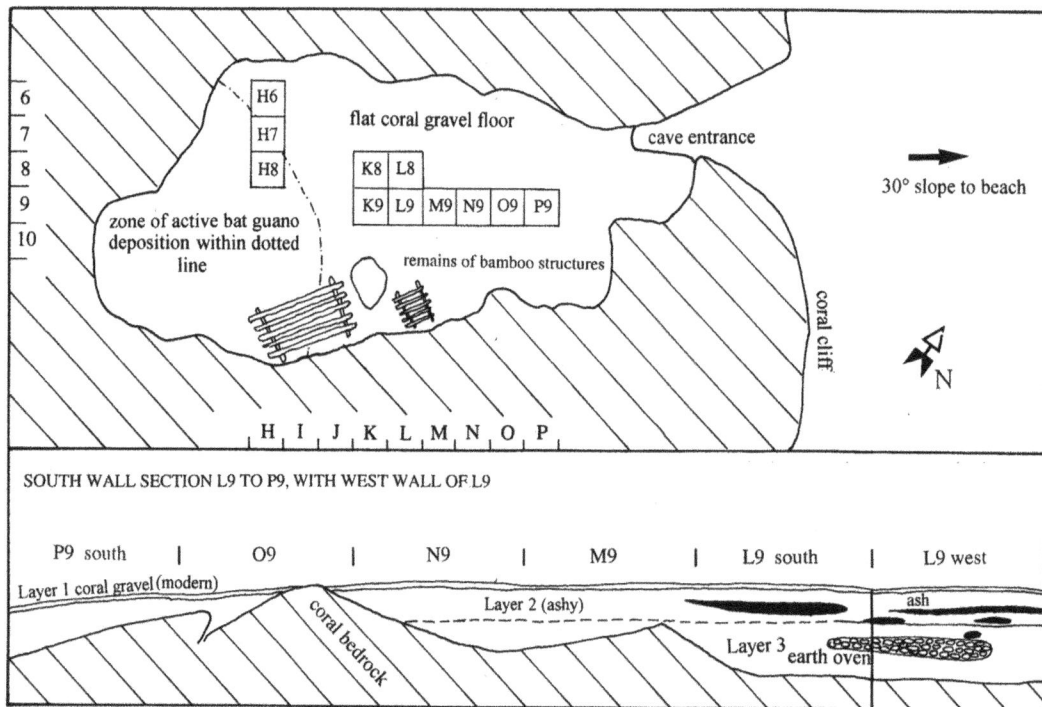

Figure 2.18 Plan and section of Um Kapat Papo.

Excavation squares are each 1x1 m.

Source: Peter Bellwood.

Three archaeological layers were recognised in Um Kapat Papo. Layer 1 is simply the modern coral gravel floor and is not considered further. Layer 2 is a brown-ashy deposit, for the most part between 10–15 cm thick, reaching 20 cm in places. Layer 3, which extends down to the coral bedrock of the cave, is a greyish-brown soil with no signs of ash, except where ash has been disturbed downwards from Layer 2 above (the deposits have occasional tree roots growing through them). Layers 2 and 3 are quite sharply differentiated to the naked eye, reflecting in part the higher densities of ash and small charcoal particles in Layer 2. There is also a well-marked shift from predominantly fine to predominantly coarse texture across the layer boundary, as shown in Table 2.6.

Table 2.6 Particle sizes of the archaeological deposit in Um Kapat Papo, before removal of calcium carbonate.

Square, Layer	Per cent particle size > 0.063 mm (coarse)	Per cent particle size < 0.063 mm (fine)	Munsell colour (after oven drying)
H8 Layer 2	35	65	10YR5/3
H8 Layer 3 (upper)	73	27	10YR4/2
H8 Layer 3 (base)	80	20	10YR5/2

Source: Peter Bellwood.

The shift reflects the fact that Layer 3, being alkaline, is to a degree concreted by calcium carbonate. The concretions themselves are small, generally of sand grain size, but their presence in Layer 3 may relate to a significantly greater age for this layer, as discussed below. After removal of calcium carbonate from the samples by solution in HCl, the coarse fractions (> 0.063 mm) of both layers were reduced to a mineral sand, accounting for only between 3.5 and 4 per cent by weight of both Layer 2 and Layer 3. This mineral sand was probably derived from the dissolution of the coral limestone and from crevices within it. Essentially, therefore, Layers 2 and 3 do not differ at all in primary grain size content and derive essentially from the decomposition of bat guano, but they do differ sharply in degree of concretion. Neither layer contains significant amounts of coral beach sand, although particles of beach sand are visible in Layer 2 owing to admixture with the imported and recent beach sand of Layer 1.

The sequence of artefactual materials from UKP is shown in Table 2.7. Pottery is generally restricted to Layer 2, but trickles into the top of Layer 3. The rare sherds below a depth of 10 cm within Layer 3 can be considered to have been trodden downwards by scuffing. Both shell and animal bones (including wallabies and phalangers) occur in fairly even densities to the base of the site.

In interpreting Table 2.7 it should be remembered that the lower spits tend to have smaller surface areas owing to the irregular surface of the bedrock. For this reason, the lessening of quantities of both shells and animal bones with depth may be more apparent than real. During excavation there was certainly no sign of any diminution in density; indeed, the greatest densities of both animal bone and marine shell seemed to be within Layer 3 rather than Layer 2.

It was also noted during excavation that there was quite a marked difference in the state of preservation of marine shell between Layers 2 and 3, suggesting that a long period of time might possibly have intervened between them. As already noted, Layers 2 and 3 are sharply differentiated visually in terms of colour and density of concretions. The suggestion that Layers 2 and 3 could be separated by quite a long interval of time is reinforced to some extent by the marine shell C14 dates, which suggest a date of c. 1500 BP for Layer 2 and c. 5000 BP for the upper part of Layer 3, at 5–15 cm within the layer. Perhaps there was a cessation of human activity between these dates, which only lie about 10 cm apart in the vertical dimension. If so, we would appear to be looking at a preceramic phase of animal and shellfish exploitation at some time between c. 7500 and 5000 BP, followed after an occupation gap by a phase of ceramic occupation after c. 2000 BP, with continuing animal and shellfish exploitation and also a more definite use of stone tools in the ceramic phase. The top 10 cm of Layer 3 seems to be a zone of mixing between these two cultural periods.

Table 2.7 Distribution of the cultural contents of Um Kapat Papo by layer and depth.

Context (depths in cm within layers)	C14 date cal. BP (all on marine shell)	Shell, gm (Squares K8, K9, L8 and L9 only)	*Pottery, no. sherds (all squares)	Manuports and cooking stones, no./gm (all squares)	Flaked stone, no. (all squares)	Animal bones gm (all squares)
Layer 2 (10–15 cm thick)						
	1765–1437 (at 15 cm)	230	218	8/1425	8	60
Layer 3						
0–10		355	53	**8/1030	3	38
10–20	5300–4900 (at 5–15 cm)	300	7	**8/1200		93
20–30		630	3			134
30–40		565	1	4/900		73
40–50		325				50
50–60	7330–7028 (at 55–65 cm)	100		2/800	1	36
60–70		135				12

* Table does not include 46 sherds found in surface Layer 1.

** The complete earth oven in Layer 3, 10–20 cm (Fig. 2.17) contained 268 cooking stones weighing 2605 kg (not included in this table).

Dates are listed in more detail in Table 1.1.

Source: Peter Bellwood.

A large earth oven about 1 m in diameter and full of non-coral beach pebbles was excavated between 15 and 25 cm depth within Layer 3 in KL9 (Fig. 2.19). The excavated portion of this earth oven (probably over 80 per cent of its area) contained 268 stones weighing a total of 26 kg, the stones being packed into a layer about 10 cm thick. The original pit dug for the earth oven was unfortunately not visible in the trench section. The stones are overlain by Layer 3 sediment, but with at least one small telltale pocket of ash, which could suggest that the pit was dug down into Layer 3 at some time during the accumulation of the ashy Layer 2. Thus, it seems likely (but not absolutely certain) that the oven belongs to the very beginning of the ceramic phase in Layer 2, c. 2000 BP. Unfortunately, no greater certainty seems possible, although the question of whether or not the oven is truly preceramic is an important one from a culture historical viewpoint.

Figure 2.19 The K9–L9 earth oven, Um Kapat Papo.

Source: Peter Bellwood.

A possible sequence of activity within Um Kapat Papo is therefore as follows:

- Preceramic occupation dated to between c. 7500 and 5000 BP, associated with exploitation of wallaby, phalanger and maritime resources, but with almost no evidence for the use of stone tools (a single blade-like flake from Layer 3 could be intrusive). The deposit can only be described as 'sparse' in cultural content, perhaps because of the relative inaccessibility of the cave. Many of the cultural materials found in Golo and Wetef during this period on Gebe (i.e. bone points, ochre, shell adzes) are absent. Between c. 5000 and 2000 BP, it is possible that the site was not regularly occupied.

- Ceramic occupation dated from c. 2000 BP onwards. The pottery in UKP resembles that of the Morotai sites (especially Tanjung Pinang) in being predominantly incised, hence a date within the past 2000 years fits well (Chapter 7). Red-slipped Neolithic pottery of Uattamdi type (c. 3500 to 2000 BP) does not occur in the site. Occupants of this phase had more access to sources of stone for tools than their predecessors. The now-extirpated wallaby appears to have survived into this phase, together with the cuscus (extant), both only in very small bone amounts. Fishing continued. A single large earth oven was found stratigraphically on the borderline between the preceramic and ceramic phases (Fig. 2.19).

Kaitutsi Cave

The cave of Kaitutsi lies 16 m inland from the beach, at the base of the coral headland called Tanjung Ben, which delimits the coastal plain upon which lies the village of Umera. It lies about 1 km from the southeastern tip of the island (Fig. 2.1). At first sight the cave looked impressive enough, being about 10 m long from drip-line to back wall and 6 m wide. However, the surface was much disturbed by pig wallows and lay only about 2 m above the present high tide level. Indeed, the surface of the cave was covered in a thin layer of clean beach sand, a sure sign that the sea had entered it in the recent past.

In order to see if the cave had any archaeological potential, a trench of 3x1 m was laid out in the approximate centre. The upper beach sand turned out to be covering a 30 cm thick layer of grey-ashy sand, mixed with pockets of pure beach sand. Pure beach sand again occurred at the base of the section, directly on bedrock. Since all cultural materials were sub-modern (plain earthenware sherds and blue-and-white ceramics of very recent appearance), Kaitutsi was deemed to be badly disturbed and of no archaeological potential. Sherds of one particular blue-and-white vessel were found throughout the deposit, up to 2 m apart and at top and bottom of the cultural layer.

The Buwawansi site complex

On our first visit to Gebe, in February 1994, exploratory boat trips were made along the southern coastline of the island. Generally, the vista was not encouraging for archaeological survey—rather barren headlands with stunted vegetation separated swampy mangrove-clad bays. No villages existed along the southern coast during our research (excepting part of the nickel-mining town of Kapaleo, including the harbour facilities opposite Fau Island), and almost the whole coastline appeared unoccupied and unutilised.

When we passed the location called Buwawansi, about 1 km north of the equator, the vista improved. Here would see a field hut, coconut trees, a sandy beach with a flat terrace behind, and numerous small tower-like raised coral massifs rising above the terrace and protruding above the inland slopes (Fig. 2.2). We stopped for a look, and immediately found pottery on the surface of the coastal terrace and eroding down the slopes from coral limestone rockshelters inland.

Because we were not carrying a plane table and telescopic alidade owing to weight restrictions on the flight from Ternate to Gebe, an approximate plan of the site complex had to be prepared with tape and compass. This was improved on the two later visits to the site (June 1994 and January 1996) and forms the basis for Figure 2.20. The site complex is about 300 m long and has an approximately west to east orientation. It is fronted by a coral sand beach in the east and a rocky coral foreshore in the west. The coastal terrace itself averages 40–60 m wide and is fairly flat, with occasional large blocks of raised coral between 10–20 m high rising from it. One of these blocks of coral, at the western end of the complex, is undercut around two sides and provides rockshelters (see Buwawansi site 3, below).

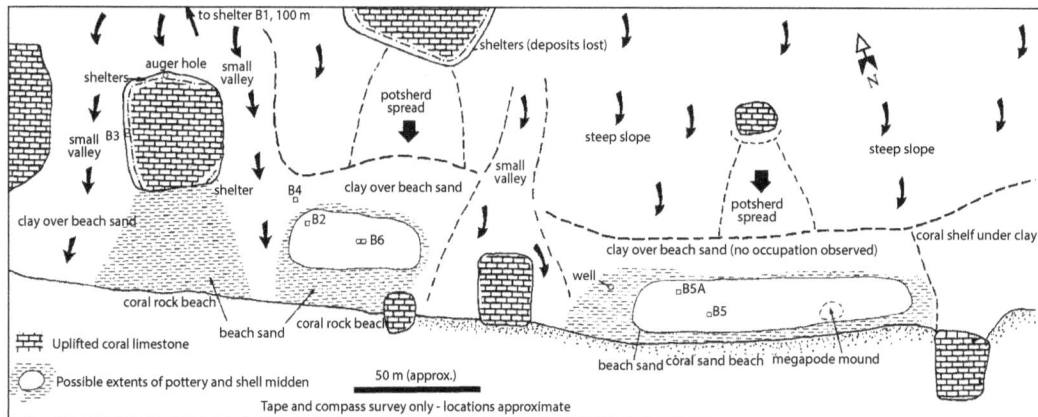

Figure 2.20 Plan of the archaeological complex at Buwawansi.
The precise location of shelter Buwawansi 1 has not been surveyed, so its position can only be approximately indicated.
Source: Peter Bellwood.

Test pits in the Buwawansi coastal terrace

In June 1994 a soil auger was taken to Buwawansi and used to drill holes in the terrace at a large number of points. As a result of this, it is possible to outline the structure of the terrace. Except where water courses run across it from the inland slopes (labelled 'small valleys' in Fig. 2.20), the terrace itself is founded on beach sand capped by 20–30 cm of cultivated topsoil, during our visits under coconut trees. The terrace has a flat modern surface approximately 1.8 m above modern high tide level and was presumably formed during a period of relatively high sea level in the past, possibly during the Middle Holocene. The beach sand is of unknown thickness— attempts to core it to its base were thwarted by the many lumps of coral.

Where water courses run across the terrace there are deep deposits of clayey and rocky soil with no apparent archaeological remains. Neither does archaeological material occur along the immediate base of the inland slopes, even though beach sand does occur there beneath the topsoil. Both these areas receive much soil wash during heavy rain and obviously become very wet and muddy.

The human occupation materials occur in areas away from frequent inundation by surface water and slope wash. These areas are two in number, a western and an eastern, both elongated ovals of well-drained topsoil over beach sand, labelled 'possible extent of pottery and shell midden' on Figure 2.20. They are separated by an area about 80 m across, which contains a coral massif and the outflow from a small gully. The two areas are about 50 and 100 m long respectively, and up to 25 m wide, thus offering a total habitable area of between 3000 and 4000 m². The occupation materials occur in the topsoil, 20–30 cm thick, in all areas heavily disturbed and eroded by cultivation activities.

Because of the obvious lack of stratigraphy and general shallowness of the deposits, excavations on the coastal terrace were limited to a few 1x1 m test pits. Square B2 ('B' for Buwawansi) produced scattered sherds to 50 cm, concentrated in the top 20 cm of topsoil, associated with a marine shell date at 20 cm of 1655–1319 cal. BP (ANU 9319), in direct association with pottery. Square B4 produced no archaeological materials because it lay off the edge of the occupied part of the terrace, although this was not realised before it was excavated. Squares B5 and B5A produced scattered potsherds to about 30 cm, associated respectively with marine shell dates of 3128–2789 and 1646–1431 cal. BP (ANU 9770 and Waikato 4630) (for details of C14 dates see Table 1.1).

Square B6, covering 2x1 m, produced the most prolific remains in terms of pottery, shells, red ochre, and even a piece of iron at 5 cm, of uncertain relationship to the pottery. Like the other squares, this one was essentially disturbed by cultivation, but in the base of the cultural layer were the remains of a scoop hearth 60 cm diameter and 10 cm deep, with ash flecks but no charcoal, and a small adjacent post hole. Large numbers of complete gastropods were found nearby, perhaps opened by heating in the fire. These finds, while of limited interest, at least imply living activities on site rather than mere dumping. B6 produced a marine shell date from 15–20 cm of 2008–1640 cal. BP (ANU 9454).

Concerning the overall time span of the terrace occupation, the C14 determinations appear to give a rather puzzling spread between c. 3000 and 1300 cal. BP. Given the relative homogeneity of the pottery in the site and the restricted depth of occupation, such a wide spread of dates seems, in reality, to be unlikely. Parallels elsewhere (Uattamdi A-B, Um Kapat Papo, Tanjung Pinang, Gua Siti Nafisah) would suggest a date for the pottery assemblage in the first 500 years CE, as discussed further in Chapter 7.

The Buwawansi rockshelters

During the 1994 research in Buwawansi, three rockshelter complexes were located. The first runs around the western and northern sides of the large coral outcrop located to the west of the terrace site (see location at left of Fig. 2.20). This outcrop is flanked by water courses during heavy rain on both its western and eastern sides, and at such times the rockshelter along its northern side receives water and washed-in soil from the slopes behind. The absence of archaeological deposits in this northern shelter was determined by drilling a core (marked as 'auger hole' on the plan— Fig. 2.20) for a depth of 2.5 m down to bedrock— this core revealed no archaeological materials at all.

Down the western side of the outcrop, however, there is a dry shelter about 35 m long by 2 m wide, which drops gently downslope through a vertical height of about 5 m from the inland side of the outcrop to the beach side. This shelter was chosen for a 2x1 m excavation, labelled B3 (i.e. Buwawansi 3) on Figure 2.20, and its contents are described below.

The second rockshelter complex discovered in 1994 was the rather impressive one, up to 5 m wide and with a possible length of about 60 m, formed around the base of the large coral massif which rises out of the top of the slope immediately inland from the terrace site B6. The shelter runs around the downslope beach side of this outcrop, and is shown in part on Figure 2.20. This shelter complex was never surveyed, because on first discovery it was obvious that every scrap of archaeological deposit that it might once have contained had fallen downslope, due to continuous erosion of the surrounding steep slopes. The shelters contained merely bare rock and sterile limestone-derived rubble and clayey soil deposits. On the slopes below this outcrop, and also on the slopes below another much smaller outcrop to the east (this one without any rockshelters), we found large numbers of scattered sherds, labelled as 'pottery spreads' on Figure 2.20. It is possible that the second outcrop also once served as a focus of habitation.

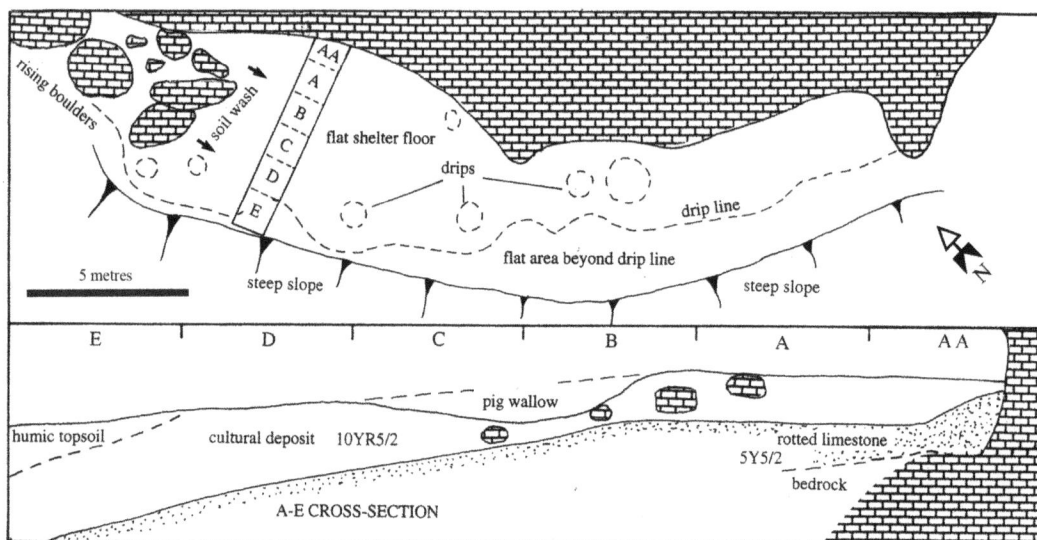

Figure 2.21 Plan and section of Buwawansi 1 rockshelter.
Source: Peter Bellwood.

The third and most important rockshelter complex was discovered in 1996, along the southwestern side of a very large coral outcrop located about 100 m inland from and north of the one with the empty shelters. This outcrop is not shown on Figure 2.20 because its location was never surveyed properly, but the plan of the shelter itself (Buwawansi 1, or B1) is given in Figure 2.21. This time, archaeological deposits did survive, but again there were considerable numbers of sherds eroding down the slopes outside the shelter, and also eroding from the deposits within it as a result of a series of aggressive roof drips that render the shelter almost uninhabitable during very heavy rain. Like Golo and Wetef, the floor of this shelter was pitted with pig wallows, but a sufficient depth of deposit survived to make excavation worthwhile.

The Buwawansi 1 excavation

The B1 shelter is about 20 m long by about 5–6 m wide (Fig. 2.21). It was excavated by means of a line of six squares running from the back wall to beyond the drip-line, denoted AA, and A to E. This line formed a single trench 6 m long by 1 m wide, which was dug in 5 cm levels using 2.5 mm sieves. Depth of deposit inside the drip-line, in Squares AA to D, was everywhere very shallow, averaging only 40 cm in the inner areas and extending to as much as 90 cm only in small holes in Squares D and E, close to and outside the drip line. Very dark greyish-brown humic topsoil (10YR3/2) occurred in Square E outside the drip-line, otherwise the whole cultural deposit was a uniform greyish-brown soil (10YR5/2), sitting on a culturally sterile layer of olive grey (5Y5/2) and white weathered limestone.

Like the deposit in Buwawansi 3, to be described below, the cultural layer in B1 is probably little more than a remnant lag deposit. Soil creeps continuously into the shelter from upslope at its north end, and prior to human occupation such soil presumably moved straight through the shelter to leave a bare floor of dissolving limestone like that exposed in the other empty shelters. With the beginning of human occupation, some degree of compaction allowed sediment to accumulate, but at all times most sediment, and perhaps the majority of the artefacts deposited in the shelter, would have slid away down the steep slopes immediately outside. This would be especially true of Square E, outside the drip-line, where both soil erosion and soil accumulation can be assumed to have been very rapid. Overall, therefore, the deposits are likely to contain only a remnant echo of the full scale of cultural activities in the shelter, yet we can still perhaps assume that this echo retains stratigraphic integrity (at least, there are no visible signs of disturbance in the deposits).

In terms of origin, as noted above, the B1 deposits are presumed to have moved down into the shelter from the rising ground surface outside to the north. In terms of grain size they vary little from top to bottom and the visible colour differences noted above can be presumed to be post-depositional in origin. Soil samples from the top of Square AA, and the top, middle and base of Square E, all showed fairly equal proportions of coarse (> 0.063 mm) and fine grains, with no change with depth.

The vertical distribution of cultural material in the B1 trench is plotted in Table 2.8. This gives raw weights for shell and sherds and plots the data by 10 cm levels below the ground surface. In general, Table 2.8 can be summarised by the comment that the density of deposition in the site differs little from top to bottom, although there is a peak in shell deposition between 30 and 50 cm in Squares D and E, which seems to overlap with the initial appearance of pottery. Beneath the pottery are thin preceramic layers, bearing shells but little else, except for one very important exception. At the very bottom of Square B (35–40 cm depth), in a small hollow in the underlying sterile layer (and thus protected from erosion), we found a heavy *Tridacna* hinge region shell adze similar to the series from Golo (Fig. 9.9). Marine shell from the same level as the adze has given a date of 9379–9007 cal. BP (Waikato 4628). But, like the Golo shell adzes, this one was presumably also cached in a hole in the cave floor, and so cannot be closely dated, except perhaps to younger than 9000 BP.

In general, the B1 deposits were a little disappointing owing to their thinness and seemingly ephemeral nature. However, the site did yield a selection of decorated pottery and the shell adze, to be described further in Chapters 7 and 9 respectively.

Table 2.8 Distribution of the cultural contents of Buwawansi 1, by depth below surface in cm.

Depth	AA		A		B		C		D		E	
	sherds	shell	sherds	shell	sherds	shell	sherds	shell	sherds	shell	sherds	shell
0-10	8	240	16	350	2	140	3	425	6	50	4	75
10-20	13	340	20	365	15	300	5	340	15	630	9	375
20-30	9	140	22	475	2	200		360	6	890	26	240
30-40				430		65*		50	4	1860	24	500
40-50				50						770	4	1820
50-60										135	3	250
60-70										25		220

Figures are weight in grams for marine shell, number of sherds for pottery.

* Not including a *Tridacna maxima* shell adze found at this level.

Source: Peter Bellwood.

The Buwawansi 3 excavation

The B3 excavation, in the first rockshelter described above, was a 2x1 m trench dug along the axis of the shelter, in two 1x1 squares (B3A and B3B). Like all other sites excavated, this was dug in 5 cm spits using 2.5 mm sieves, but the cultural contents are presented by 10 cm levels in Table 2.9. As in Buwawansi 1, the whole deposit in the two squares presumably originated in soil creep from the slope above and inland from the coral outcrop. It was obvious during the excavation that the shelter contains a gradually and continuously accumulated slope wash deposit, into which shells and sherds were occasionally discarded. The soil in the excavation section becomes lighter towards the base.

The depth of deposit reached a maximum of 140 cm at the seaward end of the trench, and was only about 100 cm deep at the upslope end. Beneath the soil lay solid bedrock. The distribution of cultural materials is interesting but not very surprising—sherds are clearly bunched at the top and fade out above 60 cm, there are absolutely no flaked lithics, and shells extend down into an apparent preceramic phase to terminate (and also to accumulate slightly) on the bedrock at 140 cm. The shells themselves were noted during excavation to be small and fragmented, and to contain lots of small gastropod opercula. Large gastropods and bivalves, so common in the terrace excavations at Buwawansi (especially Buwawansi 6), were generally rare. This suggests that such large shells rolled or were thrown downslope, and all that remains in B3 is a kind of lag deposit of small discards, left behind after casual visitation rather than continuous habitation.

This means that the B3 record is only of very limited value, except for one observation. A radiocarbon date on marine shell from 130–135 cm in B3B, close to the base of the sequence and well below any pottery, is 4271–3811 cal. BP (ANU 9453). This indicates that the soil deposits in the shelter began to build up from this date onwards. Prior to this time, the shelter presumably had a floor of bare limestone, which lay at or beneath sea level. The bedrock floor of the shelter is about 1.2 m above modern high tide, and so the local sea level around Gebe was at least a metre higher than now at 4000 BP, an observation that accords generally with the well-recorded slight retreat from a mid-Holocene high sea level in Southeast Asia generally (Sathiamurthy and Voris 2006).

Table 2.9 Distribution of the cultural contents of Buwawansi 3, by depth.

Depth (cm)	Pottery (gm)	Shell (gm)
0–10	925	1795
10–20	785	1275
20–30	190	1025
30–40	20	1300
40–50	64	975
50–60	32	575
60–70		425
70–80		600
80–90		680
90–100		220
100–110		365
110–120		125
120–130		90
130–140		230

Unfortunately, the record of sherd count for B3 can no longer be found, but the fall-off with depth is clear.

Source: Peter Bellwood.

Whatever the true age of the pottery-bearing deposits on the Buwawansi coastal terrace, the sherds they contain, as in B3, certainly postdate this C14 determination of 4271–3811 cal. BP. Nowhere in the Northern Moluccas has pottery yet been found in contexts older than the rather imprecise date of 3579–3014 cal. BP (ANU 7776) from the basal deposits in Uattamdi shelter on Kayoa Island. Thus, the calibrated date of 4271–3811 BP from the base of B3 was still very firmly in preceramic time, and at least 80 cm below the first hint of pottery in the B3 sequence.

3

Investigations on Morotai Island

Peter Bellwood, Daud Tanudirjo, and Gunadi Nitihaminoto

The island of Morotai (Fig. 3.1) is approximately 70 km long by 45 km wide. It has a particularly rugged interior (never penetrated by the research team), which lacked any substantial human settlement at the time of our research. A number of mountains rise to more than 1000 m above sea level, and these are separated by a radial drainage pattern. All modern villages are located around the coastline, especially close to where rivers reach the sea. No modern topographic maps were available for Morotai during the fieldwork, and we were obliged to use old naval charts and an unpublished series of coastal maps compiled by the Allied Geographical Section in 1944 and held in the ANU library. The most useful map available, albeit not located until after the fieldwork ended, was the 1:250,000 geological map (Peta Geologi Bersistem, Lembar Morotai) published in Bandung.

Morotai is separated from northern Halmahera by Morotai Strait (Selat Morotai), which exceeds 15 km in width. Seabed depths between the two islands are recorded variously as much as 585 m or greater than 200 fathoms (depending on the source used), according to maritime charts with depth soundings held in the National Library of Australia, so there is no possibility that both islands were ever joined by dry land connections during Pleistocene glaciations. Indeed, available information on the tectonic history of this region (Hall et al. 1988; Hall 2013) gives no reason to assume that Morotai and Halmahera were ever linked by dry land during their geological histories, although this statement can only be based on negative evidence. Morotai and the northern tip of Halmahera do share a common suite of pre-Miocene volcanic rocks, and late Oligocene to early Pliocene sedimentary rocks, but from the viewpoint of human prehistory it is most probable that a sea gap from Halmahera at least 15 km wide has always existed. The fauna of Morotai, according to Flannery (1995a), is rather impoverished. Apart from bats, the only native mammals are *Rattus morotaiensis* and *Phalanger ornatus*, both shared with Halmahera.

The rockshelters of Morotai are to be found in a zone of raised coral, which lines the southern, eastern and northeastern coasts of the island in a continuous strip up to about 5 km wide (Hall et al. 1988: Fig. 6). The sites located during our research lie in this zone, along the southern coast of Morotai from Tanjung Dehegila to Sambiki (Fig. 3.1). The topography of this raised coral coastal strip reflects the presence of a series of raised reefs that increase in height inland. The prominent but very discontinuous major coral cliff line closest to the sea is the one that contains the caves and rockshelters investigated. Although shelters and small caves do occur further inland, we were never able to locate any with good archaeological potential. We were also unable to extend our surveys north of Sambiki owing to one simple problem: there was no road at the time of the survey, and the contemporary rough sea conditions did not invite extensive boat travel. Furthermore, we found so many interesting sites on the south coast that all our available time on the island was fully occupied. Future archaeological teams might find the east and northeastern limestone coasts of Morotai worthy of attention, and indeed have recently done so with the research of Rintaro Ono and his colleagues (Ono, Aziz et al. 2017; Ono, Oktaviana et al. 2017; Ono et al. 2018) at the Early Metal Phase burial cave of Aru Manara. This new information will be addressed further in the concluding chapter of this monograph.

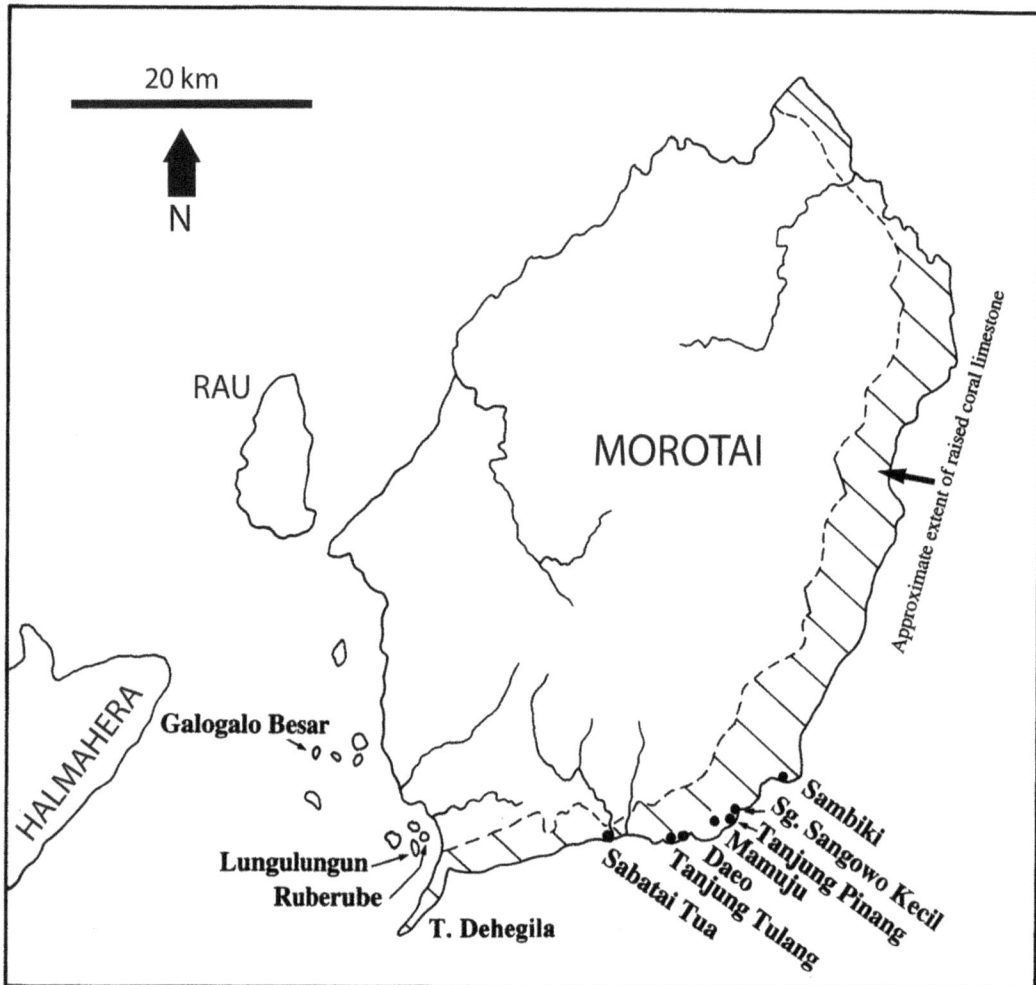

Figure 3.1 Map of Morotai, showing excavated sites.
The diagonally shaded area is raised coral limestone.
Source: Peter Bellwood.

Tanjung Pinang

The Tanjung Pinang rockshelter faces due east and is located in the side of a block of uplifted coral, about 110 m inland from the present beach. The floor of the shelter, which lies about 9 m above present high tide level, is approximately 10 m long by 4 m wide (Figs 3.2 and 3.3). Beyond the drip-line outside the shelter the ground falls quite steeply through about 4 vertical m, down a limestone rubble scree slope, which has resulted from erosion of the massif, to the level of the surrounding terrain. The massif itself is of particularly crumbly-looking rock and has doubtless decayed rapidly and extensively since being exposed to subaerial weathering. Indeed, the scree slope in front suggests that the existing shelter could once have been much larger than it is today.

Figure 3.2 Tanjung Pinang rockshelter.

A: Squares J2 to F2 (at rear) at completion, excavated in 1994. Daud Tanudirjo is standing in F2. B: The initial excavation in 1991, looking south. C: Human remains (including cranium TP5 and other cranial parts), a large *Tridacna* shell (front left) and volcanic pebbles in J2 and H2, 15–20 cm depth (upper Layer 1), 1994 excavation.

Source: Peter Bellwood.

Between the massif and the modern beach there is another very low subsidiary coral cliff, only about 2 m high or less, which presumably represents the most recent phase of uplift or sea level retreat (Holocene?) along this stretch of coast. This low cliff is too small to contain habitable shelters. The modern beach consists of a dark grey sand derived from both coral and volcanic sources, with lots of rounded beach pebbles of volcanic rock. Such pebbles were used in large numbers by the inhabitants of the shelter, both for tool making and for cooking stones (Chapter 8).

Offshore from the beach lies a shallow lagoon about 250 m wide, with a floor of coral rubble, sand and sea grass, exposed at low tide but under approximately 1.5 m of water at high tide. The reef beyond the lagoon drops off steeply, and contains potential rockshelters a few metres below modern sea level, which can be observed by snorkelling. These rockshelters contain deposits of coral rubble and coral fingers—an observation that will be returned to below. Whether the underwater shelters contain any archaeology is a question only a diving team can answer—my own suspicion is that there could be too much tidal and wave surge in the area of snorkelling visibility for coherent archaeological deposits to survive.

In 1991, three 1x1 m squares were excavated in the Tanjung Pinang shelter, denoted F3, G3 and H3. In 1994, Squares F2, G2, H2 and J2 were added directly alongside the 1991 trench (Fig. 3.3). Thus, an area of 7 m² was excavated in total, and the results will be described here as a single excavation unit. The stratigraphy is shown in Figure 3.4, which differentiates two major layers numbered 1 and 2. The shelter floor is covered by a thin layer of goat dung from the small herd belonging to the late Mr Ong Chan, who was still living in a house below the shelter when research began in 1991. Beneath the dung, which was stripped off and discarded, the floor is quite flat, hard and dry. Layer 1, approximately 80 cm thick, contains evidence of human activity throughout and is dated by a well-ordered series of marine shell C14 samples to between 10,000 and 3000 BP (Fig. 3.4, Table 3.1). Layer 2, which extends from the depth of 80 cm to the point at which massive rocks stopped excavation at 2.40 m below the surface, contains absolutely no signs of human activity. It has two rather enigmatic C14 dates on marine shell, from two points about 1.3 m apart vertically, close to the top and bottom of its profile, both of c. 40,000 cal. BP. As discussed below, these two dates presumably come from shells that dropped naturally out of crevices in the uplifted coral reef.

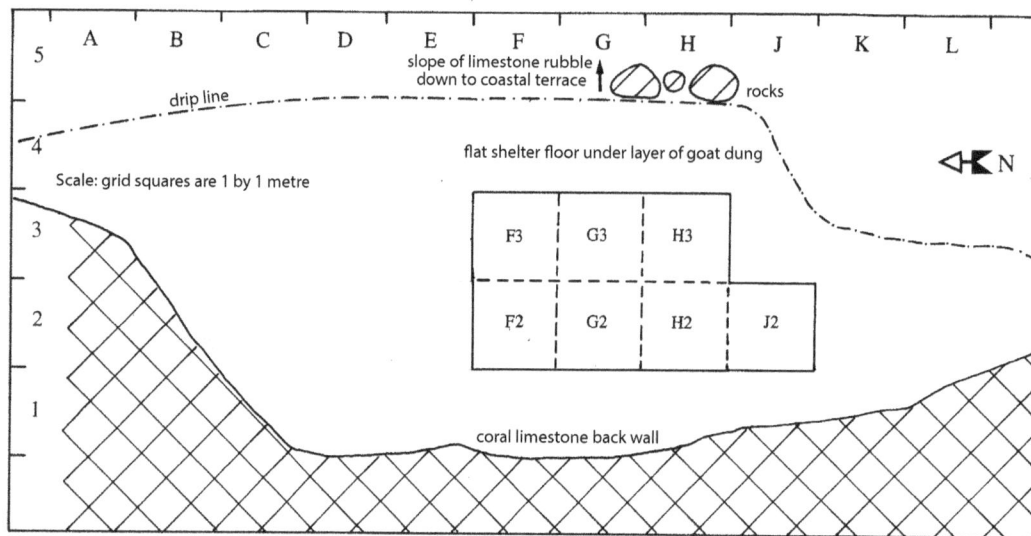

Figure 3.3 Plan of the Tanjung Pinang Shelter, showing excavations in 1991 (F3 to G3) and 1994 (F2 to J2).

Source: Peter Bellwood.

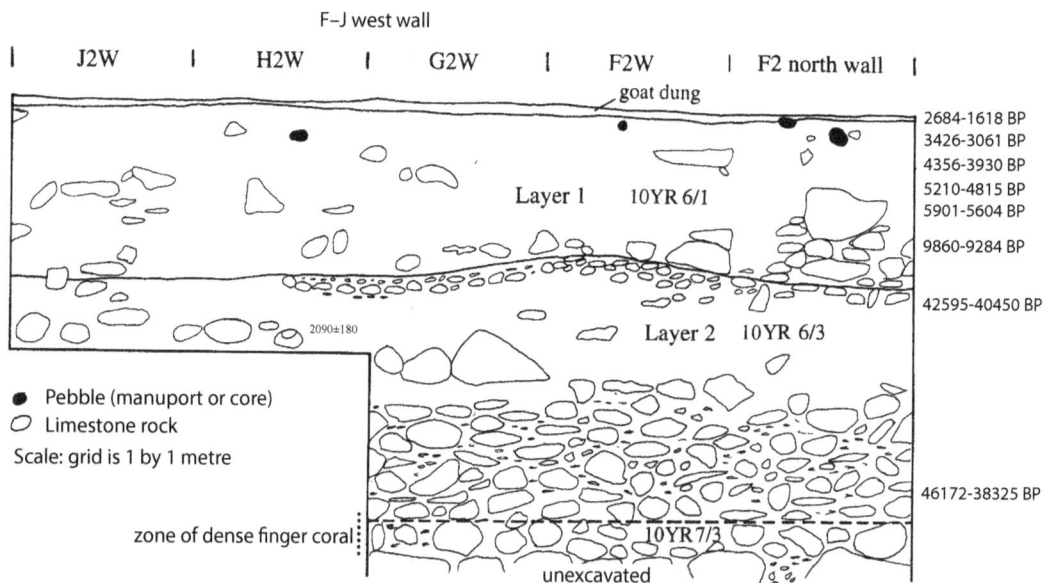

Figure 3.4 Conjoined section of Squares F2 to J2, west and north walls, Tanjung Pinang.

Dates are listed in Table 1.1.

Source: Peter Bellwood.

Layers 1 and 2 are both silty sands, similar in texture but different in colour; the interface between them is quite sharp. Layer 1 is slightly darker in colour (light grey) than Layer 2 (pale brown), which perhaps reflects the incorporation into Layer 1 of charcoal particles and other humanly created occupation materials. Charcoal particles are totally absent in Layer 2. Yet, Layer 2 does contain small amounts of marine shell, together with land snails. This poses issues of interpretation, to be examined in more detail below.

Tanjung Pinang Layer 1

As will be seen from Table 3.1, Layer 1, which extends to a depth of c. 80–90 cm below the shelter surface, contains all the positively identified artefactual material in the site. Artefacts and bones (but not marine shells or land snails) occur only in Layer 1, and are entirely absent in Layer 2. The C14 dates form a well-ordered series from roughly 9500 to 2000 cal. BP.

Marine shells occur in quantity in Layer 1, with a peak at around 10–50 cm, but fall off towards the base of the layer at about 90 cm. Most of these marine shells can be considered food discard in Layer 1, but not so the land snails of the genus *Obba*, which live in trees and probably entered the shelter fortuitously by falling from above. It will be noted that the fall-off in *Obba* from Layer 1 downwards into Layer 2 is far less marked than that for marine food shells and *Pythia* land snails. The latter like to inhabit rotten wood along the beach and drop off remarkably in the middle depths of the site, possibly because of the retreat of the coastline away from Tanjung Pinang in the millennia either side of the Last Glacial Maximum, when this coastal species would not have survived so far inland. Both land snail species inhabit the vicinity of the shelter today.

On the other hand, animal bone and flaked beach pebbles both show similar Layer 1 distributions to the marine shells, being absent in Layer 2. *Canarium* anvils seem to peak in numbers at around 20–40 cm. So also do unmodified volcanic rock beach pebbles, many probably used as cooking stones (not listed in Table 3.1), whereas lithic debitage peaks between 50 and 70 cm. All these categories relate to preceramic occupation between 10,000 and 3000 BP, seemingly most intensive between about 5500 and 3000 BP, which interestingly was also the time of intensive preceramic occupation in the cave of Siti Nafisah on Halmahera Island.

Human bones and sherds seem to reveal a different vertical distribution in Layer 1 from the above categories, with very definite peaks located *above*, rather than below, the 20 cm depth. Human bones, sherds and a number of whole *Tridacna* and other large reef shells seem to go together in this upper zone, despite difficulties of proving absolute association. The site contains many secondary burials of human crania and occasionally other bones, probably dug into very shallow pits, although no actual pit boundaries were visible during the excavation. These human bones were perhaps buried in some kind of association with the pottery and the large shells (the latter as remnants of funerary feasting?), even though the pottery is now reduced to sherd form and rather scattered, and there is no clear evidence for jar burial. Nevertheless, the finding of several large pieces of one reconstructable footed vessel in this upper zone indicates that pots might originally have been buried whole, as grave goods of some kind.

A sample of the human bone has been dated (ANU 8439) to 2684–1618 cal. BP. It will be noted that the maximum spit weight for human bone, at 10–20 cm, occurs slightly lower in depth than the maximum spit weight for pottery, which is very close to the surface of the site. This may be because the skulls were placed in shallow holes whereas the pots were originally placed on the shelter floor, later to be broken and scuffed into the topsoil. The Tanjung Pinang human bones are described by David Bulbeck in Chapter 11.

Table 3.1 Distribution of the contents of Tanjung Pinang by depth in cm. Details of the C14 dates are listed in Table 1.1.

Tanjung Pinang, depth cm	C14 date BP (hb = human bone; all others marine shell)	Total shell weight in gm (Squares F2-G2)	Obba land snails by number (Squares F2-G2)	Pythia land snails by number (Squares F2-G2)	Animal bone, all squares, gm	Non-core debitage, Squares F2 to J2 only, no./gm	Flaked beach pebbles, all squares, no./gm	Canarium anvils, all squares, no./gm	Human bone, all squares, gm	Sherd numbers, all squares (see also Table 7.5)
0-10	2684-1618 hb	3400	36	0	57	31/310	8/3775	3/1000	578	735
10-20	3426-3061	6925	69	7	0	21/227	3/635	4/1425	1265	345
20-30		10,300	70	6	14	34/355	4/1820	6/2400	623	36
30-40	4356-3930	5550	57	17	69	29/124	5/1250	4/1560		
40-50	5210-4815	2300	23	16	14	25/179	3/435	1/450		
50-60	5901-5604	1850	11	10	4	54/508	2/415			
60-70		1200	9	7	10	90/605	2/935			
70-80	9860-9284	825	39	4	3	19/95	2/80			
80-90		500	18	0	1	4/17	1/15	(layer 1/2 boundary)		
90-100	42,595-40,450	200	3	0						
100-110		600	11	0						
110-120		200	7	0						
120-130		175	7	0						
130-140		135	13	0						
140-150		20	6	0						
150-160		25	12	1						
160-170		90	38	0						
170-180		140	74	0						
180-190		80	24	2						
190-200		115	19	4						
200-210		120	6	5						
210-220		90	12	10						
220-230	46,172-38,325	115	10	14						
230-240		60	0	15						

Source: Peter Bellwood.

Observations of artefact distributions therefore point to two phases within Layer 1: an earlier with preceramic midden and flaked lithic deposition, dating overall to between 10,000 and 3000 BP; and a later one when the site was used for burial purposes with pottery grave goods, possibly from about 2000 BP onwards. Given that the flaked pebbles and debitage extend up to the surface of the site, and are hence in apparent association with the burials, one must ask if this association was culturally real, or caused by fortuitous disturbance. This issue will be discussed further in Chapter 8 since flaked lithic debitage definitely becomes rare in Neolithic and later contexts in other Northern Moluccan sites such as Uattamdi and Buwawansi, so Tanjung Pinang is a little unusual in this regard.

Tanjung Pinang Layer 2

Layer 2 poses problems of dating and interpretation. The two C14 dates of 37,500 uncal. BP, from top and bottom of the layer, are absolutely identical in their means. This suggests that primary deposition between the deaths of the dated shells must be ruled out. Otherwise, we have to explain how more than 1 m of sediment accumulated in Layer 2 almost instantaneously, whereas the same depth took 10,000 years, even with a confirmed human presence, to accumulate in Layer 1. Indeed, the very sudden jump in radiocarbon ages between >38 ka at 90–100 cm and only *c*10 ka about 10–20 cm above raises a major question. Could the interface between Layers 1 and 2 really represent a phase of non-deposition or erosion lasting for 30,000 years or more? If the dated shells from Layer 2 were *in situ* and buried immediately after death, then Layer 2 would have to be an instantaneous product at c. 40,000 BP, and such an intervening hiatus with Layer 1 above would be a certainty. One might then expect the two layers to be rather different in grain size composition, since limestone-rich Layer 2 would have undergone a great deal more weathering and solution—at least 30,000 years more than Layer 1.

To test this possibility, soil samples were taken from just above and below the Layer 1/2 interface and analysed at ANU with the help of John Magee. The results are shown in Table 3.2. According to Magee, these grain size distributions are not sufficiently differentiated to claim that the two layers are either of different origin or reflect different post-depositional histories. Essentially, it seems that the most reasonable hypothesis is to regard Layers 1 and 2 as the products of a continuous process of deposition, with the darker colour of Layer 1 reflecting simply the appearance of humans producing charcoal and bringing other organic materials into the shelter. Neither layer contains visible quantities of beach sand and both must be considered entirely terrestrial in origin, except perhaps for some of the coral fingers and lumps in the base of Layer 2.

Table 3.2 Grain size distributions by layer from Tanjung Pinang.

Layer and depth below ground level	Sand %	Silt %	Clay %	Munsell*
Analysis 1: Layer 1, 70 cm	44.89	46.04	9.10	10YR6/1
Analysis 1: Layer 2, 100 cm	59.65	32.97	7.38	10YR6/3
	>0.063 mm (coarse) %		<0.063 mm (fine) %	
Analysis 2: Layer 1, 70 cm	61		39	
Analysis 2: Layer 2, 100 cm	70		30	

* Fine fraction, oven dried.

Source: Peter Bellwood.

As already noted, Layer 2 is completely lacking in any traces of a human presence, except potentially for the marine shells, which occur continually and in quite large quantities right to the base of the site. Indeed, the shells were still continuing in gaps between the large rocks at the base when excavation ceased. *Obba* land snails continued in the same way and, as noted above, these could simply have entered the site by falling from overhanging vegetation. The strandline snail *Pythia* sp. has a different distribution, as discussed above, being totally absent in the upper half of Layer 2 (Table 3.1), presumably because the sea was much further from the site during the Last Glacial Maximum than it is today.

The Layer 2 marine shells are basically of the same reef and surge zone species as those of Layer 1 (lots of *Turbo* and *Nerita* in particular). Many are broken, some are extremely small and thus useless for food, and all below about 100 cm are surprisingly light in colour and 'clean', unlike the dirtier specimens from Layer 1. More to the point perhaps, absolutely no shells below about 95 cm below the surface are burnt, whereas in Layer 1 and into the Layer 1/2 interface there is much burnt shell. The answer seems clear, although it was not realised during the excavation (when the Layer 2 shells were thought to reflect human activity), and so could not be checked on the spot. *The shells have fallen from the shelter wall and roof due to weathering of the limestone massif.* Originally, they must have been incorporated in cracks and crevices in the living reef just as dead shells are today. This explanation was actually suggested most clearly to me by Tim Flannery after my return to Australia in 1994. Since no opportunity has arisen to go back to the site, I have been unable to examine the limestone to see if the cracks within it do indeed contain shell fragments. However, if this assumption is correct, then the Layer 2 shells have been falling into the soil matrix continuously from the shelter roof. This Layer 2 soil matrix was presumably built up continuously within the shelter, from bottom to top, after the coral massif was raised above the sea. This uplift occurred c. 40,000 years ago according to the two shell dates, but in view of the contamination problem noted above it would probably be unwise to accept this date too rigidly.

If the dates are correct, then they imply quite a rapid rate of tectonic uplift along this coastline, since regional sea levels at 40,000 BP are estimated by many authorities to have been around 90 m below present (Hope 2005). A rate of uplift approaching 2 m per millennium could be inferred from these data.

As there is no sign of a human presence in Layer 2, there seems little point in debating these geological issues further. Meanwhile, we are left with the Tanjung Pinang overall stratigraphic sequence, which I would now interpret as follows:

1. The shelter was presumably formed by wave action after the coral reef was uplifted c. 40,000 years ago. The lower half of Layer 2 contains very dense coral rubble, with increasing numbers of coral fingers towards the base. Much of this might have been incorporated within the shelter prior to uplift, when it was still beneath the sea on the outer edge of the submerged coral reef.

2. After the sea retreated due to uplift, the terrestrial soil matrix of Layer 2 began to be deposited continuously within the shelter, incorporating land snails and marine shells, the latter (at least two being c. 40,000 years old) falling down from crevices in the eroding massif itself. Roof fall was also particularly heavy during deposition of the lower part of Layer 2.

3. In the upper part of Layer 2, the quantity of roof fall decreased markedly. The strandline snail *Pythia* sp. also vanished for a time, presumably due to the onset of worldwide glacial conditions and a general lowering of sea level.

4. At the top of Layer 2, and running up into the lower part of Layer 1, there was increasing roof fall, perhaps a result of a wetter and warmer postglacial climate, human arrival, or both. Traces of human occupation start right at the base of Layer 1 at about 10,000 BP, with a few items even in the top of Layer 2, but perhaps scuffed downwards in this instance by the shelter occupants.

5. Between 5500 and 3000 BP, the shelter was used intensively by preceramic hunting and gathering populations, users of flaked stone tools, ochre, and pebble anvils, with exploitation of fish, shellfish, rodents, and phalangers.

6. After about 2000 years ago (or less), the shelter was used for secondary burial of skulls and sometimes other small bones, the bones being placed in shallow pits and in apparent association with pottery and large reef shells.

The description of the stratigraphy and cultural history of Tanjung Pinang has turned out to be something of a saga. Not all of the saga relates to human activity. But there is a moral in the saga because during the excavation of Layer 2 the archaeologists on site believed that the shellfish within the layer were reflecting human activity. Subsequent consideration has suggested they do not.

The excavation of two caves behind Daeo Village

The village of Daeo lies about 3.5 km west of Tanjung Pinang. Immediately behind the village and about 160 m inland from the head of the beach lies a coral cliff, which contains three caves. These were numbered Daeo 1 for the most westerly, Daeo 2 for the central one, and Daeo 3 (which was not excavated or mapped) for the eastern. All are quite deep from front to back and low in roof height—more cave-like than shelter-like—but whether their origin is submarine or due to wave cutting at sea level is not very evident. The latter seems most likely since the caves lack vertical roof solution holes. None are now high enough inside for standing and all three have been filled to a considerable extent with sediments. The sediment surfaces of caves 1 and 2 lie about 8 m above high tide level, and are thus at about the same absolute level as the sediment surface of the Tanjung Pinang shelter. Both are fronted by scree slopes of coral rubble, which drop down about 4.5 m to the coastal plain on which the village of Daeo is located. All in all, their altitudinal and geomorphic situations can be stated to be identical to those of Tanjung Pinang.

Daeo 2 was the second of these caves to be excavated, but since it yielded the best archaeological record we deal with it first. Daeo 1 had only a poor record in comparison and its deposits seemed to be more disturbed.

Daeo 2

This cave lies 160 m inland from the top of the beach, behind the centre of Daeo village. It measures about 3.5 m in maximum width and about 5.5 m from the drip-line to the back wall, but the roof today is only about 1 m above the floor owing to sediment fill. The cave floor itself is quite flat and very dry, but becomes damper towards the front. Within the cave, six small rectangles were laid out for excavation, each 1x0.67 m in size and labelled E4–E6 and F4–F6. The total excavation was thus a rectangle of 2x2 m (Fig. 3.5). Excavation was undertaken in 5 cm spits and all material was sieved through 2.5 mm meshes.

Daeo cave 2 contains one continuous cultural layer. This is a dark brown, clay-rich, alkaline soil, termed Layer 1. It contains many small fragments of coral, but very few large lumps. The cave roof in Daeo 2 seems to have been much less prone to roof fall than that in Tanjung Pinang. Layer 1 is 80–90 cm thick and shows no internal layering, although about two-thirds down its profile in E5 and E6 there is a layer of soft travertine/stalagmite about 5 cm thick. Another much bigger stalagmite, which presumably goes down to meet the cave floor, protrudes into the base of Layer 1 towards the wetter front of the cave in F4. These stalagmites represent periods of heavy roof dripping quite early in the sequence of human occupation, possibly about 14,000 years ago, although they could represent short-term leaks in the cave roof rather than any specific change in rainfall intensity.

The interface from Layer 1 into Layer 2 below is quite sharp. Layer 2 is a light yellowish-brown and very clayey soil, which shows no signs of human occupation. It is about 110 cm deep and becomes gradually darker (dark yellowish-brown) towards its base. It was not fully excavated but was cored to the presumed limestone bedrock by a soil auger.

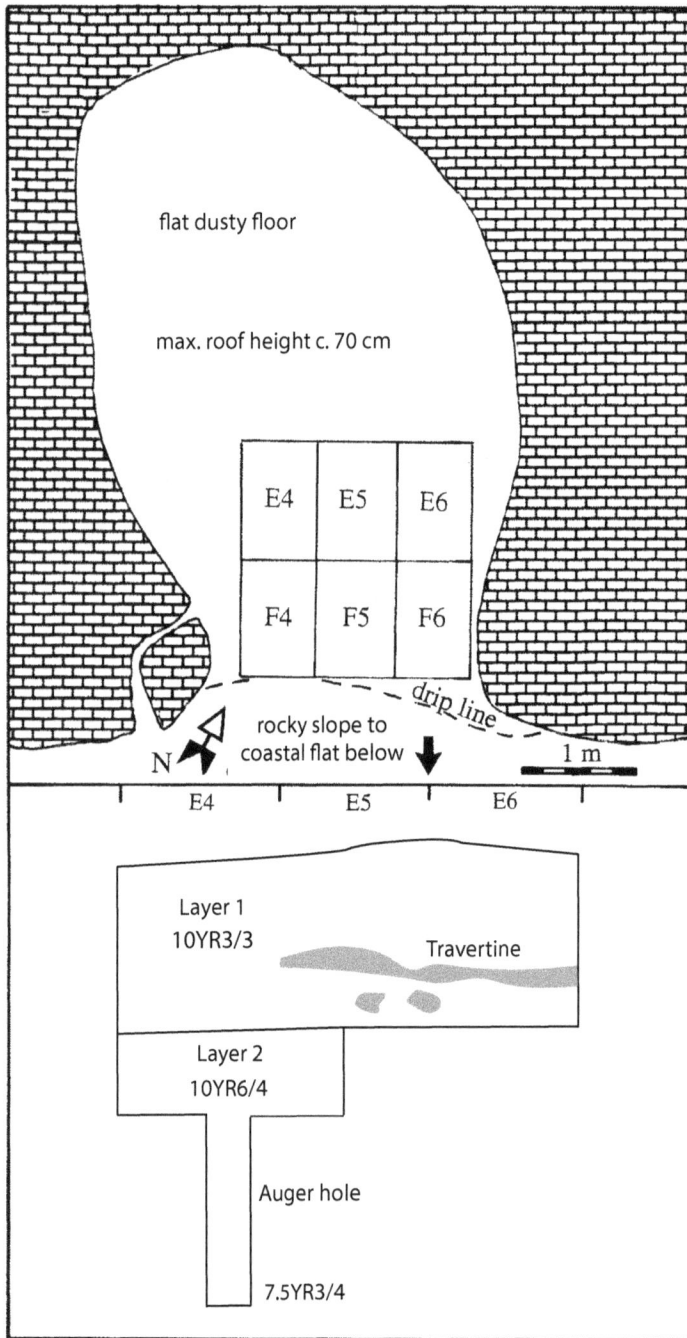

Figure 3.5 Daeo 2: plan and section.
Source: Peter Bellwood.

Layer 1 has four C14 dates. Its base may be a little older than the marine shell sample from 60–65 cm (ANU 9450), which dates to 16,767–15,889 cal. BP, and the *Canarium* charcoal from 50–55 cm, which dates to 13,065–12,731 cal. BP (OZD 768). As Table 3.3 shows, however, there is almost no cultural material below a depth of 70 cm, so there is no good reason to claim a date for first use of the cave much in excess of the oldest date of 16,000 BP. Between 20 and 25 cm, that is about one-quarter of the way down the profile, charcoal sample ANU 9452 gave a date of 6463–6194 cal. BP. These three samples are quite convincing from an age/depth perspective. However, at 55–60 cm, there is a date for charcoal sample ANU 9451 of only 1691–986 cal. BP, but in this case secondary movement downwards of the charcoal seems to be the likely explanation. Essentially, the whole of Layer 1 offers a similar cultural sequence to Layer 1 in Tanjung Pinang; that is, mainly preceramic (in this case c. 16,000 to c. 3000 cal. BP), with a thin veneer of ceramic period burial activity on the top.

From Table 3.3, it can be seen that densities are greatest for all materials, except pottery and human bone, between about 10 and 70 cm. Shells continue into culturally sterile Layer 2, as in Tanjung Pinang, and show a similar distribution in that the strandline species of *Pythia* disappears downwards towards the Last Glacial Maximum, whereas the *Obba* land snails continued to enter the deposits, albeit in smaller numbers below the appearance of humans. The small numbers of marine shells below 90 cm depth are perhaps of secondary derivation from the occupation levels above. The explanation that they have fallen naturally from the cave roof, acceptable for Tanjung Pinang, seems to be less likely (but certainly not impossible) for Daeo 2 since the rock here is much more coherent and less crumbly. If there truly was human occupation at 140 cm depth, it could only have been extremely ephemeral.

Not surprisingly, the preservation of animal bone in Layer 1 was found to improve markedly towards the protected interior of the cave in the E4–6 trench line. Bone was almost absent in F4–6, doubtless due to fluctuating dampness close to the drip-line. A similar circumstance was noted at Tanjung Pinang. However, in both shelters (and in all limestone sites excavated in Maluku) pHs were very strongly alkaline throughout.

Burnt coral pieces also occurred in Layer 1, resulting perhaps from cooking. The only *Canarium* anvil found in Daeo 2 came from quite high in the profile, in E4 at 25–30 cm depth, possibly from a late preceramic context. Human bone, mainly single teeth and small bone fragments, and potsherds have the same distribution as in Tanjung Pinang, both being concentrated at the top of Layer 1, but with the human bone having a slightly lower centre of gravity than pottery. As at Tanjung Pinang, this is perhaps because bones were placed in shallow pits scooped in the cave floor whereas pots might have been put on the cave floor itself. It is worthy of note here that an upside-down skull cap was excavated at 25–30 cm in F6 with phalanges inside; a similar situation occurred at Tanjung Pinang where one skull cap was buried upside-down and another had ribs placed inside it. It is clear that the burials in Daeo 2 and Tanjung Pinang were made by the same cultural group, perhaps at the same time and certainly within the past 2500 years. However, Daeo 2 had far less bone than Tanjung Pinang overall, and no complete skulls.

Table 3.3 Distribution of the contents of Daeo 2 by depth in cm.

Depths cm below surface	C14 cal. BP	Animal bone gm*	Manuports and cooking stones gm*	Total shell wt in gm*	Obba land snails, total no.*	Pythia land snails, total no.*	(Potentially) artefactual stone, gm	Pottery (no. of sherds)	Bone points	Human bone gm
0-10 cm		0	100	715	90	28	18	21		300
10-20		62	1300	2300	126	97	90	15		356
20-30	6463-6194 charcoal	159	2200	6375	101	34	91 + 1x400 gm Canarium anvil	1		343
30-40		204	3000	3100	205	82	135	1	1 bipoint	230
40-50		95	1650	1900	59	7	490	1	1 (?)	
50-60**	1691-986 charcoal 13,065-12,731 (Canarium charcoal)	42	1325	1500	68	13	570			
60-70	16,767-15,889 (8 Turbo opercula)	20	215	1000	40	2	370			
70-80		16	70	560	148	11	15			
80-90		6	20	170	31	3				
90-100		0	20	85	24	0				
100-110		1		95	21	1				
110-120		2		30	17	0				
120-130				25	10	0				
130-140				5	4	0				

* Below 90 cm only one-third of the excavation area was continued, into Layer 2. Actual statistics could therefore be multiplied by three from levels below 90 cm to make the data comparable in volumetric terms, although this has not been done in this table since the interface between Layers 1 and 2 was not totally flat and such action could introduce unwanted distortion of the data.

** Fragments of charred Canarium nut shell were identified to this depth, but not below.

Details of C14 dates are listed in Table 1.1.

Source: Peter Bellwood.

Daeo 1

Daeo cave 1 is larger than Daeo 2, being about 8 m from drip-line to back wall and about 5 m wide (Fig. 3.6). However, the rear of the cave is virtually filled with stalagmite, and the actual habitable area would only have been about 5x4 m, towards the front of the cave. The roof rises to a maximum of about 1.6 m above the present floor, only slightly higher than Daeo 2. Of course, both caves would have been high enough to stand up in when human occupation first began.

Daeo 1 only has one layer, cultural throughout. This is a totally dry and very loose soil, the same dark brown clayey soil as Layer 1 in Daeo 2. In Daeo 1 it sits directly on limestone bedrock at a maximum depth of 45 cm, and there is no underlying sterile clay layer. Clearly, the cave floor was bare rock when occupation began.

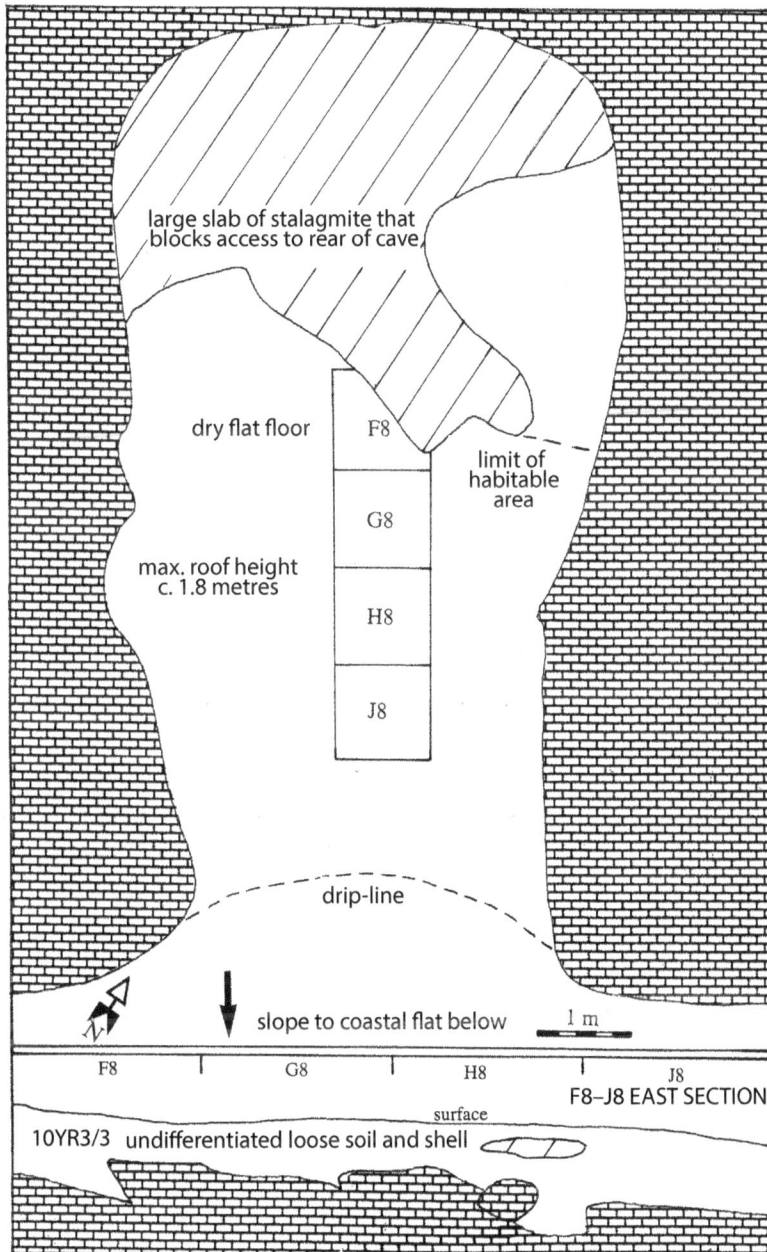

Figure 3.6 Daeo 1: plan.

Source: Peter Bellwood.

Table 3.4 Distribution of the contents of Daeo 1 by depth in cm.

Depth in cm, all squares	Human bone (gm)	Shell (gm)	Cooking stones and unmodified pebbles (no./wt gm)	Pottery sherd no.
0–5	158	5375	7/380	12
5–10	45	8975	17/1570	10
10–15	100	10,620	15/1005	1
15–20	76	7875	22/710	1
20–25	47	6230	15/960	1
25–30	26	3125	6/115	1
30–35	13	1400	4/40	
35–40		600	3/25	
40–45		350	1/450	

Source: Peter Bellwood.

A line of four 1x1 m squares was laid out from the mouth of the cave back to the stalagmite, which virtually fills the rear of the cave. As in Daeo 2, the soil was dug in 5 cm spits and sieved through a 2.5 mm mesh. The vertical distribution of cultural elements in the cave is less coherent than in Daeo 2 (Table 3.4), perhaps because Daeo 1 is totally dry within and scuffing would have been extremely easy. The greatest density of marine shell occurs at 10–15 cm, but densities do not vary greatly from top to bottom. Fewer shells occurred below 30 cm because the volume of soil is less from this depth—the bedrock rises irregularly into the cultural deposit. Cooking stones and unmodified pebbles have a similar distribution to shells. Burnt coral and burnt shells occur in small quantities throughout the deposit, and there is also some ochre. Stone tools were not found in this site. Pottery and human bone is present in only very small amounts, but in this case to quite deep within the deposit, a circumstance that suggests definite disturbance (given that both materials only occurred near the surface in Tanjung Pinang and Daeo 1). Because of the obvious potential for disturbance in Daeo 1, no C14 samples were submitted for dating. Even without the disturbance factor, Daeo 1 clearly contains little that is not represented much more clearly in Daeo 2 and Tanjung Pinang.

Tanjung Tulang

This cave is located within the coral headland, which limits the sandy beach of Daeo to the west of the village. It lies much closer to the sea than the caves of Daeo 1 and 2, and is also at a lower altitude, its floor being only between 3.5 and 4.5 m above high tide level. The cultural deposit within the cave is a loose dry humic-stained beach sand with coral pebbles, only 30 cm thick at the maximum. This cultural deposit grades into a clean beach sand of black volcanic and white coral composition, identical to that which forms the modern beach. This clean sand in turn lies on top of coral bedrock. The whole deposit is thus basically beach sand and carries an air of chronological recency, although the sea seems not to have entered the cave within living memory.

Table 3.5 Distribution of the contents of Tanjung Tulang by depth in cm.

Tanjung Tulang; Squares L5 to N5	Human bone (gm)	Shell (gm)	Pottery sherd no.
0–5	40	550	119
5–10	44	350	47
10–15	170	350	20
15–20	177	200	2
20–25	162	100	
25–30	bedrock		

Source: Peter Bellwood.

The Tanjung Tulang cave is quite large: about 15 cm long by 7 m across. The roof is about 2 m high at the front and slopes down to the back of the cave. When discovered in 1991, this cave seemed to have potential, but when excavated in 1994 the results turned out to be disappointing. A total of 4 m² was excavated, comprising a 3x1 m trench near the front of the cave and a 1x1 m square towards the rear. The cultural deposit appears to lack internal differentiation and comprises only pottery of the type found at the open site of Sabatai Tua and very fragmented human bone (Table 3.5). Possibly, as at Tanjung Pinang, secondary burials were placed in scoops within the cave floor with pottery placed above. Human bone fragments and pottery of Sabatai Tua type were also seen in at least three niches in the limestone of the headland in the vicinity of the cave. The marine shells within Tanjung Tulang could be from casual visits.

Sabatai Tua

The open archaeological site at Sabatai Tua occupies the top and seaward-facing slope of a small hill, which lies east of the modern village of Sabatai Tua. The modern village lies to the west of the Sabatai River, but the site lies across the river, on its eastern bank and immediately inland from the coastal road. Facing seawards from the site one looks down into the mouth of the Sabatai River with its flanking sand spit. This site was sketch-planned and test-pitted in 1991, but no proper survey has been carried out. The precise extent of the site is now hard to judge; it appears that no stratified deposits remain on the top of the hill and most artefacts now lie strewn around the sides of the hill as a result of soil erosion caused by gardening activities.

Informants told us that the top of the hill, a gently rounded area of about 50x40 m, is called Musi after a Tobelo man who planted coconuts here about 60 years ago. A 1x1 m test pit dug in this upper area only revealed thin disturbed soil deposits 15 cm deep sitting on sterile substrate, with no artefacts; the latter seem for the most part to have migrated downslope. About halfway down the eastern side of the hill, facing the Sabatai river mouth, lies a terrace about 80 m long by about 15 m wide, which looks as if it could be of human origin. A test pit here again yielded no definitely *in situ* archaeological materials, the few sherds recovered probably having descended down the hill from above. This terrace is called Tibi, after another Tobelo coconut planter (the inhabitants of Sabatai Tua village state that they are of mixed Tobelo and Galela descent).

The surface finds collected from Sabatai Tua comprise lots of marine shells, potsherds (including Portuguese-influenced *forna* stoves for baking sago cakes, mortars and imported glazed ceramics), and cooking stones. The earthenwares are described in more detail in Chapter 8. It may be presumed that there was once a settlement here, on the hilltop and on the lower terrace. The whole assemblage is related to that from Tanjung Pinang, Tanjung Tulang, and from surface collections made in open sites in southern Morotai.

Sambiki Tua

During a visit to Sambiki Tua village in January 1991, the team was shown a number of polished stone adzes, stated to have been found near the mosque in the village. Two more adzes were also stated to have been found somewhere in the vicinity of the Tanjung Pinang rockshelter, although no stone adzes were found during the excavations in this site. These adzes are all of untanged varieties, single-bevelled (i.e. true adzes), with rectangular or trapezoidal cross-sections. They are thus quite different from the adze kit found in association with the red-slipped pottery of the first millennium BCE in the excavations at Uattamdi on Kayoa Island (see Chapter 5). Presumably, the Morotai adzes are younger than those from Uattamdi.

On visiting the village mosque, potsherds were observed eroding out from the ground all around the building, especially where rain drips from the roof were causing soil to be washed away. The precise extent of the site could not be ascertained, but was judged to be at least 30x30 m. A 1x1 m test pit was excavated immediately behind the mosque, on its western side away from the road. This square was dug in 5 cm spits, but the soil proved too clayey and sticky for sieving and was simply hand-searched. The archaeological layer comprised the upper 40 cm of the profile; this being a pale red to light reddish-brown soil (2.5YR 6/2 and 6/4), which contained a high density of clay nodules. Some of these nodules appeared large enough to be debris resulting from pottery making on site. The sherdage in the site, mostly quite small, perhaps due to past cultivation activities, was distributed as shown in Table 3.6.

Table 3.6 Potsherd distributions by depth in cm in the Sambiki Tua site.

	0–5	5–10	10–15	15–20	20–25	25–30	30–35
Pulau Mare sherds	1						
European sherds		1	1				
Plain and red-slipped sherds	114	65	194	284	146	148	94
Incised sherds	2	2	8	1	1		
Ribbed sherds				2			
Total	117	68	201	287	147	148	94

Source: Peter Bellwood.

For now, it is only necessary to state that the Sambiki Tua pottery is a predominantly red-slipped ware that bears some resemblance to that excavated from Tanjung Pinang, but it is certainly not identical. The assemblage seems to be essentially late prehistoric, a dating confirmed by a C14 date of 1054–325 cal. BP (ANU 7784) on charcoal collected from the 15–20 cm spit. At about 30 cm a number of small postholes appeared, suggesting that the sherd disposal might have taken place within structures or beneath house floors.

4

The excavation of Gua Siti Nafisah, Kecamatan Weda, south-central Halmahera

Peter Bellwood, Gunadi Nitihaminoto, Gunadi Kusnowihardjo, and Agus Waluyo

The northern end of the southern arm of Halmahera is about 18 km wide, rugged and uninhabited in its interior. It consists mainly of late Oligocene to early Pliocene sedimentary rocks (Hall et al. 1988). In 1991, a dirt road crossed from Payahe in the west to Weda in the east, travelled by hired four-wheel drive vehicles. Weda itself, the administrative town of Kecamatan Weda, lies in a protected bay towards the northeastern limit of the arm.

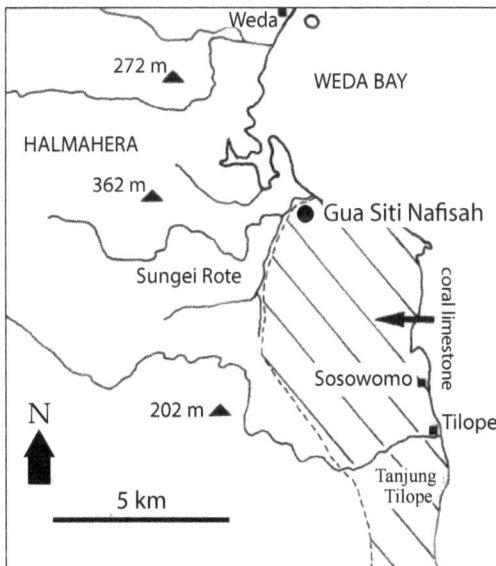

Figure 4.1 Map of the Weda region and location of Gua Siti Nafisah.

The diagonally shaded area is limestone.

Source: Peter Bellwood.

The cave of Siti Nafisah is located near an agricultural field hamlet called Nusliko, about 5.5 km south of Weda (Fig. 4.1). The cave lies on the northern side of a limestone promontory, about 120 m south of the Rote stream and about 70 m above the stream bank (and thus presumably about 75 m above sea level). This limestone promontory forms the northern limit of a broad belt of uplifted Quaternary coral limestone, about 20 km long and up to 6 km wide, that runs down the eastern coastline of the southern arm of Halmahera, through the large village of Tilope.

The cave is reached by a fairly steep rocky climb from the plantations that line the banks of the Rote stream. The promontory continues to rise above the cave to an ultimate height of just over 100 m above sea level. The story goes that the grandmother of one of our local assistants, Siraju Jalalo, once dreamt that she met an imaginary woman called Siti Nafisah in the cave—hence the name. The original name of the cave seems not to be known.

The cave is of phreatic origin, clearly indicated by blind passages in the roof that can rise up to heights of 10 m above the cave floor. In most of the occupied area the cave has a roof height of only about 3 m. It has an irregular shape, delineated in Figure 4.2, and the interior portions (inwards of Squares J10 and E12) have no traces of human occupation as far as can be observed. Prior to excavation a 1m grid was laid out for survey purposes, and three areas were eventually excavated, denoted F5–F8, J10 and E12 on the plan. The preceramic shell midden appears to be concentrated at the front of the cave, in and around Squares F5–F8, whereas the inner Squares J10 and E12 were laid out over pottery-bearing midden deposits that were visible before excavation on the cave surface.

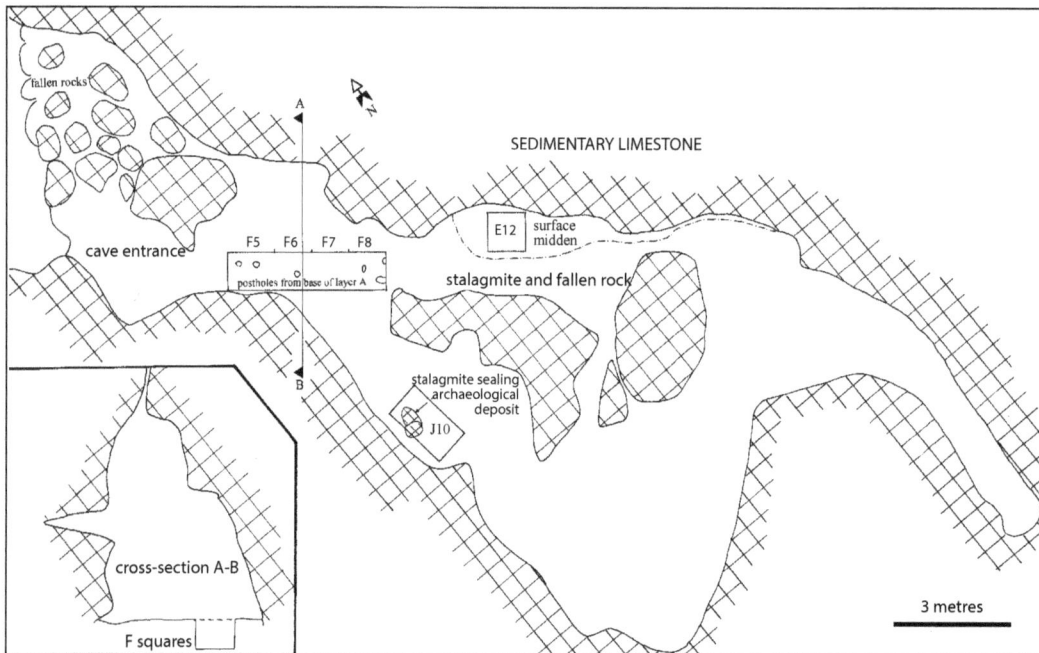

Figure 4.2 Gua Siti Nafisah: plan of the site.

Source: Peter Bellwood.

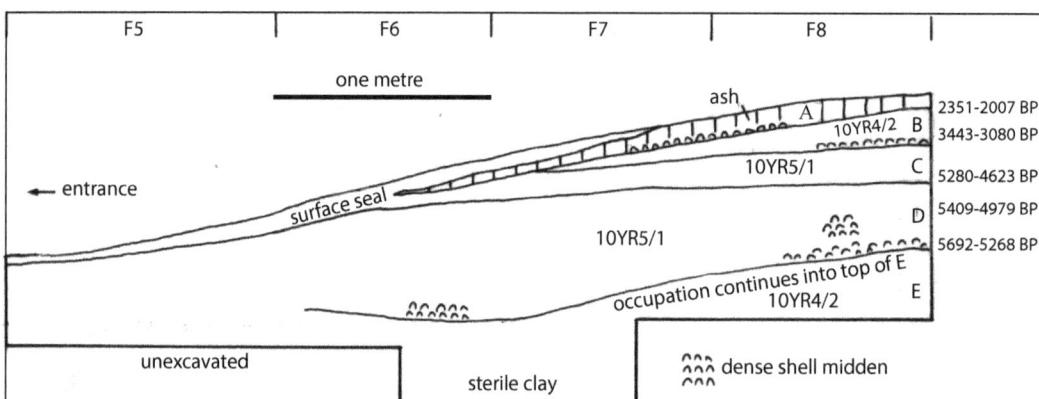

Figure 4.3 Gua Siti Nafisah: main section, Squares F5 to F8, east wall.

Details of C14 dates are listed in Table 1.1.

Source: Peter Bellwood.

The main excavation, in Squares F5–F8, covered an area of 4.25x1 m. The stratigraphic section of this trench is shown in Figure 4.3, wherein it will be seen that five layers (denoted A to E) were differentiated in the inwards portion of the trench, in Squares F7 and F8. In Square F5, towards the mouth of the cave, virtually no layer differentiation was visible at all, the deposit here being shallow (over limestone bedrock) and rather heavily concreted in places. This may reflect erosion and the effects of drips close to the cave mouth. Square F6 was similarly without clear stratigraphic differentiation, and the side closest to the cave wall was heavily disturbed by a deep area of subsidence caused by solution of the limestone and consequent sinking of cultural materials into subterranean crevices. This disturbance extended back towards J10 as a shallow trench, visible on the cave floor before excavation. Square F7 had a rather clearer stratigraphy, which became very clear in Square F8, the innermost one.

The five layers in F7 and F8 were dug in spits between 4 and 10 cm thick—the increase to 10 cm in the lower Layers D and E occurred because of time pressures and because the deposits seemed sufficiently homogeneous to allow such spit thicknesses to be excavated without loss of information. In Table 4.1, the data presented are raw counts and weights only, not densities. The figures could be converted into densities by taking spit thickness into account, but this would be unlikely to change the observation that Layers A to D have fairly continuous distributions of cultural material, while Layer E represents the sterile natural deposit that has had cultural material mixed into its top. Layers B, C and D have increasing percentages of fine fraction particles (<0.063 mm) with depth (18, 48 and 56 per cent, respectively), but this might reflect no more than post-depositional sorting caused by water from roof drips moving clay downwards through the profile.

The layers will now be described in turn:

Layer A: This is basically an ash zone 5–7 cm thick, clearly differentiated from Layer B below. Layer A contains pottery, a stone adze and fairly dense shell midden, and is of the same general age as the pottery-bearing middens in areas J10 and E12 further inside the cave. It is dated by ANU 7785 on *Anadara* shell to 2351–2007 cal. BP.

Layer B: This layer is a dark greyish-brown soil with considerable quantities of shell midden, dated by ANU 7786 on *Anadara* shell to 3443–3080 cal. BP. On its upper surface there are sherds, a stone adze fragment, and a number of postholes dug in from Layer A that are plotted on Figure 4.2. Layer B itself, below its top surface, is undoubtedly preceramic.

Layer C is a grey soil with a similar midden concentration to Layer B, dated by ANU 7787 on *Anadara* shell to 5280–4623 cal. BP. It has a sharp interface with B, but grades downwards more gradually into D below.

Layer D is also grey in colour and continues the midden in a density similar to Layers B and C above. Layer D contained many volcanic oven stones, indicating that hot stone cooking had been carried out here, even though no pit was clearly visible during the excavation. Layer D is dated by ANU 7788 and 7789, both on *Anadara* shell, to 5692–4979 cal. BP. Layers C and D appear to be essentially continuous in deposition and texture.

Layer E is a dark greyish-brown soil, which appears to be the natural pre-human deposit within the cave. Bedrock rises through it in the southern side of F5 and in the southeastern corner of F8, but in F6–F7 it was dug to a depth of 110 cm below its upper surface without reaching bedrock. In hindsight, there may be an extremely small possibility that unexcavated cultural layers could lie below Layer E, which has cultural material only in its top 15 cm, doubtless derived by downwards treading from Layer D above. Layer E also has a different grain size pattern from Layers B, C, and D. While these three layers become finer downwards, Layer E is coarser, thus reversing the trend visible in the layers of human occupation. No dates were run for Layer E.

As noted above, one of the problems encountered in this excavation was that the layers become quite invisible in Squares F5 and F6, so the following discussion of the distribution of cultural items through the stratigraphy is based mainly on Square F8, which yielded a sufficient density of material to give a reliable picture of the sequence. The question also arises of whether occupation of the site was continuous. All that can be stated here is that there is nothing in the distribution of artefacts (Table 4.1) to suggest any hiatus in occupation. During the preceramic phase the cave seems to have been occupied at a low intensity throughout, but fairly continuously. The dates are too close together to throw much light on this; all they can tell, when calibration is taken into account, is that the preceramic shell midden dates to between 5700 and 3000 BP, whereas the pottery and stone adze–bearing layer above, and the J10 pottery midden, date to less than 2400 years ago.

The Square J10, dug to a size of 1.8x1 m, was chosen for excavation around a large stalagmite that had formed on top of a shell-midden layer (indeed, the stalagmite had shells and potsherds embedded into its bottom). After removal of the stalagmite, a dense shell midden about 15–20 cm thick was revealed, with pottery throughout at a considerable density (1575 gm of pottery for the whole deposit in J10, as opposed to a total of only 230 gm for the whole of the F5–F8 area). J10 also contained animal bones, importantly of *Dorcopsis* wallaby (but not bandicoot), suggesting that wallabies survived on Halmahera until the marine shell date for the J10 midden (ANU 7790: 1598–1268 cal. BP, see Fig. 4.4). Shell density in J10 was similar to that in the densest F5–F8 preceramic midden layers, and the same shellfish species were present.

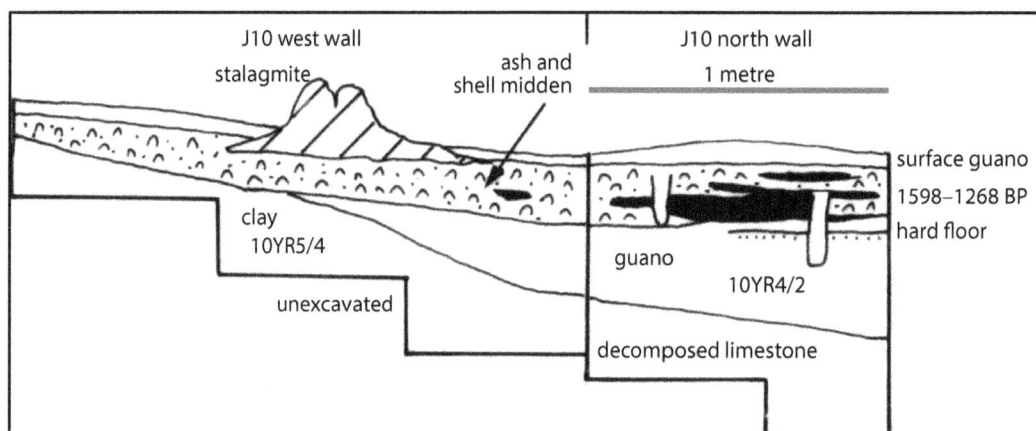

Figure 4.4 Gua Siti Nafisah: J10 section, west and north walls.
Black deposits are ash. Details of C14 dates are listed in Table 1.1.
Source: Peter Bellwood.

Table 4.1 Distribution of the contents of Gua Siti Nafisah F5-F8 by layer and depth in measured cm spits (commencing with spit A1).

Siti Nafisah: layer/spit codes and depths from surface (NB: spits are not of equal thickness)	C14 cal. BP (Anadara shell)	Stone manuports, no./gm (F8 only)	Ochre (presence only, Squares F5-F8)	Total shell weights, gm (F8 only)	Marine shell weight, gm (F8 only)	Animal bone weights, gm (F8 only)	Bone points, no. (Squares F5-F8)	Pottery, sherd no. (Squares F5-F8)
A1 (0-4)	2351-2007			2200	150	10		103
A2 (4-7)				1450	200	10		31
B1 (7-13)	3443-3080	1/150		2000	425	50	3	9
B2 (13-20)		1/200		1100	20	20		8
C1 (20-25)		3/250		1700	75	75	5	5
C2 (25-30)			*	900	100	17	2	1
C3 (30-35)	5280-4623	5/550		2250	500	85	4	1
D1 (35-40)		2/200	*	775	450	52	1	
D2 (40-50)	5409-4979	3/400**		3150	475	42	1	
D3 (50-60)		22/1900**	*	6750	50	50	1	
D4 (60-70)	5692-5268	7/650**	*	3075	200	24	2	
E1 (70-80)		2/250		400	50	30		
E2 (80-90)			*	250	50	35		

* presence of ochre

** volcanic cooking stones

Details of C14 dates are listed in Table 1.1.

Source: Peter Bellwood.

The J10 shell midden overlies a layer of dark greyish-brown bat guano, here fairly fresh and unweathered, but nevertheless alkaline, which in turn overlies a yellowish-brown clay, which grades down into rotten limestone and eventually the hard rock floor of the cave. Today, the cave has very active bat colonies in the interior and guano falls constantly. Indeed, the J10 guano layer is identical in colour and texture to the matrix of Layers A to E in Squares F5–F8, and to the soil matrix of the midden layer in J10, leaving little doubt how the bulk of the deposits in the cave originated.

In the northern part of J10 the guano contains, near its upper surface, a hard-stamped floor, which clearly represents human frequentation just prior to the deposition of the midden. An ash band on this floor, derived from a hearth (but without datable charcoal) yielded the stone adze butt drawn as Figure 8.4B. However, the suggestion made in an earlier report (Bellwood et al. 1993:30–31) that the stamped guano floor was preceramic requires modification, since a single potsherd from this ash layer was found during sieving of an ash sample to try to obtain datable charcoal (unsuccessfully) in the museum in Ternate in 1994. This adze is therefore of Neolithic and not preceramic origin.

Another 1x1 m square was dug at E12 on the plan. This simply produced a pottery-bearing shell midden layer identical to that in J10, between 5 and 18 cm deep, directly over the same red-brown clay, which occurs beneath the J10 midden. No preceramic occupation whatsoever was identified in the J10 and E12 zones of the cave interior.

Major aspects of the vertical distribution of cultural material in Gua Siti Nafisah are revealed in Table 4.1, which, together with the data from J10 and E12, indicates the following sequence:

1. Layers B, C, D, and the top of E in Squares F5–F8 represent preceramic occupation, with shellfish and marsupial exploitation at a fairly even rate over time, associated with the uses of ochre, small bone points, cooking stones, but absolutely no flaked stone tools. These layers span a period of at least 2500 years, between 5700 and 3000 BP. It is interesting to note that marsupial exploitation was apparently fairly even in intensity through this period; this differs markedly from the situation in the Gebe sites of Wetef and Golo and the Morotai site of Daeo 2, where the vertical distribution of marsupial bone resembles a bell curve with a very definite peak (Chapter 11).

2. In the upper deposits, represented by Layer A in Squares F5–F8 and by the shell middens in J10 and E12, two of the three marsupial species present in the site (the wallaby and bandicoot) continued to be present until about 2500 years ago. Their fates on Halmahera after this date remain unknown. These upper deposits contain pottery (Fig. 7.9), pig bones, two stone adzes (Fig. 8.4), shell ornaments, and even a piece of iron (on J10 surface), and clearly represent a fairly marked cultural change in the history of the site. This occurred despite the absence of any changes in patterns of shellfish exploitation. Two direct C14 dates on pig bones from this phase, both less than 2000 cal. BP, are listed in Table 1.1 and discussed in Chapter 10.

3. Occupation in the cave apparently ceased c. 1500 BP.

5

Excavations in the Uattamdi rockshelters, Kayoa Island

Peter Bellwood, Rachel Wood, Geoffrey Irwin, and Agus Waluyo

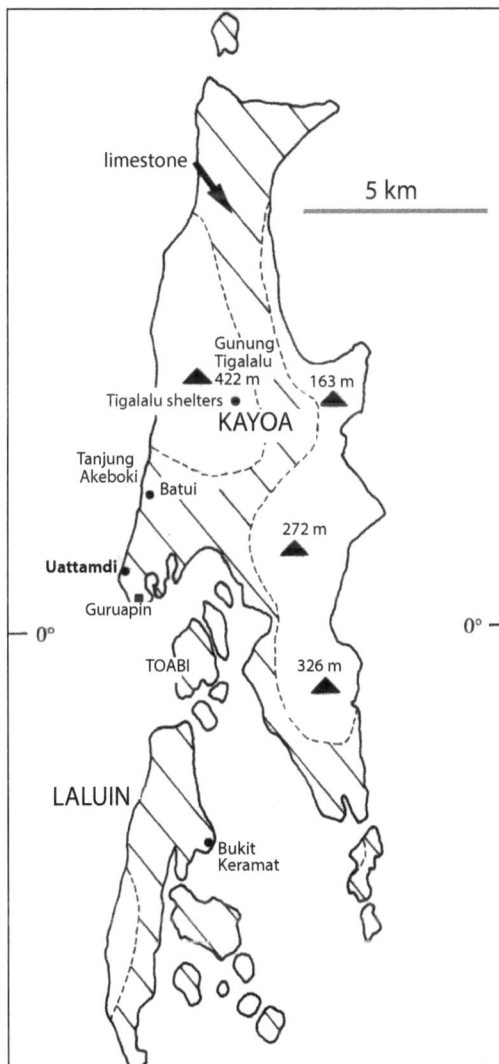

Figure 5.1 Map of Kayoa.

Diagonally shaded areas are uplifted coral limestone.

Source: Peter Bellwood.

The island of Kayoa, with neighbouring Laluin and Toabi, lies about 30 km off the western coast of the main island of Halmahera, equidistant between the volcanic islands of Makian to the north and Bacan to the south, and within the volcanic inner arc that van Bemmelen (1949:48) termed the Ternate Zone. It is about 20 km long by a maximum of 7 km wide (Fig. 5.1). Unlike the other volcanic islands, which lie to its north (especially Makian, Moti, Tidore and Ternate), Kayoa is low-lying and volcanically inactive. The highest point, Gunung Tigalalu at 422 m, is an ancient eroded volcano that still retains a definite volcanic skyline with an inner cone and outer crater rim. According to the map in Hall et al. (1988: Fig. 6), the Tigalalu volcanic rocks could be as recent as Late Pleistocene in age. Parts of eastern Kayoa consist of pre-Miocene volcanics. However, most of the island, apart from the discrete volcanic zones, is formed from uplifted Pleistocene reef limestone.

Kayoa is a slightly tilted island, with a zone of raised coral along much of its western coastline, this zone also extending southwards along the west coast of the neighbouring island of Laluin immediately to the south. A rather drowned and estuarine topography with extensive mangrove swamps lies along the eastern shoreline of both islands. Western Kayoa has coral sand beaches and coral headlands, with a series of at least three levels of raised coral reef, visible as interrupted low cliffs, lying at increasing altitudes inland. The shelter complex of Uattamdi lies in the lowest of these coral cliffs just to the north of the headland of Tanjung Pompom, 1.5 km north of the equator. It can be reached by walking trail from the town of Guruapin, the administrative centre for the *kecamatan* of Kayoa.

Uattamdi 1

The main excavated shelter of Uattamdi 1 (henceforth U1: Figs 5.2, 5.3) is located in the low cliff (here about 6 m high) of raised coral, which lies about 60 m inland from the head of the beach. Between the shelter and the beach is a flat coastal plain, today planted under coconuts, that lies at the same level as the floor of the shelter. The shelter thus has no raised deposits within, and indeed its floor is completely flat to the exterior, with a habitable area of about 50 m². In conditions of heavy rain, drips form at various places in the shelter roof, which has a fairly cracked and crumbly appearance, causing the excavation team to cast wary eyes aloft from time to time. But in general the conditions within are dry. The roof of the shelter is about 3 m high.

It should be mentioned here the modern shelter floor lies approximately 1.5–2 m above modern high tide level. Furthermore, the base of the cultural deposits lies about 1.2 m below the modern shelter surface on a sterile surface of beach sand (denoted below as Layer E). This beach sand within the shelter thus lies at the same absolute level as the modern beach. This point is stressed here because it indicates that, since occupation began in the shelter about 3500 years ago, there has been no local *relative* movement of sea level, at least not along this particular stretch of coastline. In this respect, the local sea level history at Uattamdi apparently differs from that at Buwawansi on Gebe, discussed above. At Buwawansi, sea level at 4000 BP was perhaps 1 m higher than now according to the record in Buwawansi shelter 3. Because of the likelihood of a eustatic sea level drop of approximately 1 m between 4000 and 3500 BP in Southeast Asia generally (Sathiamurthy and Voris 2006), these variations at Uattamdi and Buwawansi perhaps reflect local tectonic rather than regional eustatic movements.

The situation of basal beach sand Layer E also indicates that, at c. 3500 BP and just prior to human occupation, the active beach was within the shelter and the modern coastal plain did not exist. Presumably, this plain has developed as a result of inland soil erosion and coastal deposition since occupation in the site began. As in many Pacific islands (e.g. Kirch and Yen 1982 for Tikopia; Carson 2014 for Guam), this circumstance could reflect the environmental impact of the introduction of an agricultural economy to the island.

Uattamdi 1 was the first site to be excavated in the Moluccan program. In the 1990–91 excavation period, the 1x1 m squares D4 to D9 were excavated, followed by C4 to C7 and E4 to E9 in 1994 (Fig. 5.3). These squares, in total, cover 10 m², excavated to the culturally sterile beach sand Layer E at an average depth of 1.2 m. The square labelled AB7 in Figure 5.3 was not excavated since the deposits here were heavily concreted with calcium carbonate from the shelter wall. Deposits were sieved through 2.5 or 3 mm meshes and excavation was carried out in 5 cm spits within the five major layers in the site, these being lettered from Layer A (at the top) to the pure beach sand Layer E at the base of the site.

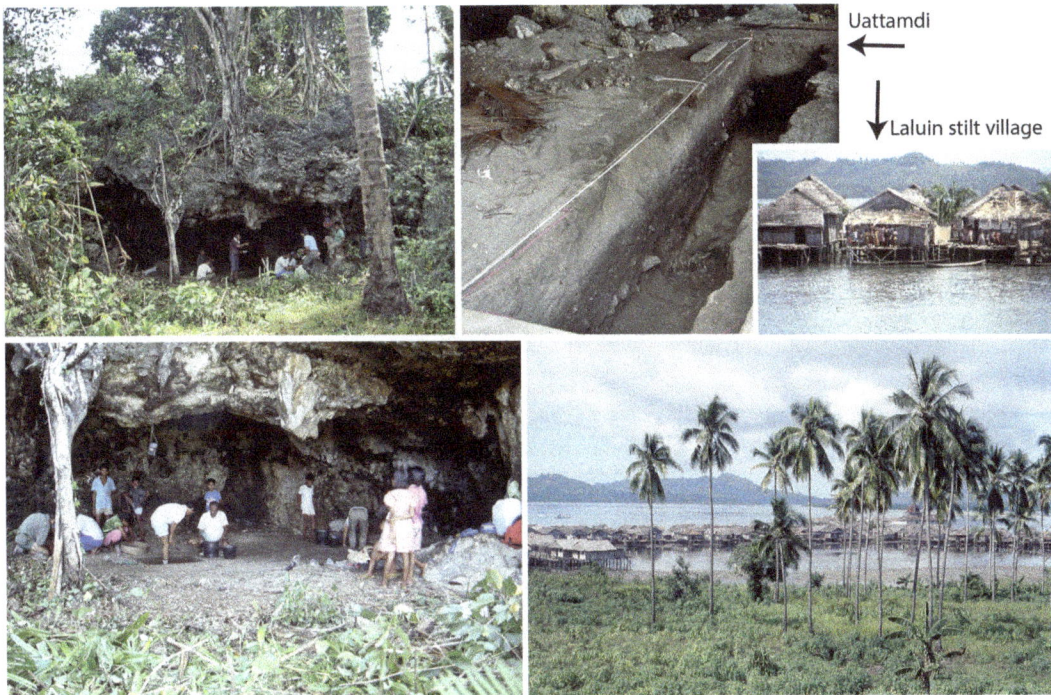

Figure 5.2 Uattamdi 1 photos.

Left and top: Uattamdi rockshelter 1, situated in a cliff of raised coral limestone, and the east wall of trench D4–D9 dug in 1991. At right, the Bajau stilt village immediately offshore from the Bukit Keramat site (see Chapter 6) on Laluin, photographed in 1991.

Source: Peter Bellwood.

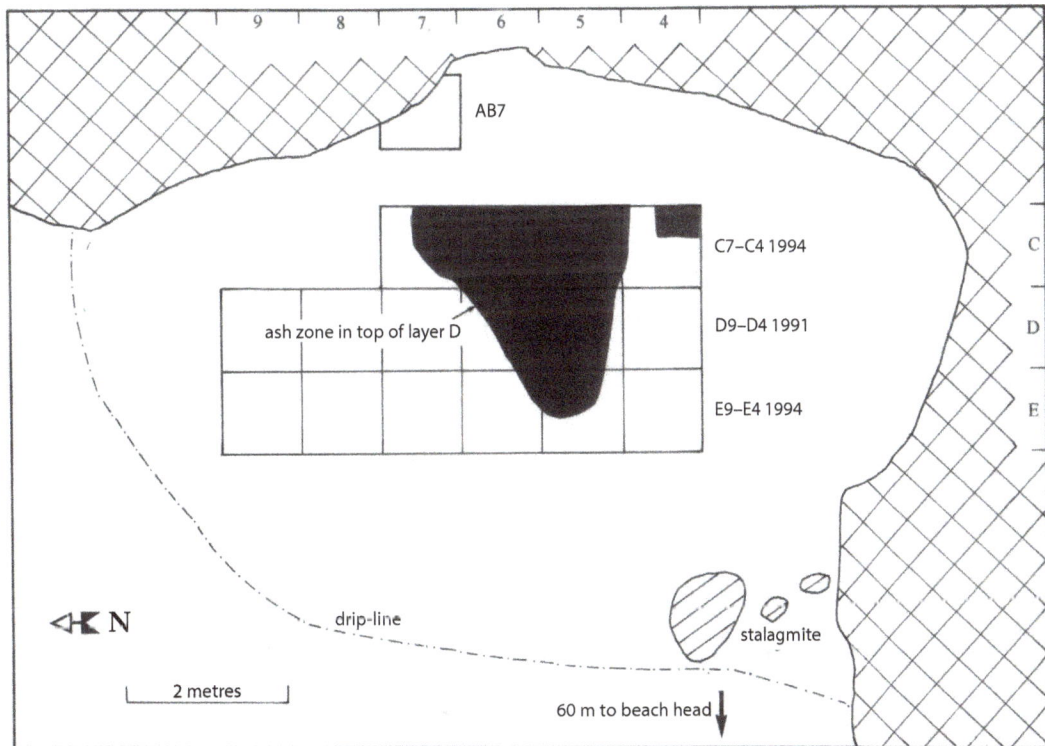

Figure 5.3 Uattamdi 1 site and excavation plan.

Source: Peter Bellwood.

The five layers in the site (Fig. 5.4) are all very sandy and clearly derive basically from a coral beach sand matrix. Simple observation suggests that they are either fairly pure beach sand (Layers E and B) or are beach sand mixed with soil from the local environment plus the debitage of human behaviour (Layers D, C and A). Grain size analyses indicate that all layers comprise over 80 per cent sand, with the most silt/clay-rich being Layer C, the richest in traces of human activity. The coarse components of each layer, after separation, are identical in visual appearance, being simply stained coral beach sand. The five layers can be described as follows, based on the section drawing in Figure 5.4, starting from the bottom:

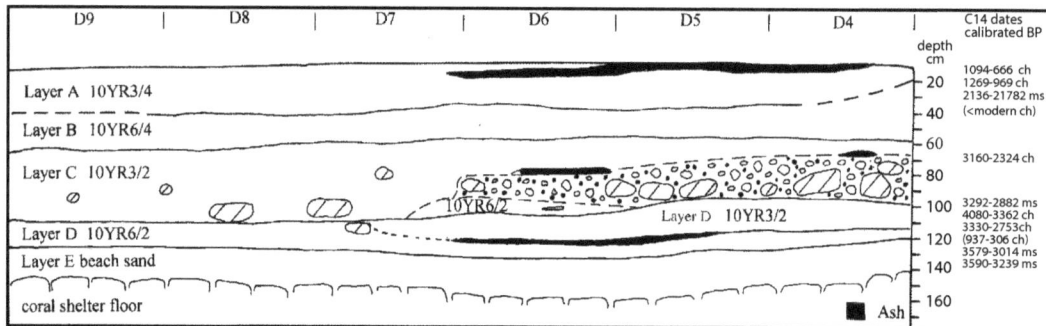

Figure 5.4 Uattamdi 1 section, Squares D4 to D9, east wall.
C14 dates are listed in Table 1.1 (ch = charcoal, ms = marine shell).
Source: Peter Bellwood.

Layer E: This is pure coral beach sand, identical to the modern beach. It contains weathered marine shells, from which the date of 3590–3239 cal. BP (ANU 9321) has been derived. Layer E is pre-human, and careful examination of it in cross-section suggests that it already had a thin veneer of dark topsoil, perhaps washed in from behind and above the shelter, before occupation began. Soil can be seen washing in during heavy rain from the south side of the shelter today. This veneer of topsoil is identified as Layer D below, and suggests that human occupation began sometime after the sea had retreated on a fairly reliable basis from the shelter. Layer E is only about 20–30 cm thick and sits directly on the coral rockshelter floor. The shelter was presumably wave-cut in origin, like many that can be seen in formation in coral headlands along the modern west coast of Kayoa, and has a fairly flat coral floor beneath the sediments. It can also be noted here that U1 has no traces of any preceramic occupation.

Layer D: This layer can be described as beach sand mixed with soil, giving a dark deposit that ranges from light yellowish-brown to very dark greyish-brown in colour. As just noted, the lighter-coloured part started life as the topsoil over the beach sand Layer E, into which the cultural material deposited by the first occupants of the site became trodden. Layer D has a sharp interface with the beach sand Layer E beneath. The main activity in Layer D was the creation of an extensive but quite thin ash deposit from hearths, as shown in Figure 5.3. This lies on the upper surface of the primary old topsoil portion of Layer D, but at the southern end of the trench these hearths are covered by a 10–15 cm deposit of dark greyish-brown soil (labelled 10YR3/2 in Fig. 5.4). It is not clear whether this extensive ash represents one large episode of activity or many superimposed small ones, but the absence of hearths elsewhere in the excavated part of Layer D suggests that the time involved in deposition could have been quite short.

The C14 dates for Layer D actually cover quite a large time span, from 4080 to 2753 cal. BP (Fig. 5.5). However, it seems most unlikely that Layer D could represent continuous activity over 1000 years, and a commencement date after 3579–3014 cal. BP based on ANU 7776 is supported by the pre-human Layer E marine shell date of 3590–3239 cal. BP (ANU 9321), as discussed above. The Bayesian chronological model (Fig. 5.5) identifies two dates within Layer D as outliers at more than 10 per cent probability. The youngest ANU 9320 is clearly too young, and is more similar in age to material from Layer A, despite being on charcoal from hearth features. ANU 10959, again on charcoal, is slightly too old, which could be a result of the old wood effect. The Bayesian model therefore suggests that Layer D dates between 3516–3058 and 3285–2769 cal. BP (start and end probability ranges given at 95 per cent probability).

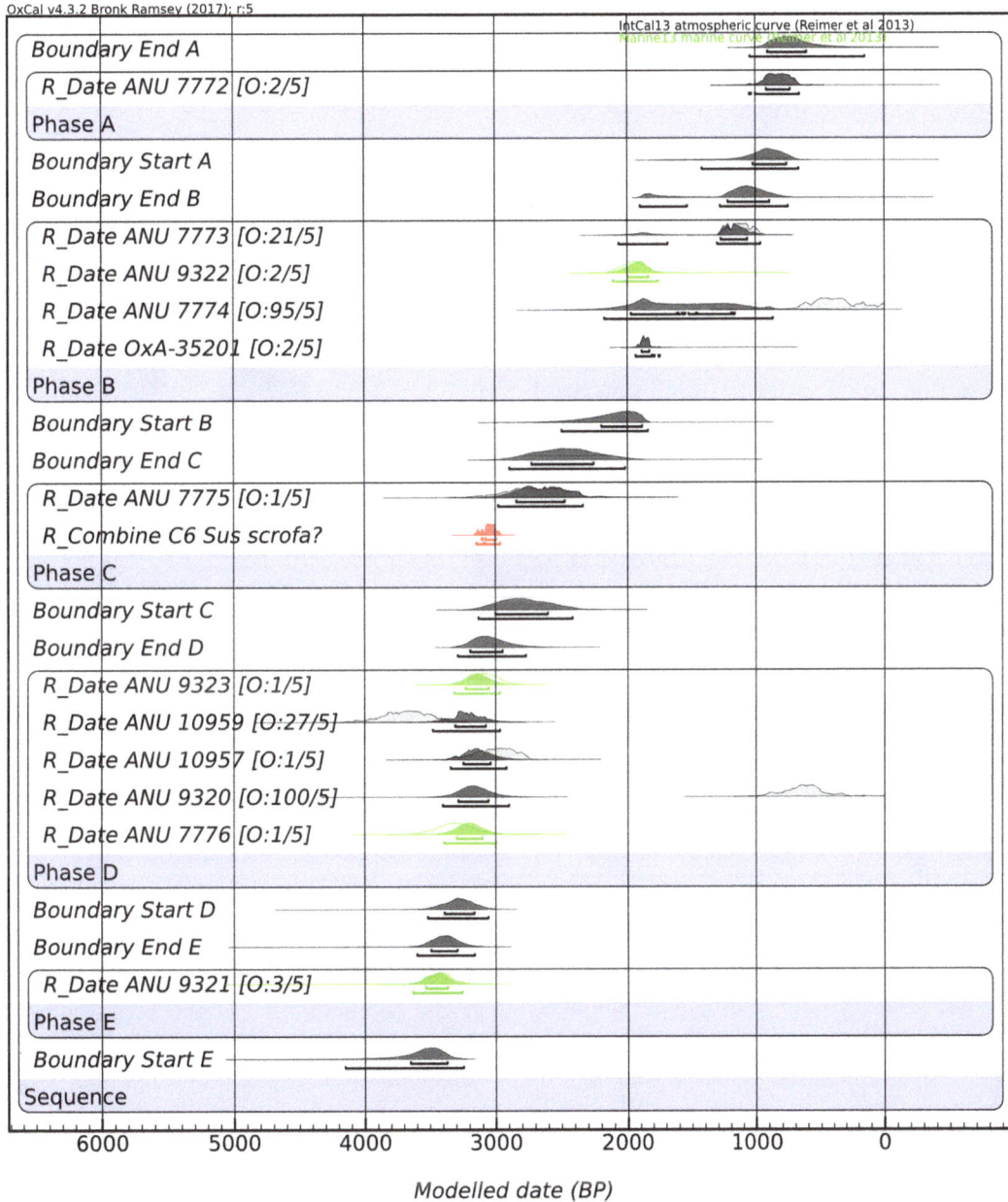

Figure 5.5 A Bayesian chronological model for Uattamdi produced using OxCal v.4.3 (Ramsey 2009).

Pale distributions denote the calibrated ages, and dark distributions the modelled ages. The two lines beneath the probability distributions represent the 68 per cent and 95 per cent probability ranges. Prior and posterior outlier probabilities are given next to the date name. Dates are calibrated against IntCal13 (grey) or Marine13 (green) (Reimer et al. 2013) with a ΔR of 0. All dates have been assigned a prior probability of 5 per cent within the General t-type Outlier Model, except for S-ANU 60005 (red), which is excluded from the model and only shown for reference due to the known problems with radiocarbon dates on tooth enamel. Details of C14 dates are listed in Table 1.1.

Source: Rachel Wood.

Layer C: This layer is a very dark greyish-brown sandy soil, within which there is a very dense layer of coral rubble, presumably derived from roof-fall, across the southern side of the trench (Figs 5.4 and 5.6). Layer C has one C14 date, of 3160–2324 cal. BP (ANU 7775), on ash likely to have contained charcoal from a hearth in spit C3, Square D7. This fits well within the general sequence of dates from the site and supports an overall date range for Layer C somewhere between c. 3000 and 2500 cal. BP. Two further radiocarbon dates on tooth enamel from a single M2 of a *Sus scrofa* mandible found in spit C6 are slightly older than ANU 7775 and similar to the age of charcoal in unit D at around 3150–2890 cal. BP. No collagen was preserved in the mandible or tooth dentine and a radiocarbon date on enamel was attempted. Radiocarbon dates on tooth enamel are notoriously unreliable, and often underestimate the true age of a sample by hundreds of years in the Holocene as groundwater carbonate is difficult to remove (Hedges et al. 1995; Grün et al. 1997; Zazzo 2014). This tooth was subjected to two pretreatment methods in an attempt to remove as much contamination as possible. Wood et al. (2016) suggested that unless enamel was heavily recrystallised, most contaminating carbonate is likely to sit at the crystal boundaries within the enamel, and they found that age increased if the sample was mechanically crushed before cleaning with acetic acid. Radiocarbon dates on finely ground Pleistocene enamel were still too young, but in the late Holocene they were indistinguishable from their known age. Dates on the tooth enamel from Uattamdi 1 do not agree with this finding, with the hand-ground sample (S-ANU 60005, 2928±29 BP) giving an age indistinguishable from that of the mechanically ground sample (S-ANU 60006, 2884±35 BP). However, this tooth enamel was extremely soft and crumbly, and has an FTIR PCI (Phosphate Crystallinity Index) of around 5.0, higher than modern *Sus scrofa* teeth with PCIs typically around 4.8 (data not shown). Combined with the radiocarbon result, this suggests that recrystallisation had occurred. Although the date is unlikely to be accurate, it does broadly agree with its stratigraphic position.

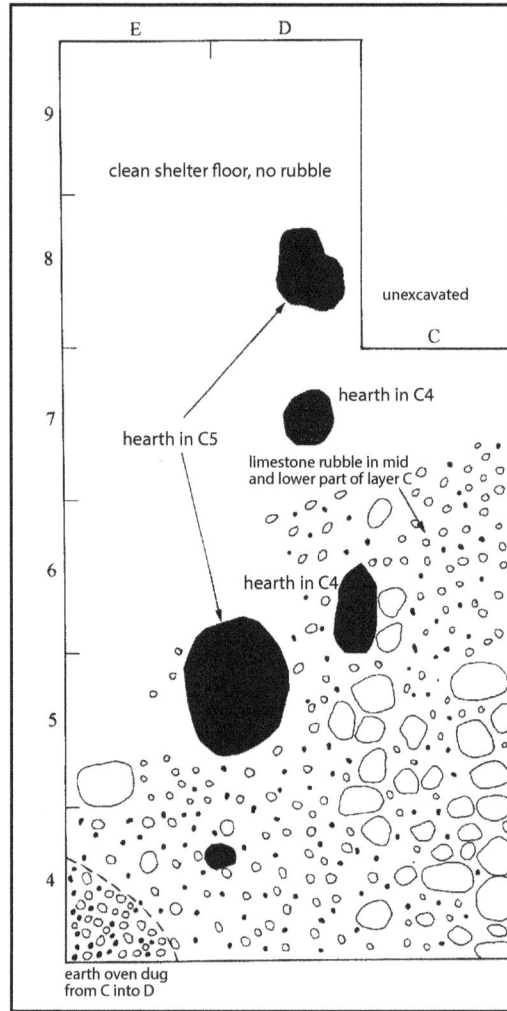

Figure 5.6 Hearths over limestone roof fall in Uattamdi 1, Layer C.

Source: Peter Bellwood.

U1 seems to have been occupied fairly frequently during the period represented by Layer C, but one major event represented in the southern part of the excavation was the appearance of the band of coral rubble mentioned above, some of very large rocks, presumably derived from an episode of roof fall. Because no rubble occurs in the northern part of the trench, and because the rubble is of even thickness, it gives the suggestion of having been piled neatly away from the major occupation area to the front (north) of the shelter. Sherds occur throughout the rubble, but presumably fell in while it was still loose and without soil matrix. Layer C immediately above the roof fall contains a number of hearths, shown in Figure 5.6. An earth oven with volcanic stones was also cut into Layer D in Square C4 from some point in Layer C, the exact point being rather hard to determine. Layer C has a very clear separation from Layer B above, but the limited number of dates from Layer B that fit the Bayesian model makes it impossible to ascertain if there was a temporal separation between the two.

Layer B: This layer is fairly pure, but slightly humic-stained coral beach sand, light yellowish-brown in colour. It was very clearly defined in the trench sections and contains many pieces of sea-borne pumice, probably resulting from the entry of a high sea (tidal wave?) into the shelter caused by an eruption with associated earthquake activity of one of the local volcanoes (Makian being the closest). There is no historically recorded eruption that fits this scenario, and Layer B was presumably deposited prior to the two C14 dates on a human cranium and marine shell (OxA 35201 and ANU 9322, respectively, see Table 1.1) that cover a 95.4 per cent range from 2136 to 1782 cal. BP. It is possible that this apparently cataclysmic event caused a local abandonment of the region for a while. This, at least, could be suggested by the cultural stratigraphy, which passes from pre-metal in Layer C to unequivocally Early Metal Phase in Layers B and A, with associated rather sharp changes in ceramic style.

Layer B had a relatively low density of cultural material compared to Layer C, and it is apparent that the shelter passed from being a zone of habitation to being a zone of burial after its deposition. Layer B contained many glass beads, pieces of metal and large burial jar sherds (see Table 5.1), all derived from jar burials, which were perhaps laid on the floor of the shelter or perhaps dug into shallow pits from the Layer B/A interface. Many of the glass beads will undoubtedly have worked down the profile by themselves, but in Squares E7–E8, six large burial jar sherds were found in obvious association at the B2 level, perhaps from the base of a smashed burial jar placed on the former shelter surface at this level. Sitting directly on top of two of the sherds and in direct touching contact with them was a complete *Turbo marmoratus* shell, a large reef gastropod that surely had some special function apart from food. This shell gave the C14 date ANU 9322 referred to above, which calibrates to c. 2000 BP. The jar burial assemblage thus presumably dates from this time, with burial activity perhaps continuing towards ANU 7773 at 1094–666 cal. BP. Many small pieces of human bone were also found in Layer B, with a partial cranium buried upside-down (Fig. 11.8), presumably in a shallow pit, in Square E4, spit B4. This cranium has been directly radiocarbon dated to 1932–1813 cal. BP (OxA 35201, 95.4%, OxCal 4.2). Layer B also has traces of occasional postholes cut into it, but no coherent plan could be traced.

Layer A: This is the sub-modern surface layer of the site, dark yellowish-brown in colour. On the modern surface are extensive ash deposits, which informants say come from sea salt evaporation activities undertaken within living memory. Otherwise Layer A, which dates to within the past 1000 years, has only a low density of cultural material, much perhaps disturbed upwards from the layer of jar burial activity at the interface between Layers A and B. It is worth noting here that shelter U1 has no sherds of the ethnographic style of pottery from Mare Island (Pulau Mare; see Mahirta 2000), and so has not been used for domestic activities for several centuries. Pulau Mare style pottery does, however, occur in the seaward shelter U2, discussed below.

The vertical distribution of material culture within Uattamdi 1

The artefact categories from Uattamdi 1 will be dealt with in more detail in later chapters, but at this point it is necessary to look at distributions through time with respect to the dated layers described above. This can be done by examining Figure 5.7 and Table 5.1. To an extent, the data are self-explanatory, but some points require emphasis. Indicators of occupation intensity in U1 are shown in Figure 5.7. In these, the data given are raw weights by layer, uncorrected to take account of layer thickness (i.e. they are quantities, not densities). In order to convert them to densities it is necessary to bear in mind that Layers A, B, C, and D are related volume-wise in ratios of approximately 4:4:7:4 respectively (i.e. A, B, and D are much the same in volume, while C is 75 per cent bigger). But even taking density into account it is obvious that volcanic cooking stones (upper chart) are most frequent in the occupation Layers C and D, and rare in the burial Layers A and B. Likewise, food shell and animal bones (middle chart) are most frequent in Layer C. So too is pottery (lower chart), which shows an interesting bimodal distribution, with the Neolithic red-slipped ware accounting for the stratigraphically deeper peak and the Early Metal Phase jar burial pottery accounting for a much smaller peak in Layer A3. Incidentally, this chart does not include the large and very heavy burial jar sherds, which would, of course, skew the results so much as to make them almost meaningless.

One may also note the sharp differentiation between a Neolithic (stone and shell) assemblage in Layers C and D, and a Early Metal Phase assemblage with a wide range of components in Layers A and B (Table 5.1). The glass beads that occur in upper Layer C appear to cross the divide, but in this case movement downwards must surely be the answer. This division is very marked and seems to fall around 2000 BP (ANU 9322) or later. Layers A and B contain all the metal, human bone, and burial jar sherds recovered from the site. Layers C and D contain all the stone tools, shell ornaments, and virtually all the red-slipped pottery.

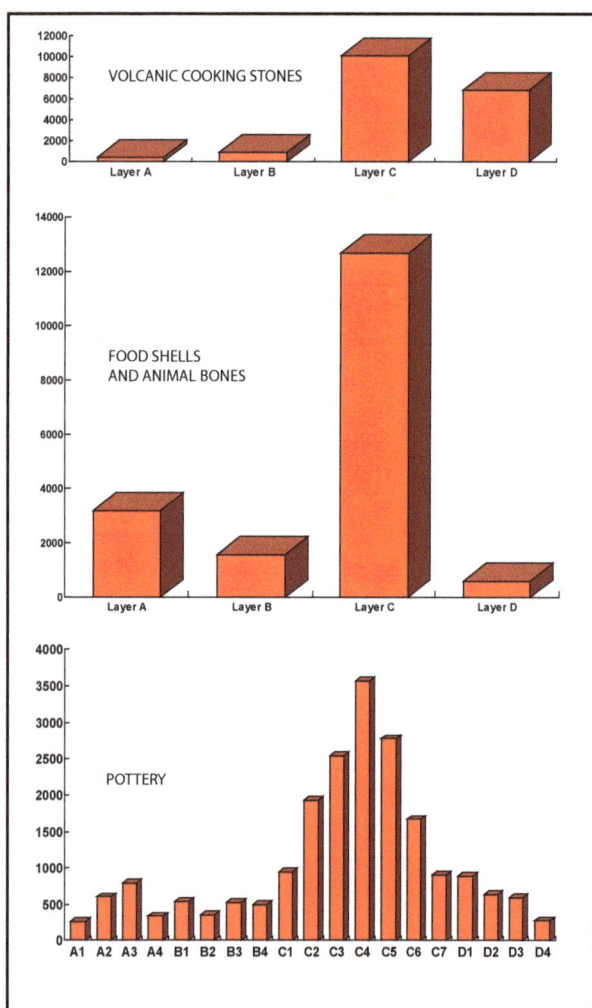

Figure 5.7 Uattamdi 1: vertical distributions of cooking stones, food shell and animal bone, and pottery sherds (excluding the jar burial vessels shown in Fig. 7.5).

Vertical axis shows weights in grams, horizontal axis shows Layers A to D.

Source: Peter Bellwood.

Table 5.1 Distribution of cultural materials by layer and 5 cm spit in Uattamdi 1 (ch = charcoal; ms = marine shell; hb = human bone; te = *Sus scrofa* tooth enamel).

Layer and 5 cm spit	C14 cal. BP	Stone adzes and adze chips	Other stone (mainly flakes)	Bone points	Shell bracelets	Shell tools	Shell beads	Glass beads	Copper/bronze	Iron	Burial jar sherds	Human bone
A1								2				
A2								1		1	3	
A3								2			8	present
A4								9	Chinese coin	1	5	present
A5	1094–666 ch							7	Chinese coin	1	5	present
B1	1269–969 ch			1			2	8			9	present
B2	2136–1782 ms 1932–1813 hb						1	17	1		13	present
B3									17			8	present
B4					1				21	1	1	3	present
C1		1 adze 1 chip	1	1				15				
C2			2	1		scraper, cut shell		13				
C3	3160–2324 ch	1 chip	2			cut shell	2	3				
C4			6	2		2 cowrie tops	2	3				
C5			3		1	cut shell, cowrie top	5					
C6	3144–2964 te	1 chip	4			scraper	3					
C7		2 chips	2		3							
D1	3293–2882 ms	1 adze	3			cowrie top						
D2	4080–3362 ch	1 adze 1 chip	1				2					
D3	3330–2753 ch	1 adze 1 chip			2	2 cowrie tops						
D4	3579–3014 ms	1 chip	1	1		shell adze						
E	3590–3239 ms	No human occupation										

Dates are listed in Table 1.1, including two dates not listed in this table that appear to be stratigraphically out of place.

Source: Peter Bellwood.

Uattamdi 2

This shelter lies 75 m west-southwest of Uattamdi 1, beneath a large block of uplifted coral that runs to the modern beach. Its surface is level with the top of the modern beach and the site is only 17.5 m inland, thus much closer to the sea than U1. This means, of course, that it is only likely to contain young archaeological deposits. A 1x1 m square was laid out in the middle of the c. 16 m² floor area of the shelter. This yielded a cultural layer only 30 cm thick, over sterile beach sand. The pottery from the shelter surface and from the cultural layer was all of the modern red-slipped and burnished Pulau Mare type (Mahirta 2000), so it is clear that this shelter does not contain deposits which are more than one or two centuries old.

6

Other explored but unexcavated sites

Peter Bellwood

The Kayoa-Laluin-Goraici region

The Bukit Keramat site is located on the eastern coastline of Laluin Island (see Fig. 5.1). This site was visited by Bellwood, Irwin, Kusnowihardjo, and Waluyo during this project in 1991, and again by Bellwood, Kusnowihardjo, and Waluyo in 1994. It is located on the top of a flat-topped limestone hill that rises to over 50 m above sea level at the end of the Tanjung Keramat peninsula, on the eastern coast of the island. It has not been surveyed, but a paced survey done in 1991 indicated an irregularly shaped occupied area on top of the hill of about 150 by 150 m, with remnant foundations of dry coral walls surviving along the northern, western, and southern sides where easy approaches exist. No walls are visible along the top of the eastern cliff, which drops down to flanking mangroves. The area yielded large quantities of local earthenware pottery, imported blue-and-white wares (mainly Chinese, presumably), and large numbers of marine shells and volcanic pebbles (for cooking?). Much material was exposed by megapode mounds, but the top of the hill also has a very thin soil layer, planted in 1991 under cassava in places, and much archaeological material seems to have eroded and fallen down the sides of the hill. It is unlikely that coherent stratigraphy survives, unless material is trapped in pockets in the limestone.

Local informants indicated that Bukit Keramat had once been a fortified dwelling place. The presences of sago cooking moulds (*forna*, a borrowing from Portuguese), ledge handles on earthenware bowls (not a feature of prehistoric Kayoa pottery), and one earthenware sago mould with a relief copy of what appears to be an element of European-style decoration (again, Portuguese?), all suggest that this site was occupied after a European presence first began in the region in the sixteenth century.

The potential for future research on this site seems small, but test-pitting will be necessary for any conclusive decision. An attractive Sama-Bajaw stilt village occupied the lagoon offshore from Bukit Keramat at the time of the research (Fig. 5.2), but whether the inhabitants were related to those who once occupied the archaeological site we do not know—such questions were not asked during our visits.

Tolimau Island, Goraici Islands: The sports field to the immediate northwest of Tolimau village produced many plain sherds of a recent variety of earthenware, including many forms paralleled in the contemporary Pulau Mare industry (Mahirta 1996). Coring of the deposit indicated that the sherds occurred throughout a topsoil layer 30 cm thick. The site yielded no decorated sherds.

Kayoa Island, Batui rockshelter: This shelter (Fig. 5.1) lies in a similar position to Uattamdi, about 50 m inland from the beach in a low coral cliff. The shelter floor covers perhaps 25 m² and would merit excavation. In 1991 we were unable to get permission from the landowner to work in the site.

Kayoa Island: Sherds of incised pottery were collected about 0.5 km south of Uattamdi, directly behind the beach. The pottery presumably belongs to the Early Metal Phase, as Layers A and B at Uattamdi. No indications were noted of any stratified deposit.

The Weda region

The cave called Batu Lubang at Sagea, located 3.5 km up the Sagea river from the coastal village of the same name (north side of Weda Bay) is spectacular, known to all inhabitants of the region and visited from time to time by speleological parties, but unfortunately of no archaeological significance. The Sagea river runs through the system and leaves no habitable area within. A small cave called Gua Jalamolo, 2.5 km from Sagea village on a north-northwest bearing, was test-pitted but yielded nothing.

A similar negative conclusion applies to several other caves visited in the Weda region. Indeed, Siti Nafisah was the only one found with any archaeological potential. Other caves, spectacular to look at but filled by periodic floodwaters, include Gua Paniki, about 3–4 km upstream from the coastal hamlet of Sidanga (north of Weda), and Gua Woye Papaya, which lies up a steep limestone gorge directly inland from Gua Siti Nafisah. A survey was also undertaken of the flat limestone region that lies immediately south of Tanjung Tilope, about 8 km south-southwest of Siti Nafisah (Fig. 4.1); no less than eight caves/shelters of various shapes and sizes were visited here during the course of a single day, but none showed high potential. All have problems of aspect and dampness, with inward-sloping floors of rock and mud, which would discourage any serious human occupation. None were seen close to the sea.

Lake Galela

While travelling to Morotai in 1991, in order to commence the Tanjung Pinang excavations, the team stopped for a day to examine the shoreline of volcanic Lake Galela to check out archaeological potential. There seems to be very little potential; the lake itself seemingly contains no shellfish and has a very steep coastline for much of its circumference, cut through an enormous thickness of volcanic ash. The impression received was that surface indications of sites are likely to be rare, and chances of locating sites will be small. The lake itself reveals no sign of a stable shoreline, except to its northeast where it abuts the lower slopes of the Tarakan Lamo volcano. It has probably changed its shape very frequently in the past according to prevailing conditions of water flow and volcanic ash deposition; it has no surface outlet and drains into the sea via subterranean seepage to the south of Tarakan Lamo.

Morotai

Non-systematic surface survey on the southern Morotai mainland and on the small islands that lie off the southeastern coast of the island (Fig. 3.1) produced the following surface indications:

- Sungei Sangowo Kecil: sherds of Sabatai Tua type were found on the west bank of the Sangowo Kecil stream, a little east of Tanjung Pinang.

- Mamuju: a flaked pebble, a *Canarium* anvil and potsherds of Sabatai Tua type were found on the surface of a bunded rice field about 1 km inland.

- A number of the small islands near Daruba were visited in 1991 for rapid surface survey, with interesting results. On Galogalo Besar, several megapode mounds near the southern tip of the island produced potsherds of the incised type typical of Tanjung Pinang (Morotai) and Um Kapat Papo (Gebe), as described in Chapter 7, in Tanjung Pinang found with human burials. A similar sherd was collected on Rube Rube Island, and this style of pottery is well dated to around 2000 BP at both Tanjung Pinang and Um Kapat Papo, and probably at Buwawansi 3 and 5 on Gebe as well. Otherwise no finds were made, apart from plain potsherds of the recent Pulau Mare type on Lungu Lungun. It is possible that some of these islands, especially those that consist only of coral sand, are of very recent formation. A few, such as Rube Rube, Ruki Rukiti, and Galogalo Besar, are of slightly raised coral and might repay more attention in the future, since it was these that yielded the c. 2000 BP sherds.

7

The earthenware pottery from the North Moluccan excavations

Peter Bellwood

The earthenware pottery from the North Moluccan excavations can be arranged into three easily recognisable chronological groups that can be briefly summarised as follows:

1. **Neolithic red-slipped pottery:** The oldest pottery recovered is a red-slipped (but otherwise undecorated) and mainly coral sand–tempered ware, represented in the research area only in the bottom two layers (C and D) of Uattamdi 1 rockshelter, Kayoa Island. This red-slipped pottery dates at Uattamdi between outer limits of c. 3350 and 2500 cal. BP (Chapter 5). It is paralleled in the mainly red-slipped but otherwise undecorated pottery excavated in contemporary and older Neolithic sites in the Talaud Islands, northern and western Sulawesi, Sabah in East Malaysia, and much further afield in the Batanes Islands and Cagayan Valley in the northern Philippines, as well as in southeastern Taiwan (Anggraeni et al. 2014; Bellwood 2011; Bellwood et al. 2011; Bellwood and Dizon 2013; Bellwood 2017:Chapters 7 and 8). The circle-, punctate-, and dentate-stamped motifs that are so characteristic of contemporary Marianas Redware and Lapita pottery (Carson et al. 2013) are so far absent during the Neolithic in the Northern Moluccas.

2. **Early Metal Phase incised, impressed, and appliqué pottery:** This is a very large and relatively unsorted category that might well occupy the whole of Moluccan later prehistory from the late Neolithic and Early Metal Phases onwards, continuing through the era of ceramic trade ware imports until the arrival of Europeans in the early sixteenth century. Much of the late Neolithic and Early Metal Phase repertoire of decorated pottery in the Northern Moluccas has incised, impressed, appliqué, and occasional red-slipped decoration, often with carinated vessel profiles. Pottery of this type occurs in the upper layers (A and B) in Uattamdi (here with metal and glass beads), in Um Kapat Papo and the Buwawansi late Neolithic site complex on Gebe, in Gua Siti Nafisah and the open site of Gorua (near Tobelo in northeastern Halmahera; Ono, Aziz et al. 2017), and in the Morotai sites, especially Tanjung Pinang and the newly excavated northeastern Morotai burial cave of Aru Manara (Ono et al. 2018). Its overall dates are probably between c. 2500 and 1000 cal. BP. This incised, impressed, and appliqué pottery is widely paralleled in a number of other roughly contemporary Island Southeast Asian Early Metal Phase sites—for example, Leang Buidane in Talaud, Sembiran in Bali, and the 'Kalanay' sites in the Philippines (Bellwood 1981, 2007; Ardika 1991; Calo et al. 2015; Solheim 2002). Sometimes associated with it is a rare vessel form with a corrugated rim, reported from Tanjung Pinang on Morotai, similar to the c. 2000–1500 BP 'corrugated ware' at Sembiran in Bali and the Anaro/Mitangeb sites in

Batanes (Bellwood and Dizon 2013:Fig. 6.10). These rims raise questions about interaction during an early phase of the spice trade, involving in the case of Sembiran a degree of early contact with India (Ardika and Bellwood 1991; Calo et al. 2015, and see below).

3. **Pottery of the Asian ceramic trade and European eras (post-1000 BP):** In our 1990s fieldwork, we also recovered quite a lot of coarse unslipped pottery, sometimes with appliqué decoration and modelling, in association with imported glazed ceramics, as in Sabatai Tua and the Tanjung Tulang rockshelters on Morotai. Also, overlapping in date with European contact (after 1512), we have the European-influenced pottery from the site of Bukit Keramat on Waidoba Island. Ethnographically and continuing today, a thick-walled handmade red-slipped and pattern-burnished ware is made exclusively on Mare Island and traded from there all over the Northern Moluccas (Mahirta 1996, 2000).

The Neolithic red-slipped pottery from Uattamdi Layers C and D

This pottery assemblage was perhaps the most significant to be discovered in the Northern Moluccas from the viewpoint of cultural history and Austronesian linguistic dispersal during the late second millennium BCE. It formed part of an introduced complex of material culture with very widespread affiliations in Island Southeast Asia and the western Pacific. This complex, as understood in the Philippines, Sabah, Sulawesi, the Talaud Islands, the Mariana Islands, and the Lapita sites of Island Melanesia and western Polynesia, included red-slipped pottery, either slipped only (as in Talaud, the Moluccas, and southeastern Indonesia generally) or additionally decorated with incised or stamped designs (as in parts of the Philippines, the Marianas, and Oceanic Lapita). It also included polished stone adzes and chisels, shell ornaments and tools, and (in some regions) domestic pigs and dogs.

This plain red-slipped style of pottery—with occasional incision or lip notching, but so far, no circle, dentate, or punctate body stamping—is the oldest style of pottery found in the Northern Moluccas. Indeed, it is the rarity of vessel body decoration other than a simple red slip, both in the Northern Moluccas and in the Talaud Islands, that gives a rather distinctive appearance to southeast Indonesian Neolithic pottery and distinguishes it very sharply from the intricately decorated Lapita Neolithic pottery that occurs to the east of the Papua New Guinea border. This type of plain red-slipped pottery is confined (so far) within the North Moluccan region to Uattamdi alone, and there is no contemporary pottery assemblage from any other site. The closest other occurrences are in the Talaud Islands, especially the rockshelter of Leang Tuwo Mane'e on Karakelong Island, about 500 km north of Kayoa (Bellwood 1981, 2017:278–279; Tanudirjo 2001), and in the Banda Islands, where Lape et al. (2018) report similar red-slipped plainware from a site on Pulau Ay. No similar Neolithic assemblage is yet reported from southeastern Indonesia, including the Aru Islands (O'Connor et al. 2005:311), although Glover (1986) reported plain and apparently mostly unslipped pottery from cave deposits in Timor Leste.

The Layer C–D assemblage from Uattamdi forms a fairly homogenous collection of red-slipped rims and body sherds, broken and dispersed into the shelter floor at a time when it was used for habitation purposes. The vertical distribution of pottery by sherd weight (Fig. 5.7, bottom) shows a very definite bell-curve, with a peak in spit C4. Although evidence of human occupation in the form of hearths goes down into Layer D, it is quite possible that the bulk of pottery deposition in the site occurred after this hearth phase, at a time when much of the excavated area was becoming piled up with limestone rubble. Absolute dating precision is not possible, but the C14 dates from the site and parallels elsewhere suggest an absolute outer date range between 3350 and 2500 cal. BP for Uattamdi Layers C and D, as discussed in Chapter 5.

The Uattamdi Layer C–D Neolithic assemblage itself shows no signs of any marked change over time, and thus appears to represent a stylistic unity. However, the likelihood of continuous scuffing (but not deep disturbance) of the shelter floor during the occupation must be borne in mind. It is very apparent from sherd matches that, at any one time, the soft dry shelter floor would have capped a disturbance zone about 10 cm deep. There are no signs of any disturbances of great absolute depth, but it is apparent that, as the shelter floor rose over time, so too a zone of sherd cycling and scuffing rose with it. Hence, it should come as no surprise to learn that, in terms of individual rim pieces of identifiable pots, those vessels that have many matching pieces tend to be distributed through several spits. Thus, four rim sherds of the notched-lip vessel illustrated as Figure 7.1(k) occurred in spits C1, C3, C5, and C6 respectively (including one each from C1 and C6 that actually fitted together). A possible 20 rim sherds of the red-slipped open bowl shown in Figure 7.1(g) occurred variously in Layers C3 to C6. The sherds of the pedestal vessel shown in Figure 7.1(I) had the same distribution. For this reason, it is safest to regard the assemblage from Layers C and D as basically a single assemblage, probably laid down over quite a short time period centred on the deposition of spit C4.

The jar burial assemblage from Layers A and B is quite separate from the older assemblage of Layers C and D, and there is almost no overlap of cultural materials, apart from a few tiny glass beads that have worked down into Layer C from above. As discussed in Chapter 5, Layer B is mainly clean beach sand that appears to represent deposition by a tsunami, an event that may well have led to a pause in occupation of the site. This younger Early Metal Phase assemblage is considered separately below.

Some of the basic characteristics of the Uattamdi Layers C and D Neolithic red-slipped assemblage are as follows:

1. Tripod/tetrapod feet, body carinations, spouts, and narrow vertical flask necks are absent in this assemblage, as (not surprisingly, perhaps) are Indian-inspired forms such as *kendi* spouts.

2. Pedestals are definitely present (Fig. 7.1(I)) on some of the unrestricted vessels with direct rims (i.e. the 'dish-on-stand' type), and there is a single-pedestal sherd with roughly cut-out decoration (not illustrated).

3. Body sherds indicate that most restricted vessels had roughly globular rather than carinated body shapes.

4. Vessel bodies are relatively thin, with a mode between 3 and 4 mm in all Layers C and D spits.

5. Vessel surface decoration is restricted almost entirely to red slip, and notching or scalloping of lips. Vessel (u) in Figure 7.1 has simple curvilinear incision, but this comes from spit C1 and thus may be of later date than the rest of the Layer C–D assemblage. The red slip seems to have been brushed on with a wad of some kind, rather than by dipping. This is apparent because of streakiness and differential slip preservation on sherd walls, the latter probably reflecting varying paint thicknesses, and also occasional painted lines. In this regard, the Uattamdi slip resembles that of Leang Tuwo Mane'e on Karakelong Island, Talaud, where red bands of paint can also occasionally be observed (Fig. 7.2).

Of the 33 Uattamdi Layer C–D reconstructable rims shown in Figure 7.1, 21 have coral sand temper and 12 have mineral (presumably volcanic) sand temper. When plotted through time, the coral and mineral sand tempers have similar distributions, although only the mineral sand temper continues into the post-Neolithic Layers A and B. Geological sourcing studies have not been carried out on the Uattamdi pottery, but some preliminary SEM analysis has been carried out on tempers by Mahirta (1996).

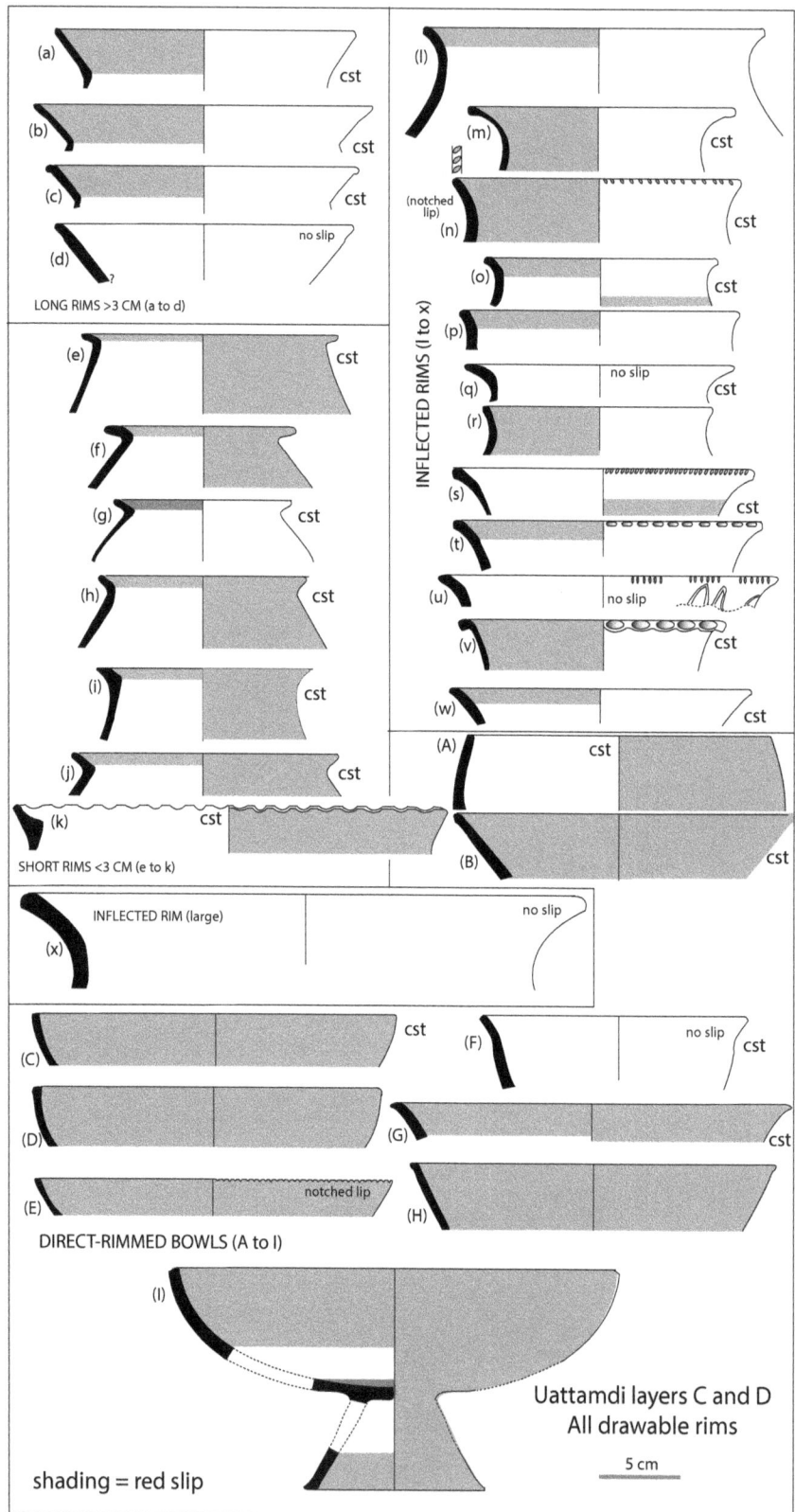

Figure 7.1 Rim sherds from Uattamdi 1 Layers C1 to D2.

cst = calcareous sand temper (others are mineral sand).

Shading = red slip (both internal and external). Unshaded vessels are not slipped.

Source: Peter Bellwood.

Table 7.1 shows the distribution of red-slipped sherds in the Uattamdi site. Clearly, percentages are highest in Layers C and D and peak noticeably around spit C4, although red-slipped sherds are found in all layers. However, some of the red-slipped sherds in Layers A and B could have been disturbed upwards from below. Table 7.2 shows the vertical distribution of rim forms and attributes through the stratigraphy, but does not include the vessels from Layers A and B that were associated with Early Metal Phase jar burials.

Three additional points about this assemblage can also be noted:

1. Two major whole vessel types are present in terms of basic forms; restricted vessels with everted rims (i.e. 'cooking pot' shapes), and direct-rimmed bowls with unrestricted profiles set on pedestals. Vessel profiles below the neck appear to be gently rounded rather than sharply angled, and there are no carinations in this assemblage.

2. Everted rims of restricted vessels reveal three variants, illustrated as long, short, and inflected in Figure 7.1. The first two variants originate from quite sharply angled eversions and the rims tend to be straight. Long rims and short rims are defined as greater and smaller than 3 cm in height/length respectively, using a simple and useful statistic originating from the analysis of Batanes pottery (Bellwood and Dizon 2013) that will be discussed further below. The third variant has a non-angular and gently inflected rim eversion attached as a continuous outwards curve. In all three variants, lips are rounded rather than squared-off. Only two of the vessels shown lack red slip altogether, and only one is incised. Rim 7.1(k) is a unique crenelated lip with an inner recess, apparently shaped to take a lid. One distinctive characteristic of all Uattamdi everted rims is that there is usually a band of red slip extending down over the inner edge of the rim. External surfaces are often red-slipped, but not always.

3. The direct rim bowls shown in Figures 7.1(A)–(I) are mostly unrestricted, except for vessel (A), which is restricted. (B) might also be a long everted rim rather than a bowl rim. These rims tend to be slipped both inside and out, a circumstance that might reflect their usage for food serving. Several of these vessels probably once had pedestals. Lips may be either squared off or rounded. Vessel 7.1(F) has a slightly inflected contour.

Table 7.1 Total sherd and red-slipped sherd distributions by spit and Layer in Uattamdi 1.

Excavation rows C and E only (not D), all spits from A to D4	Total sherds per spit (no.)	Total sherds per spit as a percentage of all sherds	Red-slipped sherds per spit (no.)	Red-slipped sherds per spit as a percentage of all red-slipped sherds	Red-slipped sherds per spit as a percentage of total sherds
A (all spits)	439	7	57	3	13
B1	174	3	25	1	14
B2	103	2	20	1	19
B3	118	2	23	1	19
B4	229	4	74	4	32
C1	239	4	83	5	35
C2	678	11	161	10	24
C3	741	12	214	13	29
C4	1070	18	351	21	33
C5	653	11	220	13	34
C6	558	9	184	11	33
C7	269	5	124	7	46
D1	280	5	74	4	26
D2	179	3	36	2	20
D3	182	3	38	2	21

Excavation rows C and E only (not D), all spits from A to D4	Total sherds per spit (no.)	Total sherds per spit as a percentage of all sherds	Red-slipped sherds per spit (no.)	Red-slipped sherds per spit as a percentage of all red-slipped sherds	Red-slipped sherds per spit as a percentage of total sherds
D4	70	1	32	2	46
Totals	5982	100%	1716	100%	

Figures are for all sherds, including body and rim pieces.

Source: Peter Bellwood.

Table 7.2 Pottery attribute distributions with depth (all squares) in Uattamdi 1 (excluding the jar burial assemblage shown in Figure 7.5).

	Long everted rims, Fig. 7.1(a)–(d), and possibly (B)	Short everted rims, Fig. 7.1(e)–(k)	Inflected everted rims, Fig. 7.1(l)–(w)	Direct rimmed bowls, Fig. 7.1(A)–(L)	Ratio of red-slipped to plain rims (total no. of rims per layer in brackets)	Notched lips (all rim sherds)	Scalloped lips (all rim sherds, possibly from one vessel)
A1	–	–	–	–	1:3 (4)	–	–
A2	–	–	–	–	2:0 (2)	1	–
A3	–	–	–	1	1:0 (1)	–	–
A4	–	–	–	–	0:1 (1)	–	–
B1	–	–	–	–	0:3 (3)	3	–
B2	–	–	–	–	2:4 (6)	4	–
B3	–	–	–	–	1:2 (3)	2	–
B4	–	–	–	–	4:3 (7)	3	–
C1	1	–	–	1	9:2 (11)	1	–
C2	2	1	2	1	12:6 (18)	3	2
C3	1	3	1	4	15:5 (20)	3	1
C4	1	3	2	6	41:13 (54)	14	1
C5	–	4	1	6	22:4 (26)	2	2
C6	–	3	3	4	22:6 (28)	2	–
C7	–	1	–	2	10:5 (15)	–	1
D1	–	1	–	1	3:1 (4)	–	–
D2	–	1	–	–	1:0 (1)	–	–
D3	–	–	–	–	(0)	–	–
D4	–	–	1	–	1:1 (2)	–	–

Source: Peter Bellwood.

Regional comparisons for the Uattamdi Neolithic pottery

It can now be asked how this early Uattamdi red-slipped pottery compares with contemporary and older Neolithic pottery from other regions of Island Southeast Asia. When the Moluccan project was running during the early and middle 1990s, the only other assemblages of this early red-slipped type were those from Madai Cave and Bukit Tengkorak, both in Sabah (Bellwood 1988, 1989), and Leang Tuwo Mane'e in the Talaud Islands (Bellwood 1981). Since 2005, important assemblages of this type have been published from Chaolaiqiao in southeastern Taiwan and the Cagayan valley on Luzon (Hung 2005, 2008), the Batanes Islands in the northern Philippines (Bellwood and Dizon 2013), and the sites of Minanga Sipakko and Kamassi in the Karama Valley of West Sulawesi (Anggraeni et al. 2014). These sites form a relatively well-dated sequence through time, with those in the north, in and close to Taiwan, being a few centuries older than those in Sulawesi and the Moluccas. The red-slipped pottery assemblages from all of these sites underwent a number of loosely in-step chronological changes, between 4200 and 2500 BP, which indicate some degree of continuing communication with respect to pottery fashion across the whole archipelago (see Fig. 7.4 below). The distances involved in this network were quite large, 2250 km from the Batanes Islands to Kayoa, for instance, so these observations might be quite relevant for understanding the establishment of this very important phase of human occupation within the Indo-Malaysian Archipelago.

Currently, an overall chronology for red-slipped but otherwise plain pottery ancestral to the type found in Uattamdi Layers C and D commenced around 4200 BP in southeastern Taiwan, Batanes, and northern Luzon. It appeared a little later to the south, c. 3500 BP in West Sulawesi, and perhaps 3350/3250 BP in the Talaud Islands. A related but clearly distinctive red-slipped tradition dominated by a prolific zonal use of dentate-, punctate-, and circle-stamped decoration characterised the northern and central Philippines, the Mariana Islands, and the Lapita sites of Island Melanesia and western Polynesia, with commencement dates in the Cagayan valley in Luzon focusing around 3800 BP (Bellwood 2017).

During the 1990s, the Uattamdi assemblage was suspected to belong to a 'Greater Lapita' complex, defining a way-station on a suggested migration route from Indonesia, around northern New Guinea, to the Bismarck Archipelago. However, the following two decades of research in the southern Moluccas and Nusa Tenggara Timur have yielded nothing to support this reconstruction, and it is now clear in hindsight that two separate migration routes were involved. One entered western Oceania and the Bismarcks via the Philippines and perhaps western Micronesia and the Admiralty Islands. The other travelled into a cul-de-sac in southeastern Indonesia, including the Moluccas, where the energy behind Austronesian expansion was gradually absorbed into an indigenous Melanesian biological and cultural world.

I elaborate on this hypothesis in the final chapter, but it must be emphasised here that the intricately stamped Philippine, Mariana, and Lapita variants of the red-slipped pottery tradition are not in evidence anywhere in southeastern Indonesia, even though we must allow for some Lapita back-movement from the Bismarcks to northeastern Borneo carrying Talasea obsidian (Bellwood 1989). There are possible parallels with dentate-stamping in Sulawesi (Anggraeni et al. 2014; Ono et al. 2019), but these could represent a separate movement from a common Philippine source region. Wherever the Lapita design system originated, its origin was certainly not in the Moluccas, and indeed it is far more likely to have resulted from direct transmission from the Philippines, possibly via the Mariana Islands (Carson et al. 2013).

I propose now to examine the above sites and regions one by one, commencing with sites closest to Maluku and moving gradually further away towards the Philippines and Taiwan. Given the absence of whole vessels and the rarity of body decoration, apart from red slip and notching around lips, it is necessary to concentrate on rim profiles. The guiding structure for this debate will be derived in part from recent observations of the assemblages from Chaolaiqiao in Taiwan, the Batanes Islands in the northern Philippines, and the Karama Valley in West Sulawesi. The earlier-excavated assemblages from Bukit Tengkorak, Leang Tuwo Mane'e, and Uattamdi can now be seen in clearer regional perspective, as will be shown below in Figure 7.4.

The relevant sites for discussion here are as follows:

1. The rockshelter of Leang Tuwo Mane'e (LTM), Talaud Islands (Bellwood 1976, 1981; Tanudirjo 2001), with a *possible* commencement date for Neolithic red-slipped pottery of c. 3500 BP (ANU 10209, marine shell, OxCal 4.2; Tanudirjo 2001:160). The LTM Neolithic pottery is shown in Figure 7.2 and in Tanudirjo (2001:Figure 5.8(a)).

2. Bukit Tengkorak Layer 3 (Early Phase), Sabah (Bellwood and Koon 1989; Bellwood 1989; Chia 2003), with a possible commencement date for Neolithic red-slipped pottery of 3200 BP (OZD 767, charcoal, OxCal 4.2). The Bukit Tengkorak Neolithic pottery is shown in Figure 7.3.

3. Minanga Sipakko and Kamassi, Karama valley, West Sulawesi (Anggraeni 2012; Anggraeni et al. 2014), with a possible commencement date for Neolithic red-slipped pottery of c. 3500 BP.

4. Torongan and Reranum Caves on Itbayat Island, and Sunget on Batan Island, northern Philippines (Bellwood and Dizon 2013), with a possible commencement date for Neolithic red-slipped pottery of c. 4200–4000 BP.

5. Chaolaiqiao, southeastern Taiwan (Hung 2005, 2008), with a possible commencement date for Neolithic red-slipped pottery of 4200 BP, based on two charcoal AMS C14 samples.

As stated, all of the above sites except for those in the Karama Valley are distinguished by a lack of pottery decoration apart from surface red slipping and lip notching, and none reveal any presence of the dentate-, punctate-, and circle-stamped styles of decoration that typified contemporary Cagayan Valley, Mariana, and Lapita sites.

Of these assemblages, the closest relations relevant for Uattamdi were undoubtedly with the Talaud site of Leang Tuwo Mane'e, illustrated here in Figure 7.2. The assemblage from LTM also has a few rims on which the red slip comes over the lip to form a band around the top of the vessel interior, as in Uattamdi. The Uattamdi C–D assemblage also resembles that from LTM and Bukit Tengkorak (Fig. 7.3) in being dominated by unthickened rims and thin-walled globular body shapes. Bukit Tengkorak has a wider range of rim cross-sections than Uattamdi or LTM, but shares with them the simple vessel forms (including ring feet) and high frequency of red slip. The complex rim forms and vessel shapes (especially carinated and narrow-necked forms) and the broad variations in surface decoration (especially horizontally zoned incision), so common in Early Metal Phase assemblages in Sabah and the Northern Moluccas, were either absent in these assemblages or, if present, occur only in rudimentary form. For comparison, some of the richly decorated Early Metal Phase pottery from Talaud and Sabah is illustrated elsewhere (Bellwood 1988, 2007:Figs 9.15 and 9.17, 2017).

Even allowing for the dating uncertainties behind these assemblages (all are small and none can be stated with certainty to be absolutely contemporary with any other), it seems a likely hypothesis that they are closely related in origin, but reflect small degrees of differentiation owing to differences in geographical location and date. It can never be proven that all were made by people who shared a close degree of ethnolinguistic relationship, but the differences between the assemblages are certainly not so great that such would be impossible. Indeed, it is interesting that stylistic change occurs in clearly visible ways through time as well as across space, and this is illustrated by the contents of Figure 7.4.

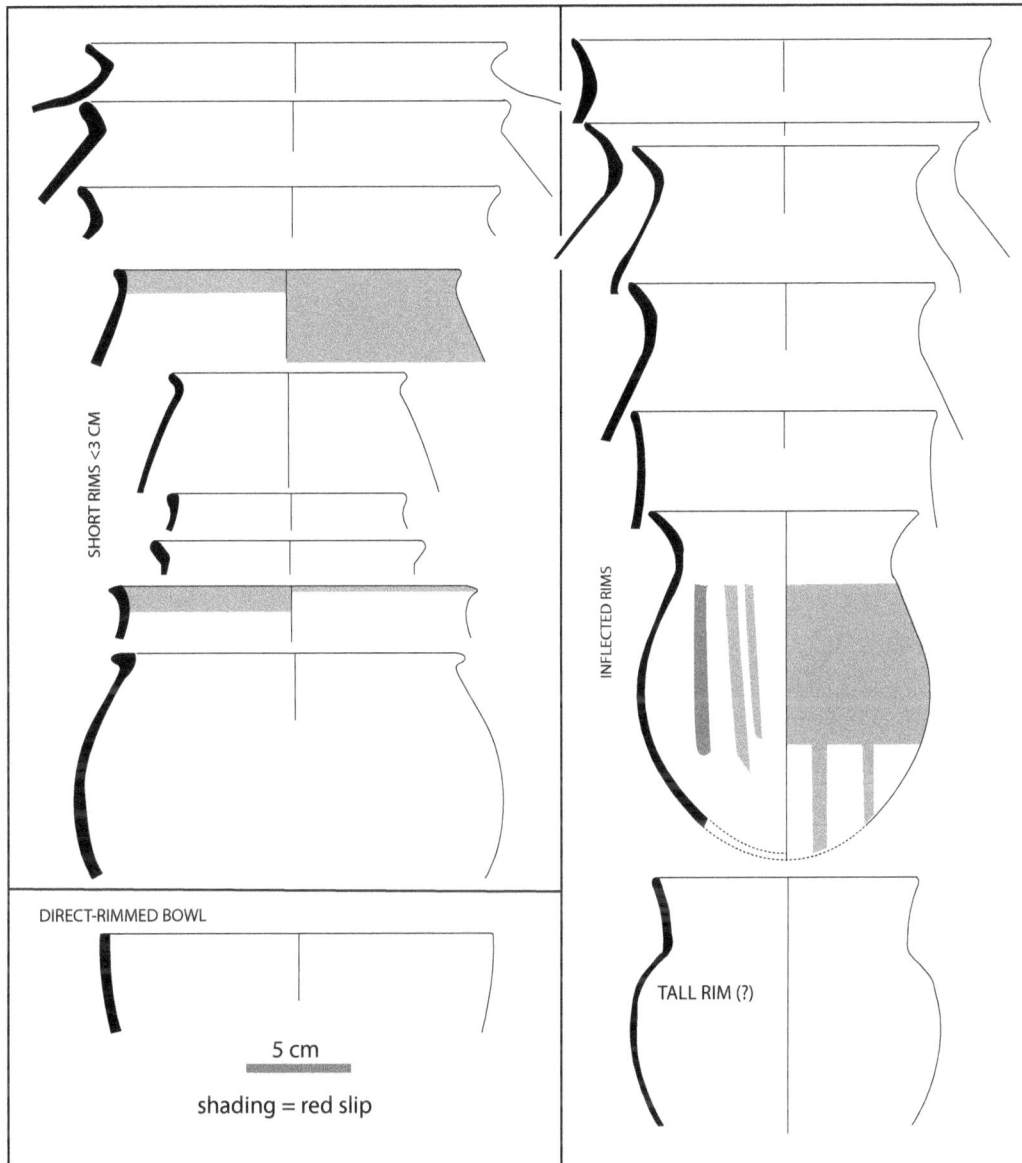

Figure 7.2 Neolithic pottery from Leang Tuwo Mane'e.

Source: Peter Bellwood.

The oldest of these red-slipped but otherwise plainware traditions is currently that from Chaolaiqiao in southeastern Taiwan, where a predominately red-slipped tradition with a very small presence of cord-marked pottery (the latter reflecting descent from the earlier Middle Neolithic fine cord-marked tradition) was excavated by Hsiao-chun Hung in 2005. Chaolaiqiao is quite tightly dated to 4200 BP, and is followed in time by the assemblages from the caves of Reranum and Torongan on Itbayat in Batanes, both also dating from about 4200 BP onwards. Following these we have the lower layers of Kamassi and Minanga Sipakko in the Karama Valley of West Sulawesi at c. 3500 BP, and then a group of sites that date roughly between 3500 and 2500 BP. These include Sunget on Batan, Bukit Tengkorak, LTM, Uattamdi, and the upper layers of Kamassi and Minanga Sipakko.

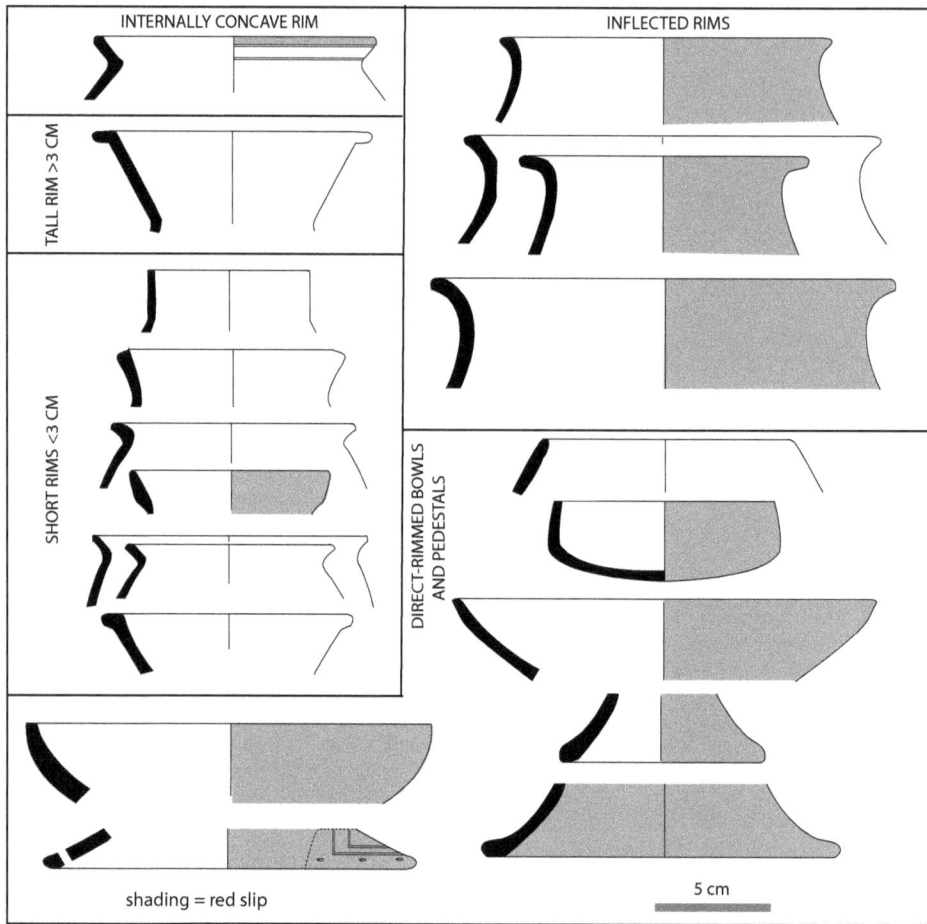

Figure 7.3 Neolithic pottery from Bukit Tengkorak.

Source: Peter Bellwood.

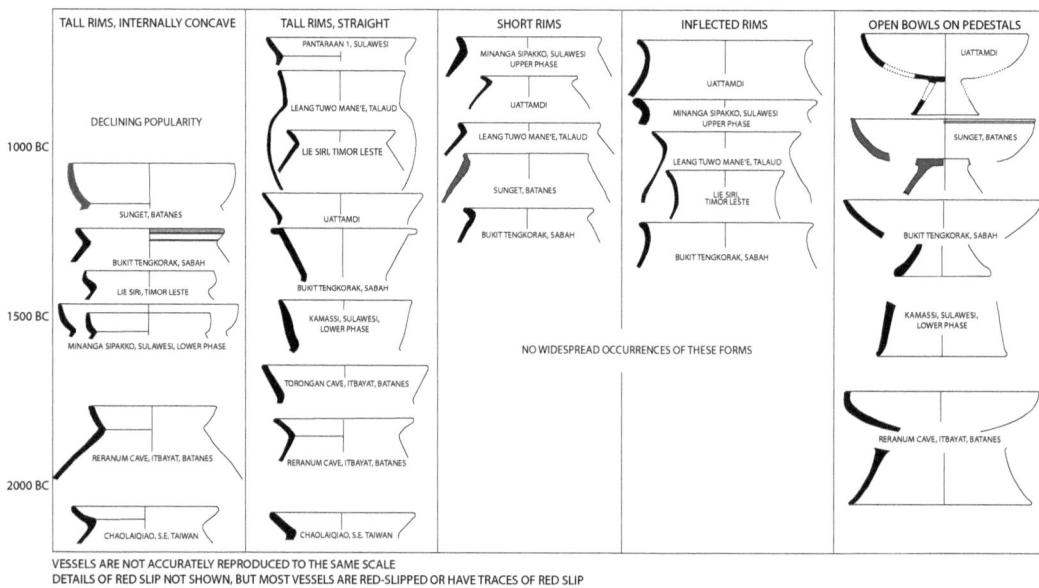

Figure 7.4 A comparison of rim forms from Taiwan to the Moluccas, 4200 to 2500 BP (here shown as 2200 to 500 BC).

Source: Peter Bellwood.

Throughout the 1000 years or more of time represented by this site sequence, and across more than 2000 km of space, it is possible to highlight some trends:

a. The earliest sites have sharply everted rims that are either concave internally or straight, but in both cases generally more than 3 cm in height/length (Fig. 7.4, the two left-hand columns) (see discussion in Bellwood and Dizon 2013:85). The internally concave rim was particularly important in Chaolaiqiao, Torongan, Reranum, and the early layers of the Karama sites, but was of diminishing importance in Bukit Tengkorak, with only a single specimen. It was absent altogether in eastern Indonesia, and its presence everywhere faded quite rapidly after 3000 BP. The long straight rim is found in all regions, but this form also diminished rapidly in frequency after 3000 BP.

b. Short rims under 3 cm in length were becoming dominant by around 3000 BP (Fig. 7.4, middle column), and it was this form that became dominant over the taller forms in the later layers of the Karama Valley sites, and also in Bukit Tengkorak and Leang Tuwo Mane'e. Most rims from Early Metal Age sites in Batanes, and Indonesia generally, tend to be of this short type, often thickened.

c. A gently inflected rather than sharply angled rim form became very popular in Leang Tuwo Mane'e and Uattamdi (Fig. 7.4, fourth column), but this form is not recorded in Chaolaiqiao and Batanes. It seems to have enjoyed its greatest popularity in eastern Indonesia.

d. Red-slipped open bowls with direct rims (Fig. 7.4, fifth column), often on quite high pedestals, occur in all phases from Reranum Cave onwards. This form has antecedents in the Neolithic of the lower Yangzi Valley (as shown in Bellwood 2017:Fig. 8.3).

Admittedly, this sequence spans a large area, a millennium or more of time, and the site components are often small in quantity and affected by chronological uncertainty. Some of the cave assemblages might contain rims that span several centuries of time. But there does seem to be a definite trend here, linking communities from Taiwan to the Moluccas in a gently evolving sequence of vessel rim form associated with red-slipped surface colouring. Both Bukit Tengkorak and the Karama sites have small quantities of stamped pottery, suggesting some degree of contact with the punctate-, dentate-, and circle-stamped pottery tradition that has recently become so significant in the archaeological sequences of northern Luzon, the Mariana Islands, and the Lapita sites of Island Melanesia. The Batanes Islands also witnessed a high popularity of circle stamping after about 3200 BP, as in the site of Sunget on Batan. But Chaolaiqiao, Reranum, Torongan, Leang Tuwo Mane'e, and Uattamdi reveal no trace of this stylistic tradition, which thus appears to have spread slightly later than the initial spread of the red-slipped plainware pottery.

This situation could suggest a scenario that might run as follows:

1. Between 4200 and 3400 BP, a tradition of red-slipped but otherwise undecorated pottery spread from southeastern Taiwan, through Batanes, presumably onwards through the Philippines and into Talaud and the Northern Moluccas. This tradition contributed directly to the Neolithic occupation of southeastern Indonesia, but did not spread further east into or beyond New Guinea.

2. After this initial movement, a sub-tradition with a strong focus on stamped decoration developed around 3800 BP, possibly initially in the northern Philippines, and spread to the Mariana Islands and Bismarck Archipelago (Carson et al. 2013), and possibly also to northern Sulawesi (Ono, Aziz et al. 2017:118; Ono et al. 2019 for Mansiri). It also spread, with a lesser emphasis on stamped forms of decoration, into eastern Borneo and northern and western Sulawesi (Anggraeni et al. 2014; Chazine and Ferrié 2008; Chia 2003), but evidently not much further. So far, traces of this tradition have not yet been found in Neolithic assemblages in other parts of Indonesia.

The Early Metal Phase jar burial assemblage from Uattamdi 1, Layers A and B (Early Metal Phase)

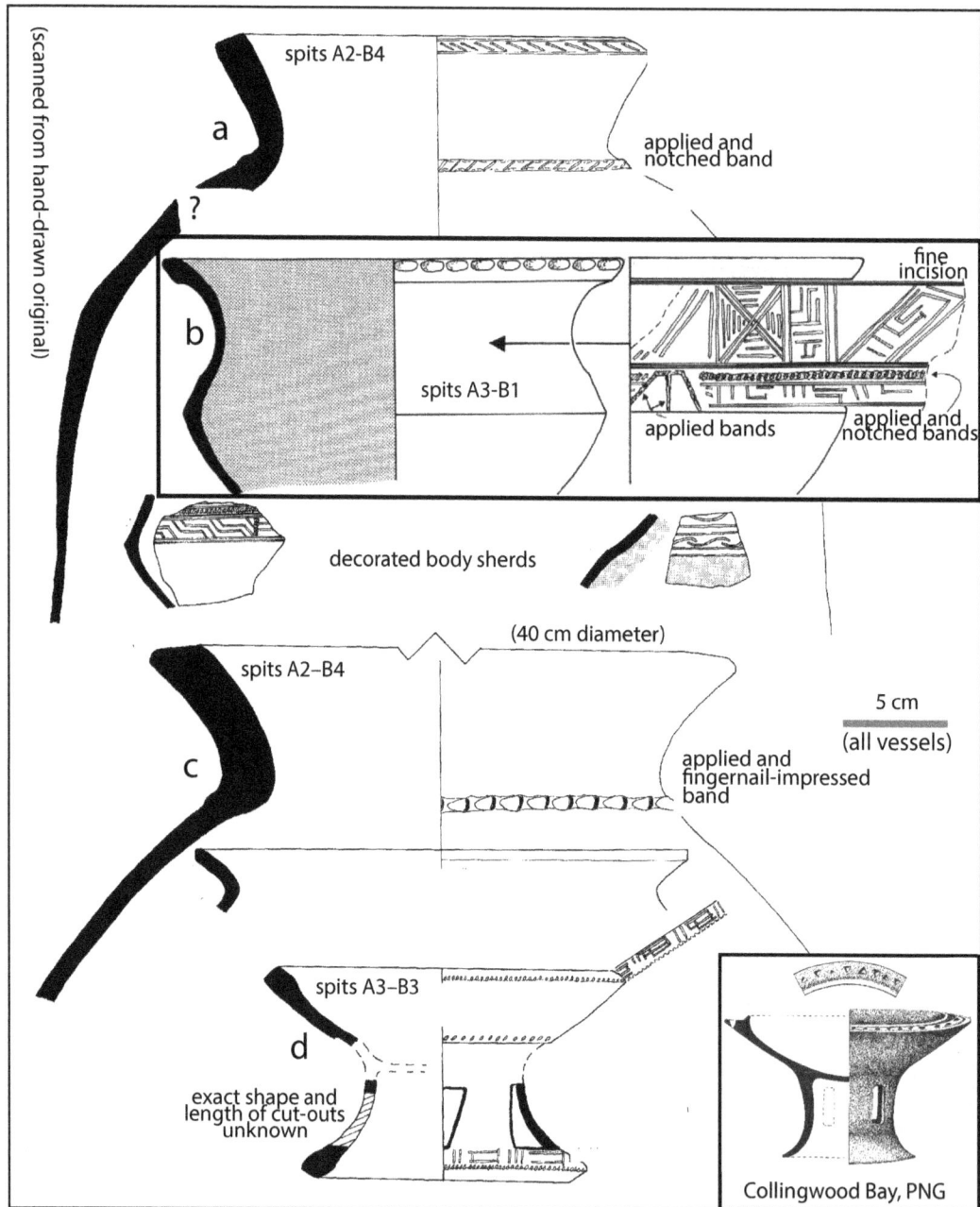

Figure 7.5 Vessels associated with jar burial in Uattamdi 1, Layers A–B (Early Metal Phase).
Shaded zones are red-slipped. The inset vessel (27.4 cm in rim diameter) is from Wawa Gardens, Rainu, Collingwood Bay, Papua New Guinea, and is reproduced courtesy of Brian Egloff (1971:Fig. 2). See also Figure 7.10.
Source: Peter Bellwood.

As noted in the Uattamdi excavation report in Chapter 5, the Neolithic assemblage in Layers C and D is sealed by the clean coral beach sand Layer B. This appears to be the result of a tidal wave, or some other event that caused large quantities of clean beach sand with pumice to be dumped inside the shelter. As shown in the histogram in Figure 5.7 (bottom), pottery sherds occur in small numbers throughout both Layers A and B. Those in the lower B spits seem to be an attenuation of the sherd distribution in Layer C beneath, whereas those in the top of B seem to be associated with a burst of jar burial activity in the shelter, with jars presumably partly buried in holes or scoops dug from the top of Layer B, later to be smashed and dispersed into upper Layer B and the overlying Layer A. The distribution of very large body and rim sherds for all Uattamdi excavated squares, of vessels likely to have been used for jar burial purposes, is as follows:

- Spit A2: 3 sherds
- Spit A3: 8 sherds
- Spits A4–A5: 10 sherds (spit A5 did not occur in all squares)
- Spit B1: 9 sherds
- Spit B2: 13 sherds
- Spit B3: 8 sherds
- Spit B4: 3 sherds
- Layers C and D: nil

This distribution indicates that the epicentre of jar burial sherdage is in spit B2, for which there is a marine shell date of 2136–1782 cal. BP (ANU 9322) and a human cranium date of 1932–1813 cal. BP (OxA 35201, see Fig. 11.8). The associations include small quantities of human bone, glass beads, bronze and iron fragments, a shell of a large *Turbo marmoratus* in direct contact with one small heap of sherds, and sherds of small and highly decorated accessory vessels. The vessels concerned are illustrated in Figure 7.5. The tops of two massive burial jars are shown as Figures 7.5(a) and (c), both with an appliqué neck band either notched or fingertip-impressed. One jar also has lip incision. These jars, and all the other vessels shown for this assemblage, have volcanic sand tempers; the coral sand tempers that dominated Layers C and D are now absent. Although similar burial jars are numerous in the Leang Buidane jar burial cave in Talaud (Bellwood 1976, 1981, 2007:Fig. 9.14), they are of slightly different shapes, and the Talaud sites also have many box-like receptacles, of a type not found at Uattamdi.

Of the small accessory vessels in Uattamdi Layer B, the sharply carinated vessel (Fig. 7.5(b)) with internal red slip and external complex incision and appliqué is most clearly paralleled in Leang Buidane in Talaud (Bellwood 1981) and Agop Atas in Sabah (Bellwood 1988:180, 183; and see illustrations of these vessels in Bellwood 2007:Figs 9.15 and 9.17), with more distant affinities amongst the non-Indian pottery from Sembiran in Bali (Ardika 1991:99) and Bukit Tengkorak in Sabah (Late Phase: Bellwood 1989). This vessel is boxed separately in Figure 7.5 and the decoration is rolled out as though flat for clarity. It has a scalloped rim with small punctuations (not shown) around the top of the lip. The dish on a stand with large pedestal cut-outs (Fig. 7.5(d)) is also paralleled in Sembiran (c. 2000–1500 BP: Ardika 1991:104), and surprisingly in eastern Papua New Guinea (Fig. 7.5(inset)), as discussed further with respect to both Uattamdi and Tanjung Pinang in the final section in this chapter. Pedestals, albeit generally with smaller or no perforations, are common during this period in eastern Indonesia (see Figs 7.10(g) and 7.10(h) for Tanjung Pinang).

All in all, the Uattamdi jar burial assemblage can be seen to have many quite specific parallels with other Early Metal Phase assemblages in Indonesia of the period between 2000 and 1000 BP. Its specific features relate it most closely to assemblages in the earlier part of this time range, closer to 2000 to 1500 BP, thus making it possibly slightly older than the Um Kapat Papo assemblage from Gebe, to be described next.

The pottery from Um Kapat Papo, Gebe Island

The Um Kapat Papo (UKP) pottery assemblage is small, but of interest because of its relative homogeneity and its association with a marine shell C14 determination of 1765–1437 cal. BP (ANU 9316). This date seems perfectly acceptable, given the nature of this pottery and parallels in other Early Metal Phase sites such as Uattamdi Layers A and B.

The most important point to note about the UKP assemblage is its unity. Although sherds occur from Layer 1 down to a depth of 25–30 cm from the top of Layer 3, it will be apparent from Table 7.3 that the vast bulk of the sherds are concentrated in Layers 1 and 2, and in the top 10 cm of Layer 3. There is a marine shell C14 date of 5300–4900 cal. BP (ANU 9317) from 5–15 cm depth within Layer 3, and a few sherds do indeed occur at this level, but it would be an insupportable inference that pottery usage in UKP actually dates from this period.

Table 7.3 The distribution of pottery by depth in Um Kapat Papo.

Layer and spit	Glazed ceramic sherds	Earthenware sherds, plain	Earthenware sherds, incised	Earthenware sherds, red-slipped	Earthenware sherds, notched lip	Total sherds
1	2	42	1	–	1	46
2, 0–5 cm		88	3	4	–	95
2, 5–10 cm	1	48	2	2	–	53
2, 10–15 cm		24	4	1	–	29
2, 15–20 cm		32	8	1	–	41
3, 0–5 cm		37	1	–	2	40
3, 5–10 cm		12	–	–	1	13
3, 10–15 cm		6	–	–	–	6
3, 15–20 cm		1	–	–	–	1
3, 20–25 cm		3	–	–	–	3
3, 25–30 cm		1	–	–	–	1

Source: Peter Bellwood.

Figure 7.6 shows two vessels from UKP (those labelled a and c, also listed in Table 7.4) for which large numbers of matching sherds are available. The sherds of both vessels come from several adjacent squares and were found in virtually all of the 5 cm spits from which pottery was derived. This circumstance, plus the general similarity of all the vessels, suggests that most were placed in the cave over a relatively short period, and that some were then scuffed and disturbed after breakage through the layers where they now occur. The pottery assemblage does not therefore reflect the presence of a stratified sequence.

The tempers and find locations of the sherds of the seven vessels reconstructed in Figures 7.6(a)–(g) are shown in Table 7.4. This list might give the impression that mineral sand tempers are more common in the site than coral sand, but this is not true. A sorting of all sherds after the excavation, including all the unmatched body sherds, indicated that approximately two-thirds of the total contain coral sand. The 5:3 predominance of mineral sands indicated in Table 7.4 thus reflects a bias resulting from the small size of the sample being considered.

Table 7.4 Tempers and find locations of the sherds of the reconstructed vessels from Um Kapat Papo, labelled as in Figure 7.6.

Vessel	Temper	Location (Square / Layer / depth in cm within Layer)	Number of sherds
a	coral sand	N9 / 1	1
		K8, L9, O9 / 2 / 0-5	3
		KL8, K9 / 2 / 5-10	2
		L9 / 2 / 10-15	4
		M9 / 2	2
		M9 / 3 / 0-5	1
		K9 / 3 / 5-10	1
b	mineral sand, laminated structure	H8 / 3 / top	unsure—could be two vessels
c	coral sand	K8 / 2 / 0-5	1
		KL8 / 2 / 5-10	1
		L9 / 2 / 10-15	1
		M9 / 2 / 15-20	2
		KL8 / 3 / 0-5	2
		KL8 / 3 / 5-15	1
		KL8 / 3 / 15-25	1
Not illustrated	mineral sand	L9 / 1	1
d	mineral sand	H6-8 / 1	1
e	coral sand	H6-9 / 2 / 0-5	10
f	mineral sand	unstratified	
g	mineral sand	H9 / 2 / 0-5	2

Source: Peter Bellwood.

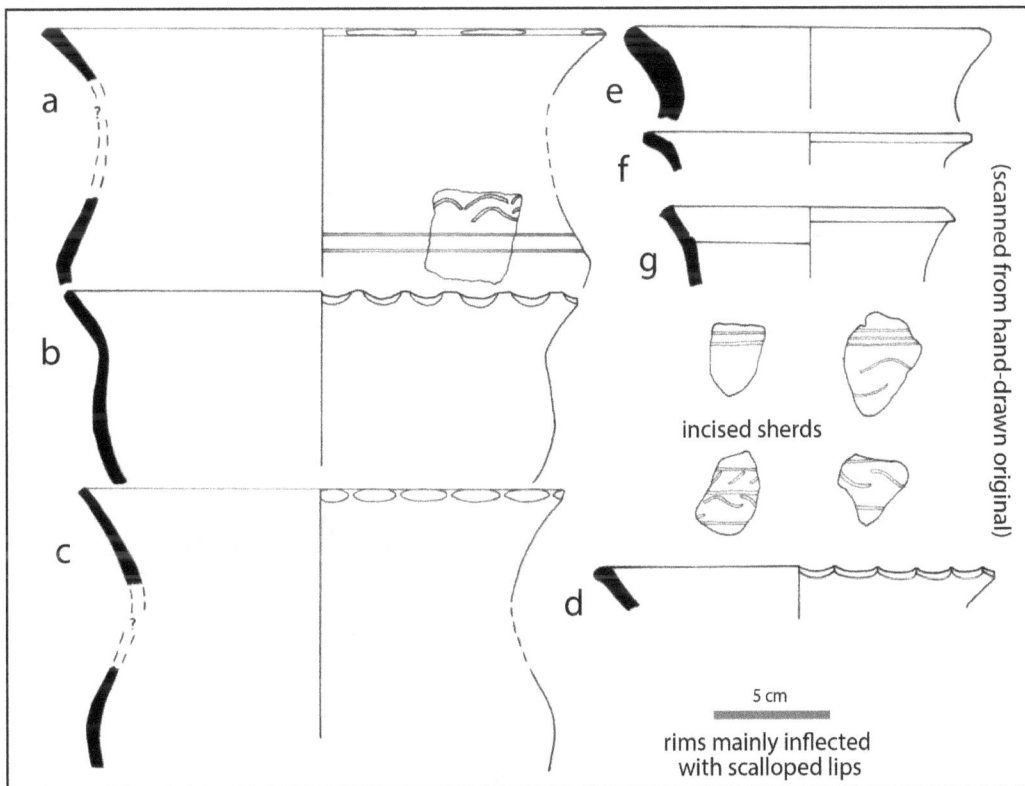

Figure 7.6 Pottery from Um Kapat Papo, Gebe Island, labelled as in Table 7.4.
Source: Peter Bellwood.

The basic design features of the UKP assemblage are simple. The represented vessels are all of restricted forms with everted rims, with long rolled-out lip indentations or scallops being common. In contradistinction to the Neolithic assemblage of Uattamdi Layers C and D, UKP has almost no red slip. Its lip cross-sections are similar to Early Metal Phase types found in Sabah and Talaud (e.g. the Atas phase in Sabah: Bellwood 1988:Chapter 11). It also, like the Early Metal Phase Layers A and B in Uattamdi, and the Early Metal Phase Sabah sites, has carinated body forms (Fig. 7.6(a)). There is also incision in UKP, of a simple curvilinear or parallel straight-line type, contained between parallel horizontal lines, which circumvent the pot. Such incised decoration is similar to that which occurs in the contemporary Moluccan assemblages from Tanjung Pinang and Buwawansi 3 (below), and also from the open site of Gorua (2300 to 2000 BP) on the northern arm of Halmahera, excavated by Rintaro Ono (Ono, Aziz et al. 2017:Fig. 3).

The UKP assemblage also contains (not illustrated) a fragment of a rim of a square or rectangular vessel (common at this time period in other Early Metal Age sites in Island Southeast Asia), and also a fragment of a flat-based plate on a foot ring (too small to reconstruct). Essentially, it fits comfortably in a time range between 2000 and 1500 BP, approximately contemporary with the pottery assemblages from Uattamdi Layers A and B, Tanjung Pinang, Siti Nafisah and Buwawansi 3. The cave of UKP, a little surprisingly, was obviously not inhabited by the makers of the Neolithic red-slipped pottery of Uattamdi type. No trace of any occupation of this phase has yet been found with certainty on Gebe, although the open site complex of Buwawansi, to be considered next, raises some possibilities.

The pottery from the Buwawansi Site Complex, Gebe

The Buwawansi pottery sample comes from four major locations, supplemented by surface finds. The four major locations are as follows:

1. The slightly inland rockshelter Buwawansi 1, which produced a few plain body sherds in the top 30 cm (Table 2.8).
2. The near-coastal rockshelter Buwawansi 3 (Table 2.9). This site produced the largest assemblage of pottery from Buwawansi (Fig. 7.7).
3. The coastal terrace open sites Buwawansi B5 and B5A.
4. The coastal terrace open site Buwawansi 6.

All the samples appear to be from one fairly homogeneous pottery tradition, characterised by incised and rare appliqué decoration. The overall time range according to the four available C14 dates with pottery associations is from 3128–1319 cal. BP, according to the calibrated ranges (OxCal 4.2) of the first four marine shell dates for the Buwawansi complex listed in Table 1.1. However, the homogeneity of the pottery and its relations with other dated Early Metal Phase assemblages suggests that a depositional time span of over 1500 years is rather unlikely. The bulk of the pottery probably dates between the 2008–1319 cal. BP time range of C14 samples ANU 9319, 9454, and Waikato 4630.

The 'Neolithic' date of 3128–2789 cal. BP (ANU 9770) from Buwawansi 5 is nevertheless quite intriguing, and raises the possibility that at least some of the pottery on the Buwawansi coastal terrace might be older, even contemporary with that from Uattamdi Layers C and D. This can only be a possibility, and none of the Buwawansi pottery shows any clear resemblance to the red-slipped plainware from the Neolithic layers in Uattamdi. Even the pottery from Buwawansi 5, with the early date of 3128–2789 cal. BP, is incised like that from all the other sites. It seems safest at present to place the Buwawansi assemblage, with those from Um Kapat Papo and Uattamdi C and D, rather firmly in the Early Metal Phase.

Buwawansi 3

The largest Buwawansi assemblage, with the best preservation, comes from rockshelter 3 (B3). Here, sherds are distributed to a depth of 60 cm, but with a rapid fall-off below the upper 20 cm (Table 2.9). The calibrated date of 4271–3811 cal. BP (ANU 9453) from the preceramic base of the site at 130–135 cm adds confidence to the above estimate of a c. 2000–1500 BP date for the pottery, for if the Buwawansi pottery were to have commenced deposition as early as 3000 years ago one would expect sherds to be found to lower levels in this shelter (assuming, of course, that the rate of deposition was fairly regular over time), and there are none.

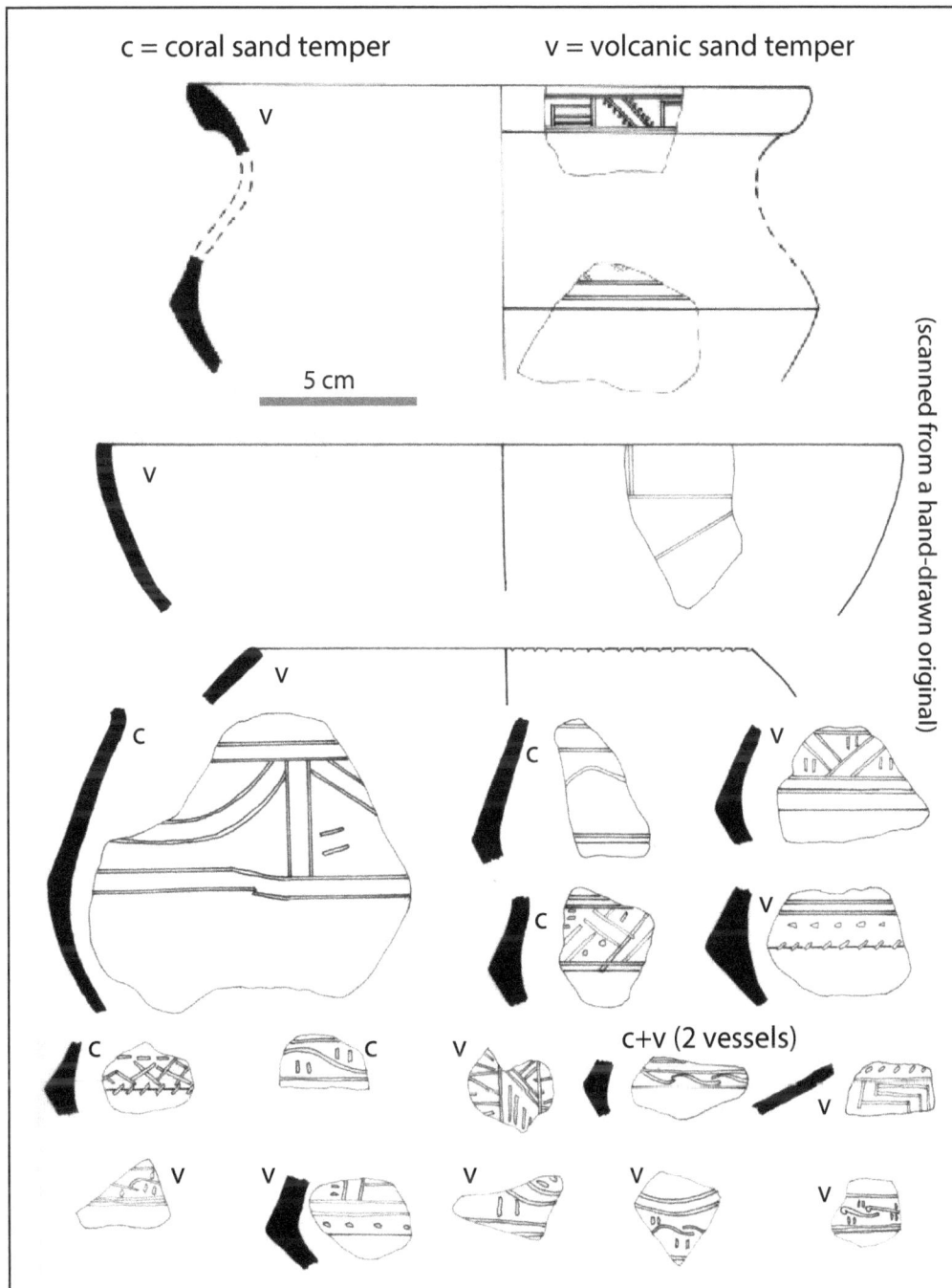

Figure 7.7 Pottery from Buwawansi 3, Gebe Island.

Source: Peter Bellwood.

Some of the diagnostic sherdage from B3 is shown in Figure 7.7, which also indicates whether tempers are coral sand or volcanic sand. The ratio of coral to volcanic temper, based on the total sample of rim sherds from the site, is 23:18. The assemblage is too small to show any significant change over time, and it is treated as a unity for descriptive purposes. The upper small carinated vessel in Figure 7.7 has an identical angular rim form to the Uattamdi vessel in Figure 7.5(c), and this angular cross-section is likewise identical to that of many rims of small carinated vessels from the Agop Atas (Mature Atas phase) and Hagop Bilo sites in Sabah, both dating to approximately c. 2000–1000 BP (Bellwood 1988), and also the rims from the Leang Buidane site in Talaud (Bellwood 1976, 1981).

It can also be seen from Figure 7.7 that sharp carinations are common, that red slipping is relatively rare, and that simple forms of zoned curvilinear and rectilinear incision dominate the decorative repertoire. One rim fragment has a red slip interior band of the type characteristic of the Uattamdi Layers C and D assemblage, but apart from this the Buwawansi 3 assemblage has the hallmarks of belonging to the Early Metal Phase. The absence of metal in the site may reflect no more than economic scarcity—Gebe is a very remote island.

Buwawansi 5 and 5A, and Buwawansi 6

The two roughly oval areas of beach sand marked on Figure 2.20 were test-pitted by four 1x1 m squares. On the western area, Square B2 produced very little, but B6 was quite rich in pottery distributed down to about 30 cm depth, with the greatest concentration towards the base. A count of B6 decorated body and rim sherds revealed 85 coral sand tempered sherds, and 35 volcanic sand tempered. Squares B5 and B5A had similar distributions of material.

Basically, the decorated sherds from the Buwawansi 5 and 6 squares are extremely close to those from Buwawansi 3, with horizontal incised zones of simple straight line and curvilinear incision, interspersed with the little trademark 'inverted commas' that appear to be a *leitmotif* of the Buwawansi and also the Tanjung Pinang assemblages. Similar inverted commas are found on Early Metal Phase pottery from Gorua on Halmahera and Aru Manara on Morotai, as discussed below (Ono, Aziz et al. 2017; Ono, Oktaviana et al. 2017; Ono et al. 2018). A number of these Buwawansi 5 and 6 sherds are drawn in Figure 7.8, together with a number of unusual sherds that merit attention, particularly in terms of unusual rim forms and modelled/appliqué decoration, the latter including the illustrated animal head that appears to have been modelled on to the rim of a small pot.

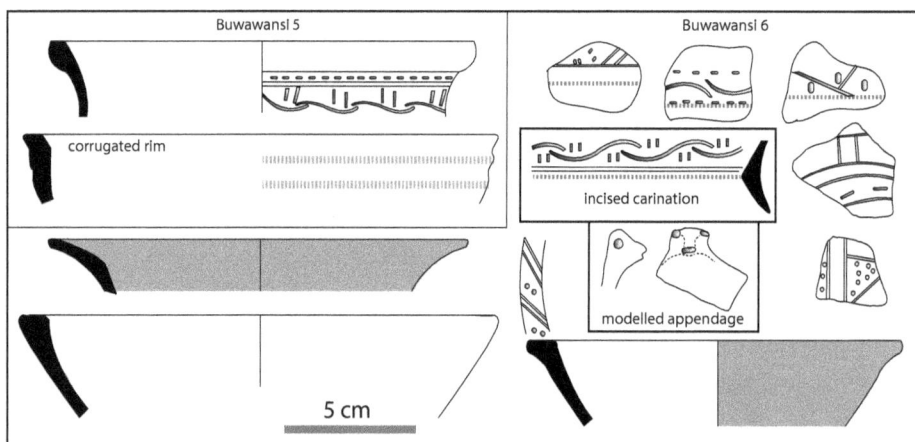

Figure 7.8 Pottery from Buwawansi 5 and 6, Gebe Island.
Shaded zones are red-slipped.
Source: Peter Bellwood.

One very important presence in Buwawansi 5 is a single corrugated rim, similar to two specimens of similar date from Tanjung Pinang on Morotai, and many more from sites in the Batanes Islands and Bali, the latter with clear signs of early Indian contact. I return to this issue again below, since the implication is that the Moluccas were brought into westerly trading spheres around 2000 years ago, an observation of no small importance for discussions connected with the origins of the Eurasian spice trade.

A unique sherd from Golo Cave

The excavations in Golo Cave yielded only 28 small plain body sherds, which do not require further comment. But one large rim sherd of a completely reconstructable vessel was found on the surface of the cave in a small recess at the back. It is illustrated here (Figure 7.9, top), since its incised surface decoration is intricate and skilfully executed. No similar pottery with exactly this type of sloping diagonal decoration was found in any other Moluccan sites, but from the vessel shape and thickened rim we suspect a date in the Early Metal Phase, possibly similar in date to the assemblage from Leang Buidane on Salebabu in the Talaud Islands (Bellwood 1981). The figures in the Leang Buidane report show many similar rims, although the Buidane body decoration differs.

The pottery from Gua Siti Nafisah, Halmahera

Excavation trench J10 at the back of Gua Siti Nafisah cave produced most of the pottery that was excavated in 1991, associated with a marine shell C14 date of 1628–1598 cal. BP (ANU 7790). Several of the reconstructed vessels in Figure 7.9 had matching sherds from both J10 and from Layer A in the F5–F8 trench, and the assemblage as whole appears to be stylistically unified, perhaps deposited over a relatively short period. Tempers appear to be of volcanic sand.

The Gua Siti Nafisah pottery has a small amount of red-slipped and incised decoration, and in our first report (Bellwood et al. 1993:29) we suggested an affinity with late Lapita pottery in Melanesia. In fact, the Gua Siti Nafisah pottery is perhaps 500–1000 years younger than the demise of Lapita decoration and, with the benefit of hindsight, this comparison now seems unwarranted. Given the date for J10, this pottery is clearly a regional facies of the North Moluccan Early Metal Phase. It belongs with the contemporary assemblages from Tanjung Pinang and Aru Manara on Morotai, and especially Buwawansi and Um Kapat Papo on Gebe. Gua Siti Nafisah yielded several tiny fragments of notched and scalloped rims like those shown in Figure 7.6 from Um Kapat Papo (all too small for useful illustration), and two body sherds show simple incised patterns between horizontal incised lines that are very similar to specimens from Um Kapat Papo and Buwawansi shown in Figures 7.6 to 7.8.

The Gua Siti Nafisah pottery assemblage appears to be distinctive in its emphasis on the production of direct-rimmed bowls, both restricted and unrestricted, and sometimes carinated in profile. No other North Moluccan assemblage carries this emphasis, and the Uattamdi 1 Layers A and B Metal Phase pottery with its everted rims is more closely related to the Early Metal Phase pottery from other regions to the north and west, such as Talaud and Sabah (Bellwood 1981, 1988, 2017). The Gua Siti Nafisah assemblage therefore has a distinctive local flavour.

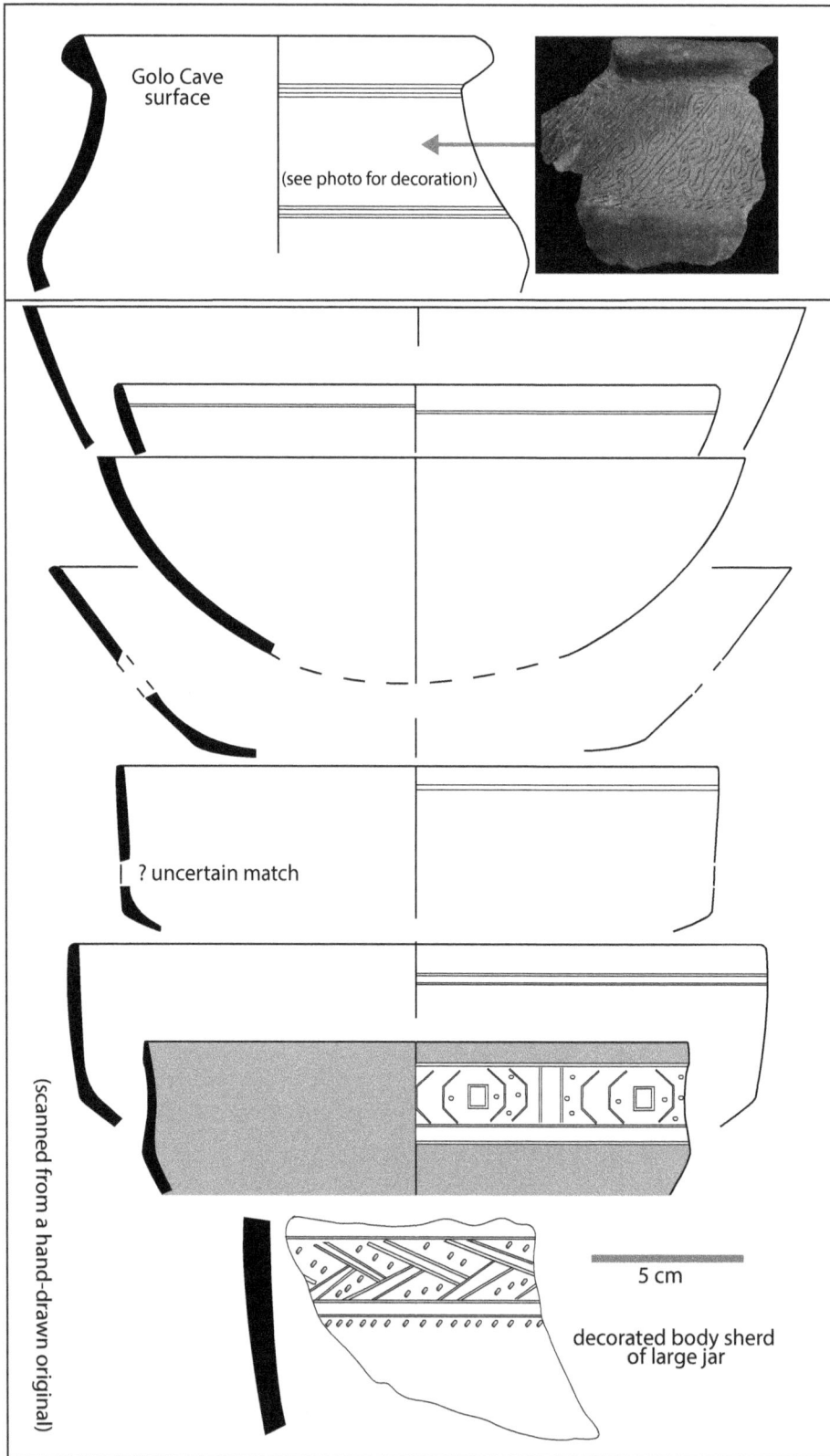

Figure 7.9 Pottery from Golo Cave (Gebe—upper vessel) and Gua Siti Nafisah Cave (eastern Halmahera—lower group).

Shaded zone is red-slipped.

Source: Peter Bellwood.

The pottery from the Morotai sites

The pottery excavated in association with the human burials from Tanjung Pinang (see Chapters 3 and 11) reveals a style of incised decoration very similar to that from Um Kapat Papo, Buwawansi, and Gua Siti Nafisah, and to a lesser extent Uattamdi Layers A and B, particularly in its focus on both linear and curvilinear motifs created from paired incised lines (Fig. 7.10, lower left). Unlike Uattamdi, there is no sign of jar burial at Tanjung Pinang, and the pottery seems to have been placed in association with secondary burials, including skulls, placed in shallow pits dug into the shelter floor (Fig. 3.2). As noted in Table 3.1, it was concentrated in the top 25 cm of the site, and details of vertical distribution by 5 cm spit are given in Table 7.5. Very little pottery was recovered from the Daeo rockshelters, but Daeo 2 produced a possible corrugated body sherd and the rim of a vessel resembling the dish on stand form from Tanjung Pinang (Figs 7.10(g) and 7.10(h)) discussed below.

Table 7.5 Vertical distribution of selected pottery features in Tanjung Pinang by 5 cm spit.

Depth cm	Weight gm	Total sherd number	Ribbed bowl rims (number)	% ribbed	% incised
0–5	1125	360	8	12	2
5–10	1460	375	23	14	7
10–15	625	218	11	14	3
15–20	361	127	7	20	2
20–25	115	36	3	10	10
Totals	3686	1116	52		

Source: Peter Bellwood.

The Tanjung Pinang tempers appear to be the same types of volcanic and coral sand that occur in the other Morotai and Gebe sites, and the general similarities in the predominantly incised decoration are very apparent when the sherds drawn in Figures 7.6 to 7.10 are compared. Tanjung Pinang has similar scalloped lips to Um Kapat Papo, although all these assemblages are rather small, and the parallels could be deemed rather impressionistic. However, the jar burial assemblage from Uattamdi A and B (Fig. 7.5), with its parallels with Leang Buidane in the Talaud Islands (Bellwood 1981), seems to stand a little apart from these other Morotai and Gebe assemblages.

The Tanjung Pinang human bone date of 2684–1618 cal. BP (ANU 8439) matches closely the dates for pottery from Buwawansi and Um Kapat Papo, and emphasises the apparent appearance of pottery-making traditions across the Northern Moluccas beyond Uattamdi in the time interval from c. 2500 to 1600 BP. The new Japanese–Indonesian excavations of the Gorua open site in northern Halmahera and the Aru Manara burial cave in northeastern Morotai by Rintaro Ono and his team (Ono, Aziz et al. 2017; Ono, Oktaviana et al. 2017; Ono et al. 2018) provide much supporting detail for this view. The pottery here was found mixed with secondarily deposited human bones, some cremated, with no clear signs of formal jar burial. Bronze and glass artefacts place the Aru Manara assemblage within the Early Metal Phase, as do the 13 radiocarbon dates from the site, some directly on human bones and teeth. These suggest major burial activity between 2700 and 2000 BP, and perhaps later. Gorua is dated by six charcoal C14 dates to 2300 to 1700 BP. The Aru Manara pottery has some interesting zoomorphic and anthropomorphic decoration, associated with circle-stamping and punctation, that is not paralleled precisely in any of the sites reported here. However, the Aru Manara pedestalled dish form, and the use of paired incised lines with 'inverted commas' as seen commonly in the pottery from Tanjung Pinang, Gorua, Um Kapat Papo, and Buwawansi, are deserving of comment. The similarities are so precise as to suggest that all of these Halmahera, Morotai, and Gebe pottery assemblages belong to this approximate Early Metal phase time span.

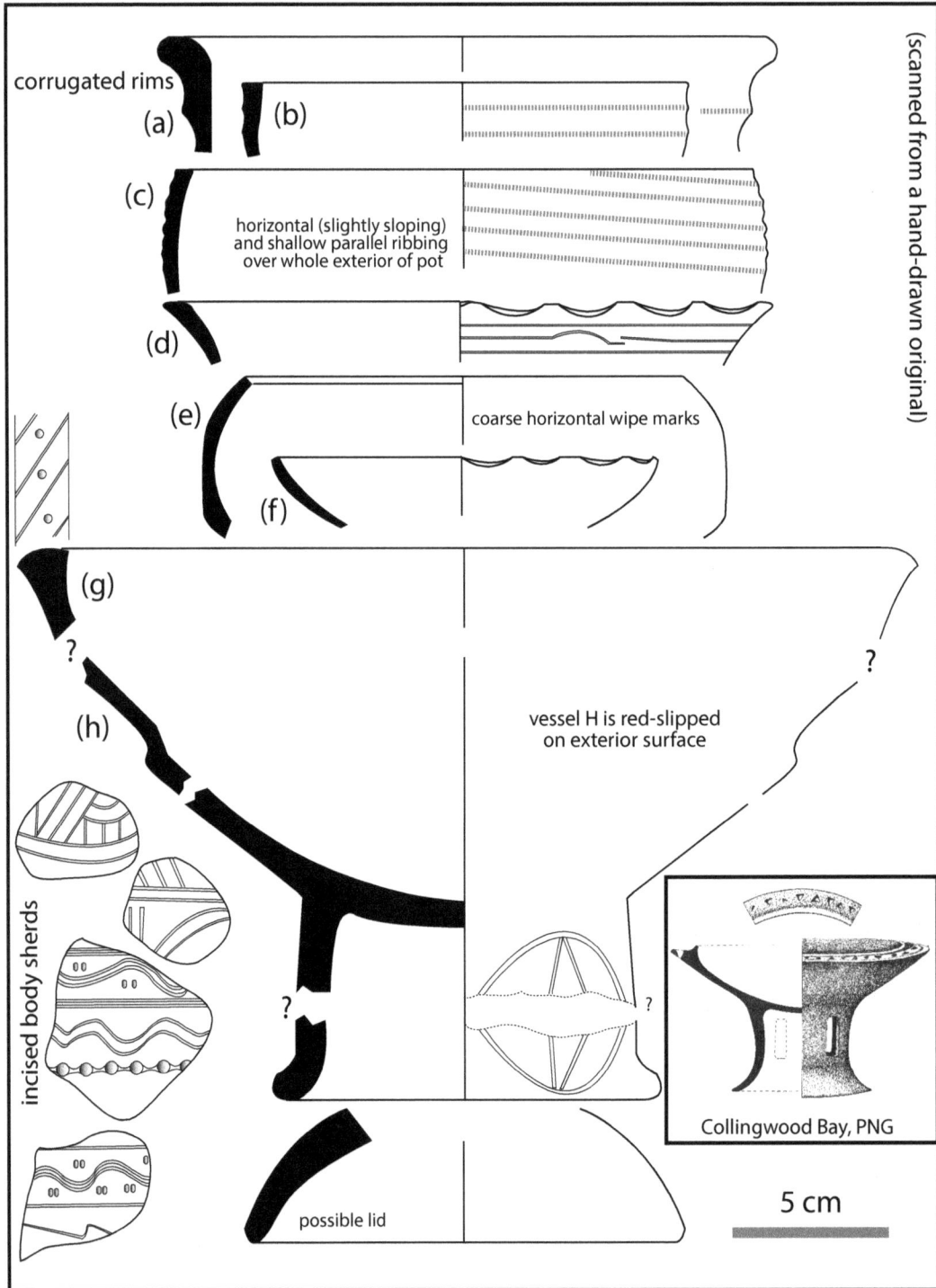

Figure 7.10 Pottery from Tanjong Pinang, Morotai, c. 2000 BP.

The inset vessel (27.4 cm in rim diameter) is from Wawa Gardens, Rainu, Collingwood Bay, Papua New Guinea, and is reproduced courtesy of Brian Egloff (1971:Fig. 2). See also Figure 7.5.

Sources: Peter Bellwood, Brian Egloff, and University of Hawai'i Press.

However, there are also hints that aspects of this kind of incised and applied decoration could have extended later in time, into the period of ceramic import that presumably overlapped in time with the Song and Ming dynasties in China, or early to mid-second millennium CE. These hints come from the sites of Sabatai Tua and Tanjung Tulang, in southeastern Morotai.

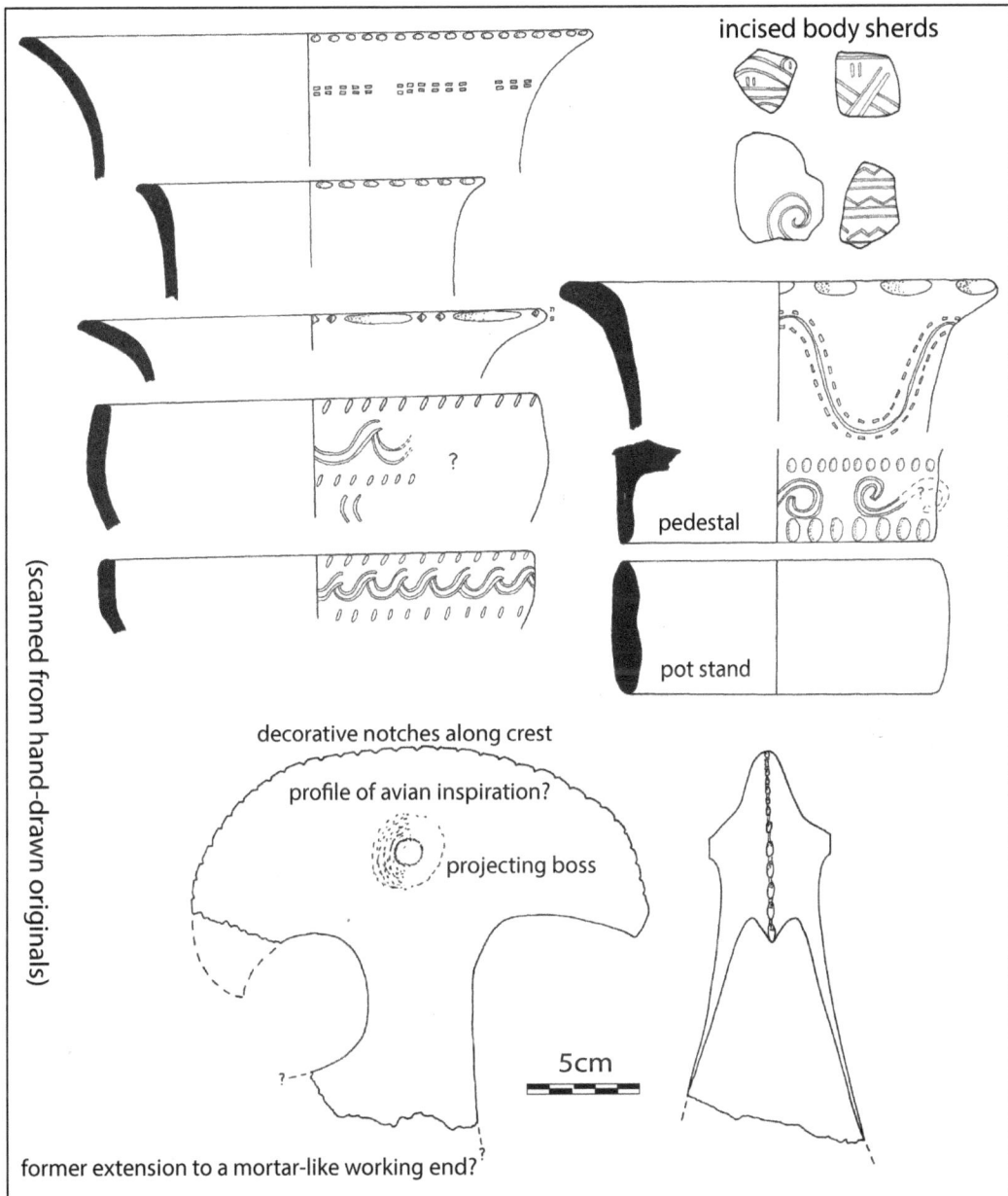

Figure 7.11 Pottery from Sabatai Tua, Morotai.
Source: Peter Bellwood.

Sabatai Tua was an open site on a hilltop, evidently eroded such that the sherds had all come to rest together on top of a thin surface soil. Because a few imported ceramic sherds were found on the site, together with sherds of the ethnographic type of sago mould called a *forna* (of Portuguese origin), Sabatai Tua was regarded as relatively young when first published in 1993 (Bellwood et al. 1993:28–29). However, some of these sherds of younger appearance could have been intrusive within this mixed surface assemblage. The pottery parallels with earlier sites such as Tanjung Pinang and Ara Manara suggest that Sabatai Tua may hold a mixture of sherds from different periods, some of which might indeed be as much as 2000 years old, or more.

The assemblage from Sabatai Tua is shown in Figure 7.11, in which it can be seen that the presence of double-line incision and lip scalloping here resembles the assemblages from Buwawansi, Um Kapat Papo, Aru Manara, and Tanjung Pinang. But Sabatai Tua also has many modelled pieces from non-containers, and one, of uncertain function and apparently modelled as a bird's head, is shown also at the base of Figure 7.11. This specimen seems to be unique. Sabatai Tua has also produced several legs and supports of pottery stoves, together with rounded pieces that might be the working ends of pottery pestles, possibly used in food preparation. Similar pieces, not illustrated, were found with imported ceramic sherds in the burial cave of Tanjung Tulang.

Pottery and the Northern Moluccas during the Early Metal Phase

Apart from the unique and much older red-slipped pottery from Uattamdi on Kayoa, other regions of the Northern Moluccas all reveal their first pottery traditions around 2500 BP. These other regions now include eastern Halmahera (Siti Nafisah), northern Halmahera (Gorua), Gebe (Um Kapat Papo, although Buwawansi might have older ceramic occupation), and now Morotai (Tanjung Pinang, Sabatai Tua, and Aru Manara). As noted in Chapter 6, sherds similar to those from Tanjung Pinang were also collected from the surfaces of two small raised coral islands off southern Morotai, namely Galogalo Besar and Rube Rube. The implication here is that pottery making was initiated at some point after 2700 BP beyond the zone of the older red-slipped pottery in regions that were previously preceramic, spreading across much of the Northern Moluccas. One might wonder why.

A hint about the reason why could come from two observations about these assemblages and their long-distance parallels. The first is that both Tanjung Pinang and Buwawansi 5 have rims with prominent horizontal corrugations that are strikingly similar to those from Mitangeb and Anaro in the Batanes Islands between Taiwan and Luzon, and also from the site of Sembiran on Bali (Bellwood and Dizon 2013:94; Ardika 1991; and see this volume Fig. 7.8, second down on left; Figs 7.10(a) and 7.10(b); and Fig. 7.12). Sembiran has attracted attention in recent years owing to the large quantities of c. 2000 BP Indian Rouletted Ware found there (Ardika and Bellwood 1991; Ardika et al. 1997; Calo et al. 2015). I am tempted to suggest that this distinctive form of corrugated pottery, a form that I have never observed in any preceding Neolithic assemblages in Island Southeast Asia, or in any succeeding post-1500 BP Early Metal Phase ones, is a marker of activity and contact across Island Southeast Asia, involving both Indian stimulus *and* trade in Taiwan nephrite (Hung 2017:333–335; Hung and Bellwood 2010; Hung et al. 2007) during the centuries around the turn of the Common Era. Of course, the Moluccan Spice Trade comes to mind as one possible reason for all this contact, but this remains surmise. Tanjung Pinang also has many sherds of a direct-rimmed and slightly restricted bowl form, shown in Figures 7.10(b–c), that carry shallow and roughly horizontal surface corrugations on their exteriors. Perhaps these reflect a locally made extension of the same stylistic idea.

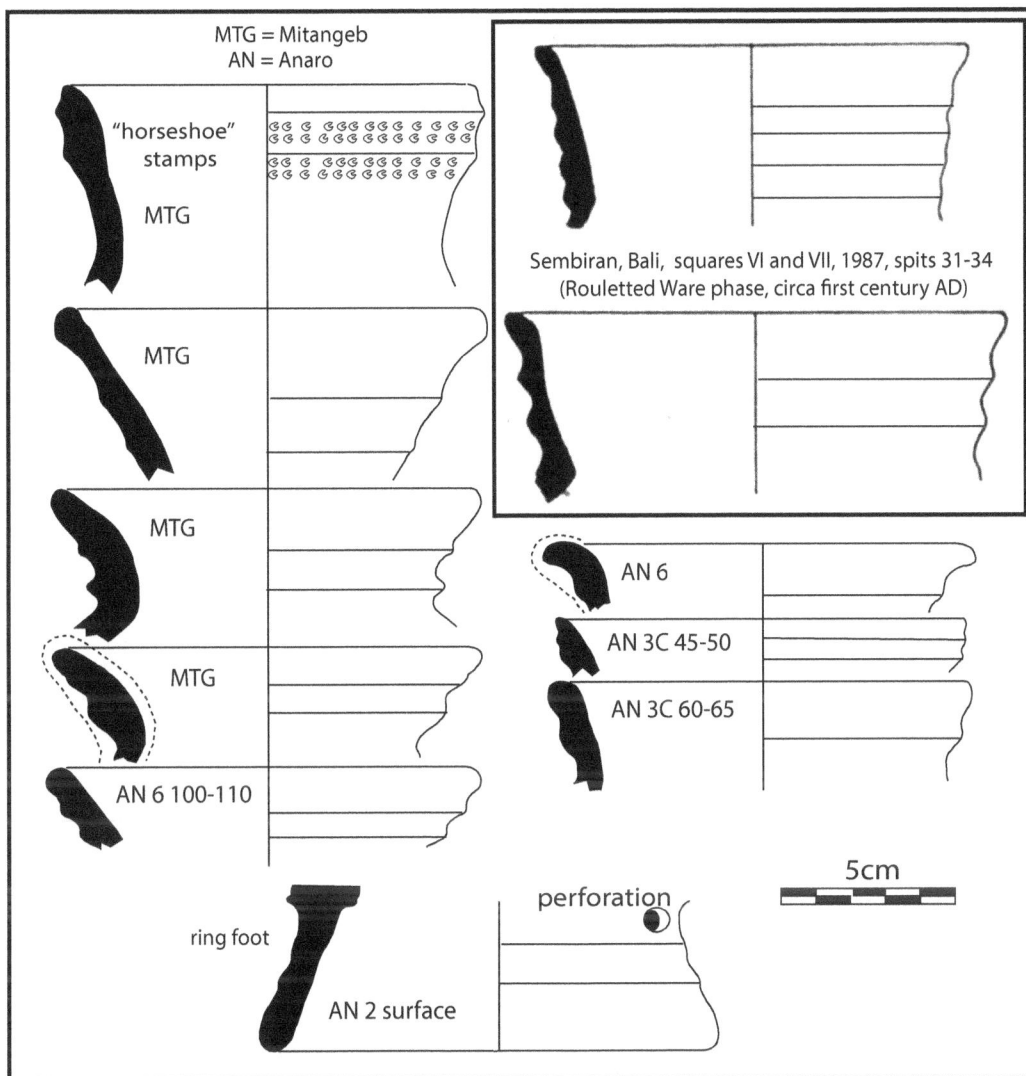

Figure 7.12 Corrugated rims from Mitangeb and Anaro (Batanes), and Sembiran (Bali).

From Bellwood and Dizon 2013, Figure 6.10. The Sembiran sherds are redrawn from Ardika 1991, Figure 5.4. Dotted lines indicate the presence of red slip.

Source: Peter Bellwood.

The second observation about long-distance parallels involves both Uattamdi 1 (Layers A and B) and Tanjung Pinang. Both of these sites have produced open bowls on stands, with cut-outs through the stand in the case of the Uattamdi specimen (Fig. 7.5(d)). Both have broad lips with incised decoration, although in the case of the specimen from Tanjung Pinang it is not absolutely certain that the rim labelled as (g) in Figure 7.10 fits the body labelled (h) (they are similar in fabric). However, similar vessels without pedestal cut-outs occur in Aru Manara (Ono et al. 2018:Figs 3 and 6). Interestingly, there are strong resemblances with a 27 cm diameter vessel published by Brian Egloff from his investigations in the Collingwood Bay region of eastern Papua New Guinea (Egloff 1971, 1979), and shown inset in both Figures 7.5 and 7.10. The Collingwood Bay vessel is not clearly dated, but in my commentary long ago on this research (Bellwood 1978:266–267) I noted the likelihood of connections between Island Melanesia and Island Southeast Asia in the general Early Metal Phase time period, although at that time the most likely connections appeared to be with Solheim's Novaliches complex in the Philippines (Solheim 2002:120), rather than with the Northern Moluccas, which at that time had seen no archaeological investigation.

Now, with the benefit of 40 years of further discovery, we can extend these relationships into the Northern Moluccas, and from the Moluccas back westwards and northwards into other regions of Island Southeast Asia. What has long been termed the 'Early Metal Phase', 'Bronze–Iron Age', or often simply 'Iron Age' in Island Southeast Asian archaeology could turn out to have been a period of remarkable contact and trade-based activity, focused on the centuries around the turn of the Common Era, with repercussions extending as far as India, Island Melanesia, and beyond. The extent of this 'beyond' in a Pacific direction could be marked by very positive similarities in certain types of New Zealand Maori and Iron Age Philippine nephrite artefacts, as discussed by me elsewhere (Bellwood and Hiscock 2018:Fig. 9.22). In my view, these similarities after 2000 BP are too strong to reflect mere chance, and of course far too late in time to reflect Neolithic migration patterns more than a millennium beforehand. But actual group-to-group contact remains just as likely as a more diffuse and so far undemonstrated concept of shared artistic ancestry.

It would perhaps be unwise to push these comparisons too far. But Pacific Island archaeologists in particular should be critical of the idea that distant Oceanic islands, once settled during Lapita times or later, were thereafter beyond the range of any long distance contact with Island Southeast Asia. In fact, I doubt that any modern archaeologist would hold such a view (see, for instance, Addison and Matisoo-Smith (2010) for an argument against it that involves Polynesian origins). The ability of ancient peoples to cross long distances at sea becomes ever more apparent as research proceeds.

In Chapter 13, these suggestions are discussed further, especially with respect to the likely spread of pottery into Papuan-speaking communities on Morotai, Halmahera, and Gebe around 2000 years ago from an earlier Austronesian-influenced node of pottery making activity in the islands west of Halmahera (for instance, Uattamdi). Linguistic evidence for contacts between the Moluccas and eastern Papua New Guinea will also be discussed. The early spice trade again beckons as a potential stimulus for such movements.

8

Lithic and other non-ceramic artefacts

Peter Bellwood, Geoffrey Irwin, and Daud Tanudirjo

During the course of the North Moluccan project, non-ceramic artefacts were recovered in only small numbers, with rather limited raw material or stylistic variation. Flaked stone tools were especially rare in comparison with many other pre-Neolithic locations in Southeast Asia. The site of Siti Nafisah produced no flaked stone at all, despite being fairly rich to its cultural base in animal bones, bone points, and shells (Table 4.1). Our general impression during the course of the research was that good cryptocrystalline raw materials such as chert, jasper, and agate are very rare in these islands (and only one piece of obsidian was found), such that people would have had to turn to inferior volcanic and metamorphic rocks for making stone tools. Perhaps they turned to alternative materials such as shell (Szabó et al. 2007; Szabó and Koppel 2015), although we did not find many finished shell tools in pre-Neolithic contexts, except for the shell adzes from Gebe. A series of bone points from Golo, Siti Nafisah, and Uattamdi have already been analysed and published by Juliette Pasveer (Pasveer and Bellwood 2004). As with the Golo lithics (below), detailed descriptions are not repeated here, except for the shell artefacts discussed by Katherine Szabó in the next chapter.

The flaked lithics from Golo and Wetef

Golo produced both flaked stone and marine shell (some worked) in relatively small amounts to its base at 35,000 cal. BP, with a very distinct shrinkage in quantity over the course of the Last Glacial Maximum (Table 2.2). A number of worked *Turbo marmoratus* opercula from the basal layers in Golo, as well as the Golo flaked lithics made of coarse chert and metamorphic rocks, none with any particular diagnostic features, have been fully reported elsewhere by Katherine Szabó and Adam Brumm (Szabó et al. 2007). There is no retouch, and it was suggested by Brumm that many lithic items were flaked elsewhere and brought into the cave, such that large cores were absent in the deposits.

A total of 22 stone artefacts similar to those from Golo was also recovered from nearby Wetef rockshelter, Squares K3 and K4. They were made on a range of volcanic, metamorphic, and chert-like rocks of generally low quality, available nearby in central and eastern parts of Gebe. Flaked stone was most frequent in Layer D, but smaller quantities occurred in Layers B and C, without indication of technological change. The most common type at Wetef was flake shatter (n=12), followed by simple unifacial flakes (n=9). There were no formal cores and only one hammerstone, which weighed 116.9 gm.

Table 8.1 Flaked stone artefacts from Wetef.

Item no.	Depth cm	Type¹	Length²	Breadth³	Thickness	Weight	Cortex⁴	Platform	Platform Crushing	Bulb	Scar	Scar Type	Bipolar
W05	45-50	S	31.8	15.8	11.4	5.4	N				unifacial	hinge	
W06	50-55	S	48.1	31.4	9.4	9.8	N				unifacial	step	
W07	160-165	F	30.6	22.5	4.9	5.5	N	Y	N	pronounced	unifacial	hinge	N
W08	195-200	S	23.8	23.2	8.6	6.8					unifacial	step	
W09	220-225	S	44.1	20	9.9	15.7					unifacial	step	
W13	25-30	S	32.2	19.6	10.6	8.4	N				unifacial	step	
W14	145-150	F	25.9 (snapped)	38.8	7.9	11.8	N	N		N	unifacial	step	
W15	145-150	S	31.9	28.8	12.4	12.1	water worn				unifacial	step/hinge	
W16	145-150	S	40	21.2	14	15.7					unifacial	hinge	possible
W17	140-145	F	60.3	35.9	16.2	39.4	N	Y	N	diffuse	unifacial	step	N
W18a	165-170	S	52.2	21.2	8	11.7	N				unifacial	step	
W18b	165-170	S	46.6 (snapped)	38.7	22.3	45.4	N				unifacial	step	
W19a	190-195	F	29.2	27.2	8.8	7.2	N	N		N	unifacial	step	N
W19b	190-195	F	29.9	40.8	9	20.2	N	Y	Y	diffuse	unifacial	step	N
W20	195-200	F	34.8	35.4	10.4	16.7	N	Y	N	pronounced	unifacial	step	N
W21	195-200	S	30.4	23.9	12.7	11.2	N				unifacial	step	
W22	200-205	S	27.1	19.3	6.5	5.6	N				unifacial	step	
W23	205-210	H	55.5	54.5	32.8	116.9	3				crushing	step	
W24	205-210	F	45.8	30.8	19.6	37.3	2	Y	Y	diffuse	unifacial	step	N
W25	210-215	F	31.9	24.3	4.9	6.2	2	Y	Y	diffuse	unifacial	feather	N
W26	210-215	F	31.5	27.6	7.3	8.8	1	N	Y	diffuse	unifacial	feather	N
W27	230-235	S	40.6	21.6	15.1	15.4	N				unifacial	step-bidirectional	

1 Type: F = flake, S = shatter, H = hammer; 2 Length: measurement (mm) along axis of percussion; 3 Breadth: max. dimension (mm) at right angles to length; 4 Cortex: 1 = 0–10% cover, 2 = 11–50%, 3 = 51–90%, 4 = 91–100%. N = no; Y = yes.

Source: Clayton Fredericksen.

The Wetef lithic collection was examined in Auckland by Clayton Fredericksen and the results of his study are presented in Table 8.1. Artefacts (not illustrated here) were technologically straightforward with no evidence of formal tools or intentional retouch. Knapping involved freehand unifacial flaking with a hard hammer, and there was only one example of possible bipolar flaking. No flake or debitage measured less than 23.8 mm in maximum dimension, suggesting that many flakes could have been struck elsewhere, as with the Golo assemblage (Szabó et al. 2007). Possible use-wear on artefacts W14 and W20 was observed under X10 magnification, and there were red/brown residues on W14, W24, and W26. Cortex remained on three flakes and the hammerstone. The primary aim of the lithic technology in both Wetef and Golo was the production of simple steep-edged flakes, probably for cutting and scraping.

The Morotai beach-pebble and flake industry

As noted in Chapter 3, Layer 1 in the Tanjung Pinang rockshelter contained an industry of flaked beach pebbles and struck debitage, together with a large number of unflaked and apparently unmodified beach pebbles that presumably served as manuports of uncertain function (Figs 8.1 and 8.2). Many of these items were left in the Sultan Palace Museum in Ternate in 1994, but the debitage from the 1994, 4x1 m trench F2 to J2 was brought to Canberra, as were those beach pebbles that showed definite signs of flaking. The debitage material itself is difficult to analyse since much of it shows the kind of fracturing that can often also be associated with the shattering of heated oven stones. The raw material is also very coarse volcanic or metamorphic rock, not amenable to use wear analysis. But quite a few pieces show definite conchoidal flaking, and some have edge abrasion indicating intentional use. None are retouched, and none have any features (e.g. blade morphology or backing) that could be defined as diagnostic at a cultural level.

In Chapter 3, the issue was raised of whether or not this industry continued in use into the late phase of skull and pottery deposition in the site. This will always be uncertain, since some of the skulls are sufficiently well preserved to indicate burial in pits deep enough to remove them from the activities of scavengers such as pigs and dogs, both presumably present on Morotai by 2000 years ago. So, quite deep disturbance is obvious for such preservation to have occurred. The same problem occurs in Daeo 2, where a similar beach pebble–based lithic industry (not described separately in this report) occurs with human bones in the upper spits, and also continues below the bones to the base of the site. Such flaked lithics were, however, not found in the open sites that we excavated on Morotai (Sabatai Tua, Sambiki Tua), or even in the pottery-bearing cave of Tanjung Tulang, so it appears most unlikely that pebble industries of this kind continued in use more recently than 2000 years ago. Furthermore, purely flaked, as opposed to ground or polished, lithics were rare in all the non-Morotai Neolithic deposits that we excavated in the Northern Moluccas, for instance in Uattamdi, Buwawansi, and the Neolithic layer in Siti Nafisah. Um Kapat Papo produced only 12 pieces of flaked stone in total—too few for any useful statement to be made.

Figure 8.1 Lithics from Tanjung Pinang.
(a)–(c): unifacially flaked pebbles; (d)–(e) and (g): steeply flaked pebbles; (f): horsehoof core with battered edges; (h): large flake with flake scar on dorsal surface (Sumatralith); (i)–(k): flaked pieces of chert; (l): *Canarium* anvil.
Source: Peter Bellwood.

Figures 8.1 and 8.2 illustrate a number of flaked lithic pieces from Tanjung Pinang. Items (a) to (c) are simple unifacially flaked pebbles, of a form typical of other contemporary pebble industries such as the Indochinese and Sumatran unifacial Hoabinhian. This is probably coincidental, reflecting no more than a focus on a use of pebbles as raw materials. Items (d), (e), and (g) are steep-edged and rather scraper-like pebble tools. Item (f) is a battered horsehoof core of very coarse volcanic rock. Items (d) to (g) resemble early tools in Australia, being generally in the steep-edged and horsehoof mode, but again the parallels might be coincidental since at this very basic level of pebble flaking the chances of overlap in form are obviously very high indeed. Item (h) is a small unifacial Sumatralith, to use a Hoabinhian terminology, made on a fairly large flake that still preserves its ventral surface. Items (i), (j), and (k) are of coarse red-brown chert, a flaked chunk and two blade-like flakes. Since the latter were rare in Maluku Utara (e.g. Fig. 8.2) it is best to regard them also as fortuitous. The Moluccas certainly have not produced any traces of a backed blade-like flake and microlith industry such as the Toalian in southwestern Sulawesi.

Item (l) in Figure 8.1 is a form of stone anvil found quite commonly in the Northern Moluccas, being a river or beach pebble with a pounded hollow on each side. Informants suggested these might have been used to open the very hard-shelled nuts of the *Canarium* tree genus. The stratigraphy associated with these anvils in Tanjung Pinang (no less than 20 in this site; Table 3.1) and Golo suggests that they originated in preceramic times, possibly in the late Pleistocene, given that one coral specimen came from a depth of 200 cm in Golo, possibly with an age of 30,000 years. One of the Tanjung Pinang specimens (different from the one in Fig. 8.1) is drawn for clarity in Figure 8.2 (lower-right inset).

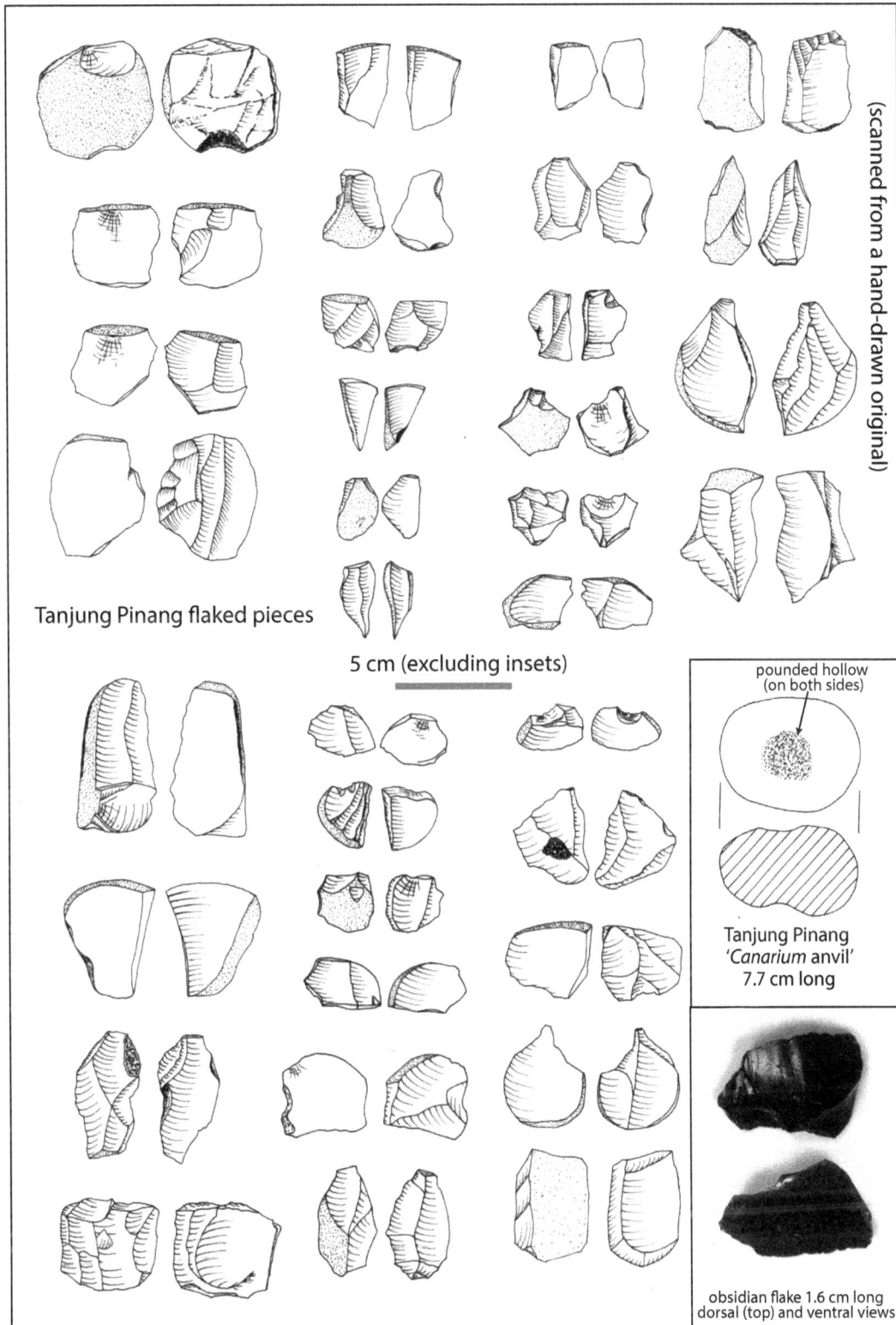

Figure 8.2 Flaked lithics struck from beach pebbles, a *Canarium* anvil and an obsidian flake from Tanjung Pinang.

Insets are not to scale.

Source: Daud Tanudirjo, Christian Reepmeyer, and Peter Bellwood.

Figure 8.2 shows a number of flaked pieces from Tanjung Pinang, many with some remaining cortexed beach pebble exterior. None of these flakes have stone adze polish of the type visible on some of the stone flakes from Neolithic Uattamdi (below). None shows positive retouch, and while occasional pieces have blade-like proportions it appears that these result from intentional unidirectionality of flaking, rather than any specific intention to produce a blade industry. The item at top left in Figure 8.2 has a quite heavily worked notch.

One remarkable Tanjung Pinang find from a depth of 15–20 cm in Square F3 was a small piece of obsidian, 16 mm long by 12 mm wide (Fig. 8.2, lower-right inset), and possibly associated with the human skull burials since it was found at their level in the site. This piece was examined initially during the 1990s by Wal Ambrose at ANU, who recorded a density of 2.271 for the raw material, then by Glenn Summerhayes, now of the University of Otago, who was unable at that time to trace the piece by geochemical sourcing to any known origin. However, in 2014, the piece was sent to Christian Reepmeyer at James Cook University, who was able to use the current obsidian database for Island Southeast Asia and Melanesia to make the following statement:

> Geochemical fingerprinting of the obsidian artefact points to one of the West Fergusson sources, most likely to the sub-source of Kukuia in the D'Entrecasteaux group. The second sub-source in this group, the Fagalulu source, can be excluded based on its higher Sr-values. Multivariate statistical analysis excluded all known Indonesian and Philippine sources (Christian Reepmeyer, email 25 January 2017).

West Fergusson obsidian is reported in small quantities from surface collections along the Sepik coastline of northwestern Papua New Guinea (Golitko et al. 2012), apparently from post-Lapita cultural contexts. The Tanjung Pinang occurrence is its first potential identification in an Indonesian archaeological site, and the significance of this will be discussed in Chapter 13. Added to the Golo and Wetef shell adzes with their Admiralty Island parallels (see below), and the Uattamdi and Tanjung Pinang pottery with its Collingwood Bay parallels (Chapter 7), it is becoming clear that periodic episodes of interaction involving the Moluccas did occur along the coastlines of or around the island of New Guinea from mid-Holocene times onwards. However, it is equally important to note that the Talasea and Admiralty obsidian sources so important in linking northern Borneo (Bukit Tengkorak, see Bellwood 1989) and the western Melanesian islands during Lapita times (c. 3000 BP) are completely absent (so far) in the Northern Moluccas, as also is any trace of any early Lapita connection in pottery decoration.

The Neolithic stone assemblage from Uattamdi 1

The lithic tools from Uattamdi 1 were restricted in distribution to Neolithic Layers C and D inside the rockshelter, and absent in the Metal Age jar burial Layers A and B above. Table 5.1 shows the stratigraphic distribution of the recovered assemblage: three complete adzes, one adze bevel, eight adze chips and other fragments with polish on one surface, and 25 unpolished flakes, cores and other debitage. The common occurrence of polished stone in this assemblage, compared with its complete absence in Tanjung Pinang, supports the comment above that the Tanjung Pinang pebble industry is likely to be entirely preceramic in date.

The three complete adzes are shown in Figure 8.3: (a) is a partially polished lenticular cross-sectioned adze of dark basalt, with a definite asymmetric adze (not axe) bevel on the side facing up in the right-hand drawing; (b) is a well-polished chisel of a similar basalt, again asymmetrically bevelled; and (d) is an edge-ground cutting tool made on a long piece of limestone, with an oval cross-section, that shows no sign of flaking. Its general shape is axe-like, but this specimen is clearly somewhat *ad hoc* in origin.

Item a was found in Square D8 in Layer C9, quite close to the base of the site and within range of a date around 3000 BP or before. Adzes of this untanged and lenticular-sectioned type also exist in contemporary Lapita sites in Island Melanesia (e.g. Kirch and Yen 1982:Fig. 92 for the Kiki Lapita phase in Tikopia), but their distribution in Indonesia is quite difficult to track owing to rarity of sufficiently detailed reports. There appear to be none in the northern Philippines or Taiwan (Hung 2004; Bellwood and Dizon 2013), so this form could be specific to Southeast Indonesia and western Oceania. I am not aware of any such close parallels elsewhere in Indonesia. Lenticular-sectioned slate adzes occur in the Kalumpang sites (Minanga Sipakko and Kamassi) in West Sulawesi, but these sites also have tanged and quadrangular-sectioned forms (van Heekeren 1972:Plates 98–99; Anggraeni 2012:Fig. IV.47) that do not occur in the Moluccas.

A small butt fragment (not illustrated) of a planilateral-sectioned adze from Uattamdi Square E5, Layer C6, also resembles a complete Lapita adze illustrated by Green (1979:Fig. 2.4) from Nenumbo, Main Reef Islands, Southeast Solomons. The Uattamdi chisel (item (b), from Layer D1) is an interesting piece with widespread parallels as far away as the Batanes Islands and Pitcairn in Polynesia (Bellwood and Dizon 2013:Fig. 8.5). Another very small (14 mm long) bevel fragment from a similar chisel was found in Square C7, Level D1 (not illustrated). The Pitcairn specimen is also drawn as item (c) in Figure 8.3.

In 2015, Matthew Spriggs at ANU showed Peter Bellwood a number of stone adzes found with late Lapita pottery on a coral reef in the DES site on Nissan Island, between New Ireland and Bougainville in eastern Papua New Guinea. The adzes are of the same untangled lenticular and planilateral-sectioned forms present at Uattamdi, and there are also chisels with oval or plano-convex cross-sections. These similarities are quite striking, especially given the movement of Talasea obsidian from New Britain into the site of Bukit Tengkorak in Sabah at the same time (Bellwood 1989). However, the perspective discussed in Chapter 7, and reinforced in the concluding Chapter 13, is that this does not necessarily demand an origin for the Lapita complex as a whole in the Moluccas.

The flaked pieces shown as (e) to (o) in Figure 8.3 are quite varied in raw material and are described in the caption to the figure. Items (e), (k), and (l) each show one polished adze surface. Quartzite core (m) and chert flake (o) both show signs of heavy use wear. No blade-like forms are present and there is no intentional retouch, but these flakes are interesting in that they document a continuing usage of such items into the Neolithic in the Northern Moluccas. While this might seem rather a trivial observation, it takes on relevance in light of the rarity of flaked stone tools in many Neolithic sites to the west and north—for instance the Kalumpang sites in West Sulawesi, and the Batanes Islands (Anggraeni et al. 2014; Bellwood and Dizon 2013:Fig. 8.1). In the north Moluccan context these items might reflect a continuation of preceramic technology into a lithic environment dominated by polished adze and chisel production.

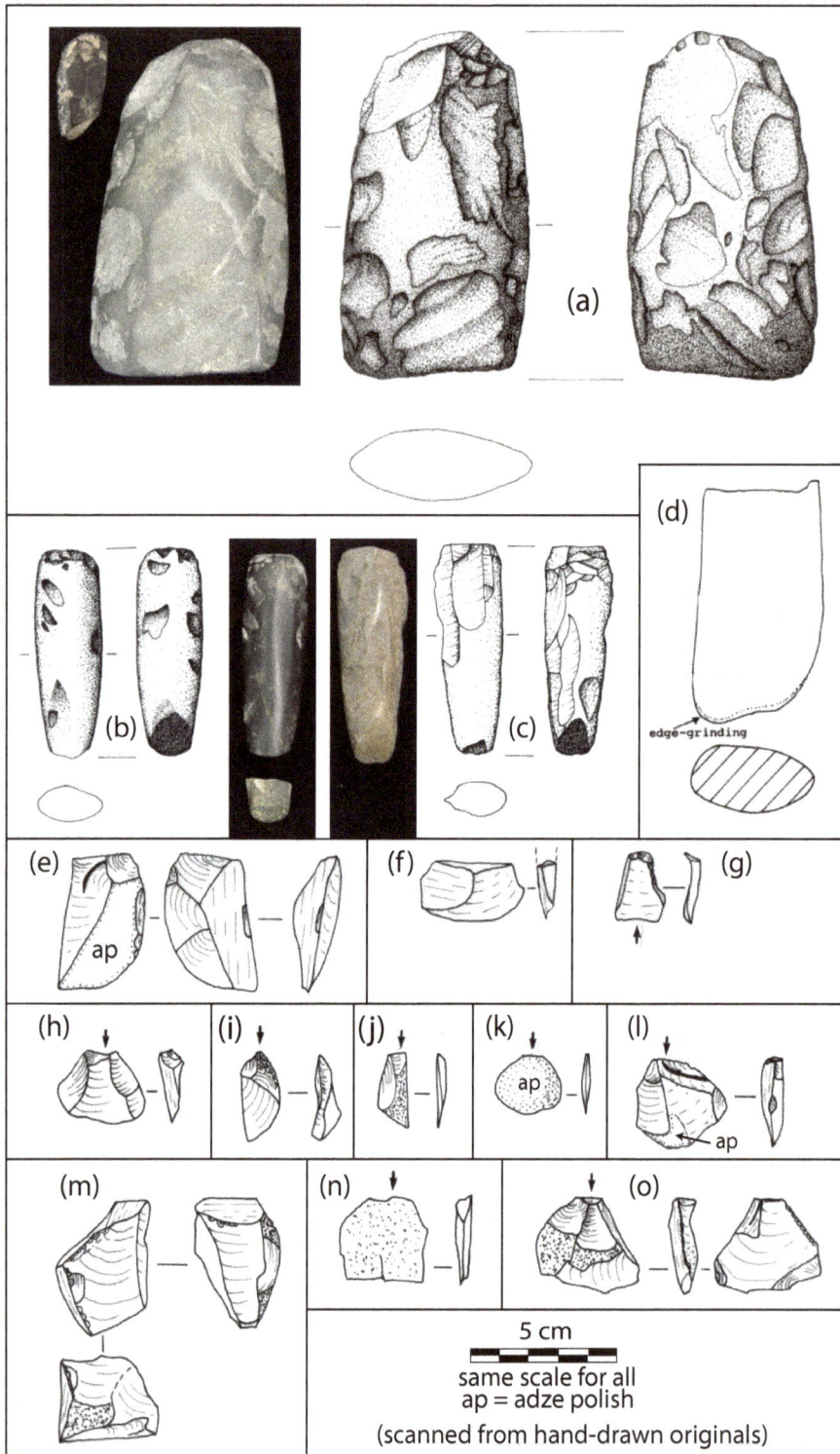

Figure 8.3 Stone artefacts from Uattamdi 1.

(a): lenticular-sectioned adze of basalt, with a separate planilaterally-sectioned adze fragment at top left; (b): oval-sectioned chisel of basalt, with a separate but almost identical chisel bevel shown below the photograph; (c): basalt chisel of the same shape from Pitcairn Island, eastern Polynesia (Harry Maude Collection, ANU); (d): edge-ground axe-like tool of unflaked limestone; (e): basalt chunk broken from adze; (f): flake of volcanic rock; (g): quartzite flake; (h)–(j): chert flakes; (k): basalt adze flake; (l): basalt flake struck from adze; (m): quartzite core; (n): quartzite flake; (o): chert flake with use wear.

Source: Katherine Szabó (drawings of basalt adzes) and Peter Bellwood.

Two Neolithic stone adzes from Gua Siti Nafisah, Halmahera

Although Gua Siti Nafisah produced no flaked lithics at all, the Neolithic deposit in this cave produced two segments of polished stone adzes (Fig. 8.4). Item (a) is a butt or blade fragment (there is a possible bevel at the top of the drawing) of a paler grey volcanic rock than the adzes from Uattamdi. Its cross-section tends towards plano-convex rather than symmetrically lenticular, but in its degree of flaking and general shape it resembles the Uattamdi adze shown in Figure 8.3(a). This adze came from Layer B1 in Square F8, from which there is a date of 3443–3080 cal. BP (ANU 7785). If this date is applicable to the adze, then it is very close in date to the specimen from Uattamdi. However, the bulk of the pottery in the site was at a higher level, and more likely associated with the dates of 2351–2007 and 1598–1268 cal BP (Tables 1.1 and 4.1).

The other adze butt is an unusual fragment made on a strongly laminated rock, perhaps metamorphic, which appears to have been hammer-dressed rather than flaked into shape (Fig. 8.4(b)). This came from Square J10, at the base of the stratigraphy beneath the shell midden dated 1598–1268 cal. BP. The cross-section is again lenticular, like the other Uattamdi and Siti Nafisah examples, and the butt is quite strongly tapered.

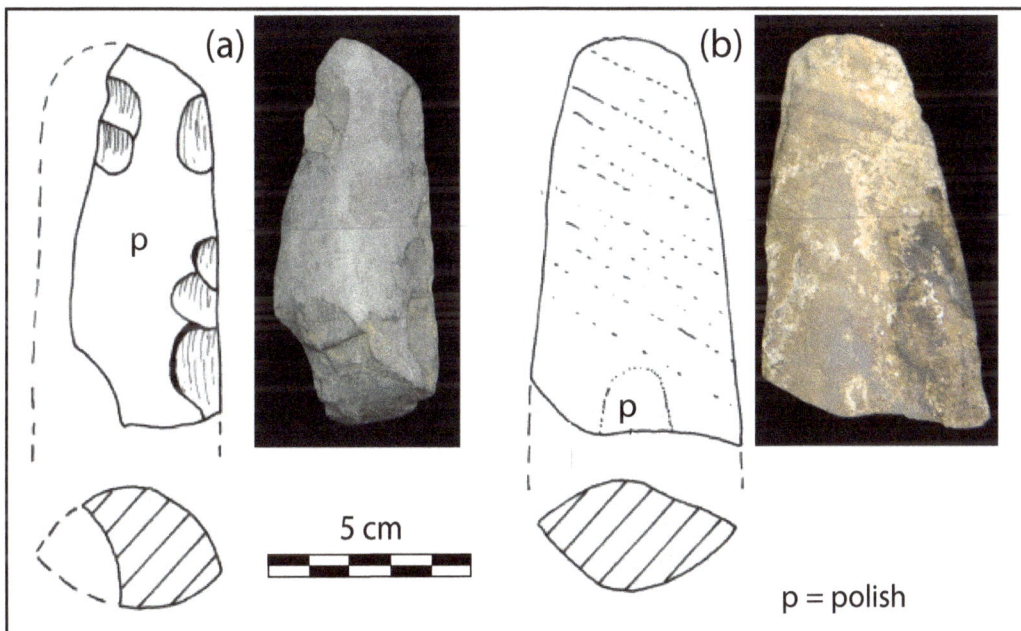

Figure 8.4 Stone adze segments from Gua Siti Nafisah, Halmahera.

(a): paler grey volcanic rock, flaked and polished; (b): laminated and possibly metamorphic rock, hammer-dressed rather than flaked, but also polished.

Source: Peter Bellwood.

Facetted ochre pieces from the Golo Cave burial pit

As noted in Table 2.3, the Golo Cave extended burial (2314–1415 cal. BP – ANU 11818) was placed in a grave filled with soil mixed with powdered-red ochre (hematite), together with the discarded ochre pieces from which the powder had been ground. Roughly 80 of these ochre pieces were recovered from within the grave fill, and a number of them were quite large, tabular in shape, with one ground flat surface from which the ochre powder had been scraped. A sample of 15 of the larger pieces are shown in Figure 8.5. The two pieces at bottom right have narrow grooves made by scratching with a pointed tool.

Figure 8.5 Ground ochre tablets from the Golo Cave burial fill.
The two specimens at bottom right have linear incisions.
Source: Peter Bellwood.

The shell adzes from Golo, Wetef, and Buwawansi

The shell artefacts from the Gebe excavations are dealt with in detail in the next chapter by Katherine Szabó. But two shell adze topics require discussion here. Wetef rockshelter produced a number of *Cassis* shell adzes not described in the next chapter, so they are described here first by Geoffrey Irwin. After this, we discuss the chronologies for the numerous Golo shell adzes, especially the *Hippopus* and *Tridacna* ones, which pose difficult problems.

Cassis shell adzes from Wetef rockshelter

Several complete and broken shell adzes made from the lip of *Cassis* shell, of the same form as at Golo (Fig. 8.6, compare Fig. 9.5 for Golo), were found at Wetef, all in Layer B1. One complete adze near the top of the layer measured 112 mm long and another, from the bottom of Layer B1 and illustrated in Figure 8.6, was 105 mm long, 35 mm wide at the bevel, and 23 mm thick. A third near-complete adze, missing part of the butt end and evidently burnt in a fire, came from the middle of Layer B1. In addition, there were seven other fragments of *Cassis* adze, some from the butt or the bevel, and others from the mid-section. Some of these pieces could have come from the same artefacts, but not all. Several of these fragments appear to have been broken in use and several had been subsequently discoloured by heat from fires.

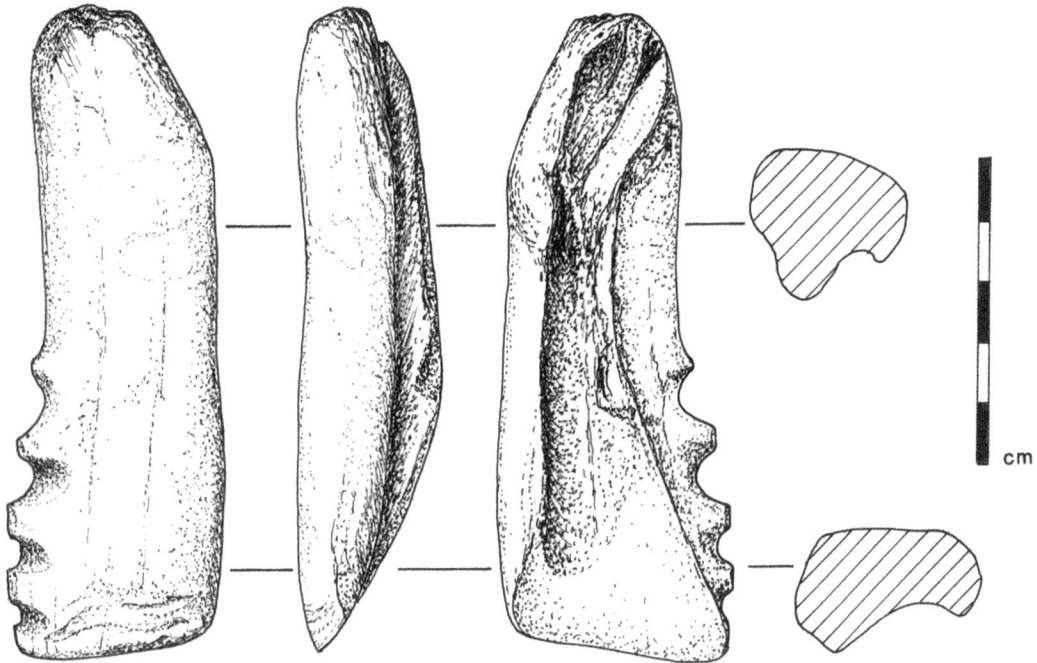

Figure 8.6 A *Cassis* shell adze from Wetef.
Source: Geoffrey Irwin.

The distribution of these shell adzes is problematical. None were contemporary with the potsherds of Layer A, although *Cassis* shell adzes are widespread in Oceania where they are always contemporary with pottery (e.g. Kirch and Yen 1982:226 for Tikopia; Carson 2014:Fig. 10.11 for House of Taga, Mariana Islands; Galipaud et al. 2016 for Pain Haka, Flores). Unlike Golo, none appeared during excavation to have been cached from above, and it is perhaps unlikely that broken pieces would have been deliberately buried, or that they all could have been carried down into Layer B1 by disturbance. Unfortunately, none of the Wetef samples submitted for direct radiocarbon dating produced a result. Their apparent preceramic context is anomalous. Or it could raise the possibility that these artefacts have a greater antiquity in Maluku and Island Southeast Asia than further east. However, a positive claim for this at present would be unwarranted.

Dating the Golo shell adzes

There are hints of external contacts reaching Gebe Island during the middle Holocene in the form of six non-*Cassis* ground clam shell adzes from preceramic contexts. These include three from Golo and one from Buwawansi made from the ventral hinge regions of large *Tridacna* clam shells (*T. maxima* or *T. gigas*), and two from Golo made from the ventral hinge regions of large *Hippopus hippopus* clam shells (Figs 8.7, 9.4, and 9.9). Four of these adzes (three *Tridacna* and one *Hippopus*) are described in more detail by Katherine Szabó in Chapter 9.

The *Tridacna* examples are paralleled closely by *Tridacna* adzes with similar hollow backs in late Pleistocene or early Holocene layers in Pamwak Cave in the Admiralty Islands (Fig. 8.7), located to the north of the Papua New Guinea mainland and about 2000 km due east of Gebe (Fredericksen et at. 1993; Schmidt 1996). The two Golo and Pamwak adzes shown in Figure 8.7 are identical in manufacturing technique, although the Pamwak example illustrated appears to have heavy cutting-edge use wear, and so is shorter than that from Golo, which shows only slight signs of use. The Pamwak adzes are dated indirectly to between 5500 and 11,000 BP (Fredericksen et al. 1993; Schmidt 1996). Daud Tanudirjo (2001) also reports such *Tridacna* adzes from the Sula Islands that lie east of Sulawesi, and Sue O'Connor informs us (pers. comm. May 2019) that similar *Tridacna* and *Hippopus* adzes have been found in Timor. Alfred Pawlik and colleagues (2015) have recently published information on other ground shell adzes of a similar Holocene and pre-Neolithic date from the Philippines and eastern Indonesia, although the Golo–Pamwak parallel appears to be the closest at present in terms of actual shape and cross-section, especially in the choice of shell used and the emphasis on the hollow back. The Golo and Pamwak specimens are indeed almost identical.

Figure 8.7 *Tridacna* shell adzes (photographed from both sides) from Golo M4 135–140 cm (top) and Pamwak Cave (Square 2, spit 4), Manus, Admiralty Islands (bottom).

Source: Peter Bellwood. Pamwak adze courtesy of Matthew Spriggs.

The Golo clam shell adzes were found in a level proxy-dated between 12,000 and 9000 years ago based on C14 dates from nearby food shells, and indeed I attributed this date to them in the second edition of my *Prehistory of the Indo-Malaysian Archipelago* (Bellwood 2007: Plate 25). However, since the majority of these tools were complete and undamaged, a moment's thought will indicate that they were all cached in holes in the cave floor, presumably by itinerant visitors who intended to reuse them during some future visit to the site. Therefore, they must have been younger than the stratigraphic dates just given, perhaps by several millennia. Exactly how old were these large clam shell adzes?

The obvious course of action, applied some years after the excavations finished, was to radiocarbon date the actual shells from which the Golo adzes were made. The results came as something of a surprise. One of the *Tridacna* adzes from 135–140 cm (a depth dated stratigraphically to c. 12,000 years ago) gave a reading of 38,984–34,638 years BP (OZD775), indicating that the maker did not use a new shell but found one either in a beach deposit or eroding from one of the many uplifted segments of Pleistocene coral reef that line the Gebe shoreline, especially on the northern side of the island. The same applied to one of the Neolithic *Cassis* adzes from the site, found with pottery in the upper layers (30–35 cm) and certainly younger than 3500 years on typological grounds, yet with a direct C14 date on the shell of 10,621–10,246 years ago (OZD773). A third *Hippopus* specimen from 145–150 cm (Fig. 9.4(a)) actually gave a younger date than the c. 12,000 years expected, of only 7176–6771 years (OZD774), confirming that it had probably been cached in a hole. This one was quite possibly made of fresh shell.

What can we conclude from these dates? That for the *Hippopus* specimen of c. 7000 BP seems a reasonable estimate for its manufacture, given that the Golo *Tridacna* and *Hippopus* adzes predated the appearance of pottery in the site and lay a little below the oldest animal bones, which also apparently commenced deposition around 7000 years ago (see Chapter 10). These *Tridacna* and *Hippopus* shell adzes, therefore, are certainly not Neolithic—they document indigenous late Palaeolithic enterprise and no doubt ocean crossing if we are to explain the Gebe and Admiralty parallels. None of the Admiralty specimens have been directly dated, but, as stated above, the excavators (Frederickson et al. 1993) obtained terminal Pleistocene to middle Holocene dates from the sediments in which they were found, suggesting an actual age during the Holocene for the adzes themselves. However, whatever the precise date for these shell adzes, which may always be uncertain owing to the problems with direct dating of shell, it is interesting that absolutely no other crafted (as opposed to simply flaked) shell artefacts occurred in the Northern Moluccan pre-Neolithic—no beads, no bracelets, no fish-hooks.

Glass beads from Uattamdi 1

The Uattamdi 1 Neolithic shell beads are discussed by Katherine Szabó in Chapter 9, but examination of Table 5.1 will indicate that 118 glass beads of the Early Metal Phase were also recovered from the Uattamdi excavations, concentrated in Layer B with the burial jar sherds. A few had also worked their way downwards through the stratigraphy into the upper part of Layer C, with its Neolithic pottery. The shell beads, on the contrary, were found mainly in Layers C and D, with only three in Layer B. The Uattamdi glass beads were not analysed chemically and have now been returned to Indonesia, but in the interests of future comparative research I have located a series of 35 mm colour print photos of the Uattamdi shell, stone, and glass beads taken during the 1990s, and scanned and inserted them into Figure 8.8. Not all the glass beads found in Uattamdi 1 are shown, but the photograph shows all the bead types that were present. All of glass were monochrome Indo-Pacific beads in the terminology of Peter Francis (1990, 2002).

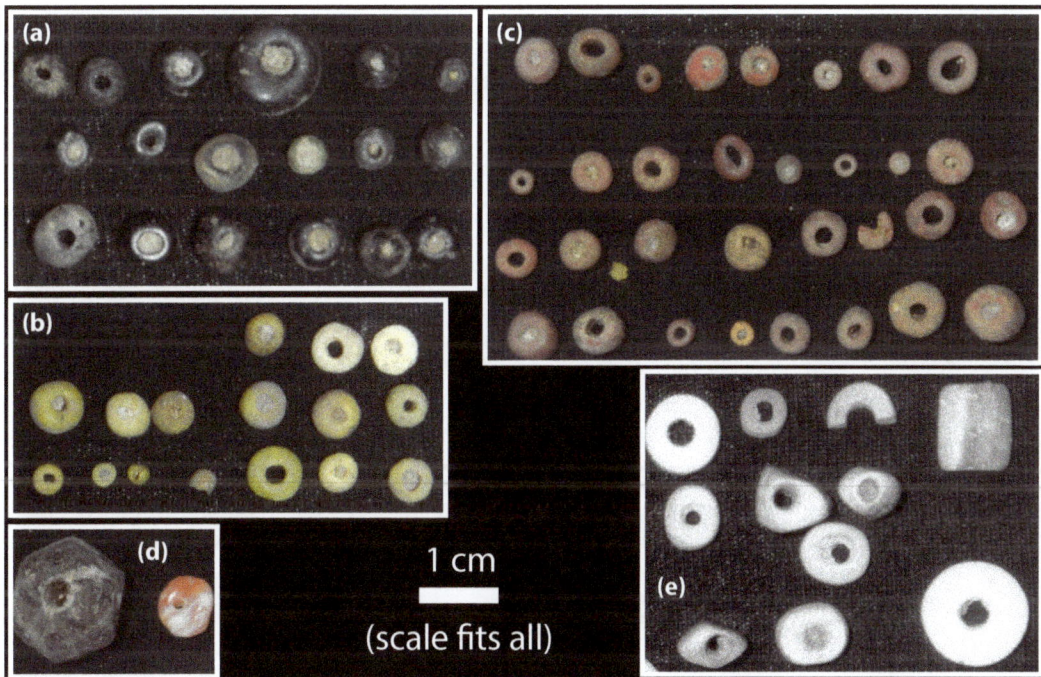

Figure 8.8 Monochrome glass beads (a–c), two stone beads (d), and shell beads (e) from Uattamdi 1.
These are scanned archival photos.
Source: Peter Bellwood.

9

Worked shell from the Northern Moluccas

Katherine Szabó

Introduction

The Northern Moluccas occupy a pivotal geographical zone at the interface of the Island Southeast Asian and Melanesian spheres. Whether one looks at genes, languages, Holocene animal translocations, or the archaeological record, it is clear that the cultures through time on these islands have both been shaped by, and have contributed to shaping, the complex fusion of influences that characterises the Asia/Pacific margin. The project reported on in this monograph intensively investigated this area for the first time, and uncovered a rich range of sites spanning c. 35,000 years of the islands' history.

There are few constants in the archaeological record that can be tracked through time. The vertebrate record of the Northern Moluccas shows dramatic shifts at different points in the past, and the ceramic record is necessarily restricted to the last few thousand years. The pre-eminence of lithic technology in the study of human cultural change through time is due to its global presence as a robust archaeological constant, but in Island Southeast Asia, and the Northern Moluccas in particular, another constant has emerged: shell technology.

From the earliest archaeological deposits at the oldest excavated site, Golo Cave, a range of shell technologies were in use ranging from the formal to the expedient (Szabó et al. 2007; Szabó and Koppel 2015). In contrast, associated lithic technologies were found to be non-standardised and uncomplicated in their manufacture (Szabó et al. 2007). While, to some extent, the early diversification of shell technologies at Golo Cave can be seen as a response to the low-quality lithic materials that were locally available, this in itself does not provide an adequate explanation. The diversity of shell-working from the lowest levels at Golo, both in terms of materials used and reduction techniques employed, clearly implies that a broad tradition of shell-working was well established by the time the site was initially occupied. Additionally, the techniques applied to various types of shell diverge from those applied to lithic material, confirming that shell was no simple technological substitute for stone.

The range of stratified sites excavated as part of this archaeological project provides snapshots through time of the rise and decline of a variety of shell-working traditions. Some have clear links beyond the Northern Moluccas whilst others are seemingly idiosyncratic. The shell artefacts will be reported upon site by site, with temporal patterning and extra-Moluccan associations being considered in the discussion section.

Background and methods

Worked shell was recovered from a range of sites excavated as part of this project. The largest sample comes from the longest sequence at Golo Cave. However, Uattamdi also yielded a range of artefacts from mid to late Holocene deposits. Smaller numbers were identified from Buwawansi, Siti Nafisah, and Tanjung Tulang. All artefacts are itemised along with their provenance details in Table 9.1.

The majority of the worked shell items reported on here were identified in the field individually as special finds and bagged according to provenance. It is thus possible that some minimally worked or unmodified-utilised shell was overlooked in this process. From the sample of shell artefacts available for study, the approach to the separation of potentially worked shell in the field seems to have been cautious, but the overall degree of potential bias in identification and retention is unclear. Only the Golo Cave sample also had associated shell midden samples that were readily available for study, and much of the Pleistocene worked shell identified came from the midden samples. Not all midden from the Golo Cave excavations was brought back to Australia, but a full sequence from Square M4, as well as additional samples collected for potential radiocarbon dating, was accessible.

Table 9.1 Worked shell identified from Northern Moluccan archaeological sites.

Square	Depth (cm)	Species	Artefact type
Golo Cave, Gebe			
Surface		*Cassis cornuta*	Reworked adze
M9	0–5	*Cassis cornuta*	Adze
M7	5–10	*Turbo marmoratus*	Cut fragment
N6	5–10	*Cassis cornuta*	Adze
N6	10–15	*Cassis cornuta*	Adze
M7	10–20	*Turbo marmoratus*	Operculum artefact
M4	15–20	*Cassis cornuta*	Adze fragment
N6	15–20	*Cassis cornuta*	Adze
M6	20–25	*Cassis cornuta*	Adze
N6	25–30	*Cassis cornuta*	Adze
LM6	25–30	*Cassis cornuta*	Adze
M7	35–40	*Cassis cornuta*	Adze
M5	40–45	*Cassis cornuta*	Adze fragment
M5	40–45	*Conus* sp.	Modified spire
M5	40–45	*Conus* sp.	Modified spire
M6	50–55	*Cassis cornuta*	Adze
M5	50–55	*Cassis cornuta*	Worked lip fragment
L6	55	*Cassis cornuta*	Adze
M8	55–60	*Turbo marmoratus*	Worked fragment
M6	60–65	*Cassis cornuta*	Adze fragment
M5	75–80	*Turbo marmoratus*	Cut fragment
N6	100	*Hippopus hippopus*	Rib-portion adze
M6	100	*Tridacna* sp.	Rib-portion adze
M5	100–110	*Turbo marmoratus*	Operculum artefact
LM6	125–130	*Tridacna* sp.	Rib-portion adze
M4	135–140	*Tridacna gigas*	Rib-portion adze
LM6	145–150	*Hippopus hippopus*	Rib-portion adze
M4	170–180	*Turbo marmoratus*	Operculum artefact

Square	Depth (cm)	Species	Artefact type
M4	180–185	*Pinctada margaritifera*	Cut fragment
M4	185–190	*Scutellastra flexuosa*	Utilised shell
M4	190–200	*Turbo marmoratus*	Operculum artefact
LM6	195–200	*Turbo marmoratus*	Reduced shell
M4	200–205	*Scutellastra flexuosa*	Three utilised shells
M4, LM6	200–210	*Turbo marmoratus*	Four operculum artefacts
M4	205–210	*Scutellastra flexuosa*	Utilised shell
LM6	210–220	*Turbo marmoratus*	Reduced shell
M5, LM6	210–220	*Turbo marmoratus*	Two operculum artefacts
M5	220–230	*Turbo marmoratus*	Four operculum artefacts
M5	230–240	*Turbo marmoratus*	Three operculum artefacts
Uattamdi, Kayoa			
D1	Spoil	*Cypraea tigris*	Perforated dorsum
C7	B6	*Isognomon isognomum*	Worked and utilised valve
D4	C2	*Isognomon isognomum*	Shaped valve
C6	C3	*Pinctada maxima*	Worked and utilised valve
D5	C3	*Asaphis violascens*	Shaped fragment
D4	C3	*Nautilus* sp.	Cut septal wall fragment
D8	C4	*Placuna ephippium*	Cut fragment
D9	C5	*Conus* sp.	Ring fragment
C5	C5	*Trochus niloticus*	Ring fragment
C5	C5	*Spondylus or Chama* sp.	Ground bead
C5	C5	*Spondylus or Chama* sp.	Ground bead
D9	C6	*Pinctada maxima*	Worked and utilised valve
D8	C7–8	*Trochus niloticus*	Ring fragment
D8	C7–8	*Trochus niloticus*	Ring fragment
C7	D3	*Cypraea tigris*	Ground dorsum
C7	D4	*Hippopus hippopus*	Shaped fragment
Buwawansi, Gebe			
B1 Square B	35–40	*Tridacna gigas*	Rib-portion adze
B4/5	Surface find	*Conus* sp.	Complete ring
Tanjung Tulang, Morotai			
N5	15–20	*Placuna placenta*	Shaped valve
N5	15–20	*Melo* sp.	Utilised lip
Siti Nasifah, Halmahera			
F5	A1	*Nautilus* sp.	Cut body fragment

Source: Katherine Szabó.

For sites other than Golo Cave, shell pieces identified as worked were either formal and highly modified artefacts or fragments of known raw materials (e.g. *Turbo marmoratus*, *Pinctada* spp.) with possible evidence of cutting or shaping. Both categories were studied with the aid of a Dino-Lite Premier AD7013MT portable digital microscope to assess finer details of clearly or potentially worked surfaces. The confirmation of a fragment as 'worked' required distinct evidence of tool use, human-mediated fracture or use-wear traces not able to be replicated by the action of taphonomic processes. Human-mediated fracture also potentially took in any shells that were deliberately broken to extract the flesh for consumption, and a discussion of such shells is presented below within the Uattamdi results.

Given that shell midden was available for study for Golo Cave, the analytical procedures followed were different from the other assemblages. Shell from Pleistocene archaeological assemblages is frequently minimally worked, and thus presents obstacles for the identification, analysis, and interpretation of any shell artefacts. An extended discussion of these issues has been presented in Szabó (2013). All shell available from the Golo Cave excavations was studied, and unusually shaped pieces as well as fragments from known major raw materials (e.g. *Tridacna* spp.) were separated for further analysis. In order to assess accurately the presence and nature of shell-working, technological studies (e.g. Szabó et al. 2007), and extensive experimental programs (e.g. Szabó and Koppel 2015) were undertaken, and aspects of these are ongoing.

Results of analysis

Golo Cave

Aspects of the worked shell from Golo Cave have already been the subject of a number of specialist papers (Szabó et al. 2007; Szabó 2013; Szabó and Koppel 2015), which have begun to reveal the extent and nature of early shell-working at the site. This published work will not be reiterated in detail here, but summaries of the findings are given along with additional discussion of other shell artefacts present in the Golo samples and a précis of ongoing research.

During the course of sorting the midden shell, a number of flakes and seemingly shaped pieces of *Turbo marmoratus* operculum were identified. Further investigation confirmed that the large (c. 500 gm in weight) opercula had been deliberately shaped through the removal of sequential flakes from the perimeter using direct percussion (Figs 9.1(a) and 9.1(b)) (Szabó et al. 2007). Some of the resulting flakes also showed signs of retouch (Fig. 9.1(c)). Initially, it was hypothesised that this distinctive knapped shell technology represented a technological transfer from lithic materials in the absence of good stone resources. However, detailed study revealed that the *T. marmoratus* operculum knapping techniques were more complicated and structured than those seen in associated lithic artefacts at Golo Cave. This, coupled with an associated diversity in shell-working technologies in the lowermost levels of the site, confirmed that shell technologies were separate from those seen in stone and that they must have had an ancestry reaching before the initial occupation of Golo Cave.

Also, whilst sorting the midden, a small number of specimens of the common limpet species gathered for consumption (*Scutellastra flexuosa*) were separated for further investigation due to visible rounding of part of the shell margin. This species has a sharp, crenelated margin, and taphonomic assessments as well as experimental fracture tests demonstrated that the damage noted on the shells could not have occurred through these mechanisms (Szabó and Koppel 2015). After an experimental program, which established baseline usewear traces for a variety of material textures, five *S. flexuosa* shells were identified as showing clear modification as a result of sustained human use. As with the *T. marmoratus* operculum artefacts, all of these shells derived from the lowermost Golo Cave deposits. Two shells displayed edge-faceting that indicated they had been used to scrape a hard material, with a further shell having edge rounding consistent with experimental specimens generated through the scraping of fresh bone (Figs 9.2(a) and 9.2(b)). The remaining two specimens had discrete patches of attritional wear on their dorsal surfaces—particularly on the elevated radial ribs. Experimental specimens used to scoop coconut flesh from the shell showed similar wear, but the restriction of abrasion to the elevated rib surfaces with little alteration to the intervening furrows indicates that the material being worked was less malleable than coconut flesh. Full details of all experiments and results are reported in Szabó and Koppel (2015).

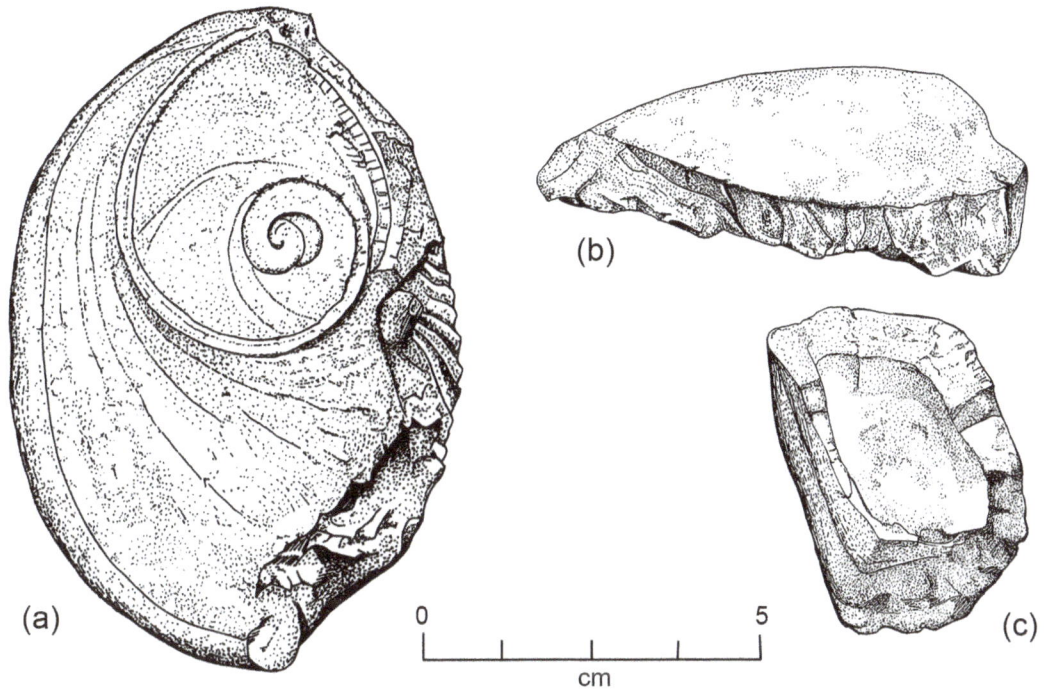

Figure 9.1 Worked *Turbo marmoratus* operculum fragments from Golo Cave.

(a) operculum shaped by sequential flaking of the perimeter, Square L6–M6 200–205 cm; (b) bending-initiated operculum flake, Square M5 230–235 cm; (c) retouched fragment of operculum, Square L6–M6 200–205 cm.

Source: Katherine Szabó, drawings by Fernando Lero.

Figure 9.2 *Scutellastra flexuosa* modified tool from Golo Cave.

(a) limpet modified through use, Square M4 200–205 cm; (b) modified portion of the same specimen at 25x magnification.

Source: Katherine Szabó.

In addition to the expedient *S. flexuosa* tools and the knapped *T. marmoratus* operculum artefacts, a further worked shell was identified from below 190 cm at Golo Cave. A reduced *Turbo marmoratus* shell was recovered from LM6 at 210–220 cm depth, with another excavated from 195–200 cm in the same unit. Both shells have had a hole knocked through the penultimate whorl on the ventral surface, but the 195–200 cm deep example also has extensive reduction of the shell from the aperture back into the body whorl, as well as at the apex and upper whorls (Figs 9.3(a) and 9.3(b)). While the hole in the centre of the shell seems to have been generated through freehand percussion on both specimens, the further reduction seen in the 195–200 cm example has been affected through chipping with a sharp point. The notches from this activity can be seen in Figure 9.3(b).

Between a depth of 100 cm and 140 cm in Golo Cave, five giant clam adzes were recovered during the excavations (Table 2.2 and Fig. 9.4). Three are discussed here,[1] and another large *Tridacna* specimen is illustrated in Figure 8.7 in the previous chapter. Two of the specimens discussed here are manufactured from species of *Tridacna*, and one from *Hippopus hippopus*. All are made from a single rib of a valve, meaning that the cutting edge is slightly convex in profile, mirroring the shape of the shell margin. The choice of this portion of the shell for adze production is typical of preceramic sites in the eastern Indonesia and New Guinea regions (Szabó 2005). Only the poll end is present from the lowermost example recovered from 125–130 cm (Fig. 9.4(c)), but the bevels and cutting edges of both of the other specimens have many striations running perpendicular to the cutting edge (Figs 9.4(b) and 9.4(e)). The poll ends of these specimens also have extensive abrasion and polish on the most elevated portions. The morphology of the polished surfaces indicates that this wear was acquired through the rubbing of hafting apparatus rather than deliberate modification.

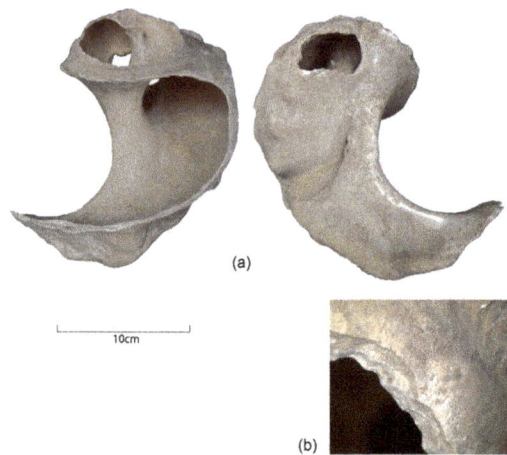

Figure 9.3 Reduced *Turbo marmoratus* shell from Golo Cave, Squares L6–M6 195–200 cm.

Inset shows the chipping near the apex at 10x magnification.

Source: Katherine Szabó.

From a depth of 65 cm upwards to the surface, 10 complete, four partial and one reworked *Cassis cornuta* adzes were recovered in Golo Cave (Fig. 9.5). This is a remarkable assemblage that is unparalleled elsewhere in Southeast Asia, with *C. cornuta* being a raw material more traditionally associated with the Pacific Islands. A number were also found in the upper deposits of Wetef Cave (see Chapter 8). All of the adzes are manufactured from the robust, thickened lip of the shell, with patches of grinding restricted to the bevel and sometimes parts of the lateral edges. The bevels of most specimens seem to have been ground using a cylindrical or convex grinding stone, meaning that the bevels are mostly convex in profile. The bevels are ground from the interior surface of the adze, with a minimum of smoothing on the outer/dorsal surface.

---

1   One *Tridacna* and one *Hippopus* shell adze from Golo were used in an artefact display in the School of Archaeology and Anthropology at ANU, and were inadvertently omitted from the assemblage sent to Katherine Szabó at the University of Wollongong. They are not described in this chapter, but the *Tridacna* specimen is shown in Figure 8.7 (previous chapter).

Figure 9.4 Giant clam adzes from Golo Cave.

(a) *Hippopus hippopus* adze, Square N6 100 cm; (b) usewear striations perpendicular to the cutting edge, *H. hippopus* adze, Square N6 100 cm, 40x magnification; (c) broken *Tridacna* sp. adze, Squares LM6 125–130 cm; (d) *Tridacna* sp. adze, Square M6 100 cm; (e) usewear striations perpendicular to the cutting edge, *Tridacna* sp. adze, Square M6 100 cm, 40x magnification.

Source: Katherine Szabó.

Figure 9.5 *Cassis cornuta* adzes from Golo Cave.

(a) curated adze, Square M9 0–5 cm; (b) adze, Square M6 20–25 cm; (c) adze, Square M6 50–55 cm; (d) impact flakes on bevel of a curated adze, Squares LM6 25–30 cm, 10x magnification.

Source: Katherine Szabó.

During analysis it was noted that two distinct types of *C. cornuta* adzes were present in the assemblage: a larger original form (Figs 9.5(b) and 9.5(c)) and a smaller, curated form with more variable morphology (Fig. 9.5(a)). The curated form sometimes has the bevel ground on a flat grinding slab rather than the convex grindstone detailed above. In total, five of the complete adzes from Golo are curated examples and five are non-curated. The non-curated examples, however, also have clear evidence of usewear at the cutting edge and often the poll, so they are certainly finished and used tools. The curated examples likewise show evidence of use (Fig. 9.5(d)).

Direct AMS radiocarbon dating of a *C. cornuta* adze recovered from Square M5, 30–35 cm, returned an Early Holocene date (OZD773, 9580±70 uncal. BP), which is clearly at odds with its stratigraphic position. Although none of the adzes were made of fossilised shell, as was the case with the preceramic adzes at Duyong Cave in the Philippines (Szabó 2005), it seems likely that subfossil shell was selected for their production. Thus, direct radiocarbon dating will produce spurious archaeological results, as discussed already in Chapter 8.

Two modified *Conus* sp. spires were identified during excavation—both from Square M5 at a depth of 40–45 cm. Both spires show clear evidence of rounding and attrition through the action of coastal taphonomic processes (Zuschin et al. 2003), meaning that both artefacts were collected post-mortem from the strandline as already abraded spires. Despite this, both artefacts show evidence of further modification after initial collection. The first *Conus* sp. spire (Fig. 9.6(a)) is smooth and water-rolled on both the interior and exterior surfaces. However, the apical area has been further smoothed through manual freehand abrasion. The perforation, which could be naturally formed, has been regularised through either deliberate modification or use (Fig. 9.6(b)). The second *Conus* sp. spire (Fig. 9.6(c)) differs from the first in its condition; it has been heavily burnt, which has recrystallised the shell into a blocky texture. Despite this, the apical area also shows additional smoothing (Fig. 9.6(d)).

Figure 9.6 Modified *Conus* sp. spires from Golo Cave, Square M5 40–45 cm.

(a) complete modified spire; (b) detail of perforation of complete spire, 30x magnification; (c) burnt modified spire; (d) detail of perforation of burnt spire, 25x magnification.

Source: Katherine Szabó.

The remaining pieces of worked shell from Golo Cave are a series of cut and/or shaped fragments from *Turbo marmoratus*, *Nautilus* sp. and *Pinctada margaritifera* shell. At present, experimental reduction is being undertaken with all of these taxa to categorically demonstrate the nature of working. *Nautilus* spp. in particular is a material that is dissimilar to other types of shell in that it is comprised of some microstructural types rare in other types of shell (Watabe 1988). Additionally, the shell is mechanically adapted to a range of forces different to that experienced by inshore species. Being pelagic and descending to considerable depths, water pressure is a significant force that *Nautilus* spp. shell is specifically adapted to withstand (Currey 1988:198). None of the fragments of *T. marmoratus*, *P. margaritifera*, or *Nautilus* sp. have enough in the way of shaping to indicate a final form or function. Nevertheless, the presence of cutting as a shell-working technique within both the Pleistocene and Holocene levels of Golo Cave is significant in itself (Szabó 2013).

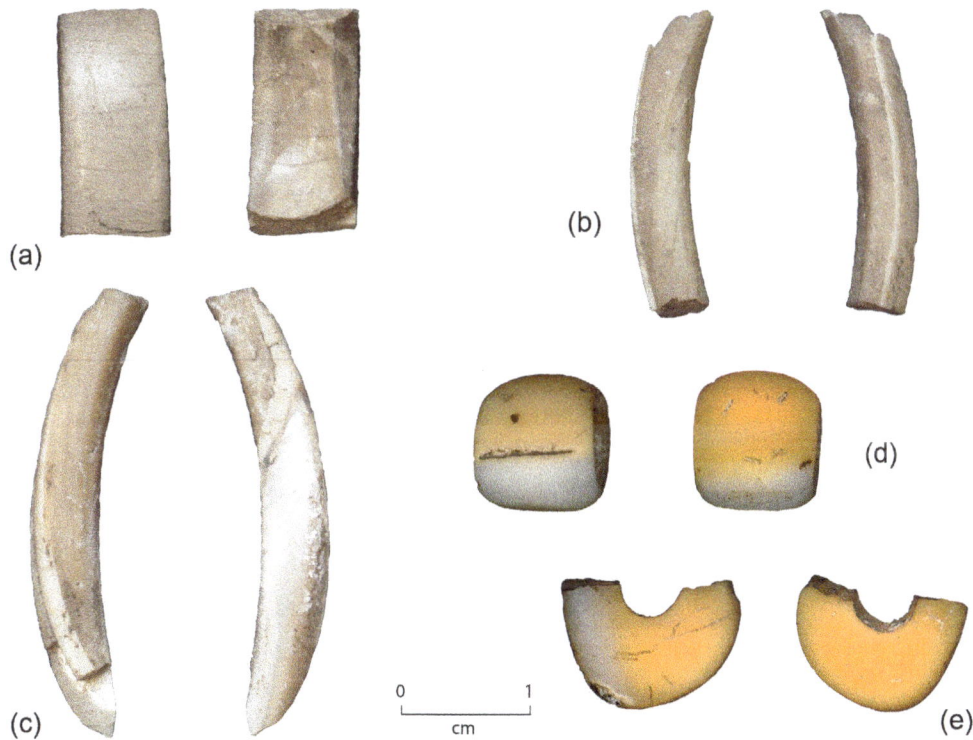

Figure 9.7 Formal shell artefacts from Uattamdi 1.

(a) *Conus* sp. ring fragment, Square D9 Layer C5; (b) and (c) *Trochus niloticus* ring fragments from different rings, Square C8 Layer C7–C8; (d) barrel bead made of *Spondylus* sp. or *Chama* sp., Square C5 Layer C5; (e) broken disc bead made of *Spondylus* sp. or *Chama* sp., Square C5 Layer C5.

Source: Katherine Szabó.

Uattamdi 1

Sixteen shell artefacts were identified during the Uattamdi 1 excavations, including both formal and expedient artefact types. All the artefacts bar one, a shaped and utilised valve of the mangrove pearl oyster *Isognomon isognomum*, derive from the lower Neolithic layer rather than the overlying Early Metal phase deposits. The overall assemblage comprises a mix of formal artefact types and expedient tools. The formal artefacts will be covered first.

Three fragments of *Trochus niloticus* ring, two fragments from Square D8 Layer C7–C8 (Figs 9.7(b) and 9.7(c)) and one from Square C5 Layer C5, were identified during excavation. Measurements indicate that they probably derive from different rings. All three are well-ground and clearly finished and used artefacts. A further ring fragment made from *Conus* sp. shell was excavated from Square D9 Layer C5 (Fig. 9.7(a)), and is also well polished and worn. Two unusual beads were also recovered from Uattamdi Layer C. They are both manufactured in the same material, with the orange-and-white mottling and surface texture suggesting that either a species of *Spondylus* or *Chama* was the raw material used. One is a squat barrel bead, fully ground and drilled end to end (Fig. 9.7(d)), and the other is half of a disc bead that is rather wedge-shaped in profile with non-parallel faces (Fig. 9.7(e)). Both are also shown in Figure 8.8. These beads have no analogues at the other Northern Moluccan sites or indeed elsewhere in Southeast Asia.

A series of dorsa from the large cowrie *Cypraea tigris* was collected from Uattamdi. In the Pacific, these are frequently—and controversially—described as 'octopus lures' based on Polynesian ethnographic examples. Archaeological specimens, however, rarely show signs of the modifications seen in the ethnohistorical artefacts, such as perforations through which to lash the cowrie dorsa to the central cane around which they are fastened. Spennemann (1993) investigated patterns of cowrie breakage in natural coastal settings and found that many modified cowries assumed to be tools could be regarded as the results of natural breakage patterns. Cowries are also collected for consumption, and given the narrow morphology of the aperture, breakage to extract the meat is common (Spennemann 1993). Experimental work undertaken as a part of my doctoral thesis (Szabó 2005) showed that it was easy to remove the dorsum of a large *Cypraea* shell with a single blow with a hammerstone to the anterior or posterior of the shell. Spennemann, recording breakage for meat extraction in Tonga, notes that in recent times an iron rod is driven through the shell and then the hole widened to extract the animal (Spennemann 1993:46). All but two examples of *Cypraea tigris* dorsa recovered from Uattamdi show no grinding, abrasion, or deliberate perforation. Indeed, most specimens show a rough notch at either the anterior or posterior end, surrounded by a zone of crushing, which indicates the dorsa were removed through the application of a single blow (Fig. 9.8(f)).

Of the two examples that show definite signs of modification beyond meat extraction, one was found in the spoil from the excavation of Square D1. Two small, parallel pierced perforations are positioned at one end of the dorsum, but given the lack of context little of interpretive value can be stated. The second is one of the deepest pieces of worked shell recovered from excavations at Uattamdi, and one of only two from Layer D (Square C7 Layer D3). A *C. tigris* dorsum, polished through handling, has been ground around the perimeter of the break surface (Fig. 9.8(a)). The angles and regularity indicate that it was ground on a flat grinding slab, although subsequent handling wear has muted and rounded the corners (Fig. 9.8(b)). There are no perforations or indications of lashing, nor do any of the edges show usewear associated with a scraping or peeling function, so its function remains unknown.

As with large cowrie shells, *Pinctada* spp. pearl oyster valves are sometimes classified as scrapers or peelers based, most commonly, on ethnographic analogy and sometimes confirmed through observations of usewear. At Uattamdi, two valves of the Golden-lipped Pearl Oyster, *Pinctada maxima*, as well as two valves of the Mangrove Pearl Oyster, *Isognomon isognomum*, have distinct modifications resulting from extended use as expedient tools. The two *P. maxima* shells are near-complete valves (Fig. 9.8(d)), with usewear striations along one or more zones of the margin (Fig. 9.8(e)) and deliberate abrasion at the hinge area to remove rough surfaces when the valve is gripped. The striations run parallel to the margin, indicating a cutting rather than scraping function. *I. isognomum* valves are less robust than *P. maxima* shells, but one near-complete valve (Square C7 Layer B6) has similar modifications to those seen in *P. maxima*, while the other worked *I. isognomum* shell (Square D4 Layer C2) has had the hinge end deliberately removed with the margins being shaped to create a spoon-like morphology. On all four valves the outer, dull prismatic exterior layer of shell has been purposefully removed, leaving only the mother of pearl layers.

Figure 9.8 Informal and expedient artefacts from Uattamdi 1.

(a) ground *Cypraea tigris* dorsum, Square C7 Layer D3; (b) detail of grinding on *C. tigris* dorsum, 40x magnification; (c) shaped *Nautilus* sp. septal wall fragment, Square D4 Layer C3; (d) *Pinctada maxima* knife, Square D9 Layer C6; (e) detail of striations parallel to edge on *P. margaritifera* knife, 30x magnification; (f) unworked *C. tigris* dorsum showing evidence of breakage for meat extraction, Square D8 Layer C5.

Source: Katherine Szabó.

Also in mother of pearl, but manufactured from *Nautilus* sp. shell, is a cut, oval fragment (Fig. 9.8(c)). It has been made from one of the inner septal (chamber) walls, with the perforation being the natural hole created by the animal to accommodate the siphuncal tube through which it regulates buoyancy. The edges of the siphuncal hole are still sharp, indicating that this artefact has seen little or no use.

A small selection of shells from other species have minor evidence of working, including a cut piece of the thin oyster relative *Placuna ephippium*, a hinge fragment of a *Hippopus hippopus* valve showing some signs of direct percussion, and a margin fragment of the common bivalve *Asaphis violascens* with deliberate knapping along the margin. Provenance details for these artefacts are given in Table 9.1.

Buwawansi

Two shell artefacts were recovered from Buwawansi. A large *Tridacna gigas* adze (Fig. 9.9(a)) is very thick and robust with a very curved cutting edge. It has been manufactured from a single rib from the thickest portion of the shell close to the hinge. The bevel area is most intensively abraded—through both deliberate modification and use—with other portions of the adze showing less attrition. The area around the poll shows high polish and abrasion of the surfaces in highest relief (Fig. 9.9(b)), and this wear pattern is most probably associated with hafting. The pit-marks on the outer surface derive from the action of marine bioeroders, including *Cliona* spp. sponges and *Lithophaga* boring mussels, on the original raw material rather than being caused by post-depositional processes.

The second artefact is a complete *Conus* sp. ring (Fig. 9.9(c)). Although it appears unfinished, with much of the second whorl still present along the interior surface, edge-rounding indicates that it has been worn extensively.

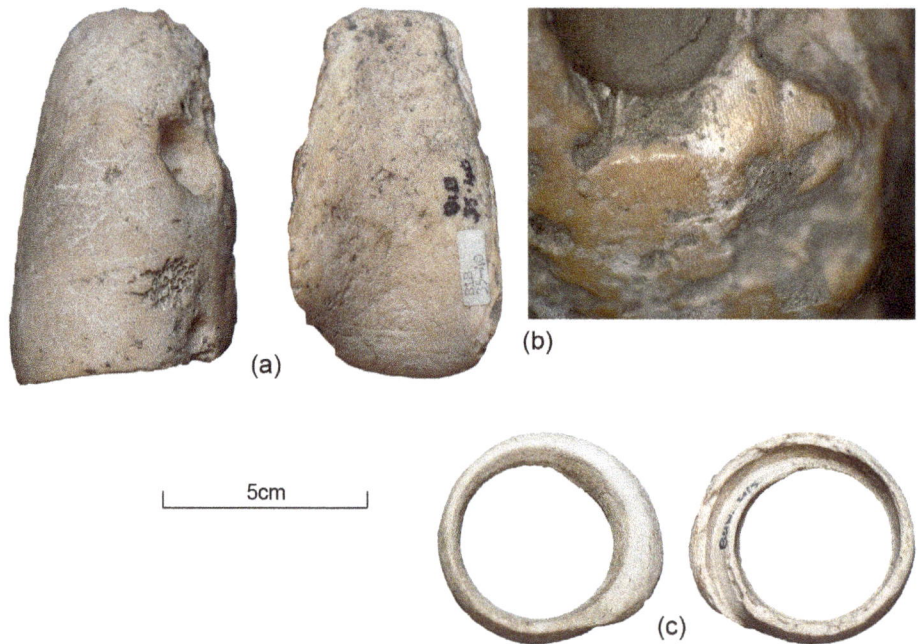

Figure 9.9 Shell artefacts from Buwawansi.

(a) *Tridacna gigas* adze, Square B 35-40 cm; (b) detail of polish and abrasion at poll end of adze, 30x magnification; (c) *Conus* sp. ring, surface find.

Source: Katherine Szabó.

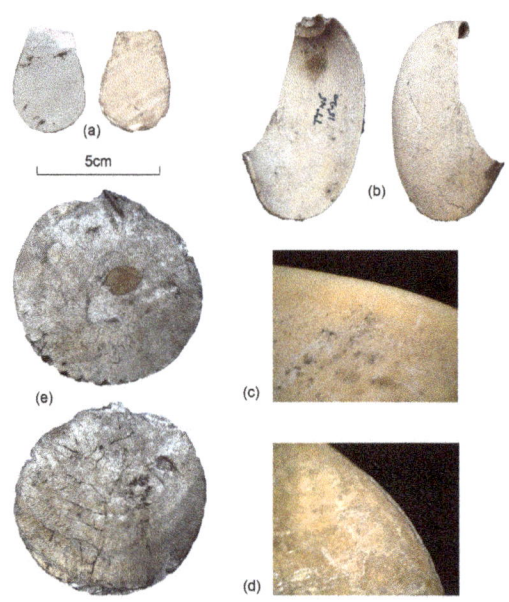

Figure 9.10 Worked shell from Gua Siti Nafisah and Tanjung Tulang.

(a) cut *Nautilus* sp. fragment, Gua Siti Nafisah Square F5 Layer A1; (b) *Melo* sp. scraper/peeler, Tanjung Tulang Square N5 15–20 cm; (c) detail of rounding at lip of *Melo* sp. scraper/peeler, 25x magnification; (d) detail of trimmed edge of *Placuna placenta* disc, 20x magnification; (e) *Placuna placenta* trimmed disc, Tanjung Tulang Square N5 15–20 cm on bedrock.

Source: Katherine Szabó.

Gua Siti Nafisah

A single piece of worked shell was identified from Gua Siti Nafisah. A teardrop-shaped cut fragment of *Nautilus* sp. was identified from the uppermost deposits in Square F5 (Fig. 9.10(a)). It is cut from the body of the shell, and the outer cream-coloured shell layer is still present. Beyond the cutting there is no further evidence of modification, either through working or use.

Tanjung Tulang

Only two pieces of worked shell were recovered from the Tanjung Tulang deposits. Both came from a depth of 15–20 cm in Square N5. The first is a section of body whorl from a small *Melo* sp. shell that retains the lip (Fig. 9.10(b)). A closer look at the central portion of the lip reveals edge-rounding and polish, with this attrition extending a couple inward into the body whorl (Fig. 9.10(c)). Although no striations are visible, this broad section of rounding and shell removal fits better with an explanation of use as a scraper or peeler than as a knife.

The second is a solid disc shaped from a complete *Placuna placenta* valve (Fig. 9.10(e)). The edges of *P. placenta* valves are highly lamellar, thin, and fragile in their natural state, and the edges of this valve have been deliberately trimmed so that the edge is both regular and more robust (Fig. 9.10(d)). There are no further indications of modification or use.

Discussion

One of the most notable aspects of the worked shell assemblages from the various Moluccan sites is the diversity in raw materials used. Many of the commonly encountered molluscan raw materials of the Island Asia-Pacific region are present, including giant clams, *Trochus niloticus*, *Turbo marmoratus*, *Nautilus* sp., and *Conus* sp., but less widespread raw materials (e.g. *Cassis cornuta, Isognomon isognomum*) appear to have had a clear role in local shell-working traditions as well. Some of these lesser-seen raw materials were used in specific locations elsewhere in the Island Asia-Pacific region, as discussed further below. The relatively large number of expedient or minimally modified artefacts expands the roster of raw materials even further.

The expedient use of shell for undertaking everyday tasks is sometimes perceived to be haphazard in the selection of raw material, simply taking a convenient shell from associated midden deposits. But the general patterning in expedient tool materials in the Northern Moluccan assemblages would seem to argue otherwise. In the earliest deposits at Golo Cave, *Scutellastra flexuosa* shells were repeatedly recycled for use from midden deposits (Szabó and Koppel 2015). The recurrent use of pearl oysters—both *Pinctada* and *Isognomon*—at Uattamdi is also suggestive. Both genera were only minimally modified, with the outer, dull prismatic layer being removed and sections of the margin being trimmed where necessary to enhance functionality. It would certainly be interesting to assess the relationship between expedient shell tool raw material choice with bigger samples of worked shell, as well as associated midden shell, to build up a picture of available resources.

There is minimal evidence for the production of formal shell artefacts at either Golo Cave or Uattamdi, with no débitage associated with the production of either giant clam or *Cassis cornuta* adzes, or *Trochus niloticus* or *Conus* sp. rings. This, however, does not mean that the production of these artefacts was not local—perhaps it was just taking place elsewhere on the nearby landscape. The standardised patterns in curation noted for the *C. cornuta* adzes at Golo Cave show that there were clear formalised traditions of artefact (re)working.

There are no molluscan raw materials that are present at all of the sites from which shell artefacts were recovered. The most ubiquitous raw material, being present at Golo Cave, Uattamdi and Gua Siti Natisaf, is *Nautilus* sp. This taxon also has the greatest longevity as a raw material based on the current evidence. As discussed above, we understand little about the finer features of *Nautilus* spp. shell as a raw material and, due to this, worked examples across the region are likely under-reported. Preceramic *Nautilus* spp. working has been recorded for Timor Leste (Glover 1986; O'Connor 2010) and Flores (van den Bergh et al. 2009) in Island Southeast Asia, and in sites on the islands of Buka and Manus in Papua New Guinea (Szabó 2005). Timor is currently the only location from which finished artefacts have been recovered and at all other locations the end points of working are currently unclear.

Aside from the intermittent appearance of worked *Nautilus* sp. shell at three sites, there was little perceptible persistence of Moluccan shell-working traditions through time. The use of *Turbo marmoratus* was virtually restricted to the Pleistocene, and giant clam use a feature of the Holocene. The use of *Cassis cornuta*, based on stratigraphic positioning, was focused upon the last few thousand years, and the current evidence of *Trochus niloticus* and *Conus* spp. use suggests a similar time depth. There is certainly no evidence at present for a preceramic lineage of local shell-working for *Conus* sp. and *T. niloticus*. These temporal horizons in approaches to shell-working and raw material selection suggest that innovations and influences were dynamic through time, and that the conservative traditions of shell-working in locations such as Timor were not a feature of the Northern Moluccan record.

As well as clear differences in shell-working traditions through time in the Northern Moluccas, there were also distinct spatial differences. Temporally, there is no analogue for Golo Cave in the Northern Moluccas outside of Gebe Island, so comparisons are difficult. The nearby Wetef rockshelter, with a similar sequence, did not have depositional conditions conducive to the preservation of worked shell before the Holocene. In the Holocene deposits at Wetef, however, *C. cornuta* lip adzes were also recovered.[2]

Conversely, Uattamdi on Kayoa Island has provided the only evidence from the Northern Moluccas of *Trochus niloticus* working; a taxon that is of central importance to shell-working across Island Southeast Asia and the western Pacific. It is also the only site in Island Southeast Asia to have yielded beads manufactured in *Spondylus/Chama* shell. Beads identified as having been produced in *Spondylus* sp. shell have been identified for some Early Lapita deposits (Kirch 1988), and this shell was also widely used in Micronesia at a rather later date (e.g. Weisler 2000).

Current evidence thus suggests that there is much diversity between the shell-working traditions of different islands and areas within the Northern Moluccas, which in turn implies that their histories of cultural influence, innovation, and contact have been different. Indeed, given the number of islands it would be surprising if local histories and trajectories were not somewhat different. It may be significant that the *C. cornuta* adzes from Golo Cave and Wetef share much stylistically with *C. cornuta* adzes found in sites in Micronesia, Polynesia, and post-Lapita Melanesia. This putative link, however, does not seem to extend beyond Gebe Island to the rest of the Northern Moluccas, and this may matter when trying to reconstruct patterns of ancient contact and influence.

The worked shell samples from the Northern Moluccan excavations are not especially large, but they are diverse and instructive. It is clear that this region has had dynamic shell-working traditions stretching back to the earliest-known deposits. Indeed, the variety and skill in shell-working displayed within the earliest deposits at Golo Cave indicates that shell-working practices were already well-developed by this point. Waves of innovation are seen periodically, when new materials, artefact types, and ideas become manifest in a change in the material record. At the moment there are several large temporal gaps in our understanding of Northern Moluccan shell-working, and the spatial diversity seen in known shell-working traditions also suggests there is much to learn by focusing on, and comparing, individual islands. The Golo Cave assemblage has already transformed the way we think about, identify, and interpret Pleistocene shell-working in Island Southeast Asia. Further samples from this critical locale will undoubtedly add still more to our knowledge of cultural development at the interface of Southeast Asia and the Pacific.

Acknowledgements

Thanks to Brent Koppel, University of Wollongong, for his assistance in the photography and reanalysis of many of the Moluccan shell artefacts. Thanks also to Peter Bellwood for information about the assemblages and the opportunity to study them.

---

2   These *C. cornuta* adzes are currently restricted to Gebe Island and Flores (Galipaud et al. 2016) within the Island Southeast Asian archaeological record (Editor).

10

Observations on the Northern Moluccan excavated animal bone and shell collections

Jennifer R. Hull, Philip Piper, Geoffrey Irwin, Katherine Szabó, Annette Oertle, and Peter Bellwood

Due to their isolation, the Northern Moluccan islands today contain only a very impoverished and mainly marsupial indigenous Wallacean vertebrate fauna that includes the cuscuses *Phalanger ornatus* and *Phalanger alexandriae* (Flannery and Boeadi 1995), the sugar glider *Petaurus breviceps* (not found so far in any archaeological contexts in the Northern Moluccas), and the large placental rodent *Rattus morotaiensis* (Flannery 1995a). These species have been supplemented by several humanly mediated introductions of placental mammal species, such as *Rattus exulans*, *R. tanezumi*, *Suncus marinus*, *Paradoxurus hermaphroditus*, *Cervis timorensis*, plus pigs and dogs (Flannery et al. 1995).

The 1990s excavations in the Moluccas produced several substantial vertebrate assemblages dating to the late Pleistocene and Holocene. The initial report on the assemblage from Gua Siti Nafisah on Halmahera was published in 1995 (Flannery et al. 1995), in which an extinct wallaby (*Dorcopsis* sp.) and a bandicoot related to the *Echymipera/Rhynchomeles* group found in the Holocene deposits of that cave were described as 'quite unexpected', and reported as occurring with the extant Moluccan cuscus species *Phalanger ornatus*. The opinion was expressed that the two extinct marsupial species were probably 'indigenous elements in the fauna'. The succeeding report (Flannery et al. 1998) announced the further discovery of wallaby bones in Golo Cave and Wetef rockshelter on Gebe, and of *Rattus morotaiensis* on Morotai.

This second report established that the wallaby was not found on Kayoa or Morotai (hence, so far only on Halmahera and Gebe), and that the bandicoot was only found in Gua Siti Nafisah on Halmahera. Further, the main author, Tim Flannery, suggested on the basis of his dental comparisons that the Halmahera and Gebe wallaby species was sufficiently close in its dentition to an extant indigenous wallaby species (*Dorcopsis muelleri mysoliae*) on Misool Island, southwest of the Bird's Head of Papua, to represent a deliberate human translocation, possibly from there. The absence of this taxon from the modern Northern Moluccan fauna and its apparently abrupt Early Holocene appearance in the archaeological record of Gebe Island thus raised important questions about the origin of this species, the potential timing of its introduction to Gebe, and the reasons for its eventual extinction.

The proposed deliberate introduction of *D. muelleri* on to Halmahera and Gebe Islands has played a pivotal role in arguments supporting human mediated animal translocation in the Late Pleistocene and Early Holocene in Wallacea and Melanesia, and the implications for behavioural complexity as expressed through seafaring (Bellwood et al. 1998; Matisoo-Smith 2007). No similar suggestions of translocation were made for the bandicoot, since the sample size was so small.

Part 1: Animal bones: All sites except Wetef (Jennifer R. Hull, Philip Piper, and Peter Bellwood)

Methods

This study deals with all the animal bones from seven sites: Tanjung Pinang with Daeo Caves 1 and 2 (Morotai Island), Uattamdi (Kayoa Island), Um Kapat Papo and Golo (Gebe Island), and Siti Nafisah (Halmahera Island). These sites provided the raw data for the Master's thesis completed at The Australian National University (ANU) by Jennifer R. Hull in 2014, under the supervision of Philip Piper and Peter Bellwood (Hull 2014). The Wetef fauna is described later in this chapter by Geoffrey Irwin. The emphases in this section are on taphonomy, tooth wear and eruption sequences, age profiling, degrees of fragmentation, and taxonomic identification of species. Altogether, a total of 16,984 fragments of bone were recovered from these seven sites, which are described individually in Chapters 2 to 5. The identifications and counts by Jennifer R. Hull for Golo Cave on Gebe are given in Tables 10.1 to 10.3.

A taphonomic analysis of the bone from each site was undertaken to identify the pre- and post-depositional processes that might have influenced preservation, following Behrensmeyer (1978) and Lyman (1994). Weathering stages were adapted from Behrensmeyer (1978) and recorded for all fragments. High-resolution images of important taphonomic indicators, significant teeth, and other selected elements were obtained with a Canon EOS 60D camera with extension tubes and a Canon EOS 700D with a 100 mm macro lens. A light microscope was used for a more detailed analysis of tooth wear and eruption sequences. Unless modern breakage was detected, maximum length was recorded for each fragment to identify fragmentation patterns. Diagnostic elements of bone were identified to the highest taxonomic level possible, using the mammal skeletal reference collections housed in the School of Archaeology and Anthropology in the ANU and the Australian Museum in Sydney, and also the fish bone comparative collection in the School of Archaeology and Natural History in the ANU.

For *Dorcopsis*, measurements of all the complete archaeological teeth were taken in terms of buccal–lingual breadth of the mesial and distal columns, and molar crown length measured from cingulum to cingulum (Pasveer 2004). These dental measurements were compared with those of dentitions of known species of *Dorcopsis* held in the storage facility at the Australian Museum in Sydney. The data were used in a series of multivariate discriminant function analyses that compared M1 and M2, M1 and M3, and M2 and M3. The aim was to determine whether the now-extirpated Gebe Island wallaby bore any metrical relationship with known extant species of wallaby. These statistical analyses were applied following Groves and Flannery (1989). For the age profiling of the assemblage, tooth eruption sequences were analysed using standards based on the detailed descriptions of eruption stages presented by van Deusen (1957). This scheme took into consideration both tooth development and eruption.

Pasveer (2004) identified seven tooth wear stages within an assemblage of *Dorcopsis muelleri* recovered from the Ayamaru region of the Bird's Head Peninsula that permitted the wear of each individual tooth to be analysed and recorded. Stage 1 shows wear but no exposed dentine, and stage 7 is where the entire surface of the tooth is a dentine 'pool'. For this study, we also included a wear stage 0, whereby the tooth exhibits no wear. Also, it was noted during the study that the molars tend to wear on the buccal lophs before the lingual, and as such the wear stages have been adapted to this description. These data enabled the determination of adult age structure as well as the developmental stages from tooth eruption data (see also Pasveer 2004) of the *Dorcopsis* community recovered from the various cave sites in the Northern Moluccas.

Taphonomic observations

Golo Cave, Gebe Island

The Golo Cave excavations produced a total of 6364 fragments of animal bone, divided between two trenches (LMN4–7, number of identified specimens (NISP): 5467; and H4–H5, NISP: 887) created from a grid of 1 m squares. Golo Squares LMN4–7 were excavated to bedrock at 240 cm. The vertebrate remains were concentrated here between 15–20 cm and 80–85 cm, and only continued to a maximum depth of 135 cm, despite cultural materials continuing to bedrock at 240 cm (Table 2.2, second column from left). Golo Squares H4 and H5 were only excavated to 90 cm and 140 cm respectively owing to the high level of the bedrock in this location, and faunal remains were not present in either below 90 cm. Golo Cave thus has no surviving animal bone from its lower layers below 135 cm, for reasons that currently remain unknown.

In Square M6 there was some evidence of mixing in the sequence, with a small concentration of modern yellow bone of unidentified mammal origin present at 30–40 cm, also in M4 at 55–60 cm. There were also fragments of mammal long bone, an acetabulum (M7, 70–75 cm) and two ribs (M5, 40–45 cm), with apparent iron oxide staining. Trench H4–H5, however, was mixed throughout with modern yellow fragments of bone from a variety of taxa.

Figure 10.1 *Dorcopsis* mandible from Golo H5, 40-45 cm, with stage 5 weathering and calcium carbonate concretion.
Source: Jennifer R. Hull.

Generally, modifications associated with sub-aerial weathering of bone in LMN4–7 were present, but fairly minimal at stages 1 or 2 (Behrensmeyer 1978), perhaps indicating relatively short exposure prior to burial. However, below 40 cm depth the proportion of bones demonstrating weathering at stage 3 and above increased. An overwhelming majority of bones in H4 H5 were highly weathered, at stage 3 or higher. This indicates that many bones in this trench probably spent a considerable duration of time in the sub-aerial zone prior to their eventual burial. Many bones also had concretions resulting from precipitation of calcium carbonate dissolved in percolating ground water (Fig. 10.1).

Burnt bone occurred throughout LMN4–7, with the highest frequency below 30 cm. Fully calcined bone occurred mostly between 30 and 70 cm. Much of the H4–5 assemblage was highly burnt, occasionally to a blue or white colour, but no concentrations of burnt bone were found. There was also evidence of butchery on several *Dorcopsis*, phalanger, lizard and pig bones, and on other unidentified mammal fragments. These cut marks occurred predominantly on limb bones and pelvic fragments.

Um Kapat Papo (UKP), Gebe Island

UKP yielded 566 fragments of animal bone that continued down to the fairly shallow bedrock at a maximum of 85 cm. This site had much less reworking in terms of bone weathering stages than Golo, with light-coloured modern bones concentrated towards the surface and darker brown bones apparently contemporary with their stratigraphic depths below. Also consistent with a more stable environment is the observation that the entire UKP assemblage is at weathering stage 3 or lower, with the majority of bones at stage 1. There was also a much lower concentration of burnt bone compared to Golo, and no calcium carbonate concretions on the bones. There are also signs of butchery at UKP—for example, a cut mark found on the antero-lateral margin close to the distal articular end of a phalanger humerus. This likely represents an attempt to separate the humerus from the radius and ulna during carcass dismemberment.

Tanjung Pinang, Morotai Island

Only 213 fragments of animal bone were recovered from Tanjung Pinang rockshelter, and whilst the trench was excavated to a depth of 240 cm, no animal bone or evidence of human occupation was recovered from Layer 2, below 80–85 cm (Chapter 3). The admixture of pieces of bone varying in colour from light yellowish-brown to dark brown in the upper 25–30 cm suggests considerable reworking of deposits. Low weathering stages (mostly stage 1) were recorded throughout the sequence, except in the upper few centimetres where higher stages were recorded, but there were no calcium carbonate concretions. No butchery or other forms of human modification to bones were identified in the assemblage, despite relatively high abundances of phalanger and fish bones.

Daeo Caves 1 and 2, Morotai Island

Daeo Cave 1 produced just 16 fragments of light yellowish-brown bone concentrated in the upper horizons. The majority demonstrated some significant weathering at stage 3, suggesting subaerial exposure. No butchery or other humanly mediated modifications were recorded, nor were there any calcium carbonate concretions.

Daeo Cave 2 produced 2145 bone fragments, varying in colour from light brown higher up to dark brown at greater depth. Some reworking and vertical movement was evident, with light coloured and apparently young yellowish-brown fragments of bone recorded to depths of 80–85 cm. The majority of bones were weathered at stage 1, suggesting only limited exposure to subaerial weathering. Three fragments of phalanger and one fragment of unidentifiable fish bone were heavily concreted with calcium carbonate. Lightly burnt fragments of bone were restricted to 15–20 cm and 75–80 cm.

Gua Siti Nafisah, Halmahera Island

Gua Siti Nafisah produced a total of 6727 bone fragments distributed between Squares F5–F8 (6441), E12 (45), and J10 (241). Deposit reworking is revealed by the modern yellow and older brown fragments found together throughout the sequence, with no apparent concentrations. Square F6 contained the highest numbers of reworked bones. There was consistent evidence of low sub-aerial weathering, with all levels containing high levels of stage 1. There were also relatively few fragments with calcium carbonate concretion, although they did appear in small pockets in spits C3, D2–D3, and E2. Cut marks occurred on the long bones of phalanger, predominantly from the 'sink area' along the southern wall of the cave entrance (Fig. 10.2) and in spit A8 of Square F6. They occurred also on bones of *Dorcopsis* (in F6 spit A4 and F8 spit D1), pig (from J10 extension, Layer C2), and reptiles.

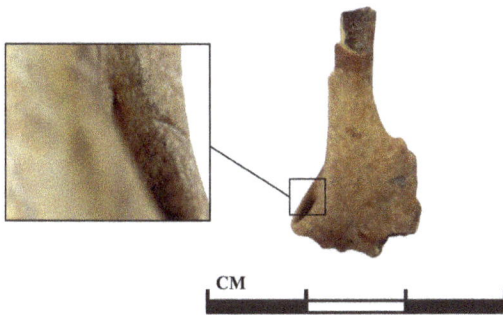

Figure 10.2 Phalanger humerus fragment from Gua Siti Nafisah (F6, sink area against cave wall) with cut mark on the medial margin of the distal end.

Source: Jennifer R. Hull.

Uattamdi, Kayoa Island

The 1244 bone fragments recovered from Uattamdi show consistent mixing between layers, and have the highest average fragment dimension, at 58.79 mm. The overwhelming majority of the fragments have stage 1 weathering, indicating rapid burial with no post-depositional taphonomic processes affecting integrity. There are no calcium carbonate concretions or evidence of butchery. The stratigraphy reveals ash layers at the top of Layer A, middle and bottom of Layer C, and the middle of Layer D, consistent with the distribution of burnt faunal remains.

Taxonomic identifications

Golo Cave, Gebe Island

In Golo Squares LMN4–7, 868 out of the total of 5467 fragments could be identified to family or higher taxonomic level (Tables 10.1–10.3). These include Osteichthyes and Elasmobranchii (NISP: 85), Reptilia (NISP: 74), *Dorcopsis* (minimum number of individuals (MNI): 21; NISP: 358), phalanger (MNI: 20; NISP: 229), Chiroptera (NISP: 96), Muridae (NISP: 16), *Sus* cf. *scrofa* (NISP: 7) and *Canis familiaris* (NISP: 2).

The *Dorcopsis* remains are dominated by fragments of upper limbs, crania, and pelves, and smaller numbers of elements such as scapulae, lower limb bones, tarsals, and vertebrae that may suggest entire carcasses were being transported to the site. The pig remains occur at 5–10 and 10–15 cm, in possible association with the supine and ochre-covered human burial directly dated to 2314–1415 cal. BP (Table 1.1, ANU 11818). There are also three possible pig fragments at 65–70 cm, but these are likely a result of disturbance. The only two dog bones from Golo were found at 50–55 and 85–90 cm, although the deeper fragment may be a modern intrusion. The *Dorcopsis* bones in this trench extended from 10–15 to 90–95 cm, with a single fragment at 100–115 cm. The uppermost fragments may have associated dates with the human burial mentioned above, and the closest associated date for the lowest fragments is from a *Nerita* marine shell dated to 12,044–11,376 cal. BP (M5 135–140 cm, Table 1.1, ANU 9769). Of the fish, two families and one sub-class were identifiable: *Serranidae*, *Scaridae*, and *Elasmobranchii*, respectively.

In Golo Squares H4–H5, 887 bone fragments were recovered. Fish remains were quite common throughout the sequence, with the highest numbers per spit (>100) between 30–35 and 50–55 cm. Below 50–55 cm, fish bones diminished in number until disappearance at 80–90 cm. *Dorcopsis* bones (MNI: 24; NISP: 150) were recorded from 25–30 cm to 75–80 cm, with a peak at 30–35 cm. Sixty-two fragments of *Dorcopsis* dentition were recovered: 45 mandibular and 17 maxillary. The *Dorcopsis* remains in this trench are also dominated by cranial and lower limb fragments. The presence of various other skeletal elements may suggest that entire carcasses were being transported to the site. The youngest phalanger bones (MNI: 6; NISP: 23) were recorded at 30–35 cm, with the highest frequency at 40–45 cm. A phalanger ulna and a *Dorcopsis* maxilla were both recorded at 80–90 cm, these being the lowest bones recovered from the sequence.

In order to verify the ages of some of the deepest and potentially oldest fragments of *Dorcopsis* at Golo, eight dental fragments were sent to the ANU AMS Radiocarbon Laboratory for C14 testing. Unfortunately, nitrogen testing of the bone indicated that insufficient collagen remained to provide an accurate date. However, two specimens were successfully dated using tooth enamel, a right maxillary fragment containing a fully erupted sequence of M2–M4 from 75–80 cm, and a left maxillary fragment containing a fully erupted P4 from 80–90 cm. These produced dates of 7675–7515 (S-ANU 36407) and 7982–7738 cal. BP (S-ANU 36409) respectively (Table 1.1).

It is recognised that tooth enamel dates are often younger than expected, due to the presences of unremoved contaminants (Zazzo 2014; Zazzo and Saliège 2011). In his recent synthesis of dates on unburnt apatite, Zazzo (2014) found that during the Holocene they are normally a few hundred C14 years too young, and beyond 8000 BP this error increases substantially (Zazzo 2014:Table 4, Figure 11). Therefore, the enamel dates for Golo *Dorcopsis* teeth should be considered minimum ages only. Nevertheless, the dating achieved the objective of demonstrating that *Dorcopsis* was present on Gebe Island from the Early Holocene onwards. Attention can also be also drawn to the two direct C14 dates on wallaby bone from Wetef rockshelter, discussed below by Geoffrey Irwin in this chapter. These are 6487–6182 (NZA 8387) and a surprisingly young 906–570 cal. BP (NZA 8369).

Table 10.1 Reptile and fish remains from Golo LMN4-7, recorded by number of individual specimens (NISP) and depth (cm).

Depth	Reptile		Fish				Unid. all bone
	Monitor Lizard	Snake	Scaridae	Serranidae	Elasmobranchi	Unid. fish bones	
0-5							1
5-10							
10-15						1	2
15-20		2				6	27
20-25	1	2				1	62
25-30	5	3				1	168
30-35	13	4		1		9	256
35-40	3	6	1			11	39
40-45	3	14		1	1	17	25
45-50	2	1			1	3	21
50-55	6	1			1	7	63
55-60		2				6	29
60-65	1	4				3	59
65-70							4
70-75							13
75-80						1	9
80-85	1						
85-90						4	
90-95						3	
95-100			2				1
100-105							
105-110							1
110-115				1		1	1
115-120						1	
120-125							
125-130							
130-135						1	
Totals	35	39	3	3	3	76	781

The right-hand column shows unidentified (unid.) remains of all species too fragmentary for any higher identification.
Source: Jennifer R. Hull.

Table 10.2 Mammal bones from Golo LMN4–7, recorded by number of individual specimens (NISP) and depth (cm).

Depth	*Dorcopsis*	Phalanger	Dog	Pig	Muridae	Peramelidae	Megachiroptera	Unid. mammal bone
?	24	2						20
0–5								5
5–10		1		1				11
10–15	4	2		3				27
15–20	17	13						90
20–25	16	23					11	84
25–30	33	27			1		4	262
30–35	38	34			2		37	525
35–40	68	49			3		1	786
40–45	63	33			2		17	773
45–50	10	6			5		1	295
50–55	22	19	1				3	325
55–60	20	8					6	200
60–65	10	5					5	183
65–70	12	4		3		1	1	74
70–75	7	1			1			38
75–80							1	24
80–85	6							24
85–90	2		1				3	28
90–95	2	2					3	17
95–100								8
100–105					1		1	4
105–110								3
110–115	1							7
115–120					1			
120–125								1
125–130								1
130–135							2	3
Total	358	229	2	7	16	1	96	3818

The counts presented here differ slightly from those in Flannery et al. (1998:Table 2) for reasons that are not entirely clear, but that may relate to differing analyst decisions about ambiguous fragments, plus the possibility that some specimens have been removed since the original bags were brought to Australia. The 1998 counts were also for post-cranial bones only.

Source: Jennifer R. Hull.

Table 10.3 Animal bones from Golo H4–H5, recorded by number of individual specimens (NISP) and depth (cm).

Depth	Reptile		Fish		Mammal					Unid. all bone
	Monitor lizard	Snake	Scaridae	Unid. fish	Pteropodidae	*Dorcopsis*	Phalanger	Muridae	Unidentified mammal	
0–5						1				
5–10				2						5
10–15				1						1
15–20				7	1				1	6
20–25		1		6						6
25–30				1		3			1	12
30–35	1					40	5		41	52
35–40				13	2	33	9	2	22	84
40–45				5		33	2	1	24	93

Depth	Reptile		Fish		Mammal					Unid. all bone
	Monitor lizard	Snake	Scaridae	Unid. fish	Pteropodidae	Dorcopsis	Phalanger	Muridae	Unidentified mammal	
45–50			1	2		12	1		52	60
50–55	1	1		3		13	5	1	33	69
55–60				1		6	1		15	5
60–65				1		3			20	7
65–70						1			2	7
70–75						1		2	3	2
75–80				1		3			15	5
80–85										
85–90				1		1	1		12	
90–95										
95–100										
Total	2	2	1	44	3	150	24	6	241	414

The right-hand column shows unidentified (unid.) remains of all species too fragmentary for any higher identification.

Source: Jennifer R. Hull.

Figure 10.3 Three *Dorcopsis* mandibles from Golo displaying different stages of tooth eruption.

Dp3 and Dp4 are fully erupted (top), M4 is beginning to erupt whilst the P4 is still in the crypt after having expelled the Dp3 and Dp4 (centre), and the fully erupted P4 (bottom).

Source: Jennifer R. Hull.

Figure 10.4 A left *Dorcopsis* mandible from Golo H5, 40–45 cm, displaying tooth wear stages on four molars (M1-6, M2-6, M3-3 and M4-2).

Source: Jennifer R. Hull.

Out of the total number of *Dorcopsis* cranial fragments, seven were determined to be of juvenile age, distinguished by an absence of P4 and the presences of Dp3 and/or Dp4. The eruption stages also indicate that the majority of individuals were adults, with all molars fully erupted (n=22). Of the seven juveniles, only five had a fully erupted M1, and three a fully erupted M2. Of the adult specimens, 11 showed evidence that the M4 was still below the jaw bone (stage 0), and seven of these exhibited a partially erupted (stage 2–3) M3. Thus, both tooth eruption patterns and tooth wear on the *Dorcopsis* molars indicate that the captured population consisted predominantly of juvenile individuals and older adults, with only a few mature adults with fully erupted M4s (Figs 10.3 and 10.4).

Um Kapat Papo, Gebe Island

The most common mammals recorded at Um Kapat Papo were *Dorcopsis* (MNI: 10; NISP: 44), phalanger (MNI: 4; NISP: 31), Osteichthyes (NISP: 30), and Muridae (MNI: 3; NISP: 40). The dog was represented by a single vertebra in Layer 3, spit 20–25 cm, and another in Layer 3, spit 25–30 cm. With the exception of a fragment of *Dorcopsis* recorded in Layer 2, macropod remains (both *Dorcopsis* and phalanger) were only recorded from Layer 3, loosely associated with a marine shell date of 7330–7028 cal. BP at 55–65 cm in Layer 3 (Table 1.1, ANU 9318). Only one fragment of Osteichthyes was identifiable to family, *Scaridae*, at Layer 3, spit 30–40 cm.

Analysis of the Gebe Island *Dorcopsis* dentition

Pasveer (2004) argued that there was strong sexual dimorphism evident in the 3rd and 4th molars between modern male (large) and female (small) *D. muelleri*. If sexual dimorphism could be ascertained in the Gebe sample, then it would have been possible to differentiate males and females and interpret the *Dorcopsis* hunted population structure. However, Pasveer's original study was based on one single sample each of male and female *D. muelleri* that were then available for study in the Australian Museum collection. In our study, the archaeological assemblage was compared to a much larger sample (45 individuals of four species) of male and female *Dorcopsis* dentitions in the Australian Museum. From this larger sample there is no evidence of sexual dimorphism in the dentition, but as noted below by Geoffrey Irwin for the Wetef *Dorsopsis* sample, and earlier by Tim Flannery and colleagues (1998), there is substantial variation in the size of fragmentary post-cranial elements that suggest sexual dimorphism in overall body size.

The sample of *Dorcopsis* cranial elements from Um Kapat Papo is quite small, but it shows similar results to Golo Cave in that the majority of individuals were adults with erupting or fully erupted M4s, with four potentially more mature in age with all teeth fully erupted and stage 4 or higher tooth wear stages. There are no examples with deciduous teeth, but there are two sub-adult mandibles, one with an erupting P4 and another with a P4 in the crypt.

Following Groves and Flannery (1989), a discriminant function analysis was undertaken to compare the archaeological dentitions of *Dorcopsis* with specimens of known species and origin held in the Australian Museum. This analysis (Fig. 10.5) used the combined measurements from the UKP and Golo adult mandibular *Dorcopsis* dentitions. Between the three tests performed, they all display a significant separation of the *D. atrata* and *D. luctuosa* samples, thus indicating that these two may be ruled out as possibilities for identification. However, the significant overlap of the archaeological samples with *D. hageni* and *D. muelleri* in all three tests would seem to indicate that the source population for the extinct Gebe wallaby is likely to have been from one of these two species. *D. muelleri* is more likely when biogeographic distributions are considered. *D. muelleri* is broadly distributed across the Bird's Head and the offshore islands of Misool, Japen, and Salawati (Flannery 1995a:79–80), whereas *D. hageni* is restricted to the northern fringes of New Guinea and absent from the Bird's Head (Flannery 1995b:144–145).

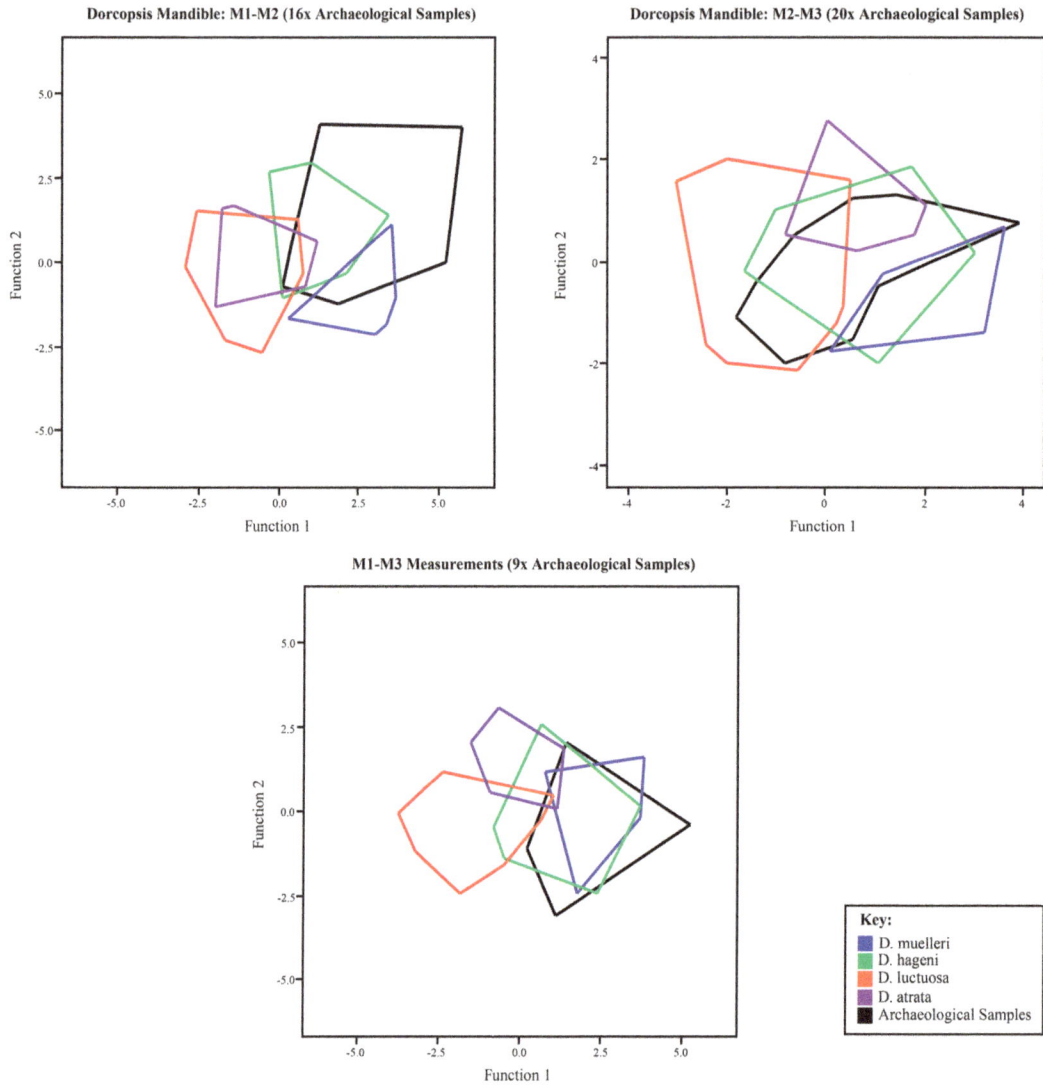

Figure 10.5 Three tests of Discriminant Function Analysis for the molar measurements (max. length, anterior and posterior breadths) for the Golo and Um Kapat Papo samples and those of four extant species of *Dorcopsis*.

Source: Jennifer R. Hull.

Tanjung Pinang, Morotai Island

Only 213 bone fragments were recovered from Tanjung Pinang, with phalanger (MNI: 6; NISP: 30) and Osteichthyes and Elasmobranchii (MNI: 6; NISP: 50) being the most numerous; two families and one sub-class were identifiable: Lethrinidae, Scaridae, and Elasmobranchii. Phalanger occurs consistently throughout the upper spits to a depth of 45–50 cm, and then decreases until it ceases to occur 80–85 cm. Only long bone fragments were found, with no cranial elements. No *Dorcopsis* bones were found at Tanjung Pinang, and there is no evidence for wallabies ever existing on Morotai. Some bat, snake, lizard, and rodent remains were recovered throughout the archaeological sequence, but these were most likely incidental introductions as part of an accumulating natural death assemblage.

Daeo Caves 1 and 2, Morotai Island

Of the 16 fragments of bone recorded from Daeo Cave 1, two rodents, one bat, and four fish fragments were identified. In Daeo Cave 2, phalanger and rodents comprised the largest proportion of the assemblage, with MNIs of 33 and 37 respectively. Also present were snakes, lizards, bats, and an unidentified intermediate-sized mammal. The highest number of phalanger remains in any given spit was 28, at 20–25 cm, with NISPs of 23 and 21 at 35–40 and 30–35 cm respectively. Small numbers of phalanger continued to 75–80 cm, where they ceased. The date of 16,767–15,889 cal. BP on a *Turbo* marine shell operculum from the 60–65 cm level in Daeo 2 (ANU 9450) thus overlaps with the oldest phalanger remains, and potentially establishes their presence on Morotai during the Late Pleistocene.

The rodent dentition from Daeo 2 (Fig. 10.6) has tooth dimensions significantly larger than any of the potentially introduced *Rattus* species, supporting the view of Flannery et al. (1995) that it was most likely the endemic *Rattus morotaiensis*. These sole cranial elements of rodent in the assemblage are from Squares E4–E5 at 10–15 cm, and hence postdate the C14 date of 6463–6194 cal. BP (ANU 9452).

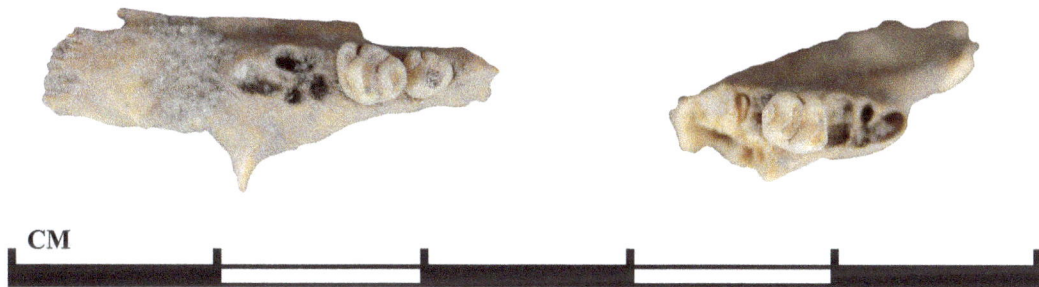

Figure 10.6 A murid rodent right mandible and left maxilla from Daeo Cave 2, E4–E6, 10–15 cm.
Source: Jennifer R. Hull.

Fish bones in Daeo 2 were confined between 20 and 45 cm, but do not occur in very large numbers. The most frequent were Scaridae (NISP: 8), Serranidae (NISP: 6) and Belonidae (NISP: 6).

Gua Siti Nafisah, Halmahera Island

Of the 6698 recovered bone fragments from Siti Nafisah, 5488 were identifiable. By far the largest proportion were bats (NISP: 5060), of which 350 cranial fragments could be identified to family or higher. This included the two genera *Hipposiderus* and *Miniopterus,* and the species *Rhinolophus euryotis* (Fig. 10.7).

With the exception of bats, the major taxa represented in Siti Nafisah were phalanger (MNI: 7; NISP: 111), Muridae (MNI: 4; NISP: 13), dog (MNI: 3; NISP: 6), *Dorcopsis* (MNI: 3; NISP: 34), pig (NISP: 7), and bandicoot (MNI: 1; NISP: 2). The dog remains were mainly metacarpals from spits A to A4, with a single metacarpal in C1. Three *Dorcopsis* incisors were submitted for C14 dating, but contained insufficient collagen.

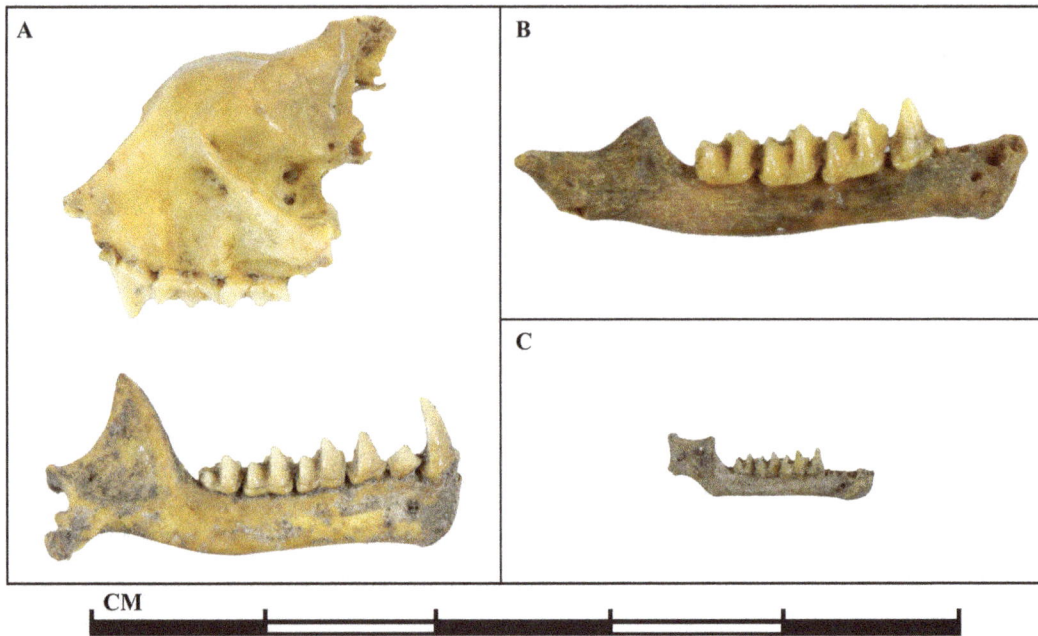

Figure 10.7 Cranial elements of *Hipposideros* (A), *Rhinolophus euryotis* (B), and *Miniopterus* (C) from Gua Siti Nafisah.

Source: Jennifer R. Hull.

Two of the pig bones came from F7 Layer D1 (an ulna) and J10 Layer C2 (a humerus—Fig. 10.8). Both show evidence of butchery and were sent to the ANU AMS Radiocarbon Laboratory for C14 testing (Table 1.1). The humerus produced a date of 1299–1187 cal. BP, but due to very low magnesium and percentage yield this date may be tenuous. The ulna produced a slightly earlier date of 1825–1699 cal. BP. Both adult and juvenile pigs were present in the site.

Other taxa represented at Siti Nafisah include reptile (NISP: 33), snake (NISP: 45), and Osteichthyes (NISP: 142), the latter including Scaridae and Labridae.

Figure 10.8 Pig distal humerus (right) exhibiting cut marks on the lateral margin, from Gua Siti Nafisah, J10, Layer C2.

This specimen has been directly C14 dated to 1825–1699 cal. BP (S-ANU 63339).

Source: Jennifer R. Hull.

Uattamdi, Kayoa Island

Of the 1191 bones recorded from Uattamdi, phalanger (NISP: 19) and Muridae (NISP: 5) occur with insignificant numbers of bat, lizard, and snake. However, there are fairly large numbers of pig (NISP: 4) and dog (NISP: 28), listed by square and spit in Table 10.4. Osteichthyes and Elasmobranchii dominate the assemblage, with 150 bones from 13 identified species (Fig. 10.11), with a further 545 being unidentified. Phalanger bones occur consistently throughout the sequence in relatively small numbers, from the surface down to the basal Layer D5. The recovered phalanger remains decreased in number with depth, but so also did most other taxa.

Table 10.4 Pig and dog bones by layer from Uattamdi 1.

Layer	Pig NISP	Dog NISP
A1		3
A2		6
A3		7
A4		10
A5		1
B1		1
B3		1
B5		1
C2	1	
C5	2	1
C6	2	
C9		2
Totals	5	33

Sources: Jennifer R. Hull and Geoffrey Clark (who identified them initially after the material was brought to ANU).

Figure 10.9 A *Sus scrofa* right mandible recovered from Layer C6 in Uattamdi, directly C14 dated from tooth enamel to 3144–2964 BP (S-ANU 60005, Table 1.1 and Chapter 5).

Source: Jennifer R. Hull.

Two fragments of the right mandible of a young adult pig were found in Uattamdi Layer C6, with an erupted M1–M2 and an M3 still in the process of erupting (Fig. 10.9). Two samples of tooth enamel have been directly dated from this mandible, with a result of c. 3000 cal. BP, as discussed in more detail by Rachel Wood in Chapter 5. This is an important date for establishing a presence of pig at the eastern edge of Island Southeast Asia, almost certainly domesticated in the absence of an indigenous wild pig species in the Moluccas, and during a peak period of Austronesian migration into Oceania. Uattamdi also has dog bones in the younger spits A1 and B5, with two vertebrae in Neolithic spit C9, the latter also potentially dating to c. 3000 BP (Fig. 10.10), although one of the C9 vertebrae sent to the ANU Radiocarbon Dating Laboratory failed the %N screening test (Stewart Fallon, pers. comm., 6 November 2018). The dog bones are predominantly carpals/metacarpals and vertebrae, with a number of refitting tibia fragments from a single context that could have belonged to one individual.

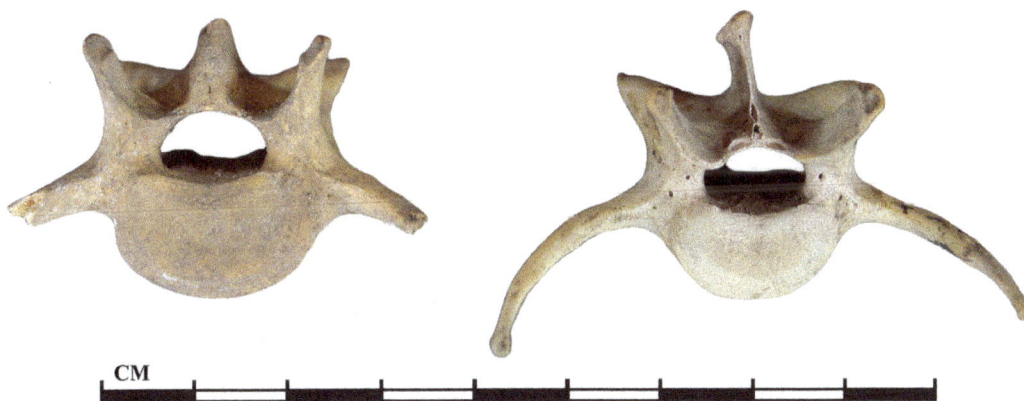

Figure 10.10 A canid vertebra (left) from Uattamdi (E7 A3) compared to a modern comparative *Canis lupus familiaris vertebra* (right) from the School of Archaeology and Anthropology, ANU.

Source: Jennifer R. Hull.

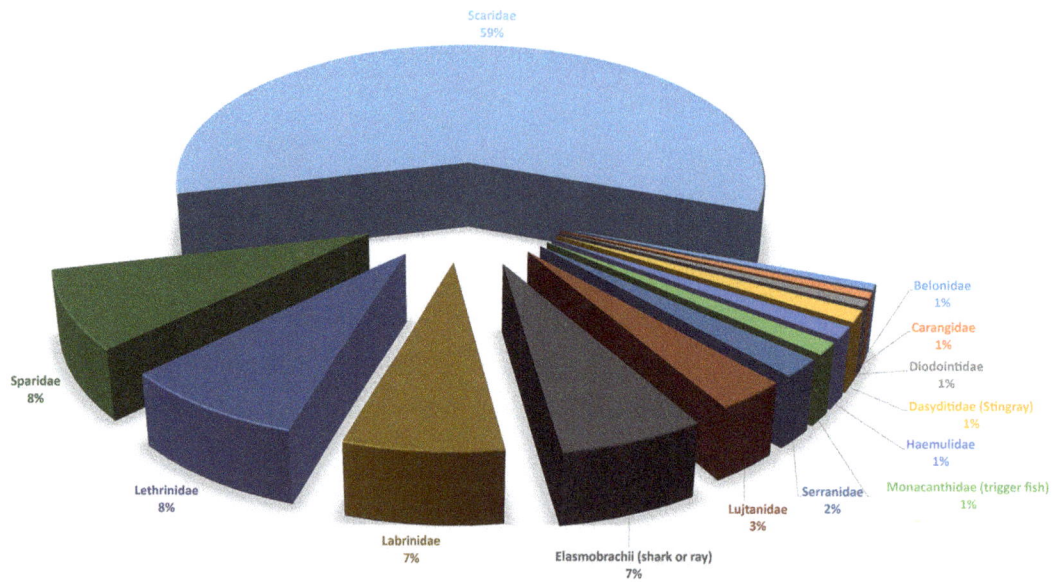

Figure 10.11 Pie chart of identified fish families from Uattamdi, all layers combined.
Source: Jennifer R. Hull.

Figure 10.12 Scaridae (left) and Lethrinidae (*Monotaxis grandoculis*, right) premaxillae from Uattamdi and Daeo Cave 2 respectively.
Source: Jennifer R. Hull.

Scaridae were clearly the dominant family in the identifiable fish remains (Figs 10.11 and 10.12), but this predominance is likely a reflection of differential survivability. Sparidae, Lethrinidae, and Labrinidae were also well-represented. The spit that seemed to have the most varied fish taxa was C3, towards the middle of the stratigraphic sequence, with a charcoal sample dated to 3160–2324 cal. BP (Table 1.1, ANU 7775).

Part 2: Wetef faunal remains (Geoffrey Irwin)

Animal bone

Wetef provided a substantial sample of animal bones of anthropogenic origin. These were identified using comparative specimens held at the Anthropology Department, University of Auckland, and the Auckland Institute and Museum. Initial sorting and quantification was done by Robin Milnes and Geoff Irwin and samples were then taken to the University of Sydney for checking by J. Peter White, with assistance from Tim Flannery, then of the Australian Museum.

Most of the bones were broken and some were burned. However, a total of 2521 identifications was made from a total NISP of 7153, i.e. 35 per cent. Of these identifications, 38.6 per cent were macropod and 26 per cent were phalanger. In both these animals all major bones were present, so we could see no evidence of selective transport or butchering, and both animals could have existed in a wild state on Gebe Island. There were bones of juvenile animals, including some small enough to be pouch young. The size range of macropod bones varied considerably, implying sexual dimorphism common among *Dorcopsis* sp., at least as far as the postcranial skeleton is concerned (see comment by Jennifer R. Hull on macropod teeth, above).

Other significant components were a range of small fish representing 22.8 per cent of the identified NISP (see below), sea turtle, bat of a size comparable to *Pteropus* sp., occasional reptiles including snake and varanid, and a few birds. No domestic animals were noted. A low rate of post-cranial bones was identified because the bone was very fragmented. However, our impression was that the unidentified bone was in much the same proportion by species as the bone identified. Summary statistics for total NISP and weights for each animal in Squares K3 and K4 are shown in Table 10.5.

Table 10.5 Summary of bone NISP and weight (gm) from Wetef K3–K4.

Square	Macropod	Phalanger	Turtle	Bat	Reptile	Fish	Bird	Unident.	Total
NISP									
K3	265	230	101	36	6	264	8	2163	3073
K4	708	425	41	99	25	310	3	2469	4080
Total	973	655	142	135	31	574	11	4632	7153
Weight									
K3	323.5	92.4	113.6	7.8	4.3	119.5	4.3	993.2	1658.6
K4	914.1	196.2	74.4	18.8	15.8	126.0	3.8	1236.6	2585.7
Total	1237.6	288.6	188.0	26.6	20.1	245.5	8.1	2229.8	4244.3

Source: Geoffrey Irwin.

Bone was virtually absent in Layer A, and the very few bones present were probably disturbed from below. A major peak in bone occurred through the levels of Layer B, which continued across the Layer B1/B2 interface. In sharp contrast, only small frequencies of bone occurred through the upper levels of Layer C. However, there was a significant increase in bone in association with the lenses of ash in Layer C2 (Fig. 2.16), dated to 9340–8974 cal. BP (Wk 4624) in the lowest band of ash in Layer C2, at a depth of 175 cm below the surface. Below this, in upper Layer D, very small quantities continued for another 20 cm, towards an associated C14 age of 12,962–12,626 cal. BP (Wk 4625). Following the deposition of the lower ash, Layer D was sealed from any later disturbance. The bone in upper Layer D could have been contemporary with this date; however, it is also possible that it was contemporary with the lower ash above, and the small quantity present in the top of Layer D had been carried down by treadage prior to the deposition of that ash. In either case, it is indicated that bone dated to the Early Holocene in Wetef.

It is interesting that both macropod and phalanger occurred as low in the site as any other animal and nothing could be deduced about their time of arrival. Below the ash at the base of Layer C, the deposit was wet and it is considered that any bone formerly in Layer D had been lost through attrition. This is similar to the case of Pamwak Cave on Manus (Fredericksen et al. 1993). If *Dorcopsis* was a translocated species from Misool near the Bird's Head of New Guinea, as suggested in Flannery et al. (1998), it was brought to Gebe no later than the Early Holocene. *Dorcopsis* was extirpated in Maluku in recent prehistory after the abandonment of Golo and Wetef caves.

Four samples of *Dorcopsis* bone from Wetef were submitted to the Rafter Radiocarbon Laboratory for AMS dating. Two samples from Layer D were found to be in a highly degraded condition and no collagen had survived. Results for the two samples dated are shown in Table 2.5. Sample NZA 8369 was collected from K4, Layer A. It was subjected to amino acid analysis and the sample was found to be moderately well to somewhat poorly preserved. The C14 age is cal. 906–570 BP. Sample NZA 8387, from K4 Layer B, was found to be extremely poorly preserved, but it produced an age of 6487–6182 cal. BP, which accords fairly well with the two wallaby bone direct dates of 8000–7500 cal. BP (discussed above) from Golo Cave.

Calculations of MNI for macropod and phalanger, based on mandibles, are shown in Table 10.6, and the details of NISP and weight of bone by 10 cm levels for K3 and K4 are shown in Tables 10.7–10.10.

Table 10.6 Macropod and phalanger MNI from Wetef.

	Macropod		Phalanger	
	L	R	L	R
K3	16	10	17	15
K4	24	23	25	37
Total	40	33	42	52

Source: Geoffrey Irwin.

Fish bone from Wetef

Fish bones were abundant in the site (NISP = 574, Table 10.11). They survived to a depth of 200 cm, as deep as the bones of any other animal; however, the distribution of fish was different. There was a major peak in the frequency of all bone through Layer B, but in Layer C1 bone was sparse. There was a clear increase again in Layer C2, but fishbone remained rare. Layer B accounted for 93.4 per cent of all fishbone with only 3.2 per cent and 0.6 per cent respectively in Layers C and D. These results may suggest that fishing became important at Wetef when rising sea levels approached modern levels.

Some 26 per cent (n=153) of the fish bones were identified to family level using comparative collections at the Anthropology Department, University of Auckland, with assistance from Simon Duff and advice from Melinda Allen. Some 11 families were present, but three families made up 75 per cent of identified specimens: Holocentridae (Soldierfishes and Squirrelfishes) 26 per cent, Muraenidae (Moray eels) 27 per cent, and Scaridae (Parrotfish) 23 per cent (Table 2.11). With one exception, represented by a single bone of Barracuda (Sphyraenidae), all families were associated with inner or outer reef habitats. The sample size is inadequate to represent the range of fishing behaviour at the site. However, ethnographic information from Pacific contexts indicates a variety of methods for capture of these fish and one method, common to all, was taking by spear.

Table 10.7 Wetef Square K3, bone NISP.

Level	Macropod	Phalanger	Bat	Turtle	Reptile	Fish	Bird	Unident	Total
0–10									
10–20				1				2	3
20–30								7	7
30–40	3	7	4			13		71	98
40–50	75	55	8	32	1	24	6	364	565
50–60	94	90	14	56	2	80		494	830
60–70	7	24	6			95		228	360
70–80	30	26	1		2	16		347	422
80–90	11	10	3	12	1	24	2	285	348
90–100	10	13				7		200	230
100–110	6	2				2		33	43
110–120	1							7	8

Level	Macropod	Phalanger	Bat	Turtle	Reptile	Fish	Bird	Unident	Total
120–130	1	1				1		14	17
130–140	3					1		12	16
140–150	3	2				1		25	31
150–160	12							32	44
160–170	7							21	28
170–180	2							19	21
180–190									
190–200								2	2

Source: Geoffrey Irwin.

Table 10.8 Wetef Square K3, bone weight (gm).

Level	Macropod	Phalanger	Bat	Turtle	Reptile	Fish	Bird	Unident	Total
0–10									
10–20				3.2				4.7	7.9
20–30								3.7	3.7
30–40	3.5	2.7	0.4			1.5		20.1	28.2
40–50	107.0	26.6	2.2	38.7	0.8	15.1	3.5	205.2	399.1
50–60	88.4	28.0	3.2	59.1	1.8	32.4		231.2	444.1
60–70	5.8	10.5	1.4			27.8		82.1	127.6
70–80	41.2	12.7	0.2		0.9	3.4		150.5	208.9
80–90	17.0	4.6	0.4	12.6	0.8	31.8	0.8	113.9	181.9
90–100	12.6	5.6				2.5		90.8	104.8
100–110	6.7	0.8				0.9		14.9	23.3
110–120	0.6							3.6	4.2
120–130	6.6	0.3				2.5		5.0	14.4
130–140	6.4					1.2		10.1	17.7
140–150	1.8	1.8				0.4		15.3	19.3
150–160	19.9							18.0	37.9
160–170	5.6							8.2	13.8
170–180	1.0							7.0	8.0
180–190									
190–200								6.1	6.1

Source: Geoffrey Irwin.

Table 10.9 Wetef Square K4, bone NISP.

Level	Macropod	Phalanger	Bat	Turtle	Reptile	Fish	Bird	Unident	Total
0–10									
10–20	1	2	3			7			13
20–30						18		10	28
30–40	33	17	2	1		10		198	261
40–50	302	129	11	27	6	38	3	378	894
50–60	105	100	15	7	2	94		304	627
60–70	73	43	24	2	1	54		428	625
70–80	66	57	5	4	6	24		346	508
80–90	45	36	24		9	20		314	443
90–100	25	13	9		1	19		174	259

Level	Macropod	Phalanger	Bat	Turtle	Reptile	Fish	Bird	Unident	Total
100–110	3					6		18	27
110–120						3		13	16
120–130	1					1		23	26
130–140	4					1		19	24
140–150	2	1				1		17	21
150–160	8	1				5		43	57
160–170	16	4						77	101
170–180	20	2						84	106
180–190	1	1				2		2	6
190–200	2	2				7		17	28
200–210	1		1			1		3	6
210–220								1	1

Source: Geoffrey Irwin.

Table 10.10 Wetef Square K4, bone weight (gm).

Level	Macropod	Phalanger	Bat	Turtle	Reptile	Fish	Bird	Unident	Total
0–10									
10–20	2.3	1.2	0.3			1.8			5.6
20–30						1.5		2.6	4.1
30–40	45.1	7.2	2.3	2.9		12.8		67.2	137.5
40–50	400.6	57.7	3.2	54.8	4.3	25.0	3.8	201.5	751.2
50–60	94.0	41.5	1.9	12.2	2.9	42.8		162.6	356.9
60–70	98.0	16.0	3.1	3.1	0.6	15.9		209.8	346.5
70–80	85.6	31.2	0.7	1.4	4.7	5.9		169.4	298.9
80–90	42.4	19.6	4.6		2.5	6.3		149.7	226.1
90–100	45.3	16.0	1.2		0.8	4.5		84.1	151.9
100–110	3.4					1.6		16.7	22.2
110–120						0.6		13.1	13.7
120–130	2.3		0.9			0.6		26.0	29.8
130–140	10.5					0.8		8.7	20.0
140–150	8.3	0.8				0.5		14	23.6
150–160	11.1	0.7				1		19.8	32.5
160–170	27.9	2.1	0.4					42.6	72.8
170–180	31.7	1.5						41.4	74.8
180–190	1.9					1		0.7	3.6
190–200	1.7	0.7				1.7		4.5	8.6
200–210	1.3		0.1			1.1		2.2	4.7
210–220								0.1	0.1

Source: Geoffrey Irwin.

Table 10.11 Wetef identified fishbone.

Layer	Acanthuridae	Balistidae	Carangidae	Holocentridae	Labridae	Lethrinidae	Lutjanidae	Muraenidae	Scaridae	Serranidae	Sphyraenidae	Total
0-10												
10-20				4								4
20-30				3		1						4
30-40		1		2				3	2			8
40-50	1			1	2			6	2			12
50-60	2			15		3	1	9	17	3		50
60-70	3		1	9		4		16	8	2	1	44
70-80	2			2		1		1	1			7
80-90		1	1	1			1	2	4			10
90-100		1		1				2	1			5
100-110						1		1		1		3
110-120										2		2
120-130						1						1
130-140												
140-150								1				1
150-160				1								1
160-170												
170-180												
180-190										1		1
190-200												
Total	8	3	2	39	2	11	2	41	35	9	1	153

Source: Geoffrey Irwin.

Zooarchaeological discussion and conclusions for Parts 1 and 2

The taphonomic processes visible in the faunal assemblages of the seven sites (excluding Wetef) analysed by Jennifer R. Hull at ANU varied considerably. The two Golo trenches on Gebe showed extensive subaerial weathering as well as significantly high concretions of calcium carbonate, often to the point of obscuring the remains. Whilst there are some examples of burning and butchery, they are not particularly common. The *Dorcopsis* remains are predominantly in the adult and mature adult age ranges, but there are some juveniles and sub-adults. The age distribution would suggest that a wild breeding population of *Dorcopsis* previously existed on Gebe Island. This would also seem to indicate a targeting of older animals, but not exclusively.

The sequence of faunal remains in these two Golo trenches does not descend as far as bedrock, a situation quite different from that with respect to marine shell, which does extend down to bedrock. This may provide an indication of severe taphonomic processes that have caused the complete destruction of bone below c. 1 m depth. This is evident in the extremely poor condition of the corroded bone fragments recovered from the deepest bone-bearing layers.

The *Dorcopsis* tooth enamel C14 dates from the lowest recorded levels with bone, at 75–80 and 80–90 cm, suggest that wallabies were definitely present on Gebe by 8000 BP, a date confirmed by one of the direct dates on wallaby bone from Wetef. Dogs and pigs are likely of Neolithic antiquity, after 3500 BP, and these introductions might have been partly responsible for the disappearance of *Dorcopsis* from Gebe by 906–570 cal. BP (Wetef rockshelter, NZA 8369).

Um Kapat Papo on Gebe revealed a very different taphonomic picture from Golo. There was far less disturbance, weathering, and calcium carbonate concretion in this site. As in Golo, evidence for butchery indicates that wallabies were eaten, although the full diet was probably dominated by fish, especially in the younger levels. No pig bones were found in UKP, and only a single fragment is likely to be dog, from Layer 3, 20–25 cm, thus relatively low and early in the sequence, which could suggest disturbance.

On Morotai Island, Tanjung Pinang exhibits low levels of disturbance and weathering, with no evidence of butchery and no presence of *Dorcopsis*. Phalanger was the dominantly recovered taxon. Fish were also a highly targeted resource, with specimens of Elasmobranchii, Scaridae, and Lethrinidae recovered. Daeo Cave 2 exhibited more disturbance and burning than Tanjung Pinang, but still with low levels of weathering.

Siti Nafisah on Halmahera is another fairly stable site with very little evidence of weathering or disturbance in the bone assemblage. Here, the burnt bones are consistent with inadvertent burning within fires associated with cooking activities, and there is more evidence of butchery than in some of the other sites. Fragmentation at this site was also less, and a much larger portion of the assemblage was taxonomically identifiable than in the other sites. The vast majority of the bones were of bat (4700/5081 fragments), unsurprising given the site is a cave, but whether bats were eaten is unclear. Aside from bats, the assemblage was dominated by phalanger, *Dorcopsis*, and reptiles (including snakes). Some dog and pig bones occur in the upper Neolithic layers. As on Gebe, it appears likely that the introduction of pig and dog may have contributed to the disappearance of the *Dorcopsis* from Halmahera. Of the fish, only Scaridae and Labridae could be identified.

The Neolithic site at Uattamdi exhibits some disturbance, sporadic evidence of burning and low levels of weathering. This site has the greatest predominance of fish bones, with the largest range of species (13) identified, with Scaridae the dominant family. Phalanger was the most common mammal, accompanied by pig and dog. The pig bones occur in the Neolithic layers in the cave, whereas dog bones occur almost throughout the sequence, which commenced around 3300 BP.

The indicators of weathering and site instability were thus highest on Gebe, whereas the Morotai and Halmahera sites had better preservation. Butchery evidence showed that phalanger, *Dorcopsis* (except on Morotai) and other taxa were being targeted as food resources. The Neolithic introductions of pig and dog roughly coincided with the decrease in *Dorcopsis* in the sequence, suggesting a possible link between the two trends.

The discriminant function analysis undertaken on the dentitions of *Dorcopsis* from Golo and Um Kapat Papo indicated that the Northern Moluccan archaeological samples were closely correlated with the Papuan *D. muelleri* and *D. hageni* dentitions in the Australian Museum, as previously noted by Flannery et al. (1998). The study was performed on the M1–M3 of nine archaeological samples. However, two other discriminant function tests (Fig. 10.5) with larger samples sizes of 16 (M1–M2) and 20 (M2–M3) teeth had a more pronounced overlap with *D. hageni*. Groves and Flannery (1989) described both *D. muelleri* and *D. hageni* as cranially and dentally very close in morphology and size. The only significant differences were in biogeographical range, with *muelleri* being present in the lowlands of West Papua as well as the islands of Misool, Salawati, and Yapen, and *hageni* in the lowlands of northern New Guinea. The current biogeographic distributions of the two species as recorded by Groves and Flannery (1989), and the statistical analyses by Flannery et al. (1998), led to the conclusion that the extinct population on Gebe Island was *D. muelleri*, potentially sourced from Misool or the mainland of New Guinea. The statistical analyses performed here, whilst somewhat inconclusive, seem to have a similar result. However, the larger dental sample analysed size here reveals considerable overlap between *D. muelleri* and *D. hageni*; as such, more data may be required to distinguish them conclusively.

The information from Wetef, analysed separately in Auckland, complements that from Golo fairly tightly. Both sites have ample evidence for human exploitation of *Dorcopsis* wallabies, phalanger cuscuses, and fish during the Holocene, but what happened prior to this? The wallabies on Gebe and Halmahera appear to be relatively unspeciated with respect to the other New Guinea extant species, and this implies a relatively recent date of introduction, in evolutionary terms. But were the introductions by natural means during periods of low sea level, or were they by human intention? Without older bone assemblages from the Northern Moluccas this mystery might never be solved fully, although analysis of ancient DNA from Moluccan and New Guinea archaeological samples could be very informative in the future. The same applies to the bones of the pigs and dogs, both species intricately involved in the history of human migration in Island Southeast Asia (Bellwood and White 2005; Oskarsson et al. 2011).

Part 3: A Late Pleistocene/Early Holocene shell midden sample from Golo Cave (Katherine Szabó and Annette Oertle)

Some of the oldest archaeological evidence for marine mollusc exploitation in the island Asia-Pacific region is evidenced by material excavated from Golo Cave. Aspects of the Golo Cave molluscan shell assemblage have already been well-reported via publications on the rich worked shell component. This includes the flaking of large, robust *Turbo marmoratus* opercula in the lowest levels of the site (Szabó et al. 2007), the repurposing of *Scutellastra flexuosa* limpets from the shell midden as scrapers in the Pleistocene (Koppel 2010; Szabó and Koppel 2015), and the deliberate shaping of *Nautilus* shell fragments also recovered from the lowest layers of the Golo deposits (Szabó 2013; Parkinson 2016). Although some details of the shell midden assemblage have been discussed as part of the presentation of data on the worked shell, including the chapter on the worked shell included in this volume, the contents and nature of the shell midden have only received partial summary in Szabó (2005).

A detailed taphonomic analysis of the Golo Cave shell midden sample, which also addresses issues of midden formation and transformation processes, is ongoing and will be published in due course. Here, we present the broad structure and nature of the Golo Cave shell midden from the available sample, particularly addressing issues of species representation and the changing nature of the molluscan assemblage through time. Key questions of interest include:

a. What sorts of molluscan resources were being transported back to Golo Cave?

b. What do these resources tell us about changes in nearby littoral environments through time?

c. What do they tell us of the utilisation of molluscan resources by Gebe human populations?

d. What are the relationships between the midden shell and the worked shell in Golo Cave?

One of the most intriguing features of the faunal record at Golo Cave is the absence of bone in the mid and lower portions of the site, despite the presence of largely well-preserved shell midden at all levels. Radiocarbon dates on midden and worked shell from the lower half of the sequence indicate that the molluscan material is not intrusive (barring the exceptional incongruous dates of the adzes manufactured on old shell). As is clearly visible in Table 2.2, shell midden is found throughout all levels of the excavated sequence, whereas negligible bone occurs below a depth of 1 m. As with the bone, shell midden densities peak between 30 and 60 cm depth. However, while bone densities fall off sharply below ~70 cm depth, the shell midden continues and is never represented in the M5 sample counted in Table 2.2 by less than 325 gm in a 10 cm spit. Whilst there could reasonably be taphonomic factors at play, as discussed above, it is hard to conceive of a taphonomic process that would eradicate all traces of a bone assemblage and yet leave the associated shell in readily identifiable condition at all levels.

Given the continuity in the presence of shell throughout the Golo sequence, an alternative would have been to look for reflections of changes in the broader landscape that could have impacted upon resource availability. The Pleistocene/Holocene transition doubtless had impacts upon the terrestrial and inshore habitats surrounding Golo Cave, and the introduction of exotic fauna by humans—whether wild or domesticated—would also have changed landscapes and interspecies relationships in both direct ways (e.g. the potential use of dogs for hunting) and indirect ways (e.g. vegetation and habitat change associated with land clearance). Additionally, as new fauna (and likely flora) were introduced into the diet and daily practices, the whole structure of the subsistence economy would have readjusted. Since shell is the only faunal material to span the whole Golo sequence, it could have provided some insight. Unfortunately, the extant shell midden sample available for analysis only covers the lower half of the site from 120 cm downwards, meaning that there is effectively no overlap with the vertebrate assemblage. Further details on the nature of the sample, and the sorts of analysis this enabled, are provided here.

Background to the sample

As briefly outlined in Chapter 9, the only complete shell midden sample retained for analysis derived from the lower half of Square M4, although sporadic samples of shell from other squares, as well as the mid-portions of M4, were retained to provide samples for radiocarbon dating. These latter radiocarbon samples tended to focus on larger, more robust species such as *Turbo setosus* and the opercula of this species as well as *T. argyrostomus*. Both the weight and the selective sampling of these shells would doubtless skew results if included, so they have been omitted from all calculations where they do not form part of the M4 shell midden assemblage from an uppermost depth of 140 cm. Only at a depth of 140 cm downwards does the M4 midden sample diversify and include all recovered taxa.

The Golo radiocarbon chronology (see Table 1.1) suggests that the zone around 130–140 cm dates to the Pleistocene/Holocene transition, taking in both the last stages of the terminal Pleistocene and the very onset of the Holocene. Thus, the shell midden assemblage presented and considered here is dominated by Late Pleistocene material with the possible inclusion of some Early Holocene shell in the uppermost spits included in the sample. The on-site spit weights recorded for midden shell from Square M5 (see Table 2.2) clearly show the highest totals for shell by some margin to be derived from the upper Holocene deposits between approximately 20 and 70 cm (Fig. 10.13). Although we assume these dense midden deposits were also present in the adjoining M4, their absence from the transported sample means that nothing can be said about the potential composition.

The absence of shell midden samples from above 140 cm necessarily means that we cannot speak to potential changes, or indeed stability, in littoral environments and/or human behaviour through time. However, we do have a valuable sample in terms of the overall faunal sequence: shell is consistently represented where bone is absent from the record. While this pattern comes across as anomalous, it is not without precedent in the region, and findings from elsewhere in the region will be considered in the Discussion section.

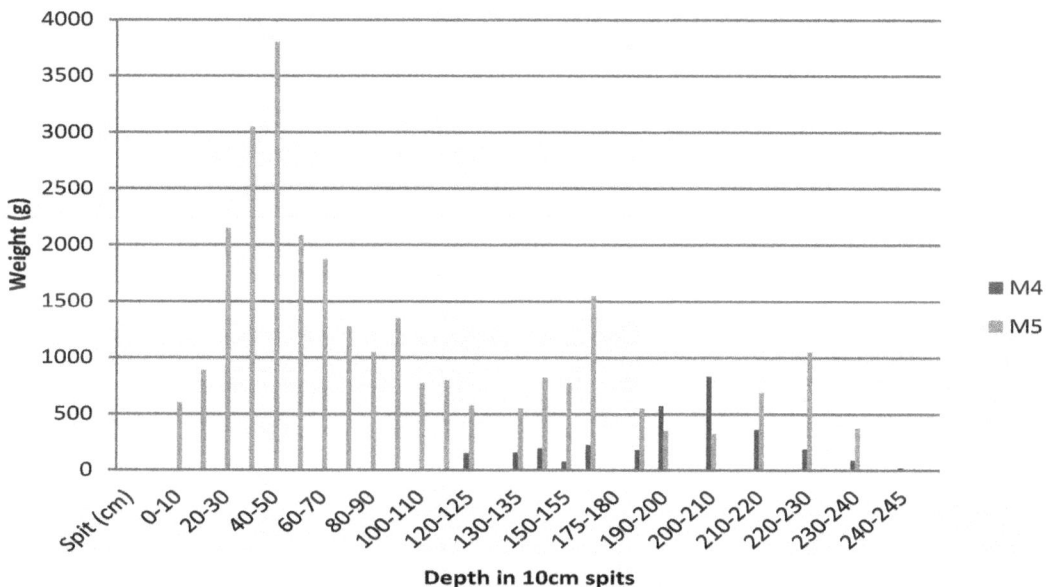

Figure 10.13 Graph to show the relative representation of shell midden (by weight) across spits in Golo Square M4 and M5.

The M5 data are taken from Table 2.2 and the M4 data derive from the research presented here. The M4 weights were recorded for each 5 cm excavation spit, so have been combined into 10 cm spit totals here for comparability with the M5 data. It should be noted that some 5 cm spits between a depth of 145 and 185 cm are missing from the transported M4 sample (see Table 10.12).

Source: Katherine Szabó and Annette Oertle.

Methods and approaches

All shell transported back to Australia was analysed by Szabó in 2002/03 and again by Oertle in 2017. Various taxa (e.g. *Scutellastra flexuosa* and *Nautilus* sp.) were studied in greater depth separately at different points in investigations of potential shell working (Szabó and Koppel 2015; Parkinson 2016).

Taxonomic identifications were made to the lowest possible level, but being careful not to assume that fragments with only genus-level identifiable features belonged to common or already identified species. Identifications were made using a wide assortment of text- and web-based resources, as well as the personal shell collection of Szabó. Taxonomy was updated and standardised using the World Register of Marine Species (WoRMS, www.marinespecies.org). Material had been pre-sieved and partially sorted during the bagging process in the field, and no further sieving was undertaken. All size classes of fragment were analysed.

To circumvent any issues of differential fragmentation, the most robust unique non-repeating elements were chosen for each taxon. For bivalves both the left and right hinges were counted, the posterior valve of chiton specimens were counted, and for gastropods the columella edge of the aperture was counted with the exception of all limpets, where the apex was used as the non-repeating element. Given that Golo Cave was excavated in 5 cm spits with no discernible stratigraphy at the depths represented by the shell sample, MNI values could not be calculated within stratigraphic units. However, a lack of discernible stratigraphy on site does not necessarily mean that different time periods are not represented in the shell sample. Therefore, to avoid inflation of totals, the highest value for either left or right hinges of bivalves *within the complete M4 sample* was used as the MNI value. This is likely to be an under-representation of occurrences, but will not overestimate numbers. Because the worked shell material was separated, analysed, and reported upon separately, the totals for worked shell objects are not represented in the numbers given here.

During the course of both the 2002/03 and 2017 analyses, running notes were made on the occurrence of various taphonomic indicators. These included the presences of:

a.   *beach-rolling/post-mortem introduction into the site*, as indicated by a muting of surface features and sculpture and the uniform rounding of edges, as well as bioerosion and/or bioadhesions such as barnacles on inner shell surfaces

b.   *burning*, as indicated by a noticeable colour change clearly distinct from staining, or shell recrystallisation clearly visible as a textural change at fracture surfaces

c.   *hermitting*, as indicated by abrasion to the interior of the aperture on gastropods, dragmarks on the outer ventral surface, and other indicators outlined in Szabó (2012)

d.   *fragmentation*, as assessed through a comparison of MNI to NISP totals.

Mention will be made of the noted presence of these indicators where relevant, although they will be dealt with more systematically and comprehensively upon the completion of Oertle's current research into taphonomic variables as they relate to the shell assemblage.

Results of analysis

A combined total of 49 species of marine gastropod, bivalve, and polyplacophoran (chiton) was identified within the M4 shell midden sample, with a further three taxa identified to higher taxonomic levels (Table 10.12). Aggregated *Turbo* spp. opercula were quantified as a group, but are not included in the species tallies. Additionally, five species of terrestrial snail were identified and these will be discussed further below. Limited numbers of decapod crustacean and echinoid urchin remains were also recovered, along with greater numbers of plates of large barnacles. These are not reported on here and are the subject of a separate study.

The four most strongly represented species total over 85 per cent of the M4 marine shell midden assemblage as calculated through MNI values. These are the limpet species *Cellana radiata* comprising 42 per cent, *Patelloida striata* 19 per cent and *Scutellastra flexuosa* 10 per cent, as well as the nerite species *Nerita plicata* comprising a further 15 per cent. Each of these four species are associated with hard-shore intertidal habitats, and the majority of the remaining marine molluscan taxa also derive from this zone, including a variety of taxa within the Muricidae and Neritidae families. Bivalves are poorly represented, totalling less than 2 per cent of the marine mollusc assemblage. However, there may be proxies for the presence of further bivalves within the gastropod component.

Species within the Muricidae are predators on other molluscs. They drill holes through the shells of their prey and extract the animal from within. The large variety of muricid species present within the M4 sample, all associated with rocky habitats, suggests that an ample source of food existed in the vicinity of collection. These muricids feed largely on nerites, limpets, barnacles, and other molluscan residents of exposed shorelines (Fiene-Severns et al. 1998), all of which are well represented within the M4 assemblage. However, this group of muricids, often known as 'rock shells', is also known by the common collective name 'oyster drills', as rock oysters are often a favoured prey item (e.g. see Tan 1993; Wright et al. 2018). Although bivalves are poorly represented overall, the best-represented taxon in the M4 sample is the rock oyster *Saccostrea* sp. Interestingly, it is only represented by right (upper) valves. As left (lower) valves are generally cemented to the substrate (or other shells), on-site extraction/processing of *Saccostrea* spp. oysters is effective in terms of time and energy, and if any parts of the shell are collected with the animal it tends to be the loose right valve (Szabó, pers. obs.). The sample is too small to make any claims with certainty, but the presence of some right valves of rock oysters, as well as numbers of predators that would inhabit those beds, indicates that oyster beds were in the vicinity of the site at the time of occupation and were exploited. Their presence may be under-represented through a tendency towards point-of-collection processing.

Despite a lack of visible stratigraphy and the presence of only the lowest metre of the M4 sequence in the shell sample, there is clearly visible vertical patterning in the distribution of shell. This is observable in Table 10.12, and is also shown graphically in Figure 10.14. Most of the shell is concentrated between a depth of 195–210 cm, but there are also noticeable peaks between 140–145 cm and 225–230 cm. If the dates for the adzes are sidelined, a depth of 140–145 cm indicates deposition at the Pleistocene/Holocene transition. Dates from 190–230 cm group around 25–35 kyr, with the exception of a couple of Early Holocene dates on *Turbo* shell. As mentioned above, other *Turbo* shell recorded here tended to have evidence of use and deposition by terrestrial hermit crabs, and their ability to confound radiocarbon sequences is well reported (Szabó 2012).

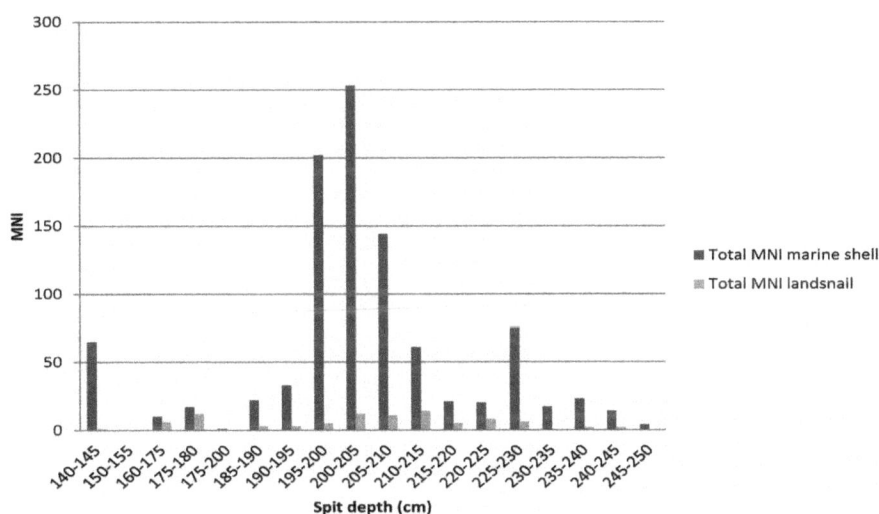

Figure 10.14 Graph to show total abundances (MNI) of marine and terrestrial molluscs per spit for Golo Square M4.

Source: Katherine Szabó and Annette Oertle.

Table 10.12 Taxon identifications and MNI totals for the marine shell midden sample from Golo Square M4, 140–250 cm.

FAMILY	SPECIES	Square M4																		
		140–145	150–155	160–175	175–180	175–200	185–190	190–195	195–200	200–205	205–210	210–215	215–220	220–225	225–230	230–235	235–240	240–245	245–250	Totals
Chitonidae	Acanthopleura spinosa									1										1
Patellidae	Scutellastra flexuosa				2		2	4	18	35	13	9	1	2	7					93
Nacellidae	Cellana radiata radiata sp.	11			7		9	19	82	100	63	28	9	14	39	6	10	8	4	409
	Patelloida striata				8		4	1	63	58	24	7	5	2	10	2	4	3		191
Haliotidae	Haliotis varia											p			1					1
Turbinidae	Turbo crassus						1													1
	Turbo setosus											1								1
	Turbo argyrostomus										1									1
	Turbo chrysostomus											1								1
	Turbo spp. operculum	2							2	2	1					2				9
Neritidae	Nerita costata	1							1											2
	Nerita polita	1		1			1	1	7	1		1				p				13
	Nerita undata	1		1			1	1		1										5
	Nerita textilis			1		1	1			p					1	1	1			7
	Nerita plicata	39		4					16	33	20	6	3	2	16	4	4	2		148
	Nerita insculpta	4																		4
	Nerita sp.									1						1	1			3
Littorinidae	Littoraria undulata	4						1												5
	Tectarius pagodus										1									1
	Tectarius cf. coronatus								1											1
Potamididae	Terebralia palustris	1																		1

FAMILY	SPECIES	140–145	150–155	160–175	175–180	175–200	185–190	190–195	195–200	200–205	205–210	210–215	215–220	220–225	225–230	230–235	235–240	240–245	245–250	Totals
Strombidae	Lambis cf. truncata							1												1
	Lambis sp.						1													1
Cypraeidae	Mauritia scurra									1										1
	Mauritia mauritania								1											1
	Mauritia arabica											1								1
	Cypraeidae spp.												1							1
Muricidae	Menathais tuberosa			1																1
	Tylothais aculeata								6	3	2	2	1							14
	Reishia bitubercularis									2	6	2					2			12
	Mancinella alouina														1					1
	Mancinella armigera									1										1
	Rapaninae sp.										1									1
	Nassa sp.	1		1																2
	Drupa morum			1																1
	Drupa clathrata									1	2	1	1							5
	Drupa ricinis						1		1		1									3
	Drupa rubiscidaeus										1									1
	Purpura persica						1		1											2
	Purpura panama									7	3	2				1				13
Terebridae	Terebra sp.									2										2
Fasciolariidae	Fusinus sp.							1												1
Tonnidae	Tonna perdix										1									1
Volutidae	Melo sp.										1									1
Ellobiidae	Pythia scarabaeus							1	1								1			3

FAMILY	SPECIES	140–145	150–155	160–175	175–180	175–200	185–190	190–195	195–200	200–205	205–210	210–215	215–220	220–225	225–230	230–235	235–240	240–245	245–250	Totals
Arcidae	Barbatia amygdalumtostum							1								1				2
	Arca navicularis									1										1
Ostreidae	Saccostrea sp.								1		2				p			1		5
Psammobidae	Asaphis violascens						1	1							p					2
Veneridae	Pitar sp.														1					1
	Periglypta sp.										1									1
	Periglypta reticulata							1												1
	Periglypta puerpera									1										1
TOTAL		65	0	10	17	1	22	33	202	253	144	61	21	20	76	17	23	14	4	

Square M4

Shell with evidence of working has not been included in this table, and gastropods with evidence of use by hermit crabs have also been removed from these MNI totals.

Source: Katherine Szabó and Annette Oertle.

Table 10.13 Table to show the MNI values for the terrestrial snail component of the Square M4 shell midden sample. Taxonomy and identifications follow Grieke (2012).

FAMILY	SPECIES	140–145	150–155	160–175	175–180	175–200	185–190	190–195	195–200	200–205	205–210	210–215	215–220	220–225	225–230	230–235	235–240	240–245	245–250	Totals
Trocho-morphidae	Videna hartmanni										4	3			2		2	2		13
Ariophantidae	Naninia aulica							3		3		2	1	1						10
Cyclophoridae	Leptopoma gebiensis												1		1					2
Camaenidae	Planispira kurri	1		6	12		3		5	6	7	9	3	7	3					62
	Papuina unicolor									3										3
TOTAL		1		6	12		3	3	5	12	11	14	5	8	6		2	2		90

Square M4

Source: Katherine Szabó and Annette Oertle.

In terms of their composition, the peaks are similar with all being comprised of combinations of the dominant four species (see Fig. 10.15). *Nerita plicata* and *Cellana radiata* are present throughout the represented sequence, but *N. plicata* is dominant in the uppermost peak (140–45 cm), while *C. radiata* dominates from 185 cm to the basal spit (250 cm). Both *Patelloida striata* and *Scutellastra flexuosa* occur from 175 cm downwards to near the base of the deposits. All four of these species are characteristic of intertidal hard-shores, and all are capable of living on exposed shores where they are subject to periodic wave action. The general lack of variation in both the dominant species, and—when all recovered marine shell midden species are considered—the hard-shore intertidal niche suggests that this habitat was accessible to the Golo inhabitants throughout the Pleistocene occupation and remained relatively stable. Nearly all identified species could have been easily gathered from the substrate and within fissures and tide pools at low tide.

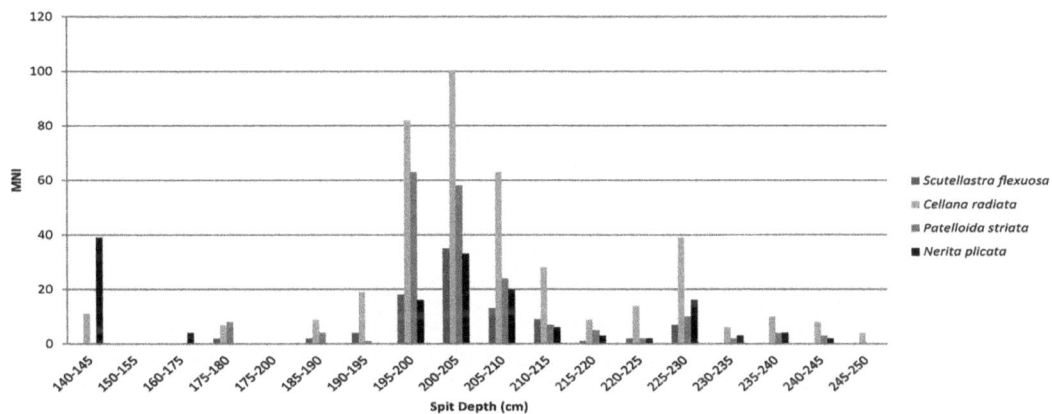

Figure 10.15 Relative abundances (MNI) of the four major molluscan species represented within the Golo Square M4 sample.

Source: Katherine Szabó and Annette Oertle.

Terrestrial snails are found in low levels in association with marine shells throughout the M4 sample. The literature on the non-marine mollusca of Gebe Island is sparse, but fortuitously a new review with additional data was published recently by Grieķe (2012). This has allowed refinement of the original identifications made as part of Szabó's 2002/03 analysis (see Table 10.13). The identified species tend to be of a moderate size, with *Planispira kurri* and *Naninia aulica* being of equivalent size, or larger than, the average nerite. *Videna hartmanni*, *Leptopoma gebiensis*, and *Papuina unicolor* are slightly smaller, but certainly not diminutive. The larger two species, and indeed all five, could viably represent a food source.

In the course of the analysis of the molluscan remains from the Niah Caves in Sarawak, Borneo, Szabó (2016) developed a series of criteria for establishing whether terrestrial snails in archaeological deposits were likely to represent a collected food source, or whether they were self-introduced into deposits. These criteria included observations about the representation of terrestrial snail species of different sizes, whether the distribution of the occurrence of land snails mapped on to, or out-grouped from, marine/freshwater shell midden stratigraphically, and whether terrestrial snail remains were predominantly found near the cave mouth. While the terrestrial snails found in the West Mouth of the Niah Caves were determined to be clearly self-introduced, the Golo Cave M4 sample is not so clear-cut. The frequencies of terrestrial snails track, rather than mirror, the abundances of marine shell (Fig. 10.14, Table 10.12). There is also a tendency towards larger species and specimens, although whether this may be an artefact of sampling is difficult to say. The small overall nature of the sample, as well as the ambiguities around chronostratigraphy, makes a definitive case for deliberate collection impossible. However, what can be said is that the M4 terrestrial snail assemblage shows none of the hallmarks characteristic of a self-introduced assemblage.

Discussion (Golo shell midden)

Although the available sample of shell midden does not capture the Holocene/Terminal Pleistocene portions of the Golo chronostratigraphic sequence, and thus cannot be directly compared with the vertebrate faunal assemblage, it does offer unique insights into Late Pleistocene subsistence at Golo where a bone record is silent. Limpets and neritids dominate, supplemented by lower numbers of other species that, for the most part, also inhabit the intertidal hard-shore. These species are able to withstand dynamic wave action, and the conditions of the coastal zone in the past seem to largely mirror those that exist today. Dwelling on rocky surfaces, and within fissures and tide pools, the species that constitute the M4 Pleistocene assemblage would have been simple to gather and provided a food source that was consistently available with the low tide.

The reliance on the hard-shore intertidal zone for the gathering of shellfish for consumption contrasts sharply with the zones necessarily exploited for the collection of molluscan raw materials for artefact production. With regards to species selected for working in the Pleistocene, *Turbo marmoratus* inhabit lagoonal habitats and, as argued in Szabó et al. (2007), the presence of the opercula as well as the lack of any evidence for bioerosion of the shells' interior or attrition caused by beach-rolling, suggests live collection. Very low occurrences of other taxa from lagoonal, subtidal habitats further demonstrate the exploitation of this zone by Pleistocene Golo occupants. Such subtidal species include the large spider conch *Lambis truncata*, the Partridge ton *Tonna perdix* and the baler shell *Melo* sp. It is possible that all of these species were collected with artefact production in mind, with *Lambis* spp. and *Melo* sp. being occasional raw materials across the region and exotic *Tonna dolium* identified within the freshwater midden at the Gan Kira entrance of the Niah Caves in Borneo (Szabó et al. 2013). The presence of fragments of *Nautilus* sp. body and septal chamber walls also indicates the collection of molluscan resources not necessarily tied to subsistence, and experimental work by Parkinson (2016) has shown clear evidence of working on some fragments. Of the array of shell species selected for artefact production, the only species that overlaps with the midden shell in type and habitat is *Scutellastra flexuosa*, which has been shown to have been occasionally repurposed from the midden as a cutting/scraping tool (Szabó and Koppel 2015).

The presence of a Pleistocene sequence where bone is entirely absent, yet molluscan shell is present and well-preserved seems highly anomalous and in want of explanation, yet this patterning is not without regional precedent. The two most notable analogies are the sequences from Leang Sarru on Salibabu Island, and earlier excavations at Leang Tuwo Mane'e on Karakelang Island, both in the Talaud group, which lies between the large Philippine island of Mindanao and Indonesian island of Sulawesi (Bellwood 1976; Ono et al. 2010; Tanudirjo 2005). The Leang Tuwo Mane'e deposits take in preceramic and ceramic material from c. 6000–1000 BP and fish bone is only reported from very recent deposits within the site, despite the presence of quantities of marine shell throughout (Bellwood 1976). The Leang Sarru sequence takes in a greater length of time, spanning from ~34,000 years through to upper earthenware-bearing deposits (Tanudirjo 2005; Ono et al. 2010). Shell midden and stone artefacts were recovered from throughout the sequence, with earthenware potsherds restricted to the upper deposits. No bone at all was recovered.

As with Golo Cave, Leang Tuwo Mane'e and Leang Sarru are limestone rockshelters, and so there would seem to be no *prima facie* reason why there should not be preservation of bone. Bellwood (1976:243) and Ono et al. (2010:323, 334) both point to the impoverished nature of the Talaud fauna with a lack of native mammals/marsupials and the dominant local terrestrial vertebrate fauna being rodents and bats/flying foxes. Presumably small reptiles, amphibians, and birds are also locally available, and fish would likewise have been accessible. Ono et al. (2010:323) suggests the fragility of fishbone could be a factor in their absence, but again the well-preserved nature of the shell requires a stronger taphonomic case to be made for the absence of bone.

Based on the current evidence from Golo Cave, coupled with Leang Tuwo Mane'e and Leang Sarru, there appears to be an economic pattern of reliance on marine invertebrate fauna during Pleistocene occupation on small, impoverished, and relatively remote Wallacean Islands. The very high totals of starch grains identified from the lowest layers of Golo Cave (see Chapter 2) may also be telling us something of the structure of Pleistocene subsistence. Rather than assuming the absence of bone is a taphonomic issue, it would be interesting to place greater focus upon understanding how such an apparently limited subsistence base supported continued occupation through the collection and study of fuller sequences. Is evidence of fishing to be found on the less exposed shores of Gebe, thus more closely aligning with records from Timor and surrounding islands (e.g. O'Connor et al. 2011; Samper Carro et al. 2016)? The repercussions of this reliance on marine invertebrate, and particularly molluscan, resources for the development and diversification of Pleistocene shell-working in the region would also benefit from a more detailed understanding of the available resources and economic behaviours of Pleistocene residents of islands such as Gebe.

11

Bioarchaeological analysis of the Northern Moluccan excavated human remains

David Bulbeck

Introduction

The Northern Moluccas form the northern apex of a triangle of small to medium-sized islands that extend to Sumba in the southwest and the Aru Islands in the southeast. These islands mark a rapid transition between indigenes with 'Melanesian' features to the east and inhabitants of predominantly 'Mongoloid' physical appearance to the north and the west. Summarising early physical anthropological research, conducted in a typological paradigm, Coon and Hunt (1965:180) wrote 'Some of the inhabitants are Negritos; others resemble Papuans. The Mongoloid element is minor'. Glinka (1981:103) emphasised the similarities between the populations across eastern Indonesia based on multivariate analysis of the recorded anthropometric data. He noted a predominantly dark brown skin colour, wavy to frizzy hair, a low incidence of epicanthic folds, low to medium stature, heads of narrow to medium breadth in shape with a very narrow forehead, and variable facial shape. Bulbeck et al. (2006) showed that recent crania from these islands have variable affinities, but predominantly with groups to the east of Wallace's Line, both 'Australoid' and Mongoloid, notably Tasmanians, Filipinos, New Britain Tolai, Guam Chamorros, and Hawaiians. The human remains excavated from the Northern Moluccas provide the opportunity to investigate whether this mixture of affinities also prevailed in prehistoric times.

Observations on the human remains also provide evidence on the palaeopathology of eastern Indonesians over the last two to three millennia. Oral pathology offers an insight into subsistence practices, while many diseases, especially those that stunt childhood growth, leave distinctive osteological markers. Some major diseases recorded during the nineteenth century in southeastern Indonesia include cholera, leprosy, malaria, sexually transmitted diseases, smallpox, and tuberculosis (Monk et al. 1997:493). In addition, two cultural practices, artificial cranial deformation and betel-nut chewing, are registered in the osteological assemblage.

Materials and methods

The researched materials include human burials dating to the last 2000–3000 years, excavated from rockshelters in the Northern Moluccas by the 'Archaeological Survey and Excavation in the Halmahera Islands, Moluccas, Indonesia' project (see Chapter 1). The identifiable individuals and unassigned remains are listed in Table 11.1. Weights were taken following cleaning and separation of associated materials that are not human bone and so may differ from the human bone weights provided in the excavation report chapters.

Table 11.1 Summary of human remains from the Northern Moluccan excavations.

Specimen	Island	Status	Weight (gm)	Estimated antiquity	Main composition	Burial mode
Golo LMN fragments	Gebe	Adults, 1 male	325	First millennium BCE?	Across skeleton	Disturbed primary extended?
Golo individual	Gebe	Male adult	1,834	2314–1415 cal. BP, ANU 11,818 on human bone	Whole skeleton	Primary extended
Tanjung Pinang 1	Morotai	Male subadult**	318	2684–1618 cal. BP, ANU 8439, apatite fraction**	Cranial	Secondary skull burial
Tanjung Pinang 2	Morotai	Male adult*	272.5	BCE/CE junction	Cranial	Secondary skull burial
Tanjung Pinang 3	Morotai	Male adult	268	BCE/CE junction	Cranial	Secondary skull burial
Tanjung Pinang 4	Morotai	Male adult*	163	BCE/CE junction	Cranial	Secondary skull burial
Tanjung Pinang 5	Morotai	Male teenager	316	BCE/CE junction	Cranial	Secondary skull burial
Tanjung Pinang 6	Morotai	Male adult*	345	BCE/CE junction	Cranial	Secondary skull burial
Tanjung Pinang 7	Morotai	Male adult	153	BCE/CE junction	Cranial	Secondary skull burial
Tanjung Pinang 8	Morotai	Male adult	360	BCE/CE junction	Cranial	Secondary skull burial
Tanjung Pinang 9	Morotai	Subadult	38.5	BCE/CE junction	Cranial	Secondary skull burial
Tanjung Pinang 10	Morotai	Male adult	69	BCE/CE junction	Cranial	Secondary skull burial
Tanjung Pinang unassigned	Morotai	Presumably from TP 1–10	1092	BCE/CE junction	Half cranial, half postcranial	From above?
Uattamdi 1	Kayoa	Male adult*	216	1932–1813 cal. BP, OxA 35,201 on human bone	Cranial	Secondary skull burial
Uattamdi 2	Kayoa	Adult/ subadult	35	BCE/CE junction	Cranial	Secondary skull burial
Uattamdi 3	Kayoa	Male adult	96	Recent	Cranial and postcranial	Secondary burial
Uattamdi 4	Kayoa	Infant	37	Recent	Mainly cranial	Secondary burial
Uattamdi 5	Kayoa	Subadult	45	Recent	Mainly cranial	Secondary burial
Uattamdi fragments	Kayoa	Infant to adult	107	First/second millennia CE	Across skeleton	Some from above Uattamdi burials?
Um Kapat Papo	Gebe	Female adult	32.5	First millennium CE	Cranial and postcranial	Secondary burials
Tanjung Tulang 1 to 3 (L5/M5/N5)	Morotai	Male adult, female adult, subadult	385	c. 1000 CE?	Cranial and postcranial	Secondary cremations
Tanjung Tulang 4 (E4/F6)	Morotai	Unsexed adult	38	c. 1000 CE?	Cranial and postcranial	Secondary cremations
Daeo 1 unassigned	Morotai	2 adults (at least 1 male), 1 subadult	347	c. 1000 CE?	Cranial and postcranial	Secondary burials, some cremation
Daeo 2 (1 to 4)	Morotai	5 adults and subadults	445	Recent	Cranial and postcranial	Secondary burials

* Identified as male from ancient DNA analysis, as also indicated on their anatomical criteria for Tanjung Pinang 1 and 6, and Uattamdi 1. Other sex assignments are based solely on anatomical criteria.

** Rachel Wood of the ANU Radiocarbon Facility comments that radiocarbon dates on apatite fractions tend to be too young, although by how much in this case is unknown. The unassigned bone submitted for ANU 8439 was collected in 1991 from the vicinities of Tanjung Pinang 1, 2, and 3.

Source: David Bulbeck.

11

Bioarchaeological analysis of the Northern Moluccan excavated human remains

David Bulbeck

Introduction

The Northern Moluccas form the northern apex of a triangle of small to medium-sized islands that extend to Sumba in the southwest and the Aru Islands in the southeast. These islands mark a rapid transition between indigenes with 'Melanesian' features to the east and inhabitants of predominantly 'Mongoloid' physical appearance to the north and the west. Summarising early physical anthropological research, conducted in a typological paradigm, Coon and Hunt (1965:180) wrote 'Some of the inhabitants are Negritos; others resemble Papuans. The Mongoloid element is minor'. Glinka (1981:103) emphasised the similarities between the populations across eastern Indonesia based on multivariate analysis of the recorded anthropometric data. He noted a predominantly dark brown skin colour, wavy to frizzy hair, a low incidence of epicanthic folds, low to medium stature, heads of narrow to medium breadth in shape with a very narrow forehead, and variable facial shape. Bulbeck et al. (2006) showed that recent crania from these islands have variable affinities, but predominantly with groups to the east of Wallace's Line, both 'Australoid' and Mongoloid, notably Tasmanians, Filipinos, New Britain Tolai, Guam Chamorros, and Hawaiians. The human remains excavated from the Northern Moluccas provide the opportunity to investigate whether this mixture of affinities also prevailed in prehistoric times.

Observations on the human remains also provide evidence on the palaeopathology of eastern Indonesians over the last two to three millennia. Oral pathology offers an insight into subsistence practices, while many diseases, especially those that stunt childhood growth, leave distinctive osteological markers. Some major diseases recorded during the nineteenth century in southeastern Indonesia include cholera, leprosy, malaria, sexually transmitted diseases, smallpox, and tuberculosis (Monk et al. 1997:493). In addition, two cultural practices, artificial cranial deformation and betel-nut chewing, are registered in the osteological assemblage.

Materials and methods

The researched materials include human burials dating to the last 2000–3000 years, excavated from rockshelters in the Northern Moluccas by the 'Archaeological Survey and Excavation in the Halmahera Islands, Moluccas, Indonesia' project (see Chapter 1). The identifiable individuals and unassigned remains are listed in Table 11.1. Weights were taken following cleaning and separation of associated materials that are not human bone and so may differ from the human bone weights provided in the excavation report chapters.

Table 11.1 Summary of human remains from the Northern Moluccan excavations.

Specimen	Island	Status	Estimated antiquity	Weight (gm)	Main composition	Burial mode
Golo LMN fragments	Gebe	Adults, 1 male	First millennium BCE?	325	Across skeleton	Disturbed primary extended?
Golo individual	Gebe	Male adult	2314–1415 cal. BP, ANU 11,818 on human bone	1,834	Whole skeleton	Primary extended
Tanjung Pinang 1	Morotai	Male subadult**	2684–1618 cal. BP, ANU 8439, apatite fraction**	318	Cranial	Secondary skull burial
Tanjung Pinang 2	Morotai	Male adult*	BCE/CE junction	272.5	Cranial	Secondary skull burial
Tanjung Pinang 3	Morotai	Male adult	BCE/CE junction	268	Cranial	Secondary skull burial
Tanjung Pinang 4	Morotai	Male adult*	BCE/CE junction	163	Cranial	Secondary skull burial
Tanjung Pinang 5	Morotai	Male teenager	BCE/CE junction	316	Cranial	Secondary skull burial
Tanjung Pinang 6	Morotai	Male adult*	BCE/CE junction	345	Cranial	Secondary skull burial
Tanjung Pinang 7	Morotai	Male adult	BCE/CE junction	153	Cranial	Secondary skull burial
Tanjung Pinang 8	Morotai	Male adult	BCE/CE junction	360	Cranial	Secondary skull burial
Tanjung Pinang 9	Morotai	Subadult	BCE/CE junction	38.5	Cranial	Secondary skull burial
Tanjung Pinang 10	Morotai	Male adult	BCE/CE junction	69	Cranial	Secondary skull burial
Tanjung Pinang unassigned	Morotai	Presumably from TP 1–10	BCE/CE junction	1092	Half cranial, half postcranial	From above?
Uattamdi 1	Kayoa	Male adult*	1932–1813 cal. BP, OxA 35,201 on human bone	216	Cranial	Secondary skull burial
Uattamdi 2	Kayoa	Adult/ subadult	BCE/CE junction	35	Cranial	Secondary skull burial
Uattamdi 3	Kayoa	Male adult	Recent	96	Cranial and postcranial	Secondary burial
Uattamdi 4	Kayoa	Infant	Recent	37	Mainly cranial	Secondary burial
Uattamdi 5	Kayoa	Subadult	Recent	45	Mainly cranial	Secondary burial
Uattamdi fragments	Kayoa	Infant to adult	First/second millennia CE	107	Across skeleton	Some from above above Uattamdi burials?
Um Kapat Papo	Gebe	Female adult	First millennium CE	32.5	Cranial and postcranial	Secondary burials
Tanjung Tulang 1 to 3 (L5/M5/N5)	Morotai	Male adult, female adult, subadult	c. 1000 CE?	385	Cranial and postcranial	Secondary cremations
Tanjung Tulang 4 (E4/F6)	Morotai	Unsexed adult	c. 1000 CE?	38	Cranial and postcranial	Secondary cremations
Daeo 1 unassigned	Morotai	2 adults (at least 1 male), 1 subadult	c. 1000 CE?	347	Cranial and postcranial	Secondary burials, some cremation
Daeo 2 (1 to 4)	Morotai	5 adults and subadults	Recent	445	Cranial and postcranial	Secondary burials

* Identified as male from ancient DNA analysis, as also indicated on their anatomical criteria for Tanjung Pinang 1 and 6, and Uattamdi 1. Other sex assignments are based solely on anatomical criteria.

** Rachel Wood of the ANU Radiocarbon Facility comments that radiocarbon dates on apatite fractions tend to be too young, although by how much in this case is unknown. The unassigned bone submitted for ANU 8439 was collected in 1991 from the vicinities of Tanjung Pinang 1, 2, and 3.

Source: David Bulbeck.

The burial modes listed in Table 11.1 suggest a focus on secondary skull burials at approximately 2000 years ago, albeit complemented by the alternative burial treatment of a primary extended inhumation in Golo Cave at a similar time, followed later by secondary burials, including burial of cremated remains at around 1000 BP.

Treatment of the burial material included mechanical cleaning of the bones and teeth. Most of this was undertaken by the author, but in some cases by Kate Stockhausen (former PhD student in the School of Archaeology and Anthropology, ANU), and in some other cases by Jennifer R. Hull during her study of the Northern Moluccan faunal material for her BA Honours research in the same school. Additional treatment of the Golo extended burial involved soaking the bone in a 3 per cent solution of acetic acid for about 24 hours to weaken the calcium carbonate crust. The treated fragments were then soaked in several changes of water to leach any acetic acid from the bone, followed by drying in air, and mechanical cleaning of the residual calcium carbonate crust.

After cleaning, the human remains were separated from any associated faunal material. The human bone elements were identified with reference to standard human anatomy atlases and the reference human skeleton held at the School of Archaeology and Anthropology, ANU. Joins between bone fragments were effected (using Tarzan's Grip®) based on matching breaks, identification to the same element, and physical proximity in the excavated deposits. The effected joins facilitated additional element identifications. When reconstruction had proceeded as far as practical, an attempt was made to assign the remains to different individuals, considering biological clues such as likely age at death and, in the context of whether the elements are juvenile or adult, a male or female status based on general size and robustness. The attempted individuation was performed primarily on the cranial material, which dominates the burial assemblage at most of the sites.

Numerous measurements and anatomical observations were undertaken following a variety of systems that have been used in recording Oriental-Pacific human remains. Most of the original observations, which were used in assessing the likely age and sex of the identified individuals (and unassigned remains), were detailed in a series of unpublished reports to Peter Bellwood. Many of the observations in these reports serve no greater purpose than to produce the list of specimens and associated information in Table 11.1, and so are not replicated here.

These original observations include Stockhausen's identifications of loose teeth, most of which I was unable to relocate, from Uattamdi, Tanjung Tulang, Daeo 1, and Daeo 2. The observations also include my notes on the extent of closure of the cranial sutures, which, along with information on whether all of the permanent teeth had erupted and the extent of wear on the erupted permanent teeth, formed the basis for assessing the age at death of the individuated burials. Only occasionally was it possible to confidently link an individual's cranial and postcranial remains, and so to assess the biological age of an individual based on postcranial indicators such as the degree of epiphyseal union of the limb bones. However, my observations on the fragments of human bone that Jennifer R. Hull extracted from the Uattamdi faunal refuse are briefly summarised here.

The observations presented here include those of value for assessing biological affinities. A number of recorded measurements are dependent on the accuracy of the reconstructions, which involve a certain degree of judgement for tasks of any greater complexity than gluing together joining fragments. Some additional measurements further required the assumption of bilateral symmetry.

In terms of analytical methodology, the exploration of the individuals' biological affinities focuses on craniometrics. The measurements reported here are those defined by Howells (1973b), excluding radii and cranial fractions. This allows statistical comparison with the populations measured by Howells (1989) as well as six series from India measured by Pathmanathan Raghavan

(Bulbeck 2013). In addition, I recorded male and female crania with 'circumferential deformation' (Lindsell 1995) from Malekula Island, Vanuatu, Melanesia. This was to provide an appropriate 'Australoid' counterpart in the comparisons for the Golo cranium, which, as described below, has marked circumferential deformation. For each compared Northern Moluccan cranium, classification formulae for the comparative series were derived for the measurements available for the Moluccan specimen, allowing the specimen's probability of classification with each of the Howells' series/Malekula to be calculated. This exercise was performed in XLSTAT using discrimination function analysis, including the option to calculate canonical variates.

The affinities of the male Moluccan crania were also explored using the anatomical characters defined by Larnach and Macintosh (1966). The characters of relevance here are those that I have found to be consistently recorded by different observers and also useful in discriminating 'Indo-Malay' crania (recent Island Southeast Asia crania northwest of eastern Indonesia) from both Australian Aboriginal and Melanesian crania (Bulbeck 2013). The Boolean expressions evaluate as 'True' for Indo-Malay crania and 'False' for Australian crania (Table 11.2) and Melanesian crania (Table 11.3). Boolean formulae are used as these may allow the classification of crania to be undertaken, even if not all of the listed characters are extant.

Table 11.2 Boolean formulae classifying Indo-Malay and Australian male crania.

Type of formula	Indo-Malay expression (Australian expression is the logical opposite)	Correctly classified	
		Indo-Malays	Australians
1. Strongest discrimination	[(Glabella not large OR Supraorbital breadth not large) AND (Sagittal keel indistinct OR Naso-frontal articulation width narrow OR Parietal bossing prominent) AND Palate module −39] OR Cranial index ×75	113/117 (97%)	176/194 (91%)
2. All Indo-Malays	(Palate module −39 OR Cranial index ×75) AND (Glabella not large OR Median frontal ridge indistinct OR Sagittal keel indistinct)	117/117 (100%)	143/199 (72%)
3. All Australians	Cranial index ×75 AND [Orbital border sharp OR Phaenozygy absent OR (Naso-frontal articulation width narrow AND Transverse occipital torus absent)]	54/117 (46%)	210/210 (100%)

Source: David Bulbeck.

Table 11.3 Boolean formulae classifying Indo-Malay and Melanesian male crania.

Type of formula	Indo-Malay expression (Melanesian expression is the logical opposite)	Correctly classified	
		Indo-Malays	Melanesians
1. Strongest discrimination	Orbital border sharp OR Transverse occipital torus absent OR (Cranial index ×75 AND Palate module −39 AND Anterior nasal spine less than Broca 4)	83/112 (74%)	416/493 (84%)
2. All Indo-Malays	Cranial index ×75 OR [Palate module −39 AND (Orbital border sharp OR Supraorbital breadth not large OR Frontal curvature index >24.7)]	117/117 (100%)	200/492 (41%)
3. All Melanesians	(Orbital border sharp OR Transverse occipital torus absent) AND (Phaenozygy absent OR Parietal bossing prominent) AND [Cranial index ×75 OR (Frontal curvature index >24.7 AND Supraorbital breadth not large AND Supramastoid crest not slight)]	27/117 (23%)	525/525 (100%)

Note: Frontal curvature index is treated as a missing observation for the Malekula crania, owing to their circumferential deformation.

Source: David Bulbeck.

As a test of the effectiveness of these formulae for classifying recent eastern Indonesian male crania, we would predict the resulting classifications to straddle the Indo-Malay and Australian/Melanesian reference samples. This is indeed found to be the case, based on a small available sample of six recent male eastern Indonesians recorded by the author (Table 11.4). For instance, while four of the six crania (three from Flores and one from Solor) are more probably Indo-Malay than Australian or Melanesian, even these crania would lie within the Melanesian range of variation, and another cranium (Gua Nempong) has a distinctly Australoid cranial morphology.

Table 11.4 Results from application of the Boolean formulae in Tables 11.2 and 11.3 to a sample of six recent eastern Indonesian male crania.

Formula	Flores, Hamy 4-1-6 09.929; Solor, MacLeay 84.45	Flores, Hamy 4-1-3 09.928, Flores, Hamy 4-1-4 09.926	Timor, MacLeay 84.42	Flores, Gua Nempong
2.1	Indo-Malay	Indo-Malay	Indo-Malay	Australian
2.2	Indo-Malay	Indo-Malay	Indo-Malay	Australian
2.3	Indo-Malay	Australian	Australian	Australian
3.1	Indo-Malay	Indo-Malay	Melanesian	Melanesian
3.2	Indo-Malay	Indo-Malay	Indo-Malay	Melanesian
3.3	Melanesian	Melanesian	Melanesian	Melanesian

Note: The Hamy expedition specimens were recorded at the Musée de l'Homme, Paris.

Source: David Bulbeck.

Multivariate metrical comparisons of the mandible from the Golo extended burial were undertaken based on the measurements presented in Table 11.8 (below). Table 11.5 lists the 107 mandibles from South Asia, Island Southeast Asia, and Melanesia recorded for the same measurements. The non-Melanesian sample sizes are small and so the comparisons treated the specimens as ungrouped individuals. The comparisons included principle components analysis, using the default settings on XLSTAT, and *k*-means clustering, performed using SAS EG. The latter analysis employed full seed replacement, as this minimises the differences in assignment of individuals to groups between different runs (Laszlo and Mukherjee 2007), with the number of clusters set at six to correspond to the six groups in Table 11.5. Also, the number of iterations was set at 20 (six iterations proved to be sufficient to satisfy the convergence criterion).

Table 11.5 Individual specimens and groups included in the mandibular metrical comparisons.

Individual/group	Group sample size	Details
Liang Lemdubu	N/A	c. 18,000-year-old female from Aru (Bulbeck 2005)
Watinglo	N/A	c. 10,000-year-old male from Papua New Guinea's north coast (Bulbeck and O'Connor 2011)
Liang Momer E	N/A	'Mesolithic' male from Flores
Liang Toge	N/A	c. 4000-year-old female from Flores
Eastern Indonesian males	7	Melolo, Sumba (2); Gua Nempong, Flores; Golo; 3 ethnographic (museum) specimens
Melanesian males	44	New Britain (19), New Ireland (1), Malekula (2), coastal Papua New Guinea including Motupore Island (22)
Melanesian females	26	New Britain (9), coastal Papua New Guinea including Motupore Island (17)
Indo-Malay males	15	Leang Buidane, Talauds (1); South Sulawesi (8); Singapore Malays (6)
Indo-Malay females	2	Provenanced only as 'Indonesia'
South Asians	9	Six males and three females from Andhra Pradesh and Sri Lanka, grouped due to minimal sexual dimorphism

Note: Unpublished data except where otherwise indicated. Criteria for sexing mandibles explained in Bulbeck and O'Connor (2011).

Source: David Bulbeck.

The available sample sizes of teeth are small, and so aggregated observations on dental metrics and oral pathology are presented in their own section towards the end of this paper. My original reports include tooth lengths and breadths recorded at the cemento-enamel junction, which can usually be taken even on very worn teeth (Snell 1949), as well as the maximum lengths and breadths that I recorded wherever interstitial wear or other effects on the teeth had not significantly reduced the dimensions available for recording. These latter observations are re-presented here to allow comparison between the Northern Moluccan burials and recorded Oriental-Pacific populations. The comparative statistic employed is Brace's (1976, 1980) 'summed tooth area', which provides a useful summary of tooth size, even though it is affected by the sexual composition and extent of interstitial wear of the available sample.

Occlusal tooth wear was recorded following Smith's (1984) system, and oral pathology following Patterson's (1984) system, with his different classes aggregated into major categories to allow condensation of the relevant information. Observations on the morphology and location of macroscopic linear enamel hypoplasia are also condensed into noting their presence at the cervical, medium, or occlusal third of the affected tooth. This is to allow an assessment of whether they probably reflect systemic arrests to childhood growth, registered by most or all of the teeth whose enamel should have been forming at the same age, or just a localised interruption to enamel formation (Hillson 1996).

Signs of pathology were also recorded on the cranial vault and other bones, based on the criteria described by Aufderheide and Rodríguez-Martin (1998).

Finally, a Penrose (1954) size and shape analysis, which separates these two components of Pearson's 'Coefficient of Racial Likeness', was undertaken on the lengths of the Golo limb bones. Penrose's statistic was chosen as a simple multivariate statistic whose conditions for application require only sample sizes, means, and standard deviations, which describes the form of most of the useful comparative data to which I have access. These (male) data come from Abe (1955), Inabe (1955), Mizoguchi (1957), and Sendo (1957) for Japanese; Genet-Varcin (1951, no standard deviations provided) for Aeta Negritos; Bergman and The (1955) for Javanese; Sarasin (1916–22) for New Caledonians and Loyalty Islanders; and Davivongs (1963a), van Dongen (1963), and Rao (1966) for Australian Aborigines.

The human remains from Golo Cave, Gebe

The oldest excavated human remains from the Northern Moluccas may be the Golo fragments from the LMN Squares. The basis for this inference is their weathered to very weathered appearance (Fig. 11.1), contrasting with the generally less weathered appearance of the extended burial, which has been directly dated to 2314–1415 cal. BP (ANU 11818). The LMN remains include fragments from two or more individuals, including what appears to be the proximal shaft of a male humerus. The inference of two individuals is based on the discrepancy between the maxilla and mandible fragments in their oral pathology and the degree of wear on the molars. The limb bone shaft fragments are quite large, especially after re-joining of adjacent segments, which suggests they may derive from disturbed primary burials rather than secondary burials.

Figure 11.1 Reconstructed limb bone fragments from Golo LMN Squares.
Source: David Bulbeck.

The Golo primary burial (Fig. 11.2) is directly radiocarbon dated to 1900±190 BP (ANU 11818), which calibrates to 2314–1415 BP at 95.4 per cent (Table 1.1). It is an adult male, with a stature when alive of around 163 cm, and an age at death of around 40 (30–50) years suggested by the dental remains (detailed towards the end of this chapter). Apart from the individual's poor state of oral health, and mild porotic hyperostosis on its extant frontal towards the midline, no signs of pathology were observed on the remains. The individual's male status is indicated by its (left) pelvic morphology—for instance, its large vertical acetabulum diameter of 56.5 mm and the small width and depth of its greater sciatic notch of 41.5 mm and 25 mm respectively (cf. Davivongs 1963b)—as well as its robust cranial morphology and large mandible.

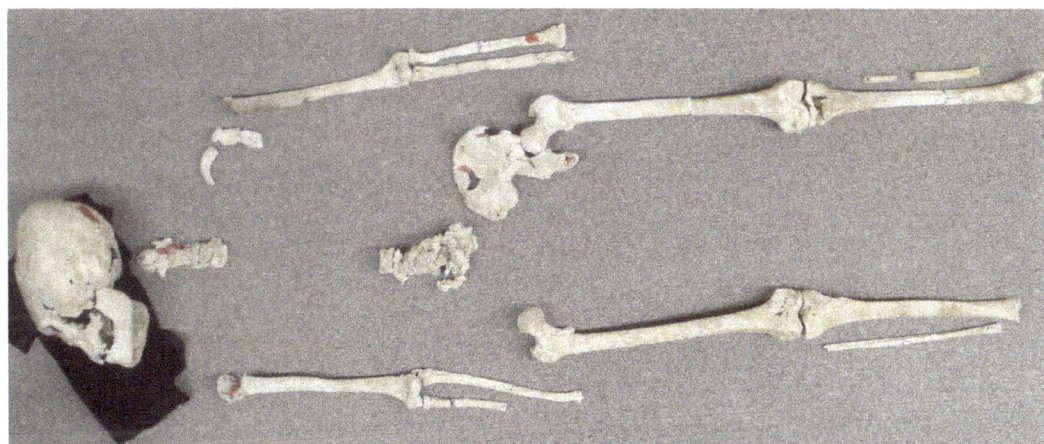

Figure 11.2 Golo extended burial after reconstruction (excluding the right pelvis, sacrificed for direct radiocarbon dating).
Source: David Bulbeck.

The Golo extended burial cranium

The extended burial has an artificially flattened frontal bone (Fig. 11.3), as registered by its small nasion-bregma subtense (more than one standard deviation below the mean recorded for any Howells' series). Other craniometric peculiarities include a very large bregma-lambda subtense, more than four standard deviations above the mean recorded for any Howells' series, associated with a vertex (highest point on the cranial vault in the Frankfort horizontal plane) that lies well posterior to bregma, producing a basion-vertex height of 156 mm, much larger than the basion-bregma height of 133 mm. Technically, the Golo individual shows circumferential erect deformation, which would have involved some sort of binding around the front and the back of its head during childhood, preventing the growing brain from filling out in these directions (Lindsell 1995).

Craniometrically, the Golo cranium clearly classifies with Malekula. Two sets of measurements were entered, the first excluding the measurements that could be taken only by assuming symmetry (Table 11.6), and the second including those measurements. In both cases, Golo registered a 100 per cent probability of being classified as Malekula. Significantly, none of the crania from the Howells' series would have been classified as Malekula. The only crania other than Golo to be classified as Malekula were the Malekula crania themselves: 16/18 (89 per cent) in the first analysis and 17/18 (94 per cent) in the second analysis. Inspection of the discriminant functions shows that a small frontal subtense and large parietal subtense—measurements both directly affected by head binding—were important for securing a 'Malekula' classification. That is, the classification obtained for the Golo cranium simply reflects this cultural practice, without of course implying that Golo might not have registered Melanesian craniometrics even in the absence of cranial deformation.

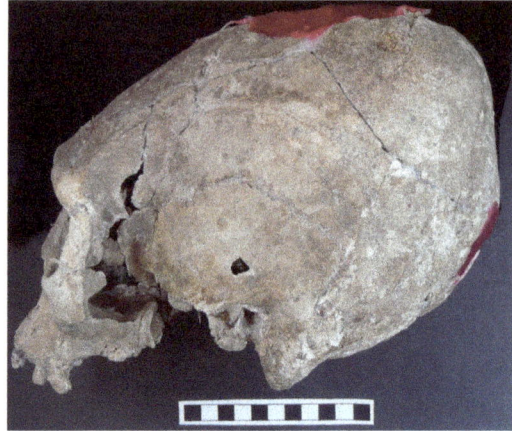

Figure 11.3 Left lateral view of the cranium from the Golo extended burial.

Source: David Bulbeck.

The observable anatomical features (Larnach and Macintosh 1966) relevant to assessing the biological affinities of the Golo cranium are presented in Table 11.7. An additional measurement required to fill the table is the palate length, which is 70 mm, to produce a palate module of 43.8 when multiplied by external palate breadth. Note that the cranium's strongly receding frontal, registered by its frontal curvature index of 15.5 (188*FRS/FRC), is not included in Table 11.7, as this shape aspect clearly reflects cultural modification rather than genetic ancestry.

The Golo cranium would be classified as Australian on all three Boolean formulae that distinguish between Indo-Malay and Australian crania, and as Melanesian on all three Boolean formulae that distinguish between Indo-Malay and Melanesian crania. Accordingly, its anatomy lies outside of the recorded range of recent Indo-Malays and entirely within the range of recent 'Australoids'.

Table 11.6 Measurements (in mm) defined by Howells (1973b) recorded on the Golo cranium.

Measurement	Acronym	Value	Comments
Glabello-occipital length	GOL	187	Dependent on accuracy of reconstruction
Nasio-occipital length	NOL	187.5	Dependent on accuracy of reconstruction
Basion-nasion length	BNL	81	Dependent on accuracy of reconstruction
Basion-bregma height	BBH	133	Dependent on accuracy of reconstruction
Maximum cranial breadth	XCB	120	Symmetry assumed to take measurement
Maximum frontal breadth	XFB	110	Symmetry assumed to take measurement
Bistephanic breadth	STB	104	
Biauricular breadth	AUB	113.5	
Minimum cranial breadth	WCB	71	Symmetry assumed to take measurement
Biasterionic breadth	ASB	124	Exceeds XCB (measured above the supramastoid crests)
Basion-prosthion length	BPL	93	Dependent on accuracy of reconstruction
Nasion-prosthion height	NPH	67	
Nasal height	NLH	49.5	Dependent on accuracy of reconstruction
Orbit height, left	OBH	35	
Orbit breadth, left	OBB	39.5	
Bijugalia breadth	JUB	112.5	
Nasal breadth	NLB	31	Dependent on accuracy of reconstruction
Palate breadth, external	MAB	62.5	
Mastoid height	MDH	30	Left side
Mastoid breadth	MDB	15.5	Left side
Bimaxillary breadth	ZMB	96	Symmetry assumed to take measurement
Zygomaxillary subtense	SSS	36.5	Symmetry assumed to take measurement
Bifrontal breadth	FMB	103	Symmetry assumed to take measurement
Nasio-frontal subtense	NAS	15	Symmetry assumed to take measurement
Biorbital breadth	EKB	102	Symmetry assumed to take measurement
Cheek height, left	WMH	20	
Supraorbital projection	SOS	13.5	
Foramen magnum length	FOL	32.5	Dependent on accuracy of reconstruction
Nasion-bregma chord	FRC	116	Dependent on accuracy of reconstruction
Nasion-bregma subtense	FRS	18	Dependent on accuracy of reconstruction
Bregma-lambda chord	PAC	115	Dependent on accuracy of reconstruction
Bregma-lambda subtense	PAS	38	Dependent on accuracy of reconstruction
Lambda-opisthion chord	OCC	114	Dependent on accuracy of reconstruction
Lambda-opisthion subtense	OCS	33	Dependent on accuracy of reconstruction

Source: David Bulbeck.

Table 11.7 Relevant anatomical observations of the Golo extended burial cranium.

Character	Observation	Binary value (Tables 10.2 and 10.3)
Maximum supraorbital breadth	110 mm	Large
Parietal bossing	Absent	Not prominent
Palate module	43.8	Large
Cranial index (100*XCB/GOL)	64.2	<75 (Narrow)
Phaenozygy	Present	Not absent
Transverse occipital torus	Medium	Present
Malar orbital border	Trace rounding	Not sharp
Anterior nasal spine	Broca 2	Less than Broca 4
Supramastoid crest	Large (left)	Not slight

Source: David Bulbeck.

The Golo extended burial mandible

The measurements taken on the Golo mandible (Fig. 11.4) are presented in Table 11.8. The measurements' loadings on Principal Components (PC) 1 to 3 in the PC analysis are presented in Table 11.9. PC 1, accounting for 45 per cent of variance, reflects size, as is usually found in PC analysis of biometric data (Joliffe 2002). PCs 2 and 3 are the main shape variables, both having an eigenvalue above 1, and respectively accounting for 19 per cent and 10 per cent of variance. A high score on PC 2 marks mandibles with a tall corpus while a low score marks mandibles with a broad corpus. In the case of PC 3, a high score reflects mandibles that are broad posteriorly in relation to corpus breadths and a low score reflects mandibles that are posteriorly narrow in relation to corpus breadths.

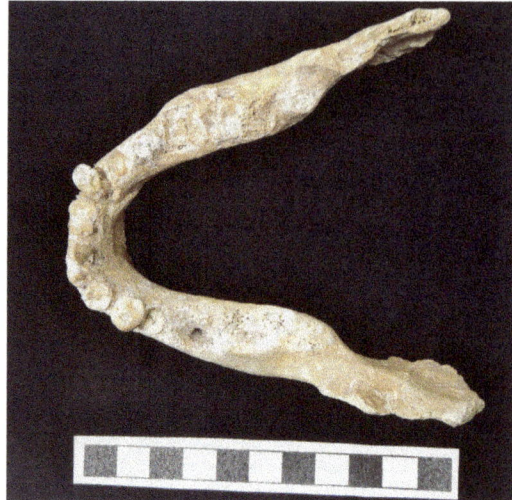

Figure 11.4 Superior view of the mandible from the Golo extended burial.
Source: David Bulbeck.

Table 11.8 Measurements on the Golo mandible included for analysis.

Measurement	Acronym	Golo value	Measurement source
Symphysis height	h1	33.5	Morant 1936
Chin height	M69	34	Bräuer 1988
Corpus height at mental foramen	M69(1)	29.5 (left)	Bräuer 1988
Corpus thickness at mental foramen	M69(3)	14 (left)	Bräuer 1988
Breadth between mental foramena	zz	53.5	Morant 1936
Corpus height between first and second molars	CHe	28	Brown 1989; Storm 1995
Corpus thickness between first and second molars	CTh	16	Brown 1989; Storm 1995
Interobliqual breadth	IOB	82.5	Jacob 1967a
Gnathion-gonion length	gngo	96.5 (left)	Morant 1936
Inferior breadth between gonia	gogo	88	Morant 1936
Outer breadth between gonia	w2	93.5	Morant 1936
Minimum ramus breadth	rb'	37	Morant 1936

Source: David Bulbeck.

Table 11.9 Loadings of the measurements for PC 1 to 3 in the Golo mandible PC analysis.

Measurement	PC 1	PC 2	PC 3
Symphysis height	0.259	0.468	0.014
Chin height	0.263	0.458	0.010
Corpus height at mental foramen	0.302	0.371	−0.021
Corpus thickness at mental foramen	0.252	−0.225	−0.468
Breadth between mental foramena	0.313	−0.179	−0.179
Corpus height between first and second molars	0.332	0.278	−0.112
Corpus thickness between first and second molars	0.214	−0.323	−0.381
Interobliqual breadth	0.316	−0.131	0.022
Gnathion-gonion length	0.336	−0.131	0.105
Inferior breadth between gonia	0.290	−0.239	0.542
Outer breadth between gonia	0.309	−0.242	0.484
Minimum ramus breadth	0.251	−0.138	−0.238

Source: David Bulbeck.

The Golo mandible scores 2.63 on PC 1. This is within the range recorded for other eastern Indonesian males (0.87 to 4.13) and Melanesian males (−2.04 to 5.41) and similar to the terminal Pleistocene male from Watinglo in Papua New Guinea (2.83). It lies above the range obtained for Indo-Malay males (−1.12 to 1.90), Indo-Malay females (−3.43 to −3.14), Melanesian females (−4.92 to 2.53), and South Asians (−5.57 to −3.15). In terms of size, the Golo mandible is quite large (and male), which is more typical of eastern Indonesian and Melanesian males than any of the other comparative series.

Figure 11.5 plots the analysed mandibles' scores on a two-dimensional plot with PCs 2 and 3 represented by the two axes. As shown there, Indo-Malay mandibles tend to have high negative to low positive scores on both PCs, Melanesian mandibles tend to have low negative to high positive scores on both PCs, while eastern Indonesian and South Asian mandibles tend to be intermediate in both respects. The Golo mandible falls within the large central area of overlap between the different series. Its shape is not diagnostic in terms of Asia-Pacific population affinities.

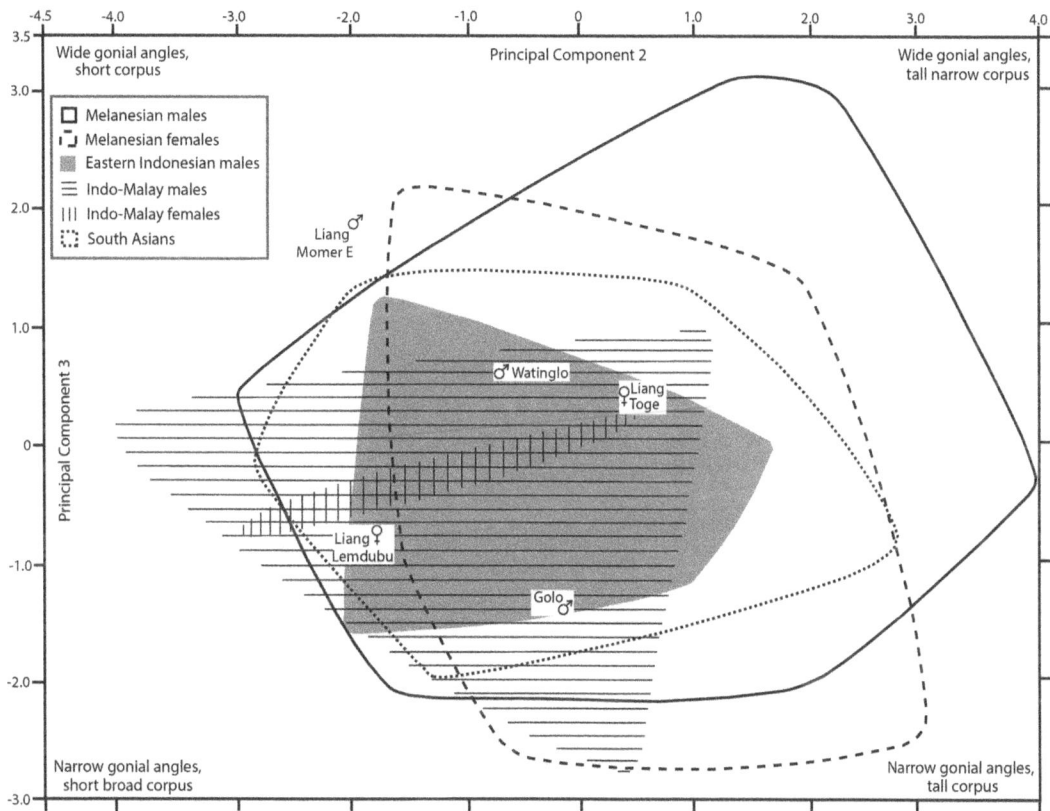

Figure 11.5 Mandibular metrical analysis, two-dimensional plot of PC 2 and 3.
Source: David Bulbeck.

Figure 11.6 plots the means of the six *k*-means clusters, which combine both size and shape in the same analysis. The implications of Figure 11.6 are summarised in Table 11.10, which also presents the membership of the six clusters. Assignment of the mandibles to the six clusters is far from random, as represented by the asterisked probability in the last column of Table 11.10. To calculate that probability, the number of combinations with the discovered membership, or a more extreme membership, was placed in the numerator, and the total number of combinations (whereby the 107 mandibles could be assigned to the six discovered clusters, 6.124 multiplied by 10 to the power of 71) was placed in the denominator. For instance, cluster 4 contained four eastern Indonesian mandibles, including Golo. The number of combinations in which this cluster of 23 mandibles could have included 4 to 7 of the eastern Indonesian mandibles is 2.278

multiplied by 10 to the power of 70. This number, divided by the total number of combinations, comes to less than 0.05, demonstrating a statistically significant over-representation of eastern Indonesian males in cluster 4 (at the conventional $p<0.05$ confidence level).

Cluster 4 also has a strong representation of Melanesian male mandibles, although not strong enough to be statistically significant. However, the probability that cluster 4 would include both four or more eastern Indonesian males and 12 or more Melanesian males is very low, 0.0019. Accordingly, k-means clustering would assign the Golo mandible to a cluster dominated by eastern Indonesian and Melanesian males.

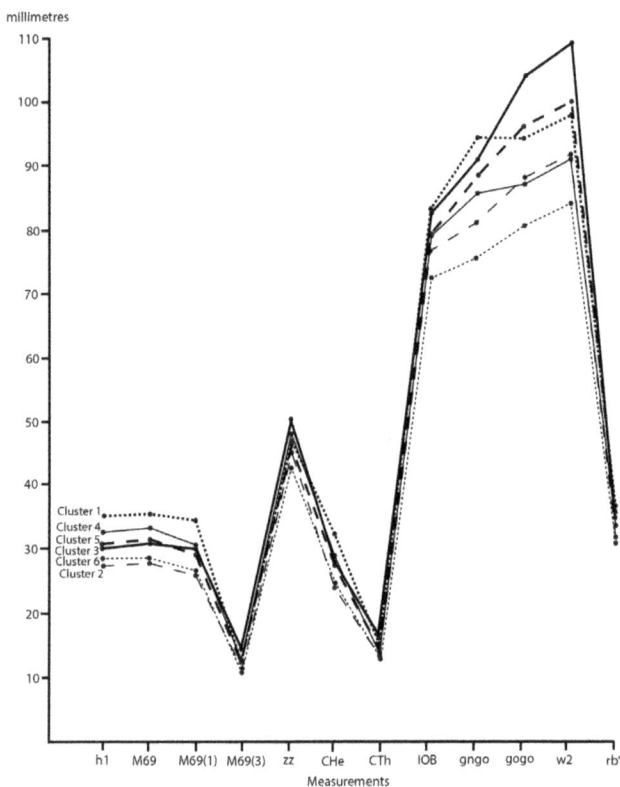

Figure 11.6 Mean mandibular measurements for clusters 1 to 6 identified by k-means analysis.
Source: David Bulbeck.

Table 11.10 Characterisation of the six k-means clusters in the mandibular metrical analysis.

Cluster	Metrical description	Composition	Asterisked probability
1	Tall anterior corpus, long corpus	4 Melanesian males*	0.0263
2	Small mandibles especially on anterior corpus heights	7 Melanesian males, 12 Melanesian females*, 1 Indo-Malay male, 1 Indo-Malay female, 2 South Asians	0.0002
3	Wide mandibles especially across gonial angles	Watinglo, Liang Momer E, 4 Melanesian males, 1 Melanesian female, 2 eastern Indonesian males, 1 Indo-Malay male	–
4	Comparatively large except across gonial angles	12 Melanesian males, 5 Melanesian females, 4 eastern Indonesian males*, 2 Indo-Malay males	0.0372
5	Comparatively large (on all measurements)	Liang Lemdubu, Liang Toge, 16 Melanesian males, 2 Melanesian females, 1 eastern Indonesian male, 11 Indo-Malay males*	0.0002
6	Small mandibles especially across gonial angles	1 Melanesian male, 6 Melanesian females, 1 Indo-Malay female, 7 South Asians*	0.0000

See text for an explanation of asterisked probability.
Source: David Bulbeck.

The Golo extended burial limb bone lengths

The limb bones of the Golo postcranial skeleton are largely complete, allowing them to be measured for their lengths as also recorded for several populations surrounding eastern Indonesia. The Golo measurements used in the analysis are presented in Table 11.11, and the square roots of the Penrose size and shape distances are presented in Table 11.12. The analysis of the square roots of the size distances is simple because they are additive, and so can be expressed in terms of the distance from the group with the shortest (or longest) limb bones. The analysis of the square roots of the shape distances was performed by finding the resultant average-linkage dendrogram and seriating the dendrogram (see Bulbeck 2013 for a detailed account of seriated dendrograms). The results of the analysis are presented in Figure 11.7.

Table 11.11 Golo limb bone measurements used in the Penrose analysis.

Measurement	Martin number	Golo's value (mm)	Comments
Femur oblique length	M2	423 (right)	Complete (left side 424 mm)
Tibia lateral condyle-malleolar length	M1	354 (right)	Complete
Fibula maximum length	M1	352.5 (right)	Estimated from the available shaft length of 267 mm
Humerus maximum length	M2	304 (left)	Complete
Radius physiological length	M2	227.5 (left)	Complete
Ulna maximum length	M1	262 (left)	Complete

Note: Martin's measurements defined by Bräuer (1988).

Source: David Bulbeck.

Table 11.12 Square roots of Penrose size (bottom-left half-matrix) and shape (top-right half-matrix) distances for limb bone lengths of Golo and the comparative Oriental-Pacific groups.

	Aeta	Loyalty Islanders	Golo	Javanese	Australians	New Caledonians	Japanese
Aeta	–	0.195	0.221	0.170	0.245	0.352	0.445
Loyalty Islanders	1.835	–	0.103	0.155	0.179	0.214	0.329
Golo	1.308		–	0.129	0.115	0.192	0.286
Javanese	0.963			–	0.100	0.224	0.293
Australians	2.068				–	0.164	0.214
New Caledonians	1.713					–	0.141
Japanese	0.361						–

Note: Golo and compared groups arranged in the seriated order for the shape distances. Size distances other than those presented can be calculated with reference to the Aeta distances (for instance, the distance between Loyalty Islanders and Golo = 1.835 – 1.308 = 0.527).

Source: David Bulbeck.

The Golo limb bone lengths are shorter than the averages recorded for the comparative southwest Pacific groups, but longer than the averages recorded for the comparative East Asian groups, especially the Aeta Negritos, who have the shortest limb bones. In terms of shape distances, Golo clusters with Loyalty Islanders and otherwise seriates adjacently to Javanese (who cluster with Australians). Golo is very different from Japanese both in terms of its longer limb bones and their different shape (Fig. 11.7). Index analysis, which is at best an approximation of the metrical drivers of the multivariate results, shows that Golo has long distal limb bones compared to its femur and humerus lengths, and a short humerus compared to its femur length (Table 11.13), contrasting with Japanese in these respects.

Bergman and The (1955) have published regression formulae for the estimation of Javanese male stature from their limb bone lengths. The similarity of Golo to Javanese in their limb bone proportions (Table 11.13) allows these formulae to be applied to Golo. The resulting estimates for Golo vary between 162 cm (fibula) and 165 cm (ulna), indicating the Golo male had a stature of around 163 cm when alive. This would fall just within the range of means of 154–163 cm recorded for living eastern Indonesian males (Keers 1948).

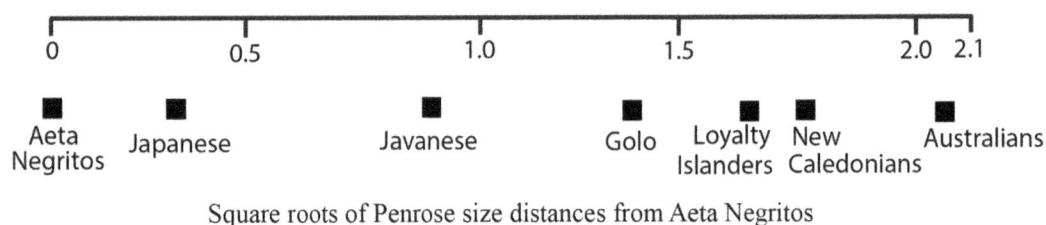

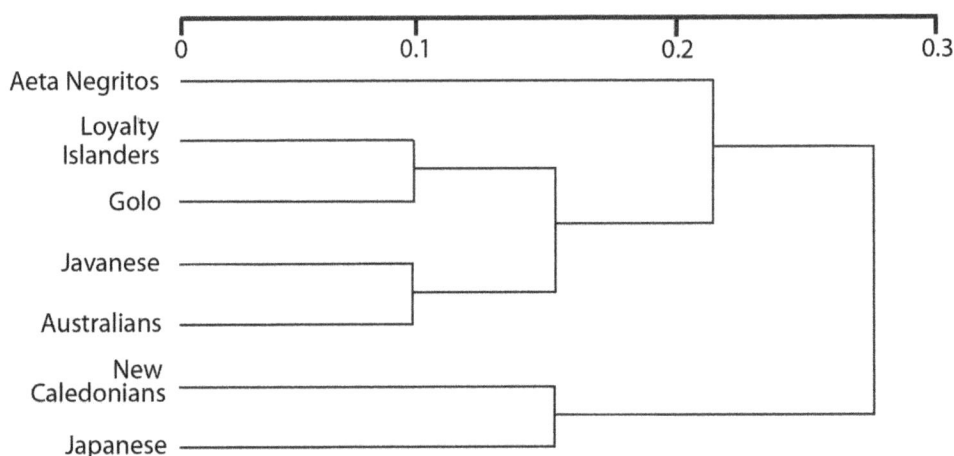

Square roots of Penrose size distances from Aeta Negritos

Seriated average-linkage dendrogram of square roots of Penrose shape distances
(coefficient of variation with a perfect seriation 96.2%)

Figure 11.7 Graphical representation of metrical comparison of Golo with six Oriental-Pacific male groups.
Source: David Bulbeck.

Table 11.13 Golo and comparative group limb bone indices based on mean measurements.

Index	Aeta	Loyalty Islanders	Golo	Javanese	Australians	New Caledonians	Japanese
Femur:tibia	84.6	86.8	83.7	83.9	84.9	84.2	79.6
Femur:fibula	81.8	84.8	83.3	82.4	83.4	82.3	80.1
Humerus:radius	75.6	75.1	74.8	75.3	76.0	72.8	70.4
Humerus:ulna	85.8	86.7	86.2	84.6	85.2	84.0	80.1
Femur:humerus	71.7	72.3	71.9	71.5	72.1	72.7	73.6

Source: David Bulbeck.

The human remains from Tanjung Pinang, Morotai

Nearly 85 per cent of the Tanjung Pinang (TP) human remains are cranial. Ten individual crania ranging in their age at death from their teens to young adulthood (30s) could be distinguished (Table 11.14). Initially, two of the adults (TP2 and TP6) were sexed as female based on their gracile anatomy, but ancient DNA analysis in Leipzig has identified them as male, and so the crania in the collection are predominantly and perhaps entirely male (Table 11.1).

The mandibular and postcranial remains are highly fragmentary or, if complete, are small elements such as carpals and tarsals. Almost every postcranial element is represented with only the clavicle, trapezoid, navicular, medial cuneiform, and intermediate cuneiform apparently absent from the nearly 600 gm of postcranial material. The postcranial assemblage includes male adult, possibly female adult (as adjudged from anatomical attributes), and subadult specimens, and was excavated in essentially the same spits as the cranial remains.

Thus, the mortuary rituals at Tanjung Pinang appear to have focused on the secondary disposal of defleshed male crania accompanied by a random assortment of non-cranial fragments and small elements. Presumably, the deceased were treated to preliminary burial or exposure to the elements at another location, before retrieval of the cranium (along with incidentally collected bone) for final burial at Tanjung Pinang.

Cranium TP1 has been directly dated to 2090±180 BP (ANU-8439) which calibrates to 2684–1618 BP at 95.4 per cent (Table 1.1). The other TP burials would also date to around 2000 years ago, as discussed in Chapter 3.

Table 11.14 Cranial thicknesses (mm) recorded on the Tanjung Pinang vaults.

Location	TP1	TP2	TP3	TP4	TP5	TP6	TP7	TP8	TP10
Mid-frontal squama						9.5	6		
Bregma	7.5	7		7.5	7	9.1	6.5		
Vertex	–	8							
Euryon	8	7		5.1	6	8.4	7	8.1	
Parietal bone	10		Quite thick						10
Lambda	11	9		7.8	5	8.9	7		

Note: TP1 to TP3 had their cranial vault thicknesses measured only at the anatomical landmarks documented by Brown et al. (1979) for Australian Aborigines, and otherwise noted impressionistically (TP3). The 10 mm parietal thickness for TP1 was recorded on a cranial vault fragment (Square F2 25–30 cm depth) that may be attributable to TP1.

Source: David Bulbeck.

Crania TP1, TP5, TP6, TP9, and TP10 all have slight to mild *cribra orbitalia* on their extant orbits, taking the form of recovery scars in the case of the adults. The orbital roofs were not preserved for TP2, TP3, TP4, or TP7. Unusually thick cranial bone was recorded for TP1, TP6, TP8, and TP10, although not for TP2, TP3, TP4, TP5, or TP7, whose cranial vault thicknesses approximate the averages recorded for Australian Aborigines (Table 11.14). TP5 also displays mild porotic hyperostosis on its frontal and upper parietal bones, and TP6 and TP7 on their upper parietal bones, while TP4 has three fistulas attributable to osteitis on its left parietal. Unfortunately, observations for porotic hyperostosis on the parietal and occipital bone of TP1 to TP3 had not been undertaken at the time these remains were returned to Jakarta. In conjunction with the frequent occurrence of macroscopic linear enamel hypoplasia on the teeth, as detailed towards the end of this chapter, the buried remains point to chronic childhood anaemia as a morbidity that afflicted the Tanjung Pinang population (cf. Aufderheide and Rodríguez-Martin 1998).

The Tanjung Pinang crania

Cranial measurements taken with a sufficient degree of accuracy for multivariate analysis are presented in Table 11.15. The classificatory probabilities of the analysed Tanjung Pinang crania are presented in Table 11.16. If the most likely classification is with an Oriental-Pacific series, this is the only classification shown, but if the most likely classification is with a series from some other part of the world, but there is also an Oriental-Pacific classification that is more probable than any other, this secondary classification is also shown.

Table 11.15 Measurements[a] in mm recorded on the Tanjung Pinang crania.

Acronym	TP1	TP2	TP3	TP4	TP5	TP6	TP7	TP8
GOL	–	173[b]	–	–	162.5[c]	170[d]	–	184[e]
NOL	–	–	–	–	162.5[f]	–	–	183[g]
BNL	–	–	–	–	–	–	–	98[h]
BBH	–	131	–	–	–	–	–	–
XCB	–	129[i]	–	125[i]	125	134.5[i]	–	137[k]
XFB	112	115[i]	–	122[i]	106	120[i]	–	–
STB	112	109[i]	–	117[i]	106	117[i]	110[i]	–
ZYB	–	–	140[i]	–	125[i]	134[m]	–	137[k]
AUB	–	115[i]	130[i]	115[i]	105[i]	109	–	132
WCB	–	–	80[i]	–	–	–	–	75
ASB	–	101[i]	120[i]	99[i]	97.5[n]	100	96[i]	117
BPL	–	–	–	–	–	–	–	109[h]
NPH	64[h]	–	–	–	63	58[h]	–	66
NLH	49	–	–	–	51	–	–	51
OBH	34.5	–	–	–	35	–	–	37
OBB	40.5	–	–	–	40[o]	–	–	40
JUB	117[h]	–	120[i]	–	115	–	120[i]	119
NLB	29.5	–	26[i]	–	23	26	25[p]	25
MAB	63.5	–	64[i]	–	60	59	63[p]	68
MDH	–	22	24	27[o]	–	23[o]	–	31
MDB	–	14	10.6	10	13	13	–	16.3
ZMB	98	–	–	–	87	–	94[i]	112
SSS	23	–	–	–	21	–	–	29
FMB	102	–	–	–	93	–	110[i]	96
NAS	15	–	–	–	12	–	–	22
EKB	101	–	–	–	97	–	108[i]	100
DKS	10	–	–	–	15[o]	–	–	13
DKB	22	–	–	–	22[h]	23	–	25
NDS	10	–	–	–	–	–	–	7
WNB	9	–	–	–	10	–	–	11
SIS	3	–	–	–	2	–	–	3
IML	–	–	–	–	33	–	38	38
XML	–	–	–	–	48	–	57	58
MLS	–	–	–	–	8	–	10	10
WMH	23	–	21[o]	–	21	25	23.5	23
SOS	7	–	–	–	2.5	–	–	5
GLS	2.5	–	–	–	2	–	–	4[p]
FRC	112	–	–	–	110	96[h]	–	–
FRS	23	17[p]	–	–	22	–	–	–
PAC	–	114	–	115[d]	104	–	117	–
PAS	–	28	–	–	23	–	25.5	–

(a) Most acronyms are detailed in Table 11.6. Other acronyms include ZYB (bizygomatic breadth), DKS (dacryon subtense), DKB (interorbital breadth), NDS (naso-dacryal subtense), WNB (least nasal breadth), SIS (simotic subtense), IML (inferior malar length), XML (maximum malar length), MLS (malar subtense), and GLS (glabella projection).

(b) Minimum estimate.

(c) Midpoint of 160–165 mm estimate.

(d) Dependent on accuracy of reconstruction.

(e) Midpoint of 182–186 mm estimate.

(f) Midpoint of 161–164 mm estimate.

(g) Midpoint of 181–185 mm estimate.

(h) Measured following estimation of the exact location of one of the anatomical points required for the measurement's definition.

(i) Symmetry assumed to take measurement.

(j) Midpoint of 133–136 mm estimate.

(k) Midpoint of 136–138 mm estimate.

(l) Midpoint of 120–130 mm estimate.

(m) Midpoint of 132–136 mm estimate.

(n) Midpoint of 95–100 mm estimate.

(o) Taken on right side.

(p) Approximate estimate, allowing for some missing bone.

Source: David Bulbeck.

Table 11.16 Classification results from discriminant function analysis of Tanjung Pinang crania.

Specimen	Most similar Oriental-Pacific series[a]	Classificatory Probability	Most similar series (if not Oriental-Pacific)	Classificatory Probability
TP 1[b]	Philippines	0.198	Dogon, Africa	0.266
TP2	Tolai	0.262	Tamil, South India	0.296
TP3	Atayal, Taiwan	0.095	Berg, Europe	0.648
TP4	None	0.000	Kannada, South India	0.738
TP5	Andamanese	0.982	NA	–
TP6	Andamanese	0.351	NA	–
TP7	Tolai, New Britain	0.502	NA	–
TP8[c]	Malekula	0.001	Santa Cruz, America	0.980

(a) Except for TP4, an Oriental-Pacific series is either the most probable or second most probable classification.

(b) Essentially identical results were obtained from the analysis that excluded NPH and JUB.

(c) In the analysis that excluded the estimated measurements, Santa Cruz was still by far the most probable classification, with Hawai'i the most likely Oriental-Pacific classification (0.006).

Source: David Bulbeck.

As shown in Table 11.16, two of the Tanjung Pinang crania would be classified as Andamanese. However, one of these (TP5) is a teenager and may not have retained Andamanese-like craniometrics into adulthood. The only other classification with an Oriental-Pacific series was with a Melanesian series (TP7). Five of the Tanjung Pinang crania would be classified with series distributed widely across the world, including India, Africa, Europe, and the New World. The last is a Mongoloid classification, in which context it is worth noting that the TP1 adolescent also has a reasonable probability of being classified as male Filipino.

Overall, particularly in the context of the small sample size of Tanjung Pinang crania and their incomplete nature, there is not a clear difference between the craniometric affinities of the Tanjung Pinang crania and those of recent eastern Indonesians. With the latter, 36 per cent would be classified with southwest Pacific series and 42 per cent with Mongoloid series, with Andamanese affinities otherwise prominent too (Bulbeck et al. 2006).

Only five of the (male) Tanjung Pinang crania have a sufficient suite of the Larnach and Macintosh (1966) characters intact for any of the Boolean expressions in Tables 10.2 and 10.3 to be evaluated. Table 11.17 presents the relevant observations and Table 11.18 summarises the results of the evaluation of the Boolean expressions. As TP1 and TP5 are adolescent, the results suggest that the Tanjung Pinang crania retained a cranial anatomy similar to that of Indo-Malays until adolescence. TP6 may have retained an Indo-Malay anatomy into adulthood, whereas TP2 and TP8 lean towards an Australoid cranial anatomy, similar in this respect to the Golo individual.

Table 11.17 Relevant anatomical observations of the Tanjung Pinang crania and their binary evaluation in terms of Tables 11.2 and 11.3.

Character	TP1	TP2	TP5	TP6	TP8
Glabella development	Martin 3 (small)	–	Martin 2 (small)	–	Martin 3 (small)
Maximum supraorbital breadth	109 mm (large)	–	101 mm (small)	–	105 mm (small)
Sagittal keeling	–	Trace (indistinct)	Absent (indistinct)	Absent (indistinct)	–
Naso-frontal articulation width	13 mm (broad)	–	11.9 mm (broad)	14.6 mm (broad)	10.7 mm (broad)
Parietal bossing	Slight (not prominent)		Slight (not prominent)	Slight (not prominent)	Absent (not prominent)
Palate module	c. 35.6 (small)[a]	–	33.6 (small)[b]	c. 35.4 (small)[c]	42.2 (large)[d]
Median frontal ridge	Trace (indistinct)	Absent (indistinct)	Trace (indistinct)	Trace (indistinct)	–
Cranial index (100*XCB/GOL)	–	–74.6 (<75, narrow)	76–78 (×75, not narrow)	c. 79 (×75, not narrow)	73–76 (not assessable on whether <75)
Transverse occipital torus	Large (present)	Small (present)	–	–	–
Malar orbital border	Rounded (not sharp)	–	Unrounded (sharp)	Rounded (not sharp)	Flattened (not sharp)
Phaenozygy	–	–	–	–	Marked (present)
Anterior nasal spine	Broca 3 or less (less than Broca 4)	–	Broca 2 (less than Broca 4)	–	Broca 1 (less than Broca 4)
Frontal curvature index	20.5 (Non-bulging, –24.7)	Low, visual estimate (Non-bulging, –24.7)	–	Low, visual estimate (Non-bulging, –24.7)	–
Supramastoid crest	–	Slight (slight)	Slight (slight)	Medium (not slight)	Medium (not slight)

(a) Relies on an estimate of c. 56 mm for palate length in addition to the Table 11.15 MAB value.

(b) Relies on a 56 mm measurement for palate length in addition to the Table 11.15 MAB value.

(c) Relies on an estimate of c. 60 mm for palate length in addition to the Table 11.15 MAB value.

(d) Relies on a 62 mm measurement for palate length in addition to the Table 11.15 MAB value.

Source: David Bulbeck.

Table 11.18 Implications of evaluation of the Boolean formulae in Tables 11.2 and 11.3 for the Tanjung Pinang crania.

Formula	TP1	TP2	TP5	TP6	TP8
2.1	Formula cannot be evaluated	Formula cannot be evaluated	More likely Indo-Malay than Australian	More likely Indo-Malay than Australian	Formula cannot be evaluated
2.2	Within the Indo-Malay range of variation	Formula cannot be evaluated	Within the Indo-Malay range of variation	Within the Indo-Malay range of variation	Formula cannot be evaluated
2.3	Formula cannot be evaluated	Within the Australian range of variation	Outside the Australian range of variation	Formula cannot be evaluated	Within the Australian range of variation
3.1	Formula cannot be evaluated	Formula cannot be evaluated	More likely Indo-Malay than Melanesian	Formula cannot be evaluated	Formula cannot be evaluated
3.2	Formula cannot be evaluated	Formula cannot be evaluated	Within the Indo-Malay range of variation	Within the Indo-Malay range of variation	Formula cannot be evaluated
3.3	Within the Melanesian range of variation	Within the Melanesian range of variation	Formula cannot be evaluated	Formula cannot be evaluated	Within the Melanesian range of variation
Inference	All affinities possible	Could be Australoid	Indo-Malay	Could be Indo-Malay	Could be Australoid

Source: David Bulbeck.

The human remains from Uattamdi 1, Kayoa

Figure 11.8 Uattamdi 1 cranial bones illustrating their thickness and porotic hyperostosis.
Source: David Bulbeck.

Five individuals were recognised amongst the Uattamdi human remains, two comprising slightly weathered bone (Uattamdi 1 and 2), and three comprising bone of fresh appearance (Uattamdi 3 to 5). Uattamdi 1 has been directly dated to 1915±27 BP (1932–1813 cal. BP), and Uattamdi 2, which is the other well-represented cranium from the excavation, probably dates to about the same time. On the other hand, Uattamdi 3 to 5 would appear to be later burials interred at the site.

Uattamdi 1, an adult male, is represented by a very peculiar posterior braincase. The maximum cranial breadth (assuming symmetry) is estimated to measure 160 mm, over 20 mm broader than any of the Golo or Tanjung Pinang crania. The cranial bone is very thick, up to 15.6 mm at inion, 12.2 mm at (right) euryon, 10 mm at lambda and 9.2 mm at (left) stephanion. Advanced porotic hyperostosis covers both surfaces of the vault, including a trabecular pattern of pinprick impressions externally and craters of up to

20 mm diameter internally (Fig. 11.8). A section of the left parietal has been cut out and this reveals thickened diploe that make up around 80 per cent of the thickness of the cranial bone, although the diploic trabeculae themselves are rather sparse and much of the diploe comprises solid bone. This lack of diploic coarsening would be unusual for anaemic sufferers except for those whose condition is caused by thalassaemia (Aufderheide and Rodríguez-Martín 1998:348; Tayles 1999:187 ff.), and this may be the appropriate diagnosis for Uattamdi 1 despite the lack of a 'hair-on-end' appearance of the diploic bone (cf. Aufderheide and Rodriguez-Martín 1998:347).

Uattamdi 2 consists of 11 cranial vault fragments from Square E9 spit B1. It is clearly a distinct individual from Uattamdi 1 as shown by the much thinner cranial vault (6.2 mm at asterion, and 7.7 mm in the vicinity of the sagittal suture), open cranial sutures, and duplication of the right postero-inferior parietal corner.

Uattamdi 3 is identified on the basis of the apparently adult fragments from Squares C4–C5, C5 spit B3, E4 spit B3, E4–E5 and E6. The parts of the skeleton represented are the right temporal, left parietal (probably), vertebral column, ribcage, left and right hands, and left and right feet. The same individual may also be represented by at least some of the adult fragments extracted by Jennifer R. Hull when she separated the human material from the Uattamdi faunal material. These adult remains include cranial vault, teeth, a hyoid bone, fragments from the entire vertebral column, ribs, scapula, humerus, radius, ulna, carpals, metacarpals, manual extremities, tibia, tarsals, metatarsals, and pedal phalanges—virtually the entire skeleton from head to toe.

Uattamdi 4 was initially recognised on the basis of apparently infantile remains from the frontal, right posterior parietal, and right temporal, from E4 spit B3, C5 spit B3 and C4–C5. The same individual may be represented by the infantile human remains extracted by Jennifer R. Hull from the Uattamdi faunal material. These include six deciduous teeth, an unfused mandibular symphysis fragment, two vertebra centra with the vertebral processes completely unfused, and miniature extremity bones present as shafts without either the base or the head attached.

Uattamdi 5 is recognised on the basis of apparently subadult but non-infantile fragments from the spits labelled as lower A and A1, comprising a partial occipital and abutting posterior parietals, additional parietal bone, and an upper rib. The remains from non-infantile children extracted by Jennifer R. Hull include the incompletely formed buds to a first molar and a third molar, a fragment from a very small superciliary region with active porotic hyperostosis on the orbital roof, and a very small sesamoid bone.

The consistently small specimens extracted by Jennifer R. Hull were recovered from all Uattamdi squares. Some were in bags that were unlabelled, or labelled only in general terms. Together they constitute 78 specimens weighing 107 gm. The generally fresh (and unburnt) condition of the bone, and the general similarity of the assemblage to the collections of highly fragmentary remains suspected to date to the Common Era from other Northern Moluccan sites (including betel-nut staining on all of the permanent anterior teeth), suggest that these Uattamdi fragments would date to the first and/or second millennia BP. This is despite these fragments' recovery from as deep as 55–60 cm. While at least some of these specimens may relate to Uattamdi 3 to 5, additional secondarily buried individuals may also be represented.

Other sites

The human remains from Um Kapat Papo, Gebe

The Um Kapat Papo human remains include a tooth, cranial vault fragments, and postcranial fragments from spits 1 and 2 of the P9 Square. Much of the postcranial skeleton is represented including the vertebral column, forearms, carpals, metacarpals, manual phalanges, patella, tibia, fibula, tarsals, metatarsals, and pedal phalanges. Some of the small bones are complete, but the larger elements are consistently represented by small fragments. The lack of duplication of any element, and the consistency with which the remains could be attributed to an adult female (epiphyses fused wherever present, small apparent size of the original bones), suggest that only one individual is represented. The fresh to quite fresh appearance of the bone, and its stratigraphic location at the same level or above the c. 2000 BP date on marine shell from the site, suggest a second millennium BP dating.

The human remains from Tanjung Tulang, Morotai

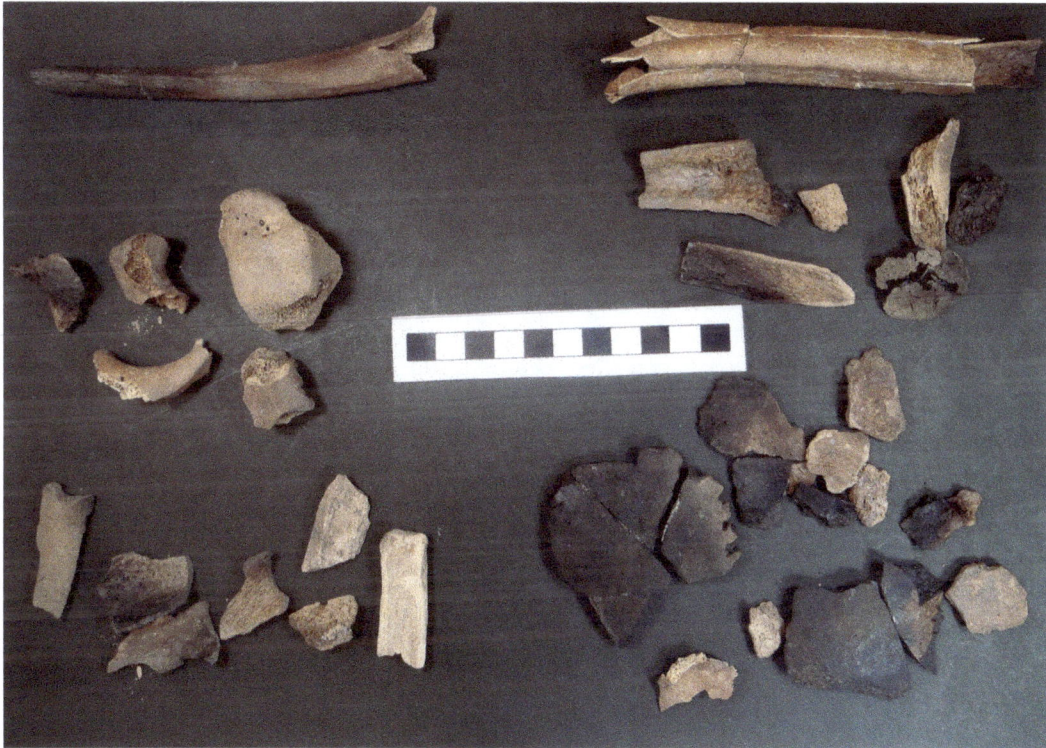

Figure 11.9 Fragments assigned to the Tanjung Tulang 2 adolescent.
Source: David Bulbeck.

Four individuals, Tanjung Tulang 1 to 4, are recognised amongst the human material excavated from the site. Tanjung Tulang 1 to 3 include an adult male (the larger adult), an adult female (the smaller adult) and a subadult represented amongst the L5/M5/N5 material (Fig. 11.9), while Tanjung Tulang 4 is an unsexed adult excavated in the E4 and F6 squares. The great majority of the human remains are burnt or singed (96 per cent by weight), and this indicates that the site was reserved for the secondary burial of cremated human remains. This use of the site apparently preceded its habitation phase, associated with the deposition of shellfish and small amounts of Sambiki Tua–type pottery, given that the main concentration of human remains was stratified beneath the major concentration of shell and pottery (see Chapter 3).

From the weathered condition of most of the bone, I would estimate the Tanjung Tulang burials date to around 1000 years ago. Similarity in age to the Tanjung Pinang burials is suggested by the dominance of cranial material (slightly over 50 per cent) in the identified Tanjung Tulang remains, the wide-scale representation of the postcranial skeleton (ribs, vertebrae, clavicle, scapula, humerus, radius, ulna, trapezoid, lunate, hamate, proximal and medial manual phalanges, pelvis, femur, tibia, fibula, talus, navicular, medial cuneiform, metatarsals, and proximal and distal pedal phalanges), and the extant status of most of the postcranial elements either as small fragments or small complete bones.

The cranial vault appears generally thick, up to 11.2 mm along the coronal suture and 11.5 mm on the occipital. Further, one of the F6 cranial vault fragments has holes on the interior surface with a 'punched out' appearance, which is suggestive of multiple myeloma (cf. Aufderheide and Rodríguez-Martín 1998). A subadult, orbital roof fragment from N5 has porotic *cribra orbitalia*, indicative of active anaemia (cf. Webb 1982). Further information on the health status of the buried Tanjung Tulang individuals might have been available if I had been able to relocate the upper left lateral incisor, upper right lateral incisor, upper right first premolar, three upper first molars, upper right second molar, lower right lateral incisor, lower canine, lower left second molar and lower left third molar mentioned in Kate Stockhausen's notes, in addition to the left second lower premolar (detailed below).

The human remains from Daeo 1, Morotai

As described in Chapter 3, Daeo 1 appears to be a disturbed site with human remains (around 350 gm) distributed throughout most of the excavated deposit, to a depth of 30–35 cm. Conceivably, the activity of burying the deceased at the site could have been a contributing factor to the disturbance of the deposit. Despite the small quantity of excavated human material, virtually the entire skeleton is represented, more or less in the expected proportions (with only the pelvic girdle missing). The assemblage consists of small fragments and a few small, complete bones, indicating the secondary burial of previously defleshed corpses. There are both fused and unfused epiphyses in the assemblage, and an unworn, lower fragmentary molar (first or second), demonstrating the representation of both adult and subadult individuals. Further, the adult postcranial material includes some extremity bones and fragments that appear to be male in their dimensions. Most of the fragments have a weathered appearance, with only small quantities recorded as burnt or as fresh, suggesting an age of perhaps 1000 years ago for the mortuary assemblage.

The recorded remains are too fragmentary to provide any biologically useful information. Information of this nature might have been possible if it had been possible to relocate the 28 human teeth identified by Kate Stockhausen in her notes. Her identifications include three upper right central incisors, indicating a minimum number of three individuals represented in the Daeo 1 assemblage.

The human remains from Daeo 2, Morotai

The description in Chapter 3 of the stratigraphy of Daeo 2 refers to a thin veneer of ceramic period burial activity on the top. This description accords well with the fresh appearance that characterises 96 per cent of the identified human bone from the site, and which indicates a first millennium BP dating for the burials. Over half of the identified bone is cranial and it includes some of the very small, delicate bones such as the palatine and concha bones. This strong representation of cranial bone suggests secondary burial of previously defleshed corpses, with a possible focus on skull burials. The postcranial material, which covers the entire skeleton apart from the pelvic girdle, includes both adult and subadult fragments and small bones (such as carpal bones). The extant cranial sutures are variably closed and fully open.

A lateral incisor in a mandible fragment was available for recording, as detailed below. In addition, the notes made by Kate Stockhausen refer to 42 teeth, which I was unable to relocate. These teeth include five upper right central incisors and five upper left lateral incisors, indicating a minimum number of five individuals represented amongst the Daeo 2 burial remains.

Northern Moluccan tooth size and morphology

Table 11.19 presents the summed average tooth area for the recorded Northern Moluccan teeth, calculated from the average tooth lengths and breadths provided in Tables 11.20 and 11.21. The summed average tooth area is the sum of the products of the average mesio-distal length and bucco-lingual breadth of each tooth class (Brace 1976). Ideally, the summed average tooth area would be based on all of the tooth classes. However, the Northern Moluccan remains that I recorded exclude any lower central incisors with measurable diameters or any lower third molars (Tables 11.20 and 11.21) so these could not be included in the calculation.

Table 11.19 Northern Moluccan summed tooth area (square millimetres), with Indo-Malaysian and Melanesian comparisons (bisexual samples except where otherwise specified).

Series	Summed tooth area (excluding lower third molars and lower central incisors)	Summed tooth area (excluding all third molars and lower central incisors)	Data source
Northern Moluccas	1229	1127	This chapter
Temperate Australians (excluding Sydney)	1230–1354	1114–1223	Brace 1980 (8 series)
New Guinea Highland males	1279	1168	Doran and Freedman 1974
Tasmanians	1262	1134	Brace 1980
Loyalty Islands	–	1117	Matsumura and Hudson 2005
Tropical Australians	1121–1226	1006–1103	Brace 1980 (7 series)
Sydney Australians	1195	1082	Brace 1980
Prehistoric Flores	1193	1075	Jacob 1967a
New Britain	1164	1056	Snell 1938
Nasioi, North Solomons	1157	1058	Bailit et al. 1968
Leang Buidane, Early Metal Phase Sulawesi	1159	1054	Bulbeck 1981
Leang Codong, Early Metal Phase Sulawesi	1136	1029	Jacob 1967a
Temiar Senoi, Malaysia	1135	1029	Bulbeck et al. 2005
Borneo 'Dayaks'	–	1025	Matsumura and Hudson 2005
Gilimanuk, Early Metal Phase Bali	1120	1014	Jacob 1967b
Batawi, Java	1105	1003	Snell 1938
Andaman Islanders	–	1003	Matsumura and Hudson 2005
Sumatrans	–	1001	Matsumura and Hudson 2005
Javanese	1087	997	Brace 1976
Melayu Malay males	1092	990	Bulbeck et al. 2005
Aboriginal Malays, Malaysia	1077	983	Bulbeck et al. 2005
Semang, Malaysia	1071	976	Bulbeck et al. 2005
Motupore Island, Papua New Guinea	1045	958	Brown 1978
Philippine Negritos	–	939	Matsumura and Hudson 2005
Tagalogs	–	880	Yap Potter et al. 1981

Source: David Bulbeck.

In addition, some of the comparative sources for average tooth lengths and breadths of recent Indo-Malaysian and Melanesian populations do not include data for third molars. Accordingly, Table 11.19 additionally presents the Northern Moluccan summed average tooth area for the dentition excluding both upper and lower third molars as well as the lower central incisors. The Northern Moluccan values are compared with the corresponding values for prehistoric (mid to late Holocene) Flores teeth, teeth from other prehistoric sites in Indonesia dating to the last two millennia BP, as well as teeth of recent Indo-Malaysians, Melanesians, Australians, and Tasmanians (see Table 11.19 for sources).

The comparative data show that the available Northern Moluccan teeth are large, with a summed tooth area that would fall within the Australian range of variation. The Northern Moluccan tooth area exceeds that recorded for tropical and Sydney-region Australians, although it is smaller than the tooth area recorded for temperate Australians (outside of the Sydney region) and Tasmanians. The Northern Moluccan tooth area is also larger than that of every comparative non-Australian series, with the single exception of New Guinea Highland males. Even this (modest) difference could be readily attributed to sexual dimorphism, because males generally exceed females from the same population in their average tooth sizes (e.g. Bulbeck 1981), and the Northern Moluccan sample includes some females notwithstanding its predominantly male composition (Table 11.1). Other series with quite large teeth include Loyalty Islanders, prehistoric Flores and, to a lesser degree, New Britain, Solomon Islanders, and the Early Metal Phase teeth from Leang Buidane in the Talaud Islands. At the other end of the scale, the smallest teeth are shown by the Semang and Philippine Negritos, the coastal Papua New Guinea sample from Motupore Island, and Philippine Tagalogs. The Motupore Island sample shows that not all Melanesians can be distinguished from Indo-Malaysians on the basis of larger teeth.

In summary, keeping in mind that the Northern Moluccan sample is small in size and irregular in its composition, we may conclude that the available data suggest large teeth, as otherwise shown by Australians, some recent Melanesian groups, and the prehistoric Flores sample.

The dental sample size is too small to propose a population affinity for the Northern Moluccan remains based on the dental morphological traits described by Scott and Turner (1997). The few observations that could be made suggest intra-population variability. For instance, with reference to the breakpoint for upper incisor shovelling in Scott and Turner (1997), the unassigned lateral incisor from Tanjung Pinang would be 'shovelled' whereas all of the other Northern Moluccan incisors would be 'unshovelled'.

Northern Moluccan tooth wear and betel-nut staining

The rate of tooth wear shown by the Northern Moluccan dental remains can be described as moderate. Around one-third of the recorded teeth are lightly worn (Table 11.22), characterised by enamel polishing or at most the creation of small dentine pools (Smith wear classes 1 to 3). However, most of these teeth either come from subadults (e.g. TP1, TP5, and TP9) or were found amongst unassigned dental remains that are suspected to include subadults. As for the adult individuals, TP3 and TP6 also have lightly worn teeth, potentially reflecting their status as young adults, whereas TP8 and especially the Golo extended burial have more heavily worn teeth. Accordingly, TP8 and the Golo individual may have died in their middle age, although compelling independent evidence for this inference is not available (for instance, the Golo extended burial is unfortunately missing its pubic processes, whose surface morphology would otherwise serve as a useful marker of biological age). It might also be noted that the tooth wear on the Golo individual is very irregular across the dentition (discussed below).

Betel-nut staining was characteristic of the Northern Moluccan anterior teeth, which are more prone than the cheek teeth to becoming stained through habitual betel-nut (*Areca catechu*) chewing. It was observed on the teeth assigned to the Golo extended burial, and on the permanent anterior Uattamdi teeth. Betel-nut staining was also observed on the extant teeth of TP1, TP2, and TP7, the anterior teeth (back to the first premolar or first molar) of TP3, TP5, TP6, and TP8, and the unassigned lateral incisor from Square J2 5–10 cm depth. The only evidence for a TP individual who was unaffected by betel-nut staining is provided by the suspected juvenile, lower left canine from Square J2 10–20 cm (TP9). Finally, the left lateral lower incisor from Daeo 2 has a strong betel-nut stain, while the second upper molar from Um Kapat Papo has a pinkish wash, though it is not diagnostic of betel-nut staining.

Northern Moluccan oral pathology

The available observations on oral pathology (Tables 11.23–11.25) suggest a difference between the Tanjung Pinang remains, characterised by sound oral health, and the Golo remains, marked by poor oral health. The TP teeth show no cases of caries, and only one case of ante-mortem tooth loss, while periodontal disease was recorded as either absent (including TP8, with its moderate tooth wear) or mild (affecting the TP5 teenager and the TP7 adult). All of these pathological traits are more developed with the available Golo material. Incipient caries was recorded on 1/3 of the unassigned Golo teeth, while 11/22 of the teeth and tooth sites from the extended burial show incipient to highly advanced caries. Similarly, ante-mortem tooth loss was recorded on 2/6 of the unassigned Golo tooth sites and 7/31 of the recordable tooth sites from the extended burial. In addition, mild periodontal disease was recorded at 5/6 of the unassigned Golo tooth sites, while mild to pronounced periodontal disease was recorded at 11/30 of the recordable tooth sites from the extended burial.

The Golo individual would have had a poorly functioning dentition at the time of death. About half of the molars had been lost ante-mortem, and the molars that remained jutted into the empty spaces left by their missing counterparts. The anterior teeth and premolars are much less affected by oral disease, but their wear pattern is uneven, with about half reduced to dentine stubs and the other half showing moderate wear. The individual had presumably used his teeth to puncture his food rather than grind it through lateral jaw excursions (as would be associated with a helicoidal occlusal plane), and probably had a diet that included both tough items and a high carbohydrate content (cf. Hillson 1996:237–239, 267, 283).

The limited available sample sizes would suggest that a diet high in carbohydrates was more a feature of the Golo than the Tanjung Pinang population. Unfortunately, too few tooth sites could be recorded from any of the other sites to assess how they might compare with Golo and Tanjung Pinang.

Table 11.20 Recorded mesio-distal diameters on Northern Moluccan permanent teeth (mm).

Tooth	GO	GE	TP1	TP2	TP3	TP5	TP6	TP7	TP8	TP9	TPU	UAT	UKP	TT4	Average
L I¹						10.3	9.7								9.6
R I¹				9.1								8.4			
L I²											7.3				6.5
R I²											5.7				
L C̲			8.8		9.3										8.5
R C̲				9.0			7.9					7.4			
L P¹						8.2	7.85		7.5			7.3			7.8
R P¹				8.1			7.8		7.8						
L P²			8.0			8.1			6.7						7.5
R P²			8.1		7.5	7.1			7.2						
L M¹						11.7	10.1		10.6			10.4, 13.2			11.2
R M¹		12.1			12.4	11.1	10.3	10.4	10.8						
L M²						9.5	10.0		10.3				10.1		9.9
R M²						9.6	9.5		10.5						
L M³							7.6		9.2			8.3, 9.7			9.0
R M³	9.05				10.2		8.1		9.7						
R I₂				5.9								6.6			6.25
L C										6.9					7.5
R C			8.0									6.5, 8.7			
L P₁		7.7													7.7
L P₂				7.1										7.0	7.05
R M₁	13.2														13.2
R M₂	12.4								11.2						11.8

GO: Golo LMN fragments; GE: Golo extended burial; TP: Tanjung Pinang, including TPU for Tanjung Pinang unassigned; UAT: Uattamdi; UKP: Um Kapat Papo; TT4: Tanjung Tulang 4.

Source: David Bulbeck.

Table 11.21 Recorded bucco-lingual diameters on Northern Moluccan permanent teeth (mm).

Tooth	GO	GE	TP1	TP2	TP3	TP5	TP6	TP7	TP8	TP9	TPU	UAT	UKP	TT4	DA2	Average
L I¹						7.5	7.8									7.7
R I¹				8.1								7.5, 7.7				
L I²		7.9									6.9					6.6
R I²											5.0					
L C̲			8.8		9.9											8.8
R C̲				9.1			8.2					7.8, 8.8				
L P¹						11.7	9.6		10.0			9.5				10.1
R P¹				10.5			9.2		10.4							
L P²		10.6	10.6			10.8			9.4			8.7				10.1
R P²		10.7			9.9	10.0			9.8							
L M¹						13.8	11.6		12.3			11.6, 12.2				12.2
R M¹		12.8			12.1		11.6	11.4	12.3							
L M²						12.8	11.9		12.5				11.4			11.9
R M²						10.3	11.55		12.6							
L M³							11.3		11.3							11.3
R M³	12.0				12.5		10.8		11.2			10.3, 10.9				

Tooth	GO	GE	TP1	TP2	TP3	TP5	TP6	TP7	TP8	TP9	TPU	UAT	UKP	TT4	DA2	Average
L I₂															6.2	6.4
R I₂				7.0								6.1, 6.2				
L C										8.1						8.2
R C			8.9									7.2, 8.7				
L P₁		8.4														8.4
L P₂			8.7											7.9		8.3
R M₁	12.5															12.5
R M₂	12.5								10.7							11.6

GO: Golo LMN fragments; GE: Golo extended burial; TP: Tanjung Pinang, including TPU for Tanjung Pinang unassigned; UAT: Uattamdi; UKP: Um Kapat Papo; TT4: Tanjung Tulang 4; DA2: Daeo 2.

Source: David Bulbeck.

Table 11.22 Recorded tooth wear (Smith's classes) on Northern Moluccan teeth.

Tooth	GO	GE	TP1	TP2	TP3	TP5	TP6	TP7	TP8	TP9	TPU	UAT	UKP	TT4	DA2
L I¹		8				3	4								
R I¹		7			2							2, 4			
L I²		4									2				
R I²		5									3				
L C		8		4		3									
R C		6			2		3					3, 5			
L P¹		8				3	3			5		1			
R P¹		8			2		3			6					
L P²		6	2				3			4		5			
R P²		8	1				3			4					
L M¹		4					3	3		5		1, 2			
R M¹		4			3	3	3	4		4					
L M²		–				2	3			3			3		
R M²		8				2	3			4					
L M³		–					2			4		1, 3			
R M³	2	–			1		2			4					
L I₁		6													
R I₁		8													
L I₂		7													5
R I₂		8		4								1, 4			
L C		5									2				
R C		5	2									1, 4			
L P₁		4													
R P₁		8													
L P₂		–	2											2	
R P₂		8													
R M₁	5	–													
R M₂	4	8								5					

GO: Golo LMN fragments; GE: Golo extended burial; TP: Tanjung Pinang, including TPU for Tanjung Pinang unassigned; UAT: Uattamdi; UKP: Um Kapat Papo; TT4: Tanjung Tulang 4; DA2: Daeo 2.

Source: David Bulbeck.

Table 11.23 Recorded caries (not recorded for teeth missing on the basis of unknown aetiology or teeth reduced to stubs) on Northern Moluccan teeth.

Tooth	GO	GE	TP1	TP2	TP3	TP5	TP6	TP7	TP8	TP9	TPU	UAT	UKP	TT4	DA2
L I¹		-				N	N								
R I¹		N			N							N, N			
L I²		N									N				
R I²		N									N				
L C̱		-		N		N									
R C̱		N			N		N					N, N			
L P¹		-				N	N		N			N			
R P¹		-			N		N		N						
L P²		N	N			N			N			N			
R P²		-	N		N	N			N						
L M¹		M				N	N		N						
R M¹		I			N	N	N	N	N			N, N			
L M²		P				N	N		N				N		
R M²		M				N	N		N						
L M³		P					N		N			N, N			
R M³	N	-			N		N		N						
L I₁		N													
L I₂		N													I
R I₂		N		N								N, I			
L C		N								N					
R C		N	N									N, N			
L P₁		N													
L P₂		-	N											N	
L M₁		P													
R M₁	I	P													
L M₂		P													
R M₂	N	M							N						
L M₃		P													
R M₃		P													

N = none; I = Incipient; M = massive; P = presumed cause of tooth loss. GO: Golo LMN fragments; GE: Golo extended burial; TP: Tanjung Pinang, including TPU for Tanjung Pinang unassigned; UAT: Uattamdi; UKP: Um Kapat Papo; TT4: Tanjung Tulang 4; DA2: Daeo 2.

Source: David Bulbeck.

Table 11.24 Recorded ante-mortem loss at Northern Moluccan tooth sites.

Tooth site	GO	GE	TP1	TP3	TP5	TP6	TP7	TP8	DA2
L I¹		N			N	N		N	
R I¹		N		N		N		N	
L I²		N			N	N		N	
R I²		N				N		N	
L C̱		N			N	N		N	
R C̱	N	N		N	X	N		N	
L P¹		N			N	N		N	
R P¹	N	N		N		N		N	
L P²		N	N		N	N		N	

Tooth site	GO	GE	TP1	TP3	TP5	TP6	TP7	TP8	DA2
R P²	X	N	N	N	N	N		N	
L M¹		N			N	N		N	
R M¹	X	N		N	N	N	N	N	
L M²		X			N	N		N	
R M²		N		N	N	N		N	
L M³		X				N		N	
R M³		–		N		N		N	
L I₁		N							
R I₁		N							
L I₂		N							N
R I₂		N							
L C		N							
R C		N	N						
L P₁		N							
R P₁		N							
L P₂		N	N						
R P₂		N							
L M₁		X							
R M₁	N	X							
L M₂		N							
R M₂	N	X				N			
L M₃		X							
R M₃		X							

X = lost ante-mortem; N = not lost ante-mortem. GO: Golo LMN fragments; GE: Golo extended burial; TP: Tanjung Pinang; DA2: Daeo 2.

Source: David Bulbeck.

Table 11.25 Recorded periodontal disease at Northern Moluccan tooth sites.

Tooth site	GO	GE	TP1	TP2	TP5	TP6	TP7	TP8	TP10	DA2
L I¹		N			M	N		N	M	
R I¹		N		N	M	N		N	M	
L I²		N			M	N		N	M	
R I²		M			M	N		N	M	
L C̲		N			M	N		N	M	
R C̲	M	M		N	M	N	M	N	M	
L P¹		N			N	N	M	N	M	
R P¹	M	N		N	–	N	M	N	M	
L P²		N	N		N	N	M	N	M	
R P²	M	N	N	N	N	N	M	N	M	
L M¹		M			N	N	M	N	N	
R M¹	M	N		N	N	N	M	N	N	
L M²		M			N	N		N		
R M²		N		N	N	N		N	N	
L M³		M				N		N	N	
R M³		–		N		N		N		
L I₁		N								
R I₁		N								

Tooth site	GO	GE	TP1	TP2	TP5	TP6	TP7	TP8	TP10	DA2
L I$_2$		N								N
R I$_2$		N								
L C		N								
R C		N	–							
L P$_1$		N								
R P$_1$		N								
L P$_2$		–	–							
R P$_2$		N								
L M$_1$		P								
R M$_1$	M	P								
L M$_2$		P								
R M$_2$	N	P								
L M$_3$		P								
R M$_3$		P								

N = None, apart from expected age-related degeneration; M = Mild, for instance, advanced dehiscences; P = Pronounced, for instance, alveolar abscesses. GO: Golo LMN fragments; GE: Golo extended burial; TP: Tanjung Pinang; DA2: Daeo 2.
Source: David Bulbeck.

Northern Moluccan general health (see also Chapter 12)

One line of insight into general health is to examine the teeth for macroscopic lines of dental linear enamel hypoplasia (LEH). These lines potentially reflect interruptions to tooth formation during childhood development. LEH was recorded on a high proportion of the Northern Moluccan teeth; for instance, all of the upper lateral incisors and first and second molars, and more than half of the upper central incisors, canines, premolars, and third molars (Table 11.26).

Further, LEH formation may reflect systemic interruptions to growth, but to have confidence in drawing that inference, observable LEH should match across different teeth that would have been forming at about the same time (Hillson 1996). Applying that criterion, we would infer that five of the eight Tanjung Pinang individuals had experienced an interruption to childhood growth. In the case of TP3, this would have occurred at a very young age, in the order of 1 year old. In the case of TP5, it would have occurred on two occasions, at the ages of around 2 years old and 6 years old. In the case of TP6, it would have occurred on three occasions, at the ages of around 2 years old, 5 years old and 12 years old. Finally, the TP1 and TP8 subadults may also have experienced an interruption to growth, respectively at approximately 6 years and 12 years of age. Susceptibility to LEH may have been increased at the time of weaning, but, if so, there is insufficient regularity in the inferred ages for LEH formation to suggest the modal age at which weaning had occurred.

With three of the five Tanjung Pinang individuals, there is evidence to relate their LEH to chronic childhood anaemia. These individuals are TP6 (*cribra orbitalia*, thick cranial bone, and porotic hyperostosis), TP1 (*cribra orbitalia* and thick cranial bone, porotic hyperostosis status unknown), and TP5 (*cribra orbitalia* and porotic hyperostosis, albeit lacking thick cranial bone). However, the same diagnosis is less convincing for TP8, which has thick cranial bone but not the other two markers, and TP7, which displays no anaemic markers. Finally, it may be noted that the TP2 and TP7 do not display either LEH or any signs of chronic childhood anaemia.

The Uattamdi assemblage resembles Tanjung Pinang in its inclusion of a proportion of individuals with osteological signs of anaemia. Although this was the case with only one of the five Uattamdi crania, the condition of this specimen (Uattamdi 1) is extreme, with a possible diagnosis of genetically determined thalassaemia. The observation of active *cribra orbitalia* on a fragmentary, juvenile orbital roof from Uattamdi confirms the case that childhood anaemia afflicted some proportion of the local population. A similar conclusion may apply to Tanjung Tulang, whose fragmentary remains included an orbital roof with active *cribra orbitalia*, examples of thick cranial vault, and a specimen with what may be advanced porotic hyperostosis.

The status of the Golo individual is ambiguous in terms of his general health prior to dying middle-aged, as the only sign of anaemia involves faint traces of porotic hyperostosis. Unfortunately, the Um Kapat Papo and Daeo assemblages are too fragmentary and/or limited in their quantity of cranial vault to provide a reliable indication of the existence or otherwise of anaemia in the populations that they represent.

Table 11.26 Macroscopic linear enamel hypoplasia observed on the Northern Moluccan teeth.

Tooth	GO	TP1	TP2	TP3	TP5	TP6	TP7	TP8	TP9	TPU	UAT	UKP	TT4	DA2	Occurrence
L I¹					I, C*	I									4/6
R I¹				0							N, N				
L I²										I					2/2
R I²										C					
L C			C		I										4/5
R C				0			C				N				
L P¹					0, C*	I		N			C				4/7
R P¹				N		I		N							
L P²		C			C			N							4/7
R P²		C		N	C			N							
L M¹						I	C	I			C, C				9/9
R M¹				0	I	I	C	C							
L M²					I	I		I				I			7/7
R M²					I	I		I							
L M³						I		I			I				5/7
R M³	N			N		I		I							
L I₂														N	2/4
R I₂			C								N, C				
L C									0, I, C*						1/3
R C		N									N				
L P₂		C													1/2
R P₂												N			
R M₁	N														0/1
R M₂	N								0, C*						1/2
Match?	N/A	Yes	No	Yes	Yes	Yes	N/A	Yes	No	No	Possible	N/A	N/A	N/A	44/62

N = none; 0 = occlusal third of tooth; I = middle third of tooth; C = cervical third of tooth. * = Multiple lines on single tooth. No observations available on many of the teeth including those from the Golo extended burial. GO: Golo LMN fragments; TP: Tanjung Pinang, including TPU for Tanjung Pinang unassigned; UAT: Uattamdi; UKP: Um Kapat Papo; TT4: Tanjung Tulang 4; DA2: Daeo 2.

Source: David Bulbeck.

Discussion

Affinities with southwest Pacific populations emerge repeatedly from the comparative analysis of the Northern Moluccan human remains. Tooth size resembles that of Australians and certain Melanesian groups (those with relatively large teeth). Craniometrically, the Malekula series from Vanuatu provides a very close match for the Golo extended burial (though this may be attributable to their shared feature of cranial deformation), and the Tolai series from New Britain provides a reasonable match for one of the Tanjung Pinang crania (TP2). In terms of cranial anatomy, the Golo cranium would be classified as either Australian or Melanesian rather than Indo-Malaysian. Metrically, the Golo mandible falls with a cluster dominated by Melanesian as well as eastern Indonesian males. Finally, the Golo limb bone proportions are most closely approached by Loyalty Islanders.

On the other hand, there would be insufficient evidence to infer a difference between Northern Moluccans and recent eastern Indonesians in their biological affinities. As for tooth size, it is undocumented for recent eastern Indonesians, and the prehistoric Flores remains recorded by Jacob (1967a) resemble the Northern Moluccan assemblage in their summed tooth area. Further, as also shown by a fair proportion of recent eastern Indonesians, the Tanjung Pinang crania include four specimens with Andamanese and 'Mongoloid' Southeast Asian craniometric affinities, even if this is more a feature of the subadults (TP1 and TP5) than the adults (true only of TP3 and TP6). As for cranial anatomy, recent eastern Indonesian males resemble Golo/Tanjung Pinang in terms of including specimens with variably Indo-Malay and southwest Pacific affinities. The mandibular metrical cluster that includes Golo is more focused on eastern Indonesians than Melanesians. Finally, recent Javanese are also very similar to Golo in their limb bone proportions, which suggests that the same may be true of recent eastern Indonesians too.

The ubiquitous presence of betel-nut staining on the recorded, permanent anterior teeth from the Northern Moluccas indicates the cultivation of betel-nut palms by 2000 BP. The poor state of oral health shown by the Golo teeth and jaws indicates a high carbohydrate component in the local diet, which may well have involved sago, an important staple today across the Northern Moluccan lowlands (Monk et al. 1997:687–689). Even though the oral health shown by the Tanjung Pinang dental arcades is generally sound, they exhibit a moderate rate of dental wear similar to that recorded for Golo. This would be more consistent with a diet that includes a substantial component of agricultural produce and/or sago (which need not be cultivated even in places where it is a staple; Ellen 2011) than the tough, fibrous diet of most hunter-gatherers. In summary, the Northern Moluccan human remains would point to the presence of arboriculture in the region for the 2000 or so years that they cover.

The Northern Moluccan human remains show a susceptibility to chronic anaemia, and in this respect are similar to the Neolithic burials from Khok Phanom Di, Thailand, which date to c. 2000–1500 BCE. The five Northern Moluccan subadults represented by their orbital roofs all exhibit active *cribra orbitalia*, similar to the rate of 77 per cent recorded for Khok Phanom Di children aged between 1 and 14 years old at death (Tayles 1999:161). Two of the four Northern Moluccan adults represented by their orbital roofs exhibit *cribra orbitalia* scars, higher than the 5 per cent recorded at Khok Phanom Di (Tayles 1999:191). Unusually thick cranial bone was recorded for one of two TP subadults, three of nine TP adults, and one Uattamdi adult, while porotic hyperostosis was observed for the Golo extended burial, one of the TP subadults, two of the six TP adults, and one Uattamdi adult. Similarly, a cranial vault thickness in excess of 7 mm was recorded for one of 16 subadults and 37 of 44 adults from Khok Phanom Di, associated in at least one case with porotic hyperostosis (Tayles 1999:187, 220–221). Tayles (1999:278–280, 319–320) accepts that malaria was endemic at Khok Phanom Di, possibly associated with thalassaemia or a functionally similar genetic mutation that confers immunity in its heterozygous expression but is severely debilitating in its homozygous expression. A similar inference would also apply to the Northern Moluccas, particularly in view of the prevalence of malaria recorded for the region during the nineteenth century.

Cranial deformation, as documented for the Golo extended burial, has been recorded for many Austronesian-speaking populations. However, the technique recorded for Sarawak, Sulawesi, the Philippines, Tahiti, and Hawai'i is fronto-occipital, rather than the circumferential deformation recorded for southern New Britain, the Solomons, and the Malekula of Vanuatu. On a broader scale, circumferential deformation occurred sporadically across Africa and Eurasia throughout the Holocene, and was also widespread across the tropical Americas after approximately 2000 BCE (Lindsell 1995). Accordingly, the circumferential deformation of the Golo cranium is suggestive of a link with Austronesian-speaking groups in Melanesia, although it may also be the result of an independently developed local custom.

Conclusions

The human remains from the Northern Moluccan excavations date from approximately 2000 years BP to the late second millennium CE. They register the practice of arboriculture throughout this period, notably *Areca catechu* (betel-nut) palms but probably also sago (to the degree it was cultivated rather than harvested 'wild'). Chronic anaemia afflicted a substantial proportion of the population, probably associated with endemic malaria. The biological affinities of the skeletal remains lie predominantly with southwest Pacific populations, although they cannot be clearly distinguished from recent eastern Indonesians in this regard. Living stature can be estimated for the 2000-year-old burial from Golo, Gebe, and at 163 cm it lies at the upper limit of the range of means recorded for recent eastern Indonesian males. The great majority of the burials are secondary, notably skull burials during the first millennium CE and secondarily buried cremations at around 1000 CE. The Golo individual, however, is distinct in being a primary inhumation, and also in displaying marked circumferential deformation, as recorded ethnographically for some Austronesian speakers in Melanesia.

Acknowledgements

The investigation of the Tanjung Pinang and Golo remains was financially supported with funding from the Australian Research Council (ARC) and The Australian National University (ANU) Faculties Research Grants Scheme. The author completed recording the Northern Moluccan remains while holding the status of Visiting Fellow at the Department of Archaeology and Anthropology, ANU. A small Culture, History and Language grant from the ANU funded my expenses associated with recording the Melolo mandibles. Two ARC Discovery Project grants, 'Contribution of South Asia to the Peopling of Australasia' (with Colin Groves) and 'The Flores hobbit—*Homo floresiensis* or microcephalic eastern Indonesian?' (with Marc Oxenham), provided financial support for recording the non-Melolo mandibles (including the Malay mandibles recorded by Daniel Rayner) and the Malekula crania. The following curators past and current provided access to the recorded museum specimens: Jakob van Brakel (Tropenmuseum, Amsterdam); Jim Specht (Australian Museum, Sydney); Alan Thorne and Jack Fenner (ANU); Barry Craig (Museum of South Australia); Jude Philp and Denise Donlon (Macleay Museum and Shellshear Museum, Sydney University); John de Vos (Leiden Natural History Museum); Rob Kruszynski (British Museum of Natural History); Philippe Menecier (Musée de l'Homme, Paris); and Ken Mowbray (American Museum of Natural History, New York).

12

Skeletal markers of health and disease in the Northern Moluccas

Bronwyn Wyatt and Justyna J. Miszkiewicz

This chapter seeks to understand how skeletal markers of systemic stress, especially those indicating childhood exposure to external or internal non-specific physiological disruptions, may have influenced longer-term growth and mortality in late prehistoric Maluku Utara. It explores the presence, severity, and distribution of pathology within the studied samples, focusing on systemic stress indicators. It discusses whether we can infer longer-term health outcomes in these populations.

The environments in which contemporary humans live are a testament to the adaptability and resilience of the ancient humans who first reached them. Many barriers of land, sea, and environmental unpredictability were overcome, shaping the responses of ancient human physiology. These responses are likely to be reflected in the surviving physical evidence representing ancient humans—their skeletal remains (Larsen 2015). By examining such remains, insights into the past biocultural experiences of individuals, and the populations from which they originated, can be gained. These insights come from skeletal markers of health and disease that allow us to infer likely diets (including the sufficiency of diet), subsistence practices, experiences of infectious diseases, and adaptations to new environments with novel challenges (Roberts and Manchester 2007).

The ancient seafaring populations of Island Southeast Asia, Melanesia, and the Pacific Islands represent groups of humans who successfully colonised new islands. Their skeletal remains are thus an important source of data for bioarchaeology and paleopathology. The Northern Moluccas islands in Indonesia (Propinsi Maluku Utara) have long been an important meeting ground between Austronesian- and Papuan-speaking populations, with exchange and modification of cultural and technological practices observed through the archaeological, linguistic, and genetic records (Bellwood 1998, 2017; Bellwood et al. 2006; Bulbeck 2008; Spriggs 1998).

Following on from Chapter 11, here the analysis of human skeletal remains recovered from the Northern Moluccan excavations is extended, by discussing skeletal markers of physiological stress in the context of age-at-death and stature. For information regarding the ancestry and antiquity of the sample, please see Chapter 11.

Materials and methods

The study sample includes human skeletal remains from five sites in the three islands of Kayoa, Morotai, and Gebe (see Table 12.1). The cultural contexts of these burials can be classified as Late Neolithic (Golo, Tanjung Pinang, and Daeo 1 and 2) and Early Metal Phase (Uattamdi). They belong to a period when pottery making was already present, with glass beads and metal artefacts (copper, iron) appearing around 2000 years ago in Uattamdi. Subsistence resources included pigs and dogs (chickens are uncertain), with presumably a range of tropical tuber, starch-bearing, and fruit/nut species such as yam, taro, banana, sago, canarium, coconut, and breadfruit. No actual plant remains were recovered during the excavations, so the plant food aspect of the diet remains rather hypothetical, but there is no reason to suspect from the regional archaeological record that cereals such as rice or millet were present in this region.

Table 12.1 Basic biological profiles for the sample.

Individual	Age-at-death	Sex	Location
Tanjung Pinang 1	Adolescent to young adult†‡§	Male	Morotai
Tanjung Pinang 2	Adult†‡§	Male	Morotai
Tanjung Pinang 3	Young adult§	Male	Morotai
Tanjung Pinang 4	Young adult†‡§	Male	Morotai
Tanjung Pinang 5	Subadult†§	Male	Morotai
Tanjung Pinang 6	Adolescent to young adult§	Male	Morotai
Tanjung Pinang 9	Subadult*	Indeterminate^	Morotai
Tanjung Pinang 10	Adult*	Male	Morotai
Tanjung Pinang Unknown 1 Adult	Adult#	Indeterminate^	Morotai
Tanjung Pinang Unknown 2 child	Child*	Indeterminate^	Morotai
Tanjung Pinang Unknown 3 subadult	Subadult#*	Indeterminate^	Morotai
Tanjung Pinang Unknown 4 subadult	Adolescent to young adult#*	Indeterminate^	Morotai
Tanjung Pinang Unknown 5 Adult	Adult#*	Indeterminate^	Morotai
Tanjung Tulang Adult 1	Adult*	Male	Morotai
Tanjung Tulang Juvenile	Subadult*	Indeterminate^	Morotai
Tanjung Tulang Adult 2	Adult*	Female	Morotai
Tanjung Tulang Adult 3	Adult*	Indeterminate^	Morotai
Daeo 1 Adult	Middle-aged adult §	Male	Morotai
Daeo 1 Juvenile	Subadult#	Indeterminate^	Morotai
Daeo 2-1 Juvenile	Subadult#*	Indeterminate^	Morotai
Daeo 2-2	Adult#*	Indeterminate^	Morotai
Daeo 2-3	Adult*	Indeterminate^	Morotai
Daeo 2-4	Adult*	Indeterminate^	Morotai
Daeo 2-5	Adult*	Indeterminate^	Morotai
Daeo 2-6	Adolescent to young adult*	Indeterminate^	Morotai
Uattamdi 1	Middle-aged adult§	Male	Kayoa
Uattamdi 2	Subadult*	Indeterminate^	Kayoa
Uattamdi 3	Adult#	Male	Kayoa
Uattamdi 4	Adolescent to young adult	Indeterminate^	Kayoa
Uattamdi 5	Child	Indeterminate^	Kayoa
Uattamdi 6	Adolescent to young adult*	Indeterminate^	Kayoa
Uattamdi 7	Adult*	Indeterminate^	Kayoa
Uattamdi 8	Child*	Indeterminate^	Kayoa
Uattamdi 9	Adult*	Female	Kayoa
Uattamdi 10	Adult*	Indeterminate^	Kayoa
Golo individual associated with cranium	Middle-aged or older adult†§	Male	Gebe

† Dental eruption (Buikstra and Ubelaker 1994)

§ Suture closure (Buikstra and Ubelaker 1994)

‡ Dental attrition (Lovejoy 1985)

Vertebral changes (Albert 1998)

* Stature or size of remains (Merchant and Ubelaker 1977; Primeau et al. 2012)

^ Remains too fragmentary for reliable estimates.

Source: Bronwyn Wyatt and Justyna Miszkiewicz.

There are remains of 36 individuals in the studied sample. Whilst most display suitable preservation for biological profile reconstruction, the largely fragmentary and incomplete nature of the sample is likely due to it being predominantly comprised of secondary cranial burials, especially from the Tanjung Pinang site on Morotai, with substantially fewer post-cranial elements recovered. Due to the uneven distribution of age groups and sexes in the sample, no inferential statistical examination is attempted, with all assessment being based on descriptive data.

Age-at-death and biological sex estimation

Following standards for the study of human skeletal remains (Buikstra and Ubelaker 1994), age-at-death was estimated using multiple methods which focus on different skeletal characteristics. The age-at-death estimates were categorised as 'infant or young child' (0 to 1 years old), 'older child' (2 to 11 years old), 'adolescent' (12 to 19 years old), 'young adult' (20 to 34 years old), 'middle-aged adult' (35 to 49 years old), and 'older adult' (50+ years old). Due to the fragmentary and largely incomplete record of the remains, multiple age-at-death estimation methods were applied in order to increase the accuracy of estimates for the available material. These included the assessment of cranial suture closure, including palatal sutures, and dental eruption patterns during human development (Buikstra and Ubelaker 1994); dental attrition by life stage as developed by Lovejoy (1985); estimation of age-at-death based on long bone diaphysis length as developed by Merchant and Ubelaker (1977); and the examination of epiphyseal union in the long bones and vertebral body surface changes using standards and criteria described by Buikstra and Ubelaker (1994).

Biological sex was estimated using standards also set out by Buikstra and Ubelaker (1994), with a further five specimens undergoing direct assessment by ancient DNA analysis. Less than half (n=13) of the sample was preserved well enough for reliable sex estimation using macroscopic examination of sex-specific characteristics of the cranium and/or pelvic remains.

Stature estimation

The estimation of stature in the recovered individuals necessitated use of multiple techniques owing to the fragmentary and incomplete state of the sample. Due to this limitation, the estimates of stature merely provide a starting point for placing these individuals into a broader context of Island Southeast Asian health and physiological attributes. Where possible, multiple methods were used to derive a likely range of stature. The assessment of stature estimates was conducted using regression equations where the maximum length of tibia and femur were available (Genoves 1967), and in some cases following the method of Trotter and Gleser (1958) for the maximum length of the humerus. Given that several of the long bones were incomplete, the method of Steele and McKern (1969) for deriving maximum lengths from bone segments was used. Metatarsal and metacarpal lengths and their relationships to stature, as described by

Meadows and Jantz (1992) and Byers et al. (1989), were also used, either as supplementary measures, or as sole measures where long bones were not available. Given the difficulties in estimating sex from co-mingled remains without cranial or pelvic bones, the stature estimation regression equations used are based on combined male and female standards. This necessitated creation of a total population average for the slope and intercept of Meadows and Jantz's (1992) methodology, thus increasing the margin of error surrounding true stature. However, where possible, this was offset by the assessment of multiple sites using different methodologies, in order to provide a likely range within which the most accurate stature might have lain.

Assessment of abnormal skeletal lesions to infer disease

The majority of the individuals in the sample were represented by their cranial vaults. These were examined macroscopically for porous changes indicative of porotic hyperostosis (PH), by locating the affected bone and describing the spread of the lesion (Rivera and Mirazón Lahr 2017). Dental defects characteristic of linear enamel hypoplasia (LEH) (Miszkiewicz 2015) were recorded on a presence/absence and severity basis. Both lesions can be linked to malnutrition and other non-specific forms of physiological health disruption in ancient humans (Miszkiewcz 2015; Rivera and Mirazón Lahr 2017). Exact frequencies and/or estimated chronology of LEH were not assessed given the fragmentary condition of the sample. Where necessary, cranial sites with potential PH and LEH lesions were also investigated with the aid of a hand magnifying glass.

Porotic hyperostosis was described using staging outlined by Schultz (1993), in which the severity and distribution of abnormal porosity to the cranial vault can range from localised to widespread. Enamel depressions indicating LEH were scored where the enamel depression was evident across the labial and buccal surfaces of the anterior and posterior teeth (Miszkiewicz 2015). Individuals were classified as affected by LEH when defects were observed on any teeth, as opposed to per tooth assessments (e.g. Oxenham 2008). This was necessary due to the incomplete nature of the available dental arcades (Goodman and Rose 1990). The LEH defects were scored by examining the occurrence of enamel growth arrests inferred from 'striping' of the labial and buccal surfaces of teeth. This was categorised as absent, single line (present), or multiple lines (present), including an approximate assessment of depth of the depressions (categorised into superficial or prominent). These should facilitate simple insights into the non-specific stress of LEH presence in the sample (Goodman and Rose 1990).

Results

The bulk of the sample comprised adolescent and young adult individuals (n=28). Represented are infants or young children (n=2), an older child (n=1), adolescents (n=13), young adults (n=15), middle-aged adults (n=4), and a single elderly adult (n=1). This results in a maximum of 36 individuals, including an estimated 14 males and two females, with the remainder classified as indeterminate (Table 12.1). Estimations of sex ratios and sex-specific differences in health and disease are not attempted.

Skeletal indicators of stress

Nine individuals (of 13 available for dental study) demonstrated some degree of macroscopically visible LEH. Six of these showed only mild depressions, localised to the buccal surfaces of teeth, and in most cases only a single affected tooth. The three individuals with more severe LEH demonstrated multiple affected teeth.

Of the 18 available cranial samples, 13 (or 72 per cent of the total crania) demonstrated lesions consistent with PH. Eight (62 per cent) showed severe or widespread lesions. One individual (Uattamdi 1) may have suffered a separate condition, given the severity of the presentation of PH. In each of the 13 individuals who demonstrate skeletal markers of PH, the cranial bones affected also demonstrate substantial thickening (Fig. 12.1, from Tanjung Pinang). The available skeletal material suggests that most individuals were affected by PH bilaterally, with the frontal and parietal cranial bones being the most commonly affected sites.

Figure 12.1 Mild porous lesions indicative of porotic hyperostosis to posterior parietal and superior occipital of Tanjung Pinang 6.

Source: Bronwyn Wyatt and Justyna Miszkiewicz.

To test whether potential differences in the resources available on Morotai, Gebe, and Kayoa might have had an effect on the skeletal health of these ancient people, the number of individuals with LEH and PH were evaluated and compared between the three islands. Kayoa and Gebe each have only a single individual with associated dental remains. No LEH was observed in the Kayoa (Uattamdi) individual, whilst the Gebe (Golo) individual demonstrated severe LEH. Eight individuals on Morotai were afflicted with LEH. The sole Gebe individual in the sample did not demonstrate skeletal alterations consistent with PH, whilst 10 individuals from Morotai and three from the Uattamdi (Kayoa) cranial remains were so affected.

Skeletal indicators of stress and their relationship with stature and age-at-death

The relationships between skeletal lesions, stature, and age-at-death can be basically assessed, but these results utilise only small samples and merely provide a potential starting point for inferring links between mortality and disease in the sample (Table 12.2). Mean estimated stature in the indeterminate group (n=7) was 165.8 cm (SD=9.3), whereas identified males (n=4) and the sole identified female (n=1) were estimated to have reached a mean of 161.8 cm (SD=7.4) and stature of 161.4 cm respectively. Stature assessment of adults found no difference in mean stature to be higher in individuals with LEH than in those without (158.4, SD=7.8 compared with 158.5, SD=12.9 respectively) (Table 12.3). On the other hand, the mean stature of individuals with PH was higher than that of unaffected individuals (165.2 cm, SD=7.6 compared with 158.4 cm, SD=7.8 respectively). However, the high standard deviations suggest cautious interpretation of the data.

Table 12.2 Stature and skeletal markers of systemic stress.

Individual	Stature (cm)	SE (cm)[a]	Porotic Hyperostosis		Linear Enamel Hypoplasia
Tanjung Pinang 1	Indeterminate^		Early stage	Bilateral superior parietal and frontal (cranium)	Mild
Tanjung Pinang 2	152.9†	±3.82	None present		Mild
Tanjung Pinang 3	Indeterminate^		Early stage	Bilateral posterior parietals (cranium)	Mild
Tanjung Pinang 4	Indeterminate^		Second stage	Bilateral posterior parietals and occipital (cranium). Possibly also microporosity of orbitals	Mild
Tanjung Pinang 5	Indeterminate^		Third stage	Bilateral posterior parietals (cranium)	Prominent, multiple
Tanjung Pinang 6	Indeterminate^		Early stage	Bilateral posterior parietals (cranium)	Mild
Tanjung Pinang 9	Indeterminate^		Third stage	Parietals and frontal (cranium)	Prominent, multiple
Tanjung Pinang 10	Indeterminate^		Third stage	Parietals and frontal (cranium)	Indeterminate^
Tanjung Pinang Unknown 1 Adult	Indeterminate^		Indeterminate^		Indeterminate^
Tanjung Pinang Unknown 2 child	Indeterminate^		Third stage	Occipital (cranium). Further cranium not available	Indeterminate^
Tanjung Pinang Unknown 3 subadult	120.5 to 128.2†	±3.82 to ±3.48	Indeterminate^		Mild
Tanjung Pinang Unknown 4 subadult	145.7‡	±7.12	Indeterminate^		Indeterminate^
Tanjung Pinang Unknown 5 Adult	174.6§		Indeterminate^		Indeterminate^
Tanjung Tulang Adult 1	158.6 to 161.0†‡	±6.98 to ±4.25	Third stage	Bilateral parietal, and frontal (cranium)	Indeterminate^
Tanjung Tulang Juvenile	132.2†	±4.25	Indeterminate^		Absent
Tanjung Tulang Adult 2	Indeterminate^		Indeterminate^		Indeterminate^
Tanjung Tulang Adult 3	Indeterminate^		Indeterminate^		Indeterminate^
Daeo 1 Adult	170.5‡	±6.42	Third stage	Parietal and occipital (cranium). Remains highly fragmentary	Indeterminate^
Daeo 1 Juvenile	Indeterminate^		Indeterminate^		Indeterminate^
Daeo 2-1 Juvenile	132.6 to 132.8†	±4.25	None present		Indeterminate^
Daeo 2-2	Indeterminate^		None present*		Absent
Daeo 2-3	167.6‡	±6.54	None present*		Absent
Daeo 2-4	159.3§	±5.30	None present*		Indeterminate^
Daeo 2-5	171.3§	±5.57	None present*		Indeterminate^
Daeo 2-6	145§	±5.30	None present*		Indeterminate^
Uattamdi 1	Indeterminate^		Final stage	Widespread and present internally (cranium).	Indeterminate^
Uattamdi 2	Indeterminate^		Third stage	Right parietal	Indeterminate^
Uattamdi 3	Indeterminate^		Early stage	Bilateral parietal, and frontal (cranium)	Indeterminate^
Uattamdi 4	163.8‡	±5.99	None present		Indeterminate^
Uattamdi 5	Indeterminate^		None present		Indeterminate^

Individual	Stature (cm)	SE (cm)ᵃ	Porotic Hyperostosis		Linear Enamel Hypoplasia
Uattamdi 6	145.9 to 152.9†	±3.51 to ±3.27	None present*		Absent
Uattamdi 7	161.7 to 164.3†	±3.51 to ±3.27	None present*		Indeterminate^
Uattamdi 8	Indeterminate^		None present*		Indeterminate^
Uattamdi 9	158.0 to 164.7†‡§	±5.28 ±6.36	None present*		Indeterminate^
Uattamdi 10	173.1 to 177.6§	±5.13 to ±5.33	None present*		Indeterminate^
Golo individual associated with cranium	162.2 to 165.7†	±3.42 to ±4.25	None present		Prominent, multiple

^ Remains too fragmentary for reliable estimates

† Steele and McKern 1969

‡ Byers, Akoshima and Curran 1989

§ Meadows and Jantz 1992, modified

* Co-mingled fragmentary remains preventing identification of skeletal material to individual

a Where a range of possible statures is presented, the SE associated with the lowest and highest estimates is presented.

Source: Bronwyn Wyatt and Justyna Miszkiewicz.

Table 12.3 Adult individuals with both stature estimates and pathology assessments.

	With LEH	Without LEH	With PH	Without PH
Number (n)	2	2	2	2
Mean stature (cm)	158.4	158.5	165.2	158.4

Source: Bronwyn Wyatt and Justyna Miszkiewicz.

The distributions of age-at-death categories with respect to stress indicators can provide further insight into skeletal health and disease in a few of the individuals (Table 12.4). The highest proportion of LEH-affected individuals were adolescents, with five of the seven individuals with dental remains affected. In young adults with dental remains, three of the five individuals demonstrated LEH, whilst the only elderly individual was also affected. No middle-aged adults with dental remains demonstrated changes to enamel consistent with LEH. With PH, each age category, except for infants and elderly adults, had individuals demonstrating its presence—in all three middle-aged adults, five of the seven adolescents, and four of the five young adults.

Table 12.4 Pathology presence by age-at-death.

	Infant	Child	Adolescent	Young adult	Middle aged adult	Elderly
LEH						
With	–	–	5	3	–	1
Without	–	–	2	2	–	–
PH						
With	0	1	5	4	3	–
Without	–	–	2	1	–	0

Source: Bronwyn Wyatt and Justyna Miszkiewicz.

Discussion

Assessment of adult stature suggests that the common experience of childhood physiological disruption did not greatly affect the overall growth of adult individuals. There was no substantial difference in individuals with LEH and those without, and a counter-intuitive difference between those with PH and those without. These findings, at least for LEH and its relationship with growth and stature, are in line with other ancient and contemporary populations (Temple 2008; Floyd and Littleton 2006). Indeed, stunted stature may be more a marker of continued exposure to stress and resource deprivation than a result of childhood disruption (Vercellotti et al. 2014). The results of this study, however, cannot provide sufficient evidence to support such a relationship due to the small sample size. Any substantial differences in LEH and PH between different age groups in the sample were not supported. The small sample sizes for older adults and young children restrict any attempt to detect differences in mortality based on childhood stress exposure. The majority of the material represented adolescents and young adults, but the degree to which this reflects true population mortality compared to burial sampling bias is unclear.

The presence of PH across the sample may reflect resource deficiencies in the population (Halcrow et al. 2014; Ortner 2003; Oxenham and Cavill 2010; Walker et al. 2009; Zuckerman et al. 2014). However, determination of specific micro-nutrient deficiencies is difficult given the incomplete skeletal material. In transitory populations, malnutrition may have been commonplace as new islands were colonised (Buckley et al. 2014). Acquired nutritional deficiencies are not the only potential cause of PH, especially within tropical environments. Porotic hyperostosis has been long linked to acquired conditions such as anemia caused by parasitic infections, or genetically determined diseases that include thalassemia and sickle cell anaemia (Rivera and Mirazón Lahr 2017). Malaria has been associated with development of porotic lesions of the cranium and orbits (Rabino Massa et al. 2000). The skeletal changes observed in individuals suffering malaria are believed to result from haemolytic anaemia induced by parasites (Nyakeriga et al. 2004). Indeed, Gowland and Western (2012) have utilised spatial epidemiology to demonstrate that the presence and severity of PH (as well as *cribra orbitalia*) tend to match the distribution of endemic malaria, which is endemic today in North Maluku (Beebe and Cooper 2000; Clark and Kelly 1993; Sternberg 1884).

Genetic studies of contemporary populations within the islands suggest a high proportion of alleles conferring protection against malarial infection, resulting in ovalocytosis and alpha-thalassemia (Hill et al. 1985). Unique forms of alpha-thalassemia have been observed with a likely Melanesian origin (Tsukahara et al. 2006). Given this, minor forms of thalassemia may be partly responsible for the high prevalence of PH within the sample. High infant and maternal mortality also reflects increased malarial presence (Soren 2003), although this sample does not have this mortality pattern. However, it is acknowledged that the PH evaluation here was solely based on macroscopic observations of few samples, with no diagnostic support using radiography of the cranial bones (e.g. to assess the extent of trabecular thickening due to potential marrow hyperplasia). A more robust differential diagnosis based on the porous lesions in the crania would be possible only with more data.

Finally, the disproportionate number of males in the Morotai sites, together with the high incidence of LEH on this island, may reflect purposeful secondary cranial burial of primarily adolescent and young adult male skulls. However, it is uncertain whether the distribution of skeletal markers of stress, age-at-death, and sex-based risk of mortality in the burial sample can be truly reflective of the broader population.

Conclusions

A basic palaeopathological assessment of this ancient Indonesian population has demonstrated the complexities of relating systemic stress exposure to longer-term health outcomes such as growth restriction or increased mortality. No clear relationship between childhood stress exposure, as indicated through LEH, and adult stature could be observed. The proportion of individuals with LEH was highest in the adolescent age group, with a decreased proportion in older age groups. This may suggest that those young individuals who would have experienced poor health, as inferred from their LEH record, may have been less likely to survive into adulthood. This is only a generalised suggestion, as assessing the direct and complex relationship between LEH and mortality requires a larger sample size. Porotic hyperostosis did not demonstrate any positive or negative relationship with stature or mortality risk, thus suggesting that the systemic causes of this condition were not uniform in their health impacts over time.

13

The Northern Spice Islands in prehistory, from 40,000 years ago to the recent past

Peter Bellwood

The previous 12 chapters have examined the results of our 1990s archaeological project in the Northern Moluccas from the perspectives of chronology, artefact sequences, animal remains, and human remains. The general goal has been to locate the Northern Moluccas within the Island Southeast Asian record of humanity since approximately 40,000 years ago. From start to finish, a number of significant questions have risen to the surface:

a. What kind of hominins first settled the Oceanic (non-landbridged) islands of the Northern Moluccas, and when?

b. Were these islands settled permanently by forager populations before the commencement of food production, or did these populations only utilise the smaller islands, such as Gebe, intermittently?

c. Were marsupials translocated from the New Guinea region to the Northern Moluccas by human intention, or did these animals disperse naturally?

d. What evidence exists within our data for interaction between the island societies of Southeast Asia (including the Moluccas) and western Oceania during the Late Pleistocene and Early Holocene, before the Neolithic?

e. How do sites such as Uattamdi fit within the picture for Neolithic dispersal around 3300 years ago through Island Southeast Asia and into Oceania? Were there links with the Lapita archaeological culture in Island Melanesia and with the initial settlement of the Mariana Islands?

f. What have been the traceable interactions between Austronesian-speaking and Papuan-speaking societies in the Northern Moluccas/New Guinea region during the past 3500 years, and especially the past 2000 years since the spice trade linking western and eastern Eurasia commenced? When did pottery making spread into the Papuan-speaking societies of Morotai and northern Halmahera? Furthermore, were the 'Spice Islands' actual sources of exported spices such as cloves around 2000 years ago, as a lot of rather loose historical inference inclines to inform us?

First, let us examine chronology. In terms of standard archaeological terminology, four overall phases (Northern Moluccas Phases 1 to 4) can be recognised in the prehistory of the Northern Moluccas. The earliest record of a potential human presence comes from Golo Cave on Gebe, with a basal date of 36,350–35,001 cal. BP (Wk 4629). Beyond this followed many millennia of Palaeolithic occupation, possibly intermittent, with bone tools and edge-ground technology for shell (but not stone) adzes appearing towards the end of this phase; indeed, during the Early Holocene rather than the Late Pleistocene in terms of current chronology. We can call this first phase *Northern Moluccas Phase 1*, let us say from 40,000 to 3500/3000 years ago, with an intensification of cultural activity during the Early and Middle Holocene.

A major change occurred associated with the oldest date of 3342 to 2971 cal. BP (ANU 7776) from Uattamdi, which marked the appearance of red-slipped pottery and the oldest shell ornaments found so far in the region. This second, Neolithic, phase apparently continued in Uattamdi until about 2000 BP, and is here termed *Northern Moluccas Phase 2*.

The first appearances of cupreous and iron artefacts and glass beads ushered in a third, metal-using, phase (*Northern Moluccas Phase 3*), again at Uattamdi, by C14 date ANU 9322, 2136 to 1782 cal. BP. This Early Metal Phase also saw the first *recorded* appearances in the region of jar burial (Uattamdi), supine orientation for an inhumation burial (Golo Cave), and a spread of earthenware potting technology into nearby previously aceramic communities on Morotai and northern Halmahera (Tanjung Pinang, Aru Manara, Gorua).

The Early Metal Phase continued onwards into the historical period (*Northern Moluccas Phase 4*), commencing in these islands in terms of direct written records with the arrival of the Portuguese in 1511 (the manuscript of Tomé Pires was written between 1512 and 1515; Cortesão 1944). One could perhaps also recognise a separate phase of importation of glazed ceramics from Chinese and other mainland sources during the early second millennium CE, but little such material was found during our excavations.

To summarise these four phases, therefore, we have the following:

Northern Moluccas Phase 1: from 40,000 to 3500/3000 BP, flaked stone and shell from the beginning, but with marsupials, bone tools, and edge-ground technology for shell adzes only appearing definitely in Holocene but pre-Neolithic contexts.

Northern Moluccas Phase 2: 3500/3000 to 2000 BP, Neolithic red-slipped pottery, shell ornaments, and pig and dog bones (no data on human burials).

Northern Moluccas Phase 3: 2000 to 500 BP, Early Metal Phase cupreous and iron artefacts, glass beads, jar burial (Uattamdi), skull burial (Tanjung Pinang), extended burial with cranial modification (Golo), spread of pottery into Morotai and Halmahera (see, on this, Ono et al. 2017, accepted), extirpation of marsupials, spice trade(?).

Northern Moluccas Phase 4: 500 BP to recent, European contact, Asian trade ceramics.

With this standard archaeological periodisation in the background, a number of important issues arise. Some can be debated fruitfully, others remain obscure, and many have been discussed in more detail in my newest book-length survey of the region (Bellwood 2017).

Some outstanding questions

What kind of hominin first settled the Oceanic (non-landbridged) islands of the Northern Moluccas, and when?

With archaic hominins attested in Java and Flores by Middle Pleistocene times, and possibly also Sulawesi and Luzon by the Late Pleistocene, one might ask if they also reached the entirely sea-girt islands of eastern Wallacea, even allowing for Pleistocene fluctuations in sea level (Hope 2005; O'Connor et al. 2017). Unfortunately, Pleistocene lithic technology in Island Southeast Asia reveals nothing about the hominin status of the makers, so we can interpret very little of a taxonomic nature from the lithic record in Golo Cave at >36,000 years ago. Neither in Golo nor in other contemporary sites in Island Southeast Asia are there Pleistocene blade, microblade, or backed tools that might give the species game away and hint whether we are dealing with *Homo erectus*, dwarfed hominins related to *Homo floresiensis*, or *Homo sapiens*.

The Pleistocene paintings in caves in Sulawesi and Borneo, the widespread terminal Pleistocene bone tools, and the eventual settlement of Australia and New Guinea by *Homo sapiens* at about 50,000 years ago or more would suggest that the first traceable Moluccans at 36,000 years ago were indeed *Homo sapiens*. But we cannot be sure, and no human remains in Moluccan sites are old enough to be of assistance. However, as Katherine Szabó has pointed out (in Szabó et al. 2007), the presence of modified shell items in the basal layers of Golo Cave suggests a potential presence of behaviourally modern *Homo sapiens* there, as opposed to an archaic hominin. But, without dated cave art and skeletons, a degree of uncertainty remains.

We might also ask just when humans, modern or otherwise, might first have settled in the Northern Moluccas, noting that it is just as likely that Halmahera was settled initially from western New Guinea, via Gebe, as from any other source region to its west (Birdsell 1977; Kealy et al. 2017). New Guinea was certainly settled by 50,000 years ago (Summerhayes et al. 2010), but this need not mean that every small island in its vicinity was settled also at this time. Indeed, Golo and Wetef were both dug to bedrock, with a maximum date of only 36,000 years ago, so we cannot argue that older material lies unexcavated beneath. Gebe is such a small island that if people really did arrive long before 36,000 years ago, we might ask where they lived without leaving traces in any of the excavated caves and rockshelters on the island. All in all, human arrival at 36,000 years ago on Gebe is the best we can do at the moment, and a claim for anything older would be unwarranted.

Were these islands settled permanently by forager populations before the commencement of food production, or did they utilise the smaller islands, such as Gebe, only intermittently?

Only Golo and Wetef on Gebe Island have sufficient time depth for analysis of this question, given the absence of Pleistocene occupation within Tanjung Pinang on Morotai, and the very limited evidence for it from Daeo 2. Indeed, there is a possibility that humans did not occupy Morotai at all until after the Last Glacial Maximum, although this is purely a negative observation that could easily be overturned by future discoveries. The Wetef dates (Table 2.5) from Gebe certainly indicate a consistent human presence during the Holocene, as they do in Golo. But Wetef had rather limited Pleistocene occupation, and Golo has some obvious problems with the distribution of C14 dates. In Table 2.2 for Golo, I have shaded the dates that appear to give a coherent sequence, and I regard all the 'rogue' marine shell dates as perhaps reflecting disturbance due to the frequent caching of shell adzes in the soft dry floor of the cave. The three direct dates on the shell adzes themselves cannot be taken seriously as indicators of stratigraphic date, as discussed in Chapter 8. If the apparent rogue dates are ignored, then the Golo sequence between 30,000 and 13,000 years ago could suggest either extremely slow deposition, or even an occupation hiatus. At this point, the Wetef date series might come to the rescue, since they do indicate occupation in the lower levels dated to c. 23,000 BP (Table 2.5). So, do these dates add up to a continuous human presence on Gebe Island from 36,000 BP onwards?

The answer is obviously uncertain. If Golo and Wetef are considered together, there is no sign of any massive hiatus across the Last Glacial Maximum, particularly when lowered sea levels are taken into account. Golo and Wetef would have been quite far inland/uphill at this time, thus perhaps not well-favoured for human occupation. But whether or not humans remained permanently on Gebe or just visited from time to time is unknown. My own intuition from the deliberate caching of shell adzes in both the Golo and Wetef Cave floors is that Gebe Island was subject to occasional visits rather than permanent occupation, but this can only remain surmise. The phytolith evidence from Golo (Tables 2.4 and 2.5) also supports a fluctuating human presence, yet indicates that Gebe Island was apparently not abandoned for any long periods during the past 35,000 years.

Were marsupials translocated from New Guinea or adjacent islands into the Northern Moluccas?

After our 1990s discoveries of marsupial bones in many excavated sites on Kayoa, Halmahera, Morotai, and Gebe Islands, the issue of human translocation of these animals came to the fore in a fairly positive way (Flannery et al. 1998). In terms of 'indigenous' fauna, it was apparent that all of these islands supported native species of marsupial cuscus (*Phalanger* sp.), and placental rodents and bats (Flannery 1995a), plus reptiles and birds. However, the finding of a few bandicoot bones in Holocene layers in Gua Siti Nafisah on Halmahera was unexpected, and even more dramatic was the finding of large numbers of wallaby bones in Gua Siti Nafisah and in the two Gebe caves of Golo and Wetef. Morotai has, to date, produced neither of these terrestrial marsupial species, but the arboreal cuscus was present there, in Daeo Cave 2.

In 1998, Tim Flannery, Peter Bellwood, Peter White and others (Flannery et al. 1998) published the conclusion that the Gebe wallaby was probably derived from translocation of the Misool Island wallaby (*Dorcopsis muelleri mysoliae*), thus from an island source just west of the Bird's Head Peninsula of New Guinea, and almost 200 km south of Gebe. This conclusion is given further statistical support from wallaby dentitions by Jennifer R. Hull in Chapter 10. No conclusions were drawn with respect to the bandicoot owing to the small size of the bone sample. The Gebe, Halmahera, and Morotai cuscuses were already regarded as indigenous species (Flannery and Boeadi 1995).

As far as the wallabies are concerned, however, there is a lingering problem with the taphonomy. Neither Golo nor Wetef have surviving animal bones in their Pleistocene layers, and the record of them starts rather unhelpfully in the Early Holocene. This is strange, given that Golo especially has stone tools and worked shells in its lower layers that suggest a human presence by 36,000 BP. These humans must have exploited some of the bony creatures of land and sea—bats, rats, lizards, small fish, and so forth, even if marsupials were then absent. Yet no animal or human bones occur in the lower layers of either site, despite the survival of shells. In fact, we have no direct fossil data on the Pleistocene fauna of the Northern Moluccan Islands at all.

So how did the three marsupial species—wallaby, bandicoot, and cuscus—actually reach these islands? Were they translocated by humans, or were they truly indigenous (i.e. endemic, self-transported)? In the case of the cuscus there appears to be no argument. They were indigenous, and belong to two endemic species: *Phalanger ornatus* on Halmahera and Morotai, and *Phalanger alexandriae* on Gebe (Flannery 1995a; Flannery and Boeadi 1995). Since these phalangers are extant species, sample sizes are sufficient for such statements to be made. But the situation is different for the locally extirpated wallabies and bandicoots, since the sample sizes are much smaller. Did humans transport them, or did they travel by themselves? We cannot be certain, but wallabies are known to be able to survive at sea at least 7 km away from land (*Canberra Times*, 14 October 1999). So, dispersal independent of humans, even during the Holocene, cannot be ruled out entirely for *Dorcopsis*.

What were the interaction levels between different island societies in Island Southeast Asia (including the Moluccas) and western Oceania during the late Pleistocene and early Holocene, before the Neolithic?

Northern Moluccas Phase 1, from 40,000 to 3500/3000 BP, with its flaked stone and shell tools, and subsequently during the Early Holocene its marsupials, bone tools, and edge-ground shell adzes, offers rather little evidence in support of frequent interaction across the eastern Indonesian archipelagoes, at least not if we focus on the Late Pleistocene. Recent discoveries of Late Pleistocene shell beads and fishhooks in Timor and adjacent islands (O'Connor 2015), plus related worked stone and bone materials with cave art in Sulawesi (Aubert et al. 2014; Brumm et al. 2017) and Borneo (Aubert et al. 2018; Fage and Chazine 2010), tell us what Late Pleistocene humans in Island Southeast Asia were capable of. But they do not attest any very obvious movement of ideas, raw materials, or of the people attached to them. There are many deep and highly significant cave sequences, such as those from Niah (Sarawak), Tabon (Palawan), Gunung Sewu (Java, many caves), Gua Harimau (Sumatra), Island Melanesia, and also the New Guinea Highlands, where such elaborate cultural and artistic creations were simply not present at all in *confirmed* Late Pleistocene contexts. To this list we can add Golo and Wetef.

During the Holocene, the tempo of inter-island contact most certainly increased. Ground and polished bone tools became common in many regions (Aplin et al. 2017), including the Northern Moluccas (Pasveer and Bellwood 2004). The ground *Tridacna* adzes of Golo and Wetef, as discussed in Chapter 8, are remarkably similar to examples from Pamwak Cave on Manus in the Admiralty Islands, 1600 km east of Gebe (Fig. 8.7). The Pamwak shell adzes are not directly dated, but the Golo ones are almost certainly Early to Mid-Holocene, and it seems reasonable to assume that the Pamwak ones might date likewise. This does suggest interaction, at least to a degree, but the supporting idea of frequent animal translocation between islands is now subject to greater doubt than it was 20 years ago.

Did the Northern Moluccas play a major role in the Neolithic dispersals from Island Southeast Asia into Western Micronesia and Island Melanesia around 3000 years ago?

I have recently addressed this issue in my recent book on the prehistory of Island Southeast Asia (Bellwood 2017), and can only reiterate that, so far, no pre–Metal Age archaeological complex with decorated pottery has been exposed anywhere in the Northern Moluccas that could be considered directly ancestral to the Lapita archaeological culture of Island Melanesia, or to the initial Marianas Redware culture of the Mariana Islands. Montenegro et al. (2016) have recently suggested a Moluccan or southern Philippine homeland for the initial settlement of the Palau Islands in western Micronesia, using wind and current simulations, and this is indeed possible given that Palau currently lacks the distinctive stamped pottery that characterises Lapita and Marianas Redware. However, it remains unlikely from an archaeological viewpoint that ancestral Lapita settlers reached the Bismarck Archipelago or the Admiralty Islands by following a route that travelled from the Northern Moluccas, along the northern coast of New Guinea, and then into Island Melanesia. Given current archaeological knowledge of the distribution of red-slipped pottery with punctate-, dentate-, and circle-stamped decoration, after 3500 BP, it is more likely that the Philippines, the Mariana Islands, and Island Melanesia were linked by migrations that did not pass through the Halmahera region. Naturally, future archaeological discoveries in the Northern Moluccas might render this observation incorrect, but we cannot interpret the archaeological record by giving priority to an absence rather than a presence.

What have been the interaction levels between Austronesian-speaking and Papuan-speaking societies in the Northern Moluccas/New Guinea region during the past 3500 years, and especially the past 2000 years since the trans-Eurasian spice trade presumably began?

The early centuries of Austronesian expansion into the Moluccas, between 3500 and 3000 BP, naturally involved some population admixture between speakers of two great language groupings on the world stage—Papuan of western Melanesia and Austronesian of Taiwan and Island Southeast Asia. The languages of the Halmahera region belong to two genetically unrelated families—West Papuan in the north (one of several Papuan language families in the New Guinea region (Ross 2005)), and Austronesian (a language family of ultimate mainland Asian origin via Taiwan) in the south (Fig. 13.1). The only linguist to offer an overall classification and discussion of the West Papuan languages has been Voorhoeve (1988). His research has been based on lexicostatistics rather than full use of the comparative method to plot shared innovations, but the results still offer a picture of considerable interest, updated from a pronoun perspective by Ross (2005).

The Papuan languages of northern Halmahera were classified into a North Halmahera Stock by Voorhoeve, this stock belonging to the West Papuan Phylum, which evidently has its greatest level of diversity in the Bird's Head region of West New Guinea (West Papua). It is thus very likely that the initial West Papuan languages of Halmahera were taken to the island by migrants from New Guinea.

How long ago might this have occurred? Since glottochronology in this region is unlikely to be a reliable technique owing to gross differences in rates of vocabulary change (Blust 2000), all that can be offered is a guestimate of several millennia based on a minimum shared cognate percentage between all pairs of languages in the North Halmahera Stock of only 21 to 28 per cent (a figure perhaps inflated by hidden borrowing: Voorhoeve 1988:182). Indeed, Voorhoeve (1994:651) once suggested that the West Papuan languages arrived in Halmahera *after* the initial Austronesian languages, but this suggestion was based on glottochronology and it has not been taken up by other linguists.

Given the archaeological record of New Guinea and Australia, it seems most likely that the West Papuan languages of Halmahera were first introduced there in the pre-Neolithic period, i.e. some time in Northern Moluccas Phase 1. Whether as long as 36,000 years ago is far less certain, and there is no visible patterning in the phylum that could possibly support or refute such an enormous antiquity. Any such patterning that might once have existed will presumably have been reduced by the genealogical levelling between the West Papuan languages to be discussed in the next paragraph. However, the fact that the establishment of Papuan language phyla in New Guinea so clearly predated the arrival of Austronesian languages in that island makes it likely that the same situation also held for the Northern Moluccas.

The remarkable point about the North Halmahera Stock languages, alluded to above, is that the largest subfamily contains languages that are very closely related—indeed, 'levelled' in linguistic parlance. This largest subfamily is termed the Halmahera Subfamily (Wurm and Hattori 1983, Map 45: Voorhoeve calls it the North Halmahera Family) and it covers the whole of northern Halmahera, Ternate, and Tidore, with the exception of part of the island of Makian. Within it all languages share over 65 per cent of basic vocabulary (100-word list). The second subfamily contains only the West Makian isolated language (Voorhoeve 1982a), which shares between 21 and 28 per cent of cognates with the languages in the Halmahera Subfamily. This suggests a situation in which the West Makian language has remained in place for many millennia, but earlier Papuan languages in northern Halmahera and Morotai have been replaced by a recent language radiation or levelling (an interpretation also followed by Yoshida 1980:Fig. 1). This radiation presumably took place sometime within the past 2000 years, given the very shallow Romance-like level of linguistic diversity between the languages concerned.

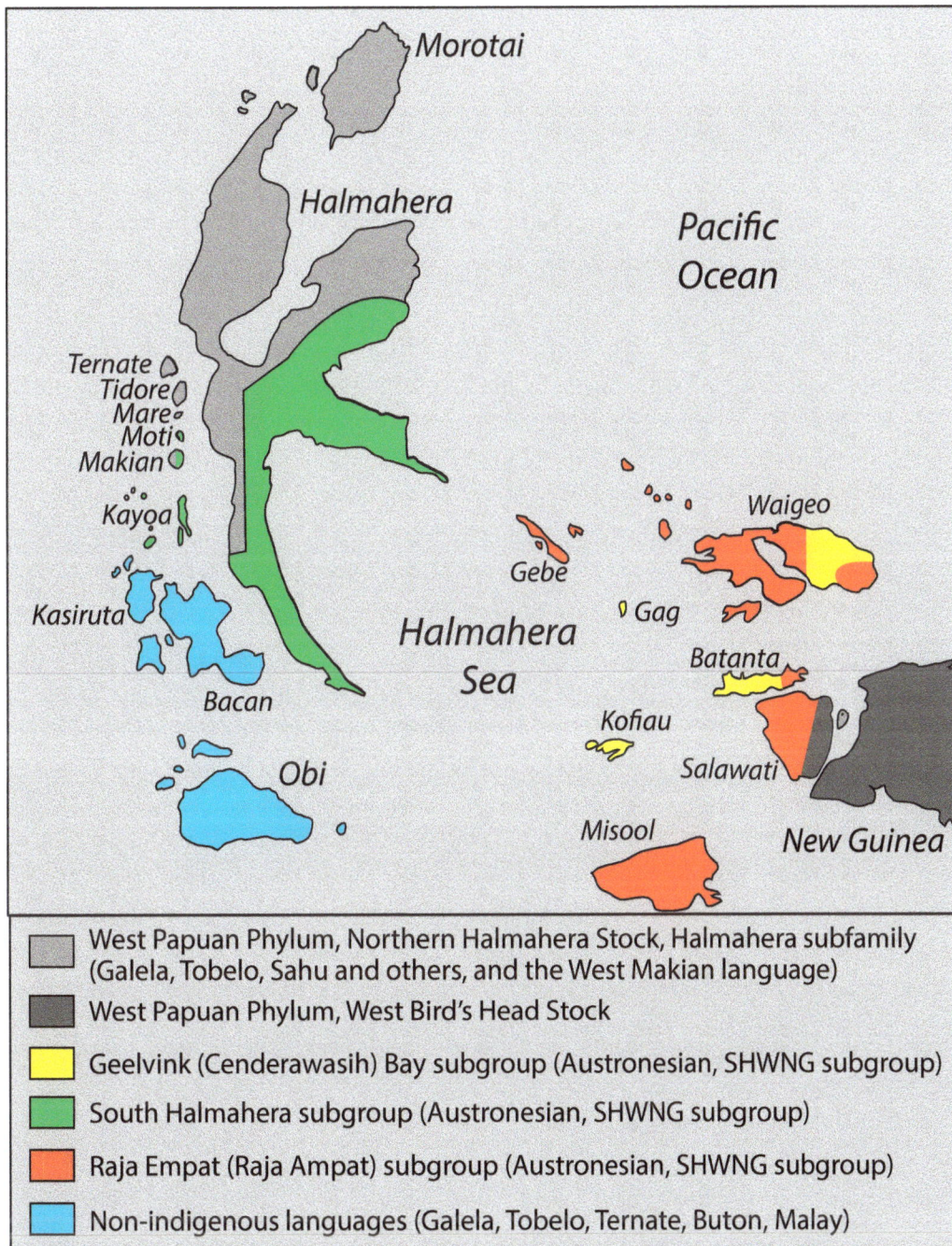

Figure 13.1 Present-day Austronesian and Papuan language groupings in the Northern Moluccas.
Source: Wurm and Hattori 1983: Map 45; Peter Bellwood.

Another very interesting observation made by Voorhoeve (1988:194) is that the North Halmahera Stock languages of Ternate, Tidore, West Makian, and Sahu, all located in the mid-western geographical portion of the Halmahera group, have adopted many elements of Austronesian grammar. Some of this borrowing was also claimed by Voorhoeve to be quite ancient, although no exact date was suggested. The locations of these four languages, perhaps not coincidentally, are all quite close to the island of Kayoa with its so-far unique assemblage of plain red-slipped pottery, polished stone adzes, pigs, and dogs dating from 3300 BP in the Uattamdi rockshelter. Was the initial enclave of Austronesian speakers at about this time localised to a relatively small area focused on the chain of small islands from Bacan up to Ternate?

There is no simple answer to this question from an Austronesian linguistic viewpoint, partly because the South Halmahera–West New Guinea (SHWNG) languages shown in Figure 13.1 also reveal considerable linguistic levelling according to Blust (2017:195–197), meaning that their current time depth is also likely to be closer to 2000 years, as with the Halmahera West Papuan languages, rather than the >3000 years BP that we would expect for initial Austronesian settlement in the Northern Moluccas. Today, the SHWNG subgroup of Malayo-Polynesian contains 40+ languages (van den Berg 2009) and is defined by about 13 linguistic innovations (Blust 1978, 1993). Its closest cousinly subgroup within the Malayo-Polynesian languages as a whole is Oceanic, rather than any of the Western Malayo-Polynesian subgroups in Sulawesi, Borneo, or the Philippines. Hence, there is a strong likelihood that it entered the Northern Moluccas from the north or east, rather than the west. In Blust's view, also followed by Kamholz (2014), the SHWNG languages represent a replacement movement from either Cenderawasih Bay or even somewhere east of it, a replacement that might mean that no descendants survive of the first layer of Austronesian languages to reach the Northern Moluccas.

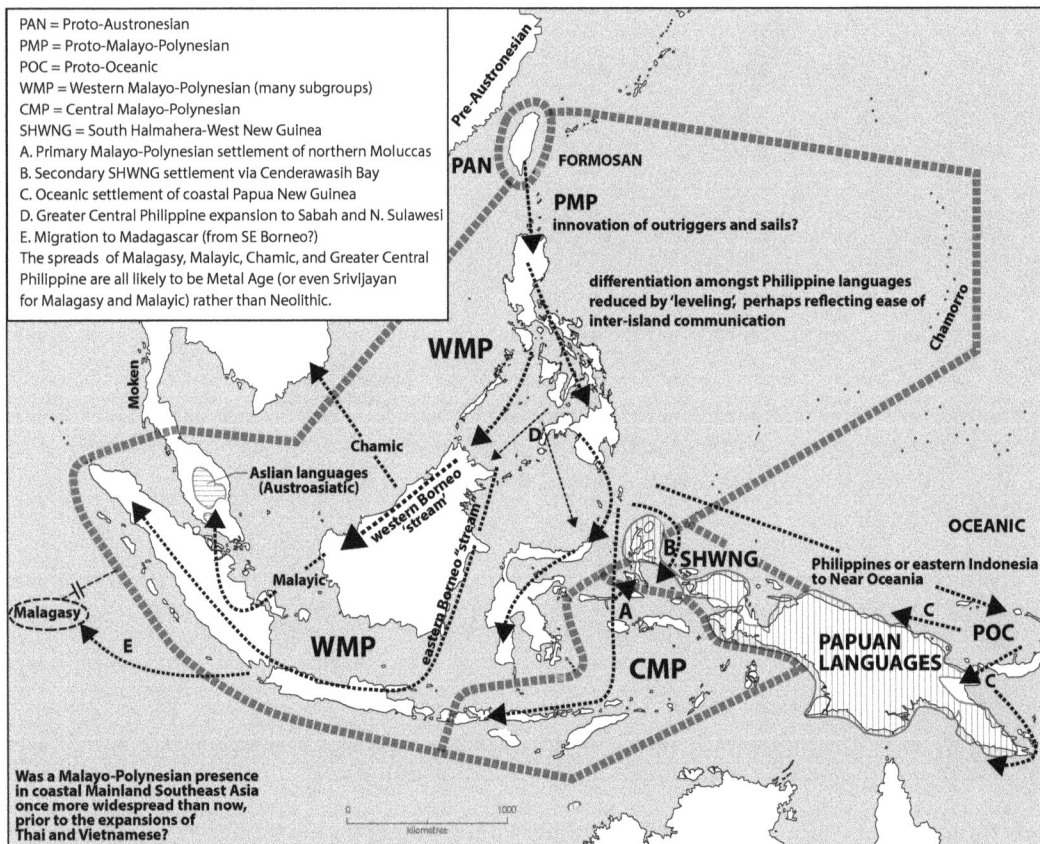

Figure 13.2 The likely migration directions of early speakers of Malayo-Polynesian languages.
Source: Peter Bellwood and Robert Blust (Bellwood 2017:Fig. 6.4).

If such a replacement really did occur quite recently, as also suggested for the Halmahera West Papuan languages, we might need to look for a combination of causes that would include secondary population movements and more recently perhaps forcible population replacement, as well as trade- and exchange-lubricated interaction (Andaya 1993). The very wide occurrence across Indonesia after 2000 years ago of characteristic incised pottery of Indonesian Metal Age style surely reflects increased communication and population movement from this time onwards, and the spice trade comes to mind.

This monograph is hardly the place to review the whole literature on the spice trade that carried cloves from Ternate and Tidore, and nutmegs from Banda, towards the Mediterranean, India, and China, starting possibly 2000 years ago (Bellwood 2017:335–337). Suffice it to say that the Roman author Pliny the Elder referred to what appear to have been cloves in 70 CE, and that actual cloves have been found in early to middle first millennium AD contexts at Segaran IIA in West Java and Mantai in Sri Lanka (Manguin and Indradjaja 2011). Furthermore, Indian pottery in quite large quantities is now well known from the sites of Sembiran and Pacung in northern Bali, dating to circa 2000 years ago or just before (Ardika and Bellwood 1991; Ardika et al. 1997; Calo et al. 2015). Neither ancient cloves nor Indian pottery have been excavated in the Moluccas, but it seems relatively certain that Indian contact could *potentially* have reached the Moluccas by 2000 years ago. So could, and did, the technological developments that are widely associated by archaeologists, linguists, and historians with a combination of Indian, Mainland Southeast Asian, early Malayo-Chamic, and Chinese trading acumen. These include metal items and metallurgy, Dong Son drums, glass beads, nephrite ornaments (although these are not yet found in the Moluccas), and probably also some new Y-chromosome haplogroups (Kusuma et al. 2016).

The Early Metal Phase, or Northern Moluccas Phase 3 in the above terminology, was thus a phase of very considerable change in the prehistory of our region. The Neolithic, or Northern Moluccas Phase 2, brought into the mix an original population of Malayo-Polynesian peoples and languages, but the Early Metal Phase probably led to some hefty stirring of the pot, and possibly the expansion of the SHWNG subgroup of Malayo-Polynesian languages as it exists today, as well as the Halmahera Subfamily of West Papuan languages.

Some further observations on cultural and genetic admixture into Near Oceania

The previous chapters have made it clear that the Uattamdi phenomenon, with its plain red-slipped pottery stone adzes, shell ornaments, and pig and dog bones, marked an external incursion into the islands west of Halmahera at around 3300 BP. It is also inferred that this incursion brought speakers of Austronesian languages, although perhaps not yet the immediate ancestors of the speakers of the SHWNG languages, from an ultimate source in Taiwan and the Philippines. So far, the Uattamdi assemblage is unique in the Northern Moluccas.

By 2000 years ago, as also discussed above, the previously preceramic inhabitants of many other regions of the Northern Moluccas, such as Morotai, Halmahera, and perhaps Gebe, adopted the use of pottery, by now of an incised and stamped style well represented in sites such as Tanjung Pinang, Aru Manara (Ono et al. 2018), Gorua (Ono, Aziz et al. 2017; Ono, Oktaviana et al. 2017), Gua Siti Nafisah, Um Kapat Papo, Buwawansi, and of course in the Early Metal Phase Layer B in Uattamdi. This spread need not have required any large-scale migration of people, but we do have the above-mentioned episodes of linguistic levelling in both the Papuan and the Austronesian languages of the Halmahera region. And this brings up the issue of ancient DNA.

In 2016, my ANU colleague Justyna Miszkiewicz extracted petrous bones from four of the Tanjung Pinang skulls, plus one from Uattamdi and one from the Golo extended skeleton (see the research reported by Wyatt and Miszkiewicz in Chapter 12). These petrous bones (Pinhasi et al. 2015) were sent to Mark Stoneking at the Max Planck Institute for Evolutionary Anthropology in Leipzig, who forwarded them to Cosimo Posth in the Max Planck Institute for the Science of Human History in Jena (Germany). The Max Planck team was able to get results that hopefully will be published in full soon. Meanwhile, I can state that the Golo skull contained no ancient DNA, but the other five from Uattamdi and Tanjung Pinang did. Perhaps not surprisingly, three of the Tanjung Pinang skulls (numbers 1, 2, and 4) carried ancient Papuan mtDNA haplogroups, whereas Tanjung Pinang skull 6 and the Uattamdi cranium had mtDNA haplogroups that are today widely associated with Austronesian-speaking populations in the Philippines and Indonesia.

The significance of these discoveries is clear, in that three of the inhabitants of Tanjung Pinang, now in the Papuan-speaking region of the Northern Moluccas, were deeply indigenous in terms of their female lines of descent, whereas one from Tanjung Pinang and one from Uattamdi reflected maternal origins further west or north within Island Southeast Asia. This was an admixed population, as illustrated also by the autosomal ancestral profiles (research in progress) of the Tanjung Pinang and Uattamdi individuals, with their shared 'Papuan' and 'Austronesian' ancestry components. All of this human material dates to around 2000–1500 years ago, and so belongs to the period of spreading material culture here associated with the arrival of the Early Metal Phase and perhaps also the early trade in spices.

This observation of population mixture in the Northern Moluccas commencing from the archaeological record around 2000 years ago is supported by a previous whole-genome autosomal DNA analysis of modern Indonesian populations by Hudjashov et al. (2017). These authors use a molecular-clock calculation to date the commencement of admixture between Papuan and Austronesian ancestral genetic components to about 2000 years ago, noting a time lag of about a millennium without strong admixture following the initial arrival of the Austronesian component, via the Philippines, into eastern Indonesia. These observations fit extremely well with the interpretation of Uattamdi as an Austronesian outlier settlement, relatively contained for almost a millennium, until Southeast Asian styles of Neolithic material culture spread fairly rapidly into regions that are currently occupied by speakers of Papuan languages.

We might now ask how far eastwards this zone of admixture spread into New Guinea coastal regions and the islands of Near Oceania. In 1982, linguist Bert Voorhoeve (C. Voorhoeve 1982b) noted a total of 31 potential borrowings between the north Halmahera West Papuan languages and the Central Papuan languages of the south coast of Papua New Guinea, almost 3000 km to the east. The latter include the modern Motu language of the Port Moresby coastline and are Oceanic (Malayo-Polynesian), not Papuan. Voorhoeve could provide no obvious historical explanation for this situation, apart from noting the possibility of long-distance sailing along the southern coastline of New Guinea by either Ternate or Tidore traders from the west seeking spices and other items, or by the ancestral Motu themselves sailing from the east. The latter were associated in the nineteenth and early twentieth centuries with multi-hulled canoe (*hiri*) voyages to exchange pots made in the Port Moresby region for sago, reaching right to the upper reaches of the Gulf of Papua, close to the Fly Delta (Dutton 1982). Indeed, finds of late Lapita sites along the Papuan southern coastline (McNiven et al. 2011) suggest that Austronesian-speaking populations might have been in that region since at least 2850 BP.

Contact between Island Southeast Asia and Island Melanesia actually has quite a deep archaeological antiquity. A millennium earlier than the Early Metal Phase in the Moluccas (c. 3000 BP), Talasea obsidian from New Britain travelled to Bukit Tengkorak in Sabah, Borneo, presumably by a Neolithic sea route to the north of New Guinea (Bellwood and Koon 1989), rather than via the Northern Moluccas, where no Talasea obsidian has ever been found. The potential Halmahera–Central Papua linguistic borrowing link discussed above appears to be younger in time, and was perhaps associated with a separate chain of connection along the south coast of New Guinea, represented by the sherds of pedestalled pottery from Uattamdi and Tanjung Pinang that resemble a pedestalled vessel found in Collingwood Bay, and the single piece of Fergusson Island obsidian from Tanjung Pinang (Chapter 8).

The evidence for late prehistoric contact between the Moluccas and the islands of Near Oceania is therefore slim, but suggestive. This is perhaps a good topic with which to end this excursion into Northern Moluccan archaeology. Whether the near future will see more discoveries in these idyllic equatorial spice-bearing islands I do not know, but I hope so, with archaeology, zooarchaeology, archaeobotany, and ancient DNA all moving forward hand-in-hand. Evidence on the plant-food elements of ancient diet will be especially welcome, as will ancient DNA from burials of a Pre-Austronesian antiquity. A non-sapient archaic hominin of hobbit morphology would be even more welcome, but I have my doubts!

References

Abe, H. 1955. Anthropological studies on the femur of Kyushu Japanese. *Jinruigaku–Kenkyu* 2(2–4):121–145.

Addison, D. and E. Matisoo-Smith 2010. Rethinking Polynesian origins: a Western-Polynesian Triple-I model. *Archaeology in Oceania* 45:1–12. doi.org/10.1002/j.1834-4453.2010.tb00072.x

Albert, A. 1998. The use of vertebral ring epiphyseal union for age estimation in two cases of unknown identity. *Forensic Science International* 97:11–20. doi.org/10.1016/S0379-0738(98)00143-1

Allen, J. 1984. In search of the Lapita homeland: Reconstructing the prehistory of the Bismarck Archipelago. *Journal of Pacific History* 19:186–201. doi.org/10.1080/00223348408572494

Andaya, L. 1993. *The World of Maluku*. Honolulu: University of Hawaii Press.

Anggraeni. 2012. The Austronesian migration hypothesis as seen from prehistoric settlements on the Karama River, Mamuju, West Sulawesi. Unpublished PhD thesis. The Australian National University, Canberra.

Anggraeni, T. Simanjuntak, P. Bellwood and P. Piper 2014. Neolithic foundations in the Karama valley, West Sulawesi, Indonesia. *Antiquity* 88:740–756. doi.org/10.1017/S0003598X00050663

Aplin, K., S. O'Connor et al. 2017. The Walandawe tradition from Southeast Asia and osseous artifact traditions in Island Southeast Asia. In M. Langley (ed.) *Osseous Projectile Weaponry*, pp. 189–208. Dordrecht: Springer.

Ardika, I.W. 1991. Archaeological Research in Northeastern Bali, Indonesia. Unpublished PhD thesis. The Australian National University, Canberra.

Ardika, I.W. and P. Bellwood 1991. Sembiran: the beginnings of Indian contact with Bali. *Antiquity* 247:221–232. doi.org/10.1017/S0003598X00079679

Ardika, I.W., P. Bellwood, I.M. Sutaba and C. Yuliathi 1997. Sembiran and the first Indian contacts with Bali: An update. *Antiquity* 71:193–195. doi.org/10.1017/S0003598X00084696

Aubert, M., A. Brumm et al. 2014. Pleistocene cave art from Sulawesi, Indonesia. *Nature* 514:223–227. doi.org/10.1038/nature13422

Aubert, M, P. Setiawan et al. 2018. Palaeolithic cave art in Borneo. *Nature*. doi.org/10.1038/s41586-018-0679-9

Aufderheide, A. and C. Rodríguez-Martin 1998. *The Cambridge Encyclopedia of Human Paleopathology*. Cambridge: Cambridge University Press.

Bailit, H., S. DeWitt and R. Leigh 1968. The size and morphology of the Nasioi dentition. *American Journal of Physical Anthropology* 28:271–288. doi.org/10.1002/ajpa.1330280316

Bedford, S., R. Blust et al. 2018. Ancient DNA and its contribution to understanding the human history of the Pacific Islands. *Archaeology in Oceania* 53:205–219. doi.org/10.1002/arco.5165

Beebe, N. and R. Cooper 2000. Systematics of malaria vectors with particular reference to the Anopheles punctulatus group. *International Journal for Parasitology* 30:1–17. doi.org/10.1016/S0020-7519(99)00171-X

Behrensmeyer, A.K. 1978. Taphonomic and ecological information from bone weathering. *Paleobiology* 4(2):150–162. doi.org/10.1017/S0094837300005820

Bellwood, P. 1975. The prehistory of Oceania. *Current Anthropology* 16:9–28. doi.org/10.1086/201515

Bellwood, P. 1976. Archaeological research in Minahasa and the Talaud Islands, north-eastern Indonesia. *Asian Perspectives* 19, Part 2:240–288.

Bellwood, P. 1978. *Man's Conquest of the Pacific*. Auckland and London: Collins.

Bellwood, P. 1981. The Buidane culture of the Talaud Islands. *Bulletin of the Indo-Pacific Prehistory Association* 2:69–127.

Bellwood, P. 1988. *Archaeological Research in South-eastern Sabah*. Kota Kinabalu: Sabah Museum Monograph no. 2.

Bellwood, P. 1989. Archaeological investigations at Bukit Tengkorak and Segarong, south-eastern Sabah. *Bulletin of the Indo-Pacific Prehistory Association* 9:122–162. doi.org/10.7152/bippa.v9i0.11286

Bellwood, P. 1998. The archaeology of Papuan and Austronesian prehistory in the Northern Moluccas, Eastern Indonesia. In R. Blench and M. Spriggs (eds) *Archaeology and Language II: Correlating Archaeological and Linguistic Hypotheses*, pp. 128–140. London and New York: Routledge. doi.org/10.4324/9780203202913_chapter_5

Bellwood, P. 2007. *Prehistory of the Indo-Malaysian Archipelago*. Revised edition. Canberra: ANU E Press. doi.org/10.22459/PIMA.03.2007

Bellwood, P. 2011. Holocene population history in the Pacific region as a model for world-wide food producer dispersals. *Current Anthropology* 52(S4):363–378. doi.org/10.1086/658181

Bellwood, P. 2017. *First Islanders*. Hoboken: Wiley Blackwell. doi.org/10.1002/9781119251583

Bellwood, P., G. Chambers, M. Ross and H-c. Hung 2011. Are 'cultures' inherited? Multidisciplinary perspectives on the origins and migrations of Austronesian-speaking peoples prior to 1000 BC. In B. Roberts and M. Van der Linden (eds) *Investigating Archaeological Cultures: Material Culture, Variability and Transmission*, pp. 321–354. Dordrecht: Springer. doi.org/10.1007/978-1-4419-6970-5_16

Bellwood, P. and E. Dizon (eds) 2013. 4000 years of Migration and Cultural Exchange: *The Archaeology of the Batanes Islands, Northern Philippines*. Terra Australis 40. Canberra: ANU E Press.

Bellwood, P., J. Fox and D. Tryon (eds) 2006. *The Austronesians: Historical and Comparative Perspectives*. Canberra: ANU E Press.

Bellwood, P. and P. Hiscock 2018. Australia and the Pacific Basin during the Holocene. In C. Scarre (ed.) *The Human Past*, fourth edition, pp. 261–302. London: Thames and Hudson.

Bellwood, P. and P. Koon 1989. Lapita colonists leave boats unburned. *Antiquity* 63:613–622. doi.org/10.1017/S0003598X00076572

Bellwood, P., A. Waluyo, Gunadi, G. Nitihaminoto and G. Irwin 1993. Archaeological research in the Northern Moluccas; interim results, 1991 field season. *Bulletin of the Indo-Pacific Prehistory Association* 13:20–33.

Bellwood, P. and P. White 2005. Domesticated pigs in eastern Indonesia. *Science* 309:381. doi.org/10.1126/science.309.5733.381a

Bergman, R. and The Tiong Hoo 1955. The length of the body and long bones of the Javanese. *Documenta de Medecina Geographica et Tropica* 7:197–214.

Birdsell, J. 1977. The recalibration of a paradigm for the first peopling of Greater Australia. In J. Allen, J. Golson and R. Jones (eds) *Sunda and Sahul*, pp. 113–168. London: Academic.

Blust, R.A. 1978. Eastern Malayo-Polynesian: a subgrouping argument. In Wurm, S.A. and Carrington, L. (eds) Second International Conference on Austronesian Linguistics, Fascicle 1, pp. 181–234. *Pacific Linguistics Series C* 61. Canberra: Department Linguistics RSPacS, The Australian National University.

Blust, R.A. 1993. Central- and Central-Eastern Malayo-Polynesian. *Oceanic Linguistics* 32(2):241–293. doi.org/10.2307/3623195

Blust, R.A. 2000. Why lexicostatistics doesn't work. In C. Renfrew, A. McMahon and L. Trask (eds) *Time Depth in Historical Linguistics*, pp. 311–332. Cambridge: McDonald Institute for Archaeological Research.

Blust, R.A. 2017. The linguistic history of Austronesian-speaking communities in Island Southeast Asia. In P. Bellwood, *First Islanders: Prehistory and Human Migration in Island Southeast Asia*, pp. 190–197. Hoboken: Wiley Blackwell. doi.org/10.1002/9781119251583

Brace, C.L. 1976. Tooth reduction in the Orient. *Asian Perspectives* 19:203–219.

Brace, C.L. 1980. Australian tooth-size clines and the death of a stereotype. *Current Anthropology* 21:141–164. doi.org/10.1086/202426

Bräuer, G. 1988. Osteometrie. In R. Knußman (ed.) Handbuch der Anthropologie. Band 1: Wesen und Methoden der Anthropologie 1. *Teil Wissenschaftstheorie, Geschichte, morphologische Methoden*, pp. 160–232. Stuttgart: Gustav Fishcer.

Bronk Ramsey, C. 2009. Bayesian analysis of radiocarbon dates. *Radiocarbon* 51(1):337–360. doi.org/10.1017/S0033822200033865

Brown, P. 1978. The Ultrastructure of Dental Abrasion: Its Relationship to Diet. Unpublished BA Hons thesis. The Australian National University, Canberra.

Brown, P. 1989. *Coobool Creek*. Terra Australis 13. Canberra: Department of Prehistory, The Australian National University.

Brown, T., S. Pinkerton and W. Lambert 1979. Thickness of the cranial vault in Australian Aborigines. *Archaeology and Physical Anthropology in Oceania* 14:54–71.

Brumm, A., M. Langley et al. 2017. Early human symbolic behaviour in the Late Pleistocene of Wallacea. *Proceedings of the National Academy of Sciences* 114:4115–4220. doi.org/10.1073/pnas.1619013114

Buckley, H., R. Kinaston et al. 2014. Scurvy in a tropical paradise? Evaluating the possibility of infant and adult vitamin C deficiency in the Lapita skeletal sample of Teouma, Vanuatu, Pacific islands. *International Journal of Paleopathology* 5:72–85. doi.org/10.1016/j.ijpp.2014.03.001

Buikstra, J. and D. Ubelaker 1994. Standards for data collection from human skeletal remains: Proceedings of a seminar at the Field Museum of Natural History. *Arkansas Archaeology Research Series* 44. Fayetteville Arkansas Archaeological Survey.

Bulbeck, D. 1981. Continuities in Southeast Asian Evolution since the Late Pleistocene. Unpublished MA thesis. The Australian National University, Canberra.

Bulbeck, D. 2005. The Late Glacial Maximum human burial from Liang Lemdubu in northern Sahulland. In S. O'Connor, M. Spriggs and P. Veth (eds) *The Archaeology of the Aru Islands, Eastern Indonesia*, pp. 255–294. Terra Australis 22. Canberra: Pandanus Press.

Bulbeck, D. 2008. An integrated perspective on the Austronesian diaspora. *Australian Archaeology* 67:31–51.doi.org/10.1080/03122417.2008.11681877

Bulbeck, D. 2013. Craniodental affinities of Southeast Asia's 'Negritos' and the concordance with their genetic affinities. *Human Biology* 85:95–134. doi.org/10.3378/027.085.0305

Bulbeck, D., R. Abdul Kadir et al. 2005. Tooth sizes in the Malay Peninsula past and present: insights into the time depth of the indigenous inhabitants' adaptations. *International Journal of Indigenous Research* 1:41–50.

Bulbeck, D. and S. O'Connor 2011. The Watinglo mandible: A second terminal Pleistocene Homo sapiens fossil from tropical Sahul with a test on existing models for the human settlement of the region. *Homo* 62:1–29. doi.org/10.1016/j.jchb.2010.10.002

Bulbeck, D., P. Raghavan and D. Rayner 2006. Races of Homo sapiens: if not in the southwest Pacific, then nowhere. *World Archaeology* 38:109–132. doi.org/10.1080/00438240600564987

Byers, S., K. Akoshima and B. Curran 1989. Determination of adult stature from metatarsal length. *American Journal of Physical Anthropology* 79:275–279. doi.org/10.1002/ajpa.1330790303

Calo, A., B. Prasetyo et al. 2015. Sembiran and Pacung on the north coast of Bali. *Antiquity* 89:378–396. doi.org/10.15184/aqy.2014.45

Carson, M. 2014. *First Settlement of Remote Oceania: Earliest Sites in the Mariana Islands.* Springer. doi.org/10.1007/978-3-319-01047-2

Carson, M., H-c. Hung et al. 2013. *The pottery trail from Southeast Asia to Remote Oceania. Journal of Coastal and Island Archaeology* 8:17–36. doi.org/10.1080/15564894.2012.726941

Carson, M. and H-c. Hung 2017. *Substantive Evidence of Initial Habitation in the Remote Pacific.* Oxford: Archaeopress.

Chang, K-c. 1969. Fengpitou, Tapenkeng, and the Prehistory of Taiwan. *Yale University Publications in Anthropology* 73.

Chazine, J-M. and J-G. Ferrié 2008. Recent archaeological discoveries in East Kalimantan, Indonesia. *Bulletin of the Indo-Pacific Prehistory Association* 28:16–22. doi.org/10.7152/bippa.v28i0.12011

Chia, S. 2003. *The Prehistory of Bukit Tengkorak.* Kota Kinabalu: Sabah Museum Monograph 8.

Clark, J. and K. Kelly 1993. Human genetics, paleoenvironments, and malaria: relationships and implications for the settlement of Oceania. *American Anthropologist* 95:612–630. doi.org/10.1525/aa. 1993.95.3.02a00040

Coon, C. and E. Hunt Jr 1965. *The Living Races of Man.* New York: Knopf.

Cortesão, A. (ed.) 1944. *The Suma Oriental of Tomé Pires.* Second Series no. 89. London: Hakluyt Society.

Currey, J. 1988. Shell form and strength. In E.R. Trueman and M.R. Clarke (eds) *The Mollusca* 11, pp. 183–210. San Diego and London: Academic Press.

Davivongs, V. 1963a. The femur of the Australian Aborigine. *American Journal of Physical Anthropology* 21:457–467. doi.org/10.1002/ajpa.1330210404

Davivongs, V. 1963b. The pelvic girdle of the Australian Aborigine: sex differences and sex determination. *American Journal of Physical Anthropology* 21:443–455. doi.org/10.1002/ajpa.1330210403

Dickerson, R. 1928. *Distribution of Life in the Philippines.* Manila: Bureau of Printing.

Doran, G. and L. Freedman 1974. Metrical features of the dentition and arches of populations from Goroka and Lufa, Papua New Guinea. *Human Biology* 46:583–594.

Dutton, T. (ed.) 1982. *The Hiri in History: Further Aspects of Long Distance Motu Trade in Central Papua.* Pacific Research Monograph 8. Canberra: Australian National University Press.

Egloff, B. 1971. Archaeological research in the Territory of Papua and New Guinea. *Asian Perspectives* 14:60–64.

Egloff, B. 1979. *Recent Prehistory in Southeast Papua.* Terra Australis 4. Canberra: Department of Prehistory, The Australian National University.

Ellen, R. 2011. Sago as a buffer against subsistence stress and as a currency of inter-island trade networks in eastern Indonesia. In G. Barker and M. Janowski (eds) *Why Cultivate? Anthropological and Archaeological Approaches to Foraging-Farming Transitions in Southeast Asia*, pp. 47–60. Cambridge: McDonald Institute for Archaeological Research.

Fage, L-H. and J-M. Chazine 2010. *Borneo: Memory of the Caves.* Caylus: Le Kalimanthrope.

Fiene-Severns, P., M. Severns and R. Dyerly 1998. *Tropical Seashells of the Philippines.* Hong Kong: Periplus Editions.

Flannery, T. 1995a. *Mammals of the South-west Pacific and Moluccan Islands.* Sydney: Reed.

Flannery, T. 1995b. *Mammals of New Guinea.* Sydney: Reed.

Flannery, T., P. Bellwood et al. 1995. Fossil marsupials (Macropodidae, Peroryctidae) and other mammals of Holocene age from Halmahera, North Moluccas, Indonesia. *Alcheringa* 19:17–25. doi.org/10.1080/03115519508619095

Flannery, T., P. Bellwood et al. 1998. Mammals from Holocene archaeological deposits on Gebe and Morotai Islands, Northern Moluccas, Indonesia. *Australian Mammalogy* 20:391–400.

Flannery, T. and Boeadi 1995. Systematic revision within the Phalanger ornatus complex (Phalangeridae: Marsupiala). *Australian Mammalogy* 18:35–44.

Floyd, B. and J. Littleton 2006. Linear enamel hypoplasia and growth in an Australian Aboriginal community. *Annals of Human Biology* 33:424–443. doi.org/10.1080/03014460600748184

Francis, P. 1990. Glass beads in Asia. Part Two. Indo-Pacific beads. *Asian Perspectives* 29:1–23.

Francis, P. 2002. *Asia's Maritime Bead Trade.* Honolulu: University of Hawai'i Press.

Fredericksen, C., M. Spriggs and W. Ambrose 1993. Pamwak rockshelter. In M. Smith et al. (eds) *Sahul in Review*, pp. 144–152. Canberra: Department of Prehistory, The Australian National University.

Galipaud, J., R. Kinaston et al. 2016. The Pain Haka burial ground in Flores. *Antiquity* 90:1505–1521. doi.org/10.15184/aqy.2016.185

Genet-Varcin, E. 1951. *Les negritos de l'île de Luçon (Philippines).* Paris: Masson.

Genoves, S. 1967. Proportionality of the long bones and their relation to stature among Mesoamericans. *American Journal of Physical Anthropology* 26:67–77. doi.org/10.1002/ajpa.1330260109

George, W. 1981. Wallace and his line. In T.C. Whitmore (ed.) *Wallace's Line and Plate Tectonics*, pp. 3–8. Oxford: Clarendon Press.

Glinka, J. 1981. Racial history of Indonesia. In H. Suzuki et al. (eds) *Asien I: Japan, Indonesien, Ozeanien*, pp. 79–113. Munich: Oldenbourg.

Glover, I. 1986. *Archaeology in Eastern Timor, 1966–67*. Terra Australis 11. Canberra: Research School of Pacific Studies, The Australian National University.

Golitko, M., M. Schauer and J. Terrell 2012. Identification of Fergusson Island obsidian on the Sepik coast of northern Papua New Guinea. *Archaeology in Oceania* 47:151–156. doi.org/10.1002/j.1834-4453. 2012.tb00127.x

Golson, J. 1972. Both sides of the Wallace Line. In N. Barnard (ed.) *Early Chinese Art and its Possible Influence in the Pacific Basin* 3, pp. 533–596. New York: Intercultural Arts Press.

Goodman, A. and J. Rose 1990. Assessment of systemic physiological perturbations from dental enamel hypoplasias and associated histological structures. *American Journal of Physical Anthropology* 33:59–110. doi.org/10.1002/ajpa.1330330506

Gowland, R. and A. Western 2012. Morbidity in the marshes: Using spatial epidemiology to investigate skeletal evidence for malaria in Anglo-Saxon England (AD 410–1050). *American Journal of Physical Anthropology* 147:301–311. doi.org/10.1002/ajpa.21648

Green, R. 1967. The immediate origins of the Polynesians. In G. Highland et al. (eds) *Polynesian Culture History*, pp. 215–240. Honolulu: Bishop Museum Press.

Green, R. 1979. Lapita. In J. Jennings (ed.) *The Prehistory of Polynesia*, pp. 27–60. Cambridge: Harvard University Press. doi.org/10.4159/harvard.9780674181267.c3

Green, R. 1991. Near and Remote Oceania—disestablishing 'Melanesia' in culture history. In A. Pawley (ed.) *Man and a Half*, pp. 491–502. Auckland: Polynesian Society.

Grieķe, K. 2012. Non-marine mollusca of Gebe Island, North Moluccas. *Vernate* 31:225–240.

Groves, C. and T. Flannery 1989. Revision of the genus Dorcopsis (Macropodidae: Marsupialia). In G. Grigg, P. Jarmen and I. Hume (eds) *Kangaroos, Wallabies, and Rat-Kangaroos*, pp. 117–128. New South Wales: Surrey Beatty & Sons Pty Ltd.

Grün, R., M. Abeyratne et al. 1997. AMS 14C analysis of teeth from archaeological sites showing anomalous ESR dating results. *Quaternary Science Reviews* 16:437–444. doi.org/10.1016/S0277-3791 (96)00093-5

Halcrow, S., N. Harris et al. 2014. First bioarchaeological evidence of probable scurvy in Southeast Asia. *International Journal of Paleopathology* 5:63–71. doi.org/10.1016/j.ijpp.2014.01.004

Hall, R. 2013. The palaeogeography of Sundaland and Wallacea since the late Jurassic. *Journal of Limnology* 72:1–17. doi.org/10.4081/jlimnol.2013.s2.e1

Hall, R., M. Audley-Charles et al. 1988. Late Palaeogene-Quaternary geology opf Halmahera, eastern Indonesia: initiation of a volcanic island arc. *Journal of the Geological Society of London* 145:577–590. doi.org/10.1144/gsjgs.145.4.0577

Hedges, R., J. Lee-Thorpe and N. Tuross 1995. Is tooth enamel carbonate a suitable material for radiocarbon dating? *Radiocarbon* 37:285–290. doi.org/10.1017/S0033822200030757

Hill, A., D. Bowden, et al. 1985. Melanesians and Polynesians share a unique alpha-thalassemia mutation. American *Journal of Human Genetics* 37:571–581.

Hillson, S. 1996. *Dental Anthropology*. Cambridge: Cambridge University Press. doi.org/10.1017/CBO 9781139170697

Hope, G. 2005. The Quaternary in Southeast Asia. In A. Gupta (ed.) *The Physical Geography of Southeast Asia*, pp. 38–64. Oxford: Oxford University Press.

Howard, A. 1967. Polynesian origins and migrations: A review of two centuries of speculation and theory. In G. Highland et al. (eds) *Polynesian Culture History*, pp. 45–102. Honolulu: Bishop Museum Press.

Howells, W. 1973a. *The Pacific Islanders*. New York: Scribner's Sons.

Howells, W. 1973b. *Cranial Variation in Man*. Cambridge, MA: Harvard University, Papers of the Peabody Museum 67.

Howells, W. 1989. *Skull Shapes and the Map*. Cambridge, MA: Harvard University, Papers of the Peabody Museum 79.

Hudjashov, G, T. Karafet et al. 2017. Complex patterns of admixture across the Indonesian Archipelago. *Molecular Biology and Evolution* 34:2439–2452. doi.org/10.1093/molbev/msx196

Hull, J. 2014. The Vertebrate Remains Recovered During the 1990–1996 Excavations of the Northern Moluccan Islands. Unpublished Master of Archaeological Science subthesis. The Australian National University, Canberra.

Hung, H-c. 2004. A sourcing study of Taiwan stone adzes. *Bulletin of the Indo-Pacific Prehistory Association* 24:57–70.

Hung, H-c. 2005. Neolithic interaction between Taiwan and northern Luzon: The pottery and jade evidences from the Cagayan Valley. *Journal of Austronesian Studies* 1(1): 109–134.

Hung, H-c. 2008. Migration and Cultural Interaction in Southern Coastal China, Taiwan and the northern Philippines, 3000 BC to AD 1. Unpublished PhD thesis. The Australian National University, Canberra.

Hung, H-c. 2017. Nephrite and other Early Metal Age exchange networks across the South China Sea. In P. Bellwood, *First Islanders*, pp. 333–335. Hoboken: Wiley Blackwell. doi.org/10.1002/9781119251583

Hung, H-c. and P. Bellwood 2010. Movement of raw materials and manufactured goods across the South China Sea after 500BCE: from Taiwan to Thailand, and back. In B. Bellina, L. Bacus, O. Pryce and J. Wisseman Christie (eds) *50 Years of Archaeology in Southeast Asia: Essays in Honour of Ian Glover*, pp. 234–243. Bangkok: River Books.

Hung H-c., M. Carson et al. 2011. The first settlement of Remote Oceania: Luzon to the Marianas. *Antiquity* 85:909–926. doi.org/10.1017/S0003598X00068393

Hung, H-c., Y. Iizuka et al. 2007. Ancient jades map 3000 years of prehistoric exchange in Southeast Asia. *Proceedings of the National Academy of Sciences of the United States of America* 104(50):19745–19750. doi.org/10.1073/pnas.0707304104

Inabe, K. 1955. Anthropological studies on the tibia and fibula of Kyushu Japanese. *Jinruigaku–Kenkyu* 2(1):1–41.

Jacob, T. 1967a. *Some Problems Pertaining to the Racial History of the Indonesian Region*. Utrecht: Netherlands Bureau for Technical Assistance.

Jacob, T. 1967b. Racial identification of the Bronze Age human dentitions from Bali, Indonesia. *Journal of Dental Research* 46:903–910. doi.org/10.1177/00220345670460054801

Joliffe, I. 2002. *Principal Components Analysis*. Second edition. New York, NY: Springer.

Kamholz, D. 2014. Austronesians in Papua: Diversification and Change in South Halmahera–West New Guinea. Unpublished PhD thesis. University of California, Berkeley. digitalassets.lib.berkeley.edu/etd/ucb/text/Kamholz_berkeley_0028E_14626.pdf

Kealy, S., J. Louys and S. O'Connor 2017. Reconstructing palaeogrography and inter-island visibility in the Wallacean Archipelago. *Archaeological Prospection*. doi.org/10.1002/arp.1570

Keers, W. 1948. An Anthropological Survey of the Eastern Little Sunda Islands. *Mededeling* 74, Afdeling Volkenkunde No. 26. Amsterdam: Koninklijke Vereeniging Indisch Instituut Amsterdam.

Kirch, P. 1988. Long-distance exchange and island colonization: the Lapita case. *Norwegian Archaeological Review* 21:103–117. doi.org/10.1080/00293652.1988.9965475

Kirch, P. and D. Yen. 1982. Tikopia. Honolulu: *Bishop Museum Bulletin* 238.

Koppel, B. 2010. Fracture and modification of Patella shell: distinguishing human working. Unpublished BA(hons) thesis. School of Earth and Environmental Sciences, University of Wollongong, Wollongong.

Kusuma, P., M. Cox et al. 2016. Western Eurasian genetic influences in the Indonesian Archipelago. *Quaternary International* 416:243–248. doi.org/10.1016/j.quaint.2015.06.048

Lape, P., E. Peterson, D. Tanudirjo et al. 2018. New data from an open Neolithic site in eastern Indonesia. *Asian Perspectives* 57:222–243. doi.org/10.1353/asi.2018.0015

Larnach, S. and N. Macintosh 1966. *The Craniology of the Aborigines of Coastal New South Wales*. Oceania Monographs 13. Sydney: University of Sydney.

Larsen, C. 2015. *Bioarchaeology*. Cambridge: Cambridge University Press. doi.org/10.1017/CBO 9781139020398

Laszlo, M. and S. Mukherjee 2007. A genetic algorithm that exchanges neighboring centres for k-means clustering. *Pattern Recognition Letters* 28:2359–2366. doi.org/10.1016/j.patrec.2007.08.006

Lindsell, P. 1995. The Distribution and Detection of Artificial Cranial Deformation. Unpublished BA(hons) thesis. University of New England, Armidale.

Lipson, M., P. Skoglund et al. 2018. Population turnover in Remote Oceania shortly after initial settlement. *Current Biology* 28:1157–1165. doi.org/10.1016/j.cub.2018.02.051

Lovejoy, C. 1985. Dental wear in the Libben population: its functional pattern and role in the determination of adult skeletal age at death. *American Journal of Physical Anthropology* 68:47–56. doi.org/10.1002/ajpa.1330680105

Lyman, R. 1994. *Vertebrate Taphonomy*. Cambridge: Cambridge University Press. doi.org/10.1017/CBO 9781139878302

Mahirta 1996. The development of the Mare pottery tradition. *Bulletin of the Indo-Pacific Prehistory Association* 20:124–132.

Mahirta 2000. The Development of Mare Pottery in the Northern Moluccas Context. Unpublished MA thesis. The Australian National University, Canberra.

Manguin, P. and A. Indradjaja 2011. The Batujaya Site. In P. Manguin, A. Mani and G. Wade (eds) *Early Interactions between South and Southeast Asia*, pp. 113–136. Singapore: Institute of Southeast Asian Studies. doi.org/10.1355/9789814311175

Matisoo-Smith, E. 2007. Animal translocations, genetic variation, and the human settlement of the Pacific. In J.S. Friedlaender (ed.) *Genes, Language, and Culture History in the Southwest Pacific*, pp. 157–170. Oxford: Oxford University Press. doi.org/10.1093/acprof:oso/9780195300307.003.0010

Matsumura, H. and M. Hudson 2005. Dental perspectives on the population history of Southeast Asia. *American Journal of Physical Anthropology* 127:182–209. doi.org/10.1002/ajpa.20067

McNiven, I., B. David et al. 2011. New direction of human colonization of the Pacific. *Australian Archaeology* 72:1–6. doi.org/10.1080/03122417.2011.11690525

Meadows, L. and R. Jantz 1992. Estimation of stature from metacarpal lengths. *Journal of Forensic Science* 37:147–154. doi.org/10.1520/JFS13222J

Merchant, V. and D. Ubelaker 1977. Skeletal growth of the protohistoric Arikara. *American Journal of Physical Anthropology* 46:61–72. doi.org/10.1002/ajpa.1330460109

Miszkiewicz, J. 2015. Linear enamel hypoplasia and age-at-death at Medieval (11th–16th centuries) St. Gregory's Priory and cemetery, Canterbury, UK. *International Journal of Osteoarchaeology* 25:79–87. doi.org/10.1002/oa.2265

Mizoguchi, S. 1957. Anthropological studies on the radius and ulna of Kyushu Japanese. *Jinruigaku–Kenkyu* 4(1–4): 237–259.

Monk, K.A., Y. de Fretes and G. Reksodiharjo-Lilley 1997. *The Ecology of Nusa Tenggara and Maluku*. Singapore: Periplus.

Montenegro, A., R. Callaghan and S. Fitzpatrick 2016. Using seafaring simulations ansd shortest-hop trajectories to model the prehistoric colonization of Remote Oceania. *Proceedings of the National Academy of Sciences* 113:12685–12690. doi.org/10.1073/pnas.1612426113

Morant, G.M. 1936. A biometric study of the human mandible. *Biometrika* 28:84–112. doi.org/10.1093/biomet/28.1-2.84

Nyakeriga, A., M. Troye-Blomberg et al. 2004. Iron deficiency and malaria among children living on the coast of Kenya. *Journal of Infectious Diseases* 190:439–444. doi.org/10.1086/422331

O'Connor, S. 2010. Continuity in shell artefact production in Holocene East Timor. In B. Bellina et al. (eds) *50 Years of Archaeology in Southeast Asia: Essays in Honour of Ian Glover*, pp. 218–233. Bangkok: River Books.

O'Connor, S. 2015. Crossing the Wallace Line. In Y. Kaifu et al. (eds) *Emergence and Diversity of Modern Human Behavior in Palaeolithic Asia*, pp. 214–224. College Station: Texas A&M University Press.

O'Connor, S., J. Louys et al. 2017. Hominin dispersal and settlement east of Huxley's Line. *Current Anthropology* 58, Supplement 17, S567-S582. doi.org/10.1086/694252

O'Connor, S., R. Ono and C. Clarkson 2011. Pelagic fishing at 42,000 years before the present and the maritime skills of modern humans. *Science* 334:1117–1121. doi.org/10.1126/science.1207703

O'Connor, S., M. Spriggs and P. Veth (eds) 2005. *The Archaeology of the Aru Islands, Eastern Indonesia.* Terra Australis 22. Canberra: ANU E Press.

Ono, R., F. Aziz, A. Oktaviana et al. 2017. The development of pottery making traditions and maritime networks during the Early Metal Age in Northern Maluku Islands. *Amerta* 35:75–148. doi.org/10.24832/amt.v35i2.256

Ono, R., A. Oktaviana, F. Aziz et al. 2017. Development of regional maritime networks during the Early Metal Age in northern Maluku Islands: A view from excavated glass ornaments and pottery variation. *Journal of Island and Coastal Archaeology* 13:98–108. doi.org/10.1080/15564894.2017.1395374

Ono, R., A. Oktaviana, M. Ririmasse, M. Takenaka, C. Katagiri and M. Yoneda. 2018. Early Metal Age interactions in Island Southeast Asia and Oceania: jar burials from Aru Manara, Northern Moluccas. *Antiquity* 92:1023–1039. doi.org/10.15184/aqy.2018.113

Ono, R., S. Soegondho and M. Yoneda 2010. Changing marine exploitation during Late Pleistocene in Northern Wallacea: shell remains from Leang Sarru Rockshelter in Talaud Islands. *Asian Perspectives* 48:318–341.

Ono, R., H. Sofian, N. Aziz et al. 2019. Traces of early Austronesian expansion to East Indonesia? New findings of dentate-stamped and lime-infilled pottery from central Sulawesi. *Journal of Island and Coastal Archaeology*. doi.org/10.1080/15564894.2018.1481897

Ortner, D. 2003. *Identification of Pathological Conditions in Human Skeletal Remains*. San Diego, CA: Academic Press.

Oskarsson, M., C. Klutsch et al. 2011. Mitochondrial DNA data indicate an introduction through Mainland Southeast Asia for Australian dingoes and Polynesian domestic dogs. *Proceedings of the Royal Society B: Biological Sciences* 279 (1730):967–974. doi.org/10.1098/rspb.2011.1395

Oxenham, M. 2008. Dental health in northern Vietnam: Pre-Metal through Early Metal periods. *Bulletin of the Indo-Pacific Prehistory Association* 22:121–134. doi.org/10.7152/bippa.v22i0.11812

Oxenham, M. and I. Cavill 2010. Porotic hyperostosis and cribra orbitalia: the erythropoietic response to iron-deficiency anaemia. *Anthropological Science* 118:199–200. doi.org/10.1537/ase.100302

Parkinson, G. 2016. Establishing traces for the working of Nautilus shell in prehistory. Unpublished BA(hons) thesis. School of Earth and Environmental Sciences, University of Wollongong, Wollongong.

Parmentier, H. 1924. Dépôts de jarres à Sa Huynh. *Bulletin de l'Ecole Francaise d'Extrême-Orient* 24:325–343. doi.org/10.3406/befeo.1924.3008

Pasveer, J. 2004. *The Djief Hunters: 26,000 years of Rainforest Exploitation on the Bird's Head of Papua, Indonesia*. Leiden & New York: A.A. Balkema Publishers. doi.org/10.1201/b17006

Pasveer, J. and P. Bellwood 2004. Prehistoric bone artefacts from the Northern Moluccas, Indonesia. *Modern Quaternary Research in Southeast Asia* 18:301–359.

Patterson, D. Jr 1984. *A Diachronic Study of the Dental Paleopathology and Attritional Status of Prehistoric Ontario pre-Iroquois and Iroquois Populations*. Ottawa: National Museums of Canada. doi.org/10.2307/j.ctv17202

Pawlik, A., P. Piper et al. 2015. Shell tool technology in Island Southeast Asia. *Antiquity* 89:292–308. doi.org/10.15184/aqy.2015.3

Penrose, L. 1954. Distance, size and shape. *Annals of Eugenics* 18:337–343.

Pinhasi, R., D. Fernandes et al. 2015. Optimal ancient DNA yields from the inner ear part of the human petrous bone. *PloS ONE* 10(6): e0129102. doi.org/10.1371/journal.pone.0129102

Posth, C., K. Nägele, et al. 2018. Language continuity despite population replacement in Remote Oceania. *Nature Ecology and Evolution* 2:731–740. doi.org/10.1038/s41559-018-0498-2

Primeau, C., L. Friis et al. 2012. A method for estimating age of Danish medieval sub-adults based on long bone length. *Anthropologischer Anzeiger* 69:317–333. doi.org/10.1127/0003-5548/2012/0168

Rabino Massa, E., N. Cerutti and M. Savoia 2000. Malaria in ancient Egypt. Chungará (Arica, Chile) 32:7–9.

Ramsey, C.B. 2009. Bayesian analysis of radiocarbon dates. *Radiocarbon* 51: 337–360. doi.org/10.1017/S0033822200033865

Rao, P. 1966. The Anatomy of the Distal Limb Segments of the Aboriginal Skeleton. Unpublished PhD thesis. University of Adelaide, Department of Anatomy, Adelaide.

Reimer, P.J., E. Bard et al. 2013. IntCal13 and Marine13 radiocarbon age calibration curves 0–50,000 years cal BP. *Radiocarbon* 55:1869–1887. doi.org/10.2458/azu_js_rc.55.16947

Rivera, F. and M. Mirazón Lahr 2017. New evidence suggesting a dissociated etiology for cribra orbitalia and porotic hyperostosis. *American Journal of Physical Anthropology* 164:76–96. doi.org/10.1002/ajpa.23258

Roberts, C. and K. Manchester 2007. *The Archaeology of Disease*. Ithaca: Cornell University Press.

Ross, M. 2005. Pronouns as a preliminary diagnostic for grouping Papuan languages. In A. Pawley et al. (eds) *Papuan Pasts*, pp. 15–66. Canberra: Pacific Linguistics.

Samper Carro, S., S. O'Connor, J. Louys, S. Hawkins and Mahirta 2016. Human maritime subsistence strategies in the Lesser Sunda Islands during the terminal Pleistocene—early Holocene: New evidence from Alor, Indonesia. *Quaternary International* 416:64–79. doi.org/10.1016/j.quaint.2015.07.068

Sarasin, F. 1916–22. *Anthropologie der New-Caledonier und Loyalty Insulaner*. Berlin: C.W. Kreidel's Verlag.

Sathiamurthy, E. and H. Voris 2006. Maps of Holocene sea leval transgression and submerged lakes on the Sunda Shelf. *The Natural History Journal of Chulalongkorn University*, Supplement 2: 1–44.

Schmidt, L. 1996. Tales Told by Shells, Changing Patterns of Molluscan Exploitation: A Shell Midden Analysis Pamwak Rockshelter Manus Island, Papua New Guinea. Unpublished BA (hons) thesis. The Australian National University, Canberra.

Schultz, M., 1993. Initial stages of systemic bone disease. In G. Grupe, A.N. Garland (eds) *Histology of Ancient Human Bone: Methods and Diagnosis*, pp. 185–203. Berlin: Springer. doi.org/10.1007/978-3-642-77001-2_12

Scott, R. and C. Turner II 1997. *The Anthropology of Modern Human Teeth*. Cambridge: Cambridge University Press. doi.org/10.1017/CBO9781316529843

Sendo, T. 1957. Anthropological studies on the humerus of Kyushu Japanese. *Jinruigaku–Kenkyu* 4(1–4): 273–296.

Skoglund, P., C. Posth et al. 2016. Genomic insights into the peopling of the southwest Pacific. *Nature* 538:510–513. doi.org/10.1038/nature19844

Smith, B. 1984. Patterns of molar wear in hunter-gatherers and agriculturalists. *American Journal of Physical Anthropology* 63:39–56. doi.org/10.1002/ajpa.1330630107

Snell, C. 1938. *Menschelijke Skeletresten uit de Duinformatie van Java's Zuidkust nabij Poeger (Z.-Banjoewangi)*. Surabaya: G. Kolff.

Snell, C. 1949. Human remains from Gol Ba'it, Sungai Siput, Perak, Malay Peninsula. *Acta Neerlandica Morpholigica Normalis et Pathologicae* 6:353–377.

Solheim, W. 1959. Introduction to Sa Huynh. *Asian Perspectives* 3:97–108.

Solheim, W. 1968. The Batungan Cave sites, Masbate, Philippines. *Asian and Pacific Archaeology Series* (Honolulu) 2:21–62.

Solheim, W. 2002. *The Archaeology of Central Philippines*. Manila: Archaeological Studies Program, University of the Philippines, Diliman.

Soren, D. 2003. Can archaeologists excavate evidence of malaria? *World Archaeology* 35:193–209. doi.org/10.1080/0043824032000111371

Spennemann, D. 1993. Cowrie shell tools: fact or fiction? *Archaeology in Oceania* 28:40–49. doi.org/10.1002/j.1834-4453.1993.tb00312.x

Spoehr, A. 1957. *Marianas Prehistory: Archaeological survey and excavations on Saipan, Tinian and Rota.* Fieldiana. Anthropology 48. Chicago: Chicago Natural History Museum Press. doi.org/10.5962/bhl.title.3552

Spriggs, M. 1984. The Lapita cultural complex: Origins, distribution, contemporaries and successors. *Journal of Pacific History* 19: 202–223. doi.org/10.1080/00223348408572495

Spriggs, M. 1998. Research questions in Maluku archaeology. *Cakalele: Maluku Research Journal* 9:51–64.

Steele, D. and T. McKern 1969. A method for assessment of maximum long bone length and living stature from fragmentary long bones. *American Journal of Physical Anthropology* 31:215–227. doi.org/10.1002/ajpa.1330310211

Sternberg G. 1884. *Malaria and Malarial Diseases.* New York: William Wood & Company.

Storm, P. 1995. The evolutionary significance of the Wajak skulls. *Scripta Geologica* 110.

Summerhayes, G., M. Leavesley et al. 2010. Human adaptation and plant use in Highland New Guinea 49,000 to 44,000 years ago. *Science* 330:78–81. doi.org/10.1126/science.1193130

Szabó, K. 2005. Technique and Practice: Shell-Working in Island Southeast Asia and the Western Pacific. Unpublished PhD thesis. The Australian National University, Canberra.

Szabó, K. 2012. Terrestrial hermit crabs (Anomura: Coenobitidae) as taphonomic agents in circum-tropical coastal sites. *Journal of Archaeological Science* 39:931–941. doi.org/10.1016/j.jas.2011.10.028

Szabó, K. 2013. Identifying worked shell: A consideration of methodological issues with particular reference to Pleistocene contexts. In G. Bailey, K. Hardy and A. Camara (eds) *Shell Energy: Mollusc Shells as Coastal Resources*, pp. 277–286. Oxford: Oxbow Books.

Szabó, K. 2016. Molluscan remains from the Niah Caves. In G. Barker (ed.) *Rainforest Foraging and Farming in Island Southeast Asia: The Archaeology of the Niah Caves, Sarawak 2*, pp. 469–484. Cambridge: McDonald Institute Monographs.

Szabó, K., A. Brumm and P. Bellwood 2007. Shell artefact production at 32,000 BP in Island Southeast Asia: thinking across media? *Current Anthropology* 48:701–724. doi.org/10.1086/520131

Szabó, K., F. Cole, L. Lloyd-Smith et al. 2013. The 'Metal Age' at the Niah Caves: c. 2000–500 years ago. In G. Barker (ed.) *Rainforest Foraging and Farming in Island Southeast Asia: The Archaeology of the Niah Caves*, Sarawak 1, pp. 299–340. Cambridge: McDonald Institute Monographs.

Szabó, K. and B. Koppel 2015. Limpet shells as unmodified tools in Pleistocene Southeast Asia: an experimental approach to assessing fracture and modification. *Journal of Archaeological Science* 54:64–76. doi.org/10.1016/j.jas.2014.11.022

Tan, K.-S. 1993. Feeding ecology of common intertidal Muricidae (Mollusca: Neogastropoda) from the Burrup Peninsula, Western Australia. In F. Wells, D. Walker and D. Jones (eds) *The Marine Flora and Fauna of Dampier, Western Australia*, pp. 173–192. Perth: Western Australian Museum.

Tanudirjo, D. 2001. Islands in Between: Prehistory of the northeastern Indonesian archipelago. Unpublished PhD thesis. The Australian National University, Canberra.

Tanudirjo, D. 2005. Long-continuous or short-occasional occupation? The human use of Leang Sarru Rockshelter in the Talaud Islands, northeastern Indonesia. *Bulletin of the Indo-Pacific Prehistory Association* 25:15–19.

Tayles, N. 1999. *The Excavation of Khok Phanom Di. A Prehistoric Site in Central Thailand.* Volume V: The People. London: The Society of Antiquaries of London.

Temple, D. 2008. What can variation in stature reveal about environmental differences between prehistoric Jomon foragers? *American Journal of Human Biology* 20:431–439. doi.org/10.1002/ajhb.20756

Terrell, J., K. Kelly and P. Rainbird 2001. Foregone conclusions? In search of Papuans and Austronesians. *Current Anthropology* 42:97–124. doi.org/10.2307/3596473

Thomas, N., H. Guest and M. Dettelbach (eds) 1996. *Observations Made During a Voyage Round the World (by Johann Reinhold Forster).* Honolulu: University of Hawai'i Press.

Trotter, M. and G. Gleser 1958. A re-evaluation of estimation of stature based on measurements of stature taken during life and of long bones after death. *American Journal of Physical Anthropology* 16:79–123. doi.org/10.1002/ajpa.1330160106

Tsang, C-h. and K-t. Li 2015. *Archaeological Heritage in the Tainan Science Park of Taiwan.* Taitung: National Museum of Prehistory.

Tsukahara, T., F. Hombhanje et al. 2006. Austronesian origin of the 27-bp deletion of the erythrocyte band 3 gene in East Sepik, Papua New Guinea inferred from mtDNA analysis. *Journal of Human Genetics* 51:244–248. doi.org/10.1007/s10038-005-0352-7

van Bemmelen, R. 1949. *The Geology of Indonesia* (2 volumes). The Hague: Government Printing Office.

van den Berg, R. 2009. Possession in South Halmahera-West New Guinea: Typology and reconstruction. In A. Adelaar and A. Pawley (eds) *Austronesian Historical Linguistics and Culture History*, pp. 327–357. Canberra: Pacific Lingustics.

van den Bergh, G., H. Meijer et al. 2009. The Liang Bua faunal remains: a 95 k.yr. sequence from Flores, east Indonesia. *Journal of Human Evolution* 57:527–537. doi.org/10.1016/j.jhevol.2008.08.015

van Deusen, H. 1957. A new species of wallaby (genus Dorcopsis) from Goodenough Island, Papua. *American Museum Novitates* 1826:1–25.

van Dongen, R. 1963. The shoulder girdle and humerus of the Australian Aborigine. *American Journal of Physical Anthropology* 29:469–488. doi.org/10.1002/ajpa.1330210405

van Heekeren, H. 1972. *The Stone Age of Indonesia.* Second edition. The Hague: Nijhoff. doi.org/10.26530/OAPEN_613383

Vercellotti, G., B. Piperata et al. 2014. Exploring the multidimensionality of stature variation in the past through comparisons of archaeological and living populations. *American Journal of Physical Anthropology* 155:229–242. doi.org/10.1002/ajpa.22552

Voorhoeve, C. 1982a. The West Makian language. In C.L. Voorhoeve (ed.) *The Makian Languages and their Neighbours*, pp. 1–74. Canberra: Pacific Linguistics D-46.

Voorhoeve, C. 1982b. The Halmahera connection: A case for prehistoric traffic through Torres Straits. In A. Halim et al. (eds) *Papers from the Third International Conference on Austronesian Linguistics*, pp. 217–239. Canberra: Pacific Linguistics C-75.

Voorhoeve, C. 1988. The languages of the North Halmaheran Stock. In *Papers in New Guinea Linguistics* 26, pp. 181–209. Pacific Linguistics Series A, No. 76. Canberra: Department of Linguistics, The Australian National University.

Voorhoeve, C. 1994. Contact-induced change in the non-Austronesian languages in the North Moluccas, Indonesia. In T. Dutton and D. Tryon (eds) *Language Contact and Change in the Austronesian World*, pp. 649–674. Berlin: Mouton de Gruyter. doi.org/10.1515/9783110883091.649

Walker, P., R. Bathurst et al. 2009. The causes of porotic hyperostosis and cribra orbitalia: A reappraisal of the iron-deficiency-anemia hypothesis. *American Journal of Physical Anthropology* 139:109–125. doi.org/10.1002/ajpa.21031

Wallace, A. 1869. *The Malay Archipelago*. London: Macmillan.

Watabe, N. 1988. Shell Structure. In E.R. Trueman and M.R. Clarke (eds) *The Mollusca* 11, pp. 69–104. San Diego CA and London: Academic Press.

Webb, S. 1982. Cribra orbitalia: a possible sign of anaemia in pre- and post-contact crania from Australia and New Guinea. *Archaeology in Oceania* 17:148–156. doi.org/10.1002/j.1834-4453.1982.tb00059.x

Weisler, M. 2000. Burial artifacts from Marshall Islands: description, dating and evidence for extra-archipelago contacts. *Micronesica* 33:111–136.

Whitmore, T. (ed.) 1981. *Wallace's Line and Plate Tectonics*. Oxford: Clarendon Press.

Wood, R., M. Duval et al. 2016. The effect of grain size on carbonate contaminant removal from tooth enamel: Towards an improved pretreatment for radiocarbon dating, *Quaternary Geochronology* 36:174–187. doi.org/10.1016/j.quageo.2016.08.010

Wood, R.E., A. Arrizabalaga Valbuena et al. 2014. The chronology of the earliest Upper Palaeolithic in northern Iberia: New insights from L'Arbreda, Labeko Koba and La Vi-a, *Journal of Human Evolution* 69:91–109. doi.org/10.1016/j.jhevol.2013.12.017

Wright, J., W. O'Connor, L. Parker and P. Ross 2018. Predation by the endemic whelk Tenguella marginalba (Blainville, 1832) on the invasive Pacific oyster Crassostrea gigas (Thunberg, 1793). *Molluscan Research*. doi.org/10.1080/13235818.2017.1420397

Wurm, S. and S. Hattori (eds) 1983. *Language Atlas of the Pacific Area, Part II*. Canberra: Australian Academy of the Humanities.

Yap Potter, R., A. Alcazaren et al. 1981. Dimensional characteristics of the Filipino dentition. *American Journal of Physical Anthropology* 55:33–42. doi.org/10.1002/ajpa.1330550106

Yoshida, S. 1980 Folk orientation in Halmahera. In N. Ishige (ed.) *The Galela of Halmahera*, pp. 19–88. Osaka: Senri Ethnological Studies 7.

Zazzo, A. 2014. Bone and enamel carbonate diagenesis: A radiocarbon prospective. *Palaeogeography, Palaeoclimatology, Palaeoecology* 416:168–178. doi.org/10.1016/j.palaeo.2014.05.006

Zazzo, A. and J. Saliège 2011. Radiocarbon dating of biological apatites: A review. *Palaeogeography, Palaeoclimatology, Palaeoecology* 310 (1–2):52–61. doi.org/10.1016/j.palaeo.2010.12.004

Zuckerman, M., E. Garofalo et al. 2014. Anemia or scurvy: A pilot study on differential diagnosis of porous and hyperostotic lesions using differential cranial vault thickness in subadult humans. *International Journal of Paleopathology* 5:27–33. doi.org/10.1016/j.ijpp.2014.02.001

Zuschin, M., M. Stachowitsch and R.J. Stanton Jr 2003. Patterns and processes of shell fragmentation in modern and ancient environments. *Earth-Science Reviews* 63:33–82. doi.org/10.1016/S0012-8252(03)00014-X

Contributors

Peter Bellwood
The Australian National University, Canberra, Australia

Doreen Bowdery
The Australian National University, Canberra, Australia

David Bulbeck
The Australian National University, Canberra, Australia

Jennifer R. Hull
The Australian National University, Canberra, Australia

Geoffrey Irwin
Auckland University, Auckland, New Zealand

Gunadi Kusnowihardjo
Balai Arkeologi, Yogyakarta, Indonesia

Justyna Miszkiewicz
The Australian National University, Canberra, Australia

Gunadi Nitihaminoto
formerly Balai Arkeologi, Yogyakarta, Indonesia (deceased)

Annette Oertle
University of Sydney, Australia

Philip Piper
The Australian National University, Canberra, Australia

Joko Siswanto
Balai Arkeologi, Manado, Indonesia

Katherine Szabó
Monash University, Melbourne, Australia, and Max Planck Institute for the Science of Human History, Jena, Germany

Daud Tanudirjo
Gadjah Mada University, Yogyakarta, Indonesia

Agus Waluyo
formerly Balai Pelestarian Cagar Budaya Daerah Istimewa Yogyakarta, Indonesia (retired)

Rachel Wood
The Australian National University, Canberra, Australia

Bronwyn Wyatt
The Australian National University, Canberra, Australia

www.ingramcontent.com/pod-product-compliance
Lightning Source LLC
Chambersburg PA
CBHW041019280326
41926CB00095B/4776